Egypt

Egypt

ART & ARCHITECTURE

Matthias Seidel and Regine Schulz
With contributions from Abdel Ghaffar Shedid
and Martina Ullmann

h.f.ullmann

Frontispiece:
Seated figure of King Chephren (p. 96/97)

Note on this Book:
Information regarding the location of works
in museums as well as concerning opening times
are subject to change.

© 2005 Tandem Verlag GmbH
h.f.ullmann is an imprint of Tandem Verlag GmbH

Original title: *Kunst und Architektur. Ägypten*
ISBN 978-3-8331-1424-3

Project Management: Ute Edda Hammer
Editors: Anna Bechinie, Jutta Buness
Layout and Typesetting: Holger Crump
Graphics: Rolli Arts, Essen
Cartography: Studio für Landkartentechnik, Norderstedt
Picture Editors: Katrin Engler, Astrid Schünemann

© 2005 for the English edition:
Tandem Verlag GmbH
h.f.ullmann is an imprint of Tandem Verlag GmbH

English-language edition translated by Peter Barton, Anthea Bell,
Richard Elliott and Eileen Martin and edited by Gabriele Bock on
behalf of Cambridge Publishing Management

Project Coordination: Lucas Lüdemann

Overall responsibility for production:
h.f.ullmann publishing, Potsdam, Germany

ISBN 978-3-8331-5281-8

Printed in China

10 9 8 7 6 5 4 3 2 1
X IX VIII VII VI V IV III II I

If you would like to be informed about forthcoming h.f.ullmann titles, you can
request our newsletter by visiting our website (**www.ullmann-publishing.com**) or
by emailing us at: newsletter@ullmann-publishing.com.
h.f.ullmann, Birkenstraße 10, 14469 Potsdam, Germany

Table of Contents

Luigi Mayer, The Obelisks of Alexandria called "Cleopatra's needles", 1804

David Roberts, The Desert near Cairo

The Pyramid Complex of King Djoser in Saqqara

Richard Lepsius, Semite
Caravan in the Tomb of
Khnumhotep at Beni Hassan

David Roberts, The Great
Court of the Temple of Horus
at Edfu

WesternThebes, View into
the Valley at Deir el-Bahri

View of the Temple Island of Philae

Papyrus with the Book of the Dead of Amenemope, 18th Dynasty

The Great Temple of Ramesses II in Abu Simbel

The History of the Pharaohs

The Predynastic and Early Dynastic Periods
(5th and 4th centuries B.C.; First and Second Dynasties, ca. 3000–2680 B.C.)

In the last phase of the late Paleolithic age, from about 10,000 B.C., a climate change occurred in North Africa that caused an expansion of the steppes and desert regions that is now the Sahara. The people who lived there were hunters and gatherers, and

from the 8th to the 7th millenium B.C. they also reared cattle. They established the first small settlements where they evolved new techniques like pottery. In flight from the encroaching desert, ever larger groups of them penetrated the fertile valley of the Nile from the 7th and 6th millenium B.C., where they found a population which lived on fishing and possibly by then crop farming as well.

The Egyptian delta had links with Asia Minor, and the first towns grew up here in the 5th and 4th millenium B.C., with associations of settlements (like Merimda Beni Salama, el-Omari, Maadi and Buto). In the south of the country the tendency to local concentration came only rather later, with the Badarian and Naqada cultures. Towards the end of the 4th millenium, however, there was strong pressure to expand, particularly from these areas, and this led to protracted hostilities between the north and south of Egypt. As writing also began to develop at this time (ca. 3200 B.C.) we know the names of the rulers even though they do not appear in the later Egyptian annals, and for that reason they are known today as the kings of the Protodynastic period, or the Dynasty 0.

The "Great White" (God) in the form of a baboon, Dynasty 0, ca. 3100 B.C., calcite, H. 52 cm, Ägyptisches Museum, Staatliche Museen Preussischer Kulturbesitz, Berlin

The best known evidence of the victory finally achieved by the people of Upper Egypt is the magnificent ceremonial palette of the last Protodynastic ruler, King Narmer, on which he is shown smiting his enemies from Lower Egypt. But the ruler to whom the final unification of Egypt is ascribed was Horus Aha, and he later entered the annals of his country as Menes, the first king of the First Dynasty.

The rulers of the first two dynasties came from Thinis in Upper Egypt, hence this early period of Egyptian history is known as the

Head of King Djedefre (from a sphinx), Fourth Dynasty, ca. 2550 B.C., Abu Roash, quartzite, H. 26.5 cm, Musée du Louvre, Paris

Thinite period. To enforce their claim to both parts of the country they set up their capital, Memphis, exactly on the border between Upper and Lower Egypt, at the southern tip of the delta. But they ordered their tombs to be built further into Upper Egypt, at Abydos, while ordering monumental secondary burial places to be constructed in Saqqara, the necropolis for Memphis. These secondary mortuaries became cult centers. Despite considerable resistance, these rulers finally succeeded in bringing peace to Egypt; they developed an efficient administration and a common theological concept that formed the basis of their claim to power.

The Old Kingdom and the First Intermediate Period

(Third to Sixth Dynasty, ca. 2680–2190 B.C.; Eighth to Tenth Dynasty, ca. 2190–2020 B.C.)

The Old Kingdom was the time of the great pyramids. These unique constructions should not be seen only as royal burial places, they were also magical and powerful symbols of creation. This concept reflected the power structure in the holy kingdom, over which the pharaoh ruled like a divinity; his regeneration after death and his ascent to heaven were the prerequisites for the continued existence of every creature in

King Chephren, Fourth Dynasty, ca. 2530 B.C.,
Giza, anorthosite gneiss, H. 17.2 cm,
Ägyptisches Museum der Universität Leipzig

this world and the other world. This is particularly clear in the burial complex of King Djoser of the Third Dynasty in Saqqara. The external form of his Step Pyramid indicates the ascent to heaven, while the arrangement of the subterranean burial chambers and the orientation of the mortuary temple point to the transition from this world to the other world. The courtyard where the festival of regeneration (the Sed festival) was celebrated, with the thrones of Upper and Lower Egypt, expresses the desire for constant renewal and for eternal life for the king and his subjects.

Although the names of the rulers of the Fourth Dynasty are well known from the pyramids they built, very few other depictions of historical events have survived. That is true for Snefru, the first king of this dynasty. It is unfortunate, as he is always referred to in later testimonies that have survived as a good king in every way. His building work was stupendous, for he had three pyramids erected, one in Meidum (the Step Pyramid), and two in Dahshur (the Bent and the Red Pyramids). But his son Cheops, who built Egypt's greatest pyramid in Giza, is described by the Greek historian Herodotus (5th century B.C.) as a veritable tyrant, although this has not so far been confirmed by any ancient Egyptian source. It may well be due to the erroneous assumption that Cheops could only have built such mighty works by oppressing the people and using slave labor. Two other kings of the Fourth Dynasty chose the plateau of Giza for their pyramids, Chephren and Mycerinus, Cheop's son and grandson. If one sees the pyramids of the Fourth Dynasty as the expression of royal power, it is striking that at the end of this period King Shepseskaf broke with this tradition. After completing the burial place for his father Mycerinus he revived the old form of the mastaba for his tomb in South Saqqara, and so went back to the beginning of the royal building tradition.

Throughout the entire Fourth Dynasty the main administration and military posts were filled with direct relatives of the king. At the head of the centrally controlled administration was a vizier, who was responsible for all internal and foreign affairs. To strengthen the king's power on earth royal seats were established throughout the land and the provincial administration was made responsible to royal officials. Particular care was taken to cultivate contacts with other countries, especially Nubia, Libya and Asia Minor, and the supplies of the goods, livestock and people needed were enforced, if necessary, with military means. Egypt was poor in timber, and cedar wood was in particular demand (among other things for coffins); it came mainly through peaceful trade with Byblos.

Queen Khentkaues, Shepseskaf's sister, was the mother of the first three kings of the Fifth Dynasty, but their father is so far not known. The Papyrus Westcar contains a legend of these births which tells that they were the fruit of the sun god Re, who appeared to their mother, so endowing the new ruling dynasty with divine legitimization. The special relation of the kings to the sun god was also evident from the new cult centers to him which almost every king now had built near Abusir.

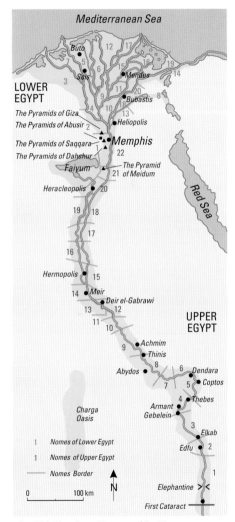

The Old Kingdom: Egypt and its Nomes

Triads of King Mycerinus (figure of the king), Fourth Dynasty, ca. 2500 B.C., Giza, graywacke, H. 96 cm, Egyptian Museum, Cairo

While Userkaf, the first king of the Fifth Dynasty, still built his pyramids in Saqqara, the rulers who followed him (Sahure, Neferirkare, Neferefre and Niuserre) chose Abusir as burial place as well. In internal politics this age brought the growing emancipation of the administration from the royal family. In foreign policy an extension of foreign trade can be traced, in the south down to Punt, the land of incense (probably Eritrea or Somalia) and in the north up to Ebla in Syria. Under Pharaoh Asosi (ca. 2405 to 2367 B.C.) one expedition is actually said to have penetrated as far as Yam (south of the third Nile cataract) and brought back ivory, incense and a "dancing dwarf."

A clear break with the cult practice came at the end of the Fifth Dynasty. The kings ceased erecting shrines to the sun god and again built their tombs in Saqqara. Unas (ca. 2360 B.C.), whose family came from the delta, was the first to have the wall of his burial chamber adorned with pyramid texts. The pronouncements were to assist the regeneration and transfiguration of the ruler. The change in the religion may possibly be connected with the growing importance of the god of the dead, Osiris, who now represented the king after death and became the guarantor of regeneration for his people. With Unas' son-in-law Teti a new dynasty, the Sixth, began, and although the rulers of this dynasty maintained the religious tradition that had started with Asosi and Unas considerable changes did take place, internally and in foreign policy. The cult centers in the provinces (like Abydos, Coptos and Thebes) became increasingly important, and their administrations began to make themselves independent. During the long reign of Pepy II, who came to the throne when he was only a child, the situation deteriorated alarmingly. The tax payments from the provinces failed to materialize with growing frequency, so that the royal treasury could no longer fulfill its obligations;

trade was also hardly protected any more, and attacks from Bedouins were frequent. Nevertheless, several expeditions to Nubia are known. Eventually economic collapse could no longer be averted. After the deaths of Pepy II and his son Nemtyemsaf II, a Queen Nitocris is believed to have come to the throne as the last ruler of the Sixth Dynasty. Whether she really existed is disputed, as is the accusation that she murdered her brother Nemtyemsaf II and later committed suicide. But certainly a number of other rulers followed. They are known as the Eighth Dynasty; they ruled from Memphis but had little influence over the rest of the country.

The last phase of the Old Kingdom and the First Intermediate Period that followed were marked by famine, invasion and incessant fighting in large parts of the country. Fear and uncertainty were widespread, traditional values lost their meaning and even many royal tombs were plundered in these violent times.

Finally, the nomarchs of Herakleopolis (Ninth and Tenth Dynasties) took the old capital of Memphis, seeing themselves as the rightful successors to the rulers of the Old Kingdom. But numerous other small political units existed at the same time, ruled by warring princes. We have a glimpse into conditions in Upper Egypt from the detailed biograpy of Ankhtifi from his tomb in Mo'alla. The self-assured prince (in the inscriptions he boastfully refers to himself as the "incomparable hero") was able, with difficulty, to main-

Pepy I, shown kneeling, Sixth Dynasty, ca. 2280 B.C.; probably Dendara, slate, H. 15.2 cm, The Brooklyn Museum of Art, New York

tain order and supplies where he held power (the second and third districts) but his military campaign in the north was unsuccessful.

The Middle Kingdom and the Second Intermediate Period

(Eleventh to Twelfth Dynasty, 2119–1793 B.C.; Thirteenth to Seventeenth Dynasty, 1793–1550 B.C)

During the First Intermediate Period a second great center of power grew up in Thebes, whose inhabitants became the main opponents of the Herakleopolites. The local rulers of Thebes were closely related to the nomarchs of Elephantine,

King Mentuhotep II (detail), Eleventh Dynasty, ca. 2020 B.C., Western Thebes, limestone, H. 53.3 cm, The British Museum, London

and this gave them access to Nubian mercenaries who supported their wars of expansion. The rulers Intef I, II and III, for example, succeeded in steadily expanding their field of influence. They took the title of king and laid claim to the whole of Egypt. Mentuhotep II finally succeeded in reuniting the country under his rule around 2040 B.C., and so putting an end to the First Intermediate Period. The Middle Kingdom had begun.

The most important task now was to stabilize the administration of the country, to strengthen the king's power, secure the external frontiers and resume trade, especially in order to obtain the urgently needed raw materials like timber and metals. Some of the artistic and intellectual elite of the old Heracleopolite kingdom did move to Thebes, and new and binding administrative structures were set up. In the deep valley of Deir el-Bahri Mentuhotep II had a unique mortuary cult center built, which included a terraced temple in the foreground. A primeval mound may have stood in the center of this. The temple was dedicated to the god Amun, who was regarded as the "king of the gods" and the direct divine reference person for the king. Within a few generations he had risen to be one of the most important divinities of Egypt, and his main shrine in Karnak later became the religious center of the country.

Amenemhet I, the last vizier of the Eleventh and the later founder of the

Twelfth Dynasty, probably first had to fight his way to power, as some of the nomarchs did not support his assumption of office. He took up the traditions of the Old Kingdom, moved the capital to the north near what is now el-Lisht, and had a traditional pyramid built there as his tomb. Although he increased Egypt's prosperity, secured the frontiers with fortifications, sent out successful expeditions and set up trading posts in Palestine, he was murdered after a conspiracy in the harem. Nevertheless, his son and co-regent

Senusret I performing the ritual run at the Sed festival before the god of fertility Min, Twelfth Dynasty, ca. 1930 B.C., Coptos, limestone, H. 105 cm, Petrie Museum, University College, London

Senusret I succeeded in maintaining his claim to the throne. The political situation had become so precarious through the assassination that it was recorded in two literary works, the "Instruction of Amenemhet II" and "The Tale of Sinuhe." Senusret I and his successors Amenemhet II and Senusret II saw their main task as strengthening central power. They were also concerned to secure the frontiers and intensify trade with central Africa, Asia Minor and the Aegean. One of the most striking testimonies to this was the treasure found in the Month temple at et-Tod, which included objects from Babylon and Crete.

To provide better military protection in Nubia and protect Egypt's interests from the mighty Kerma kingdom, Senusret III had a navigable canal cut through the first Nile cataract. The Egyptian fortifications to the north and south of the second and third Nile cataracts were enlarged and Amenemhet III completed another great project, the drainage and cultivation of the marshy oasis of Faiyum that had been started under Senusret II. This made the oasis the most fertile region in the country, and temples to the crocodile god Sobek and Renenutet, the goddess of fertility, were erected there. Amenemhet III finally actually chose the entrance to the Faiyum at Hawara for his pyramid, after abandoning building work on his first pyramid in Dahshur (where the pyramids of Amenemhet II and Senusret III stand). His

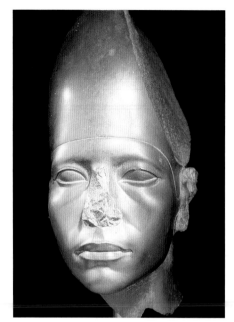

Amenemhet III, wearing the white crown, Twelfth Dynasty, ca. 1820 B.C., graywacke, H. 46 cm, Ny Carlsberg Glyptothek, Copenhagen

huge mortuary temple, which contains many internal chambers, was described as a labyrinth later in antiquity. During the second half of the Twelfth Dynasty Egypt enjoyed great prosperity at home and good relations abroad, the central administration was effective, the sciences (particularly medicine, astronomy and mathematics) innovative and in every field of the fine arts, literature and architecture masterworks were created. After the death

of Amenemhet IV and his sister Sobekneferu there appear to have been repeated battles for the throne of Egypt throughout the entire Thirteenth Dynasty; but despite all the difficulties in the royal family the administrative system was so efficient that the unity and prosperity of the country were preserved for a long time.

Around 1648 B.C., however, the country must have split up again. In the eastern delta and parts of southern Palestine an independent small trading state emerged that is called the Fourteenth Dynasty; its rulers chose Avaris as their capital. They finally succeeded in extending their field of power down to Memphis, and putting an end to the Thirteenth Dynasty. The Second Intermediate Period had begun. Six rulers established themselves in Avaris and they are known as the great Hyksos of the Fifteenth Dynasty (Greek, from the Egyptian: *hekakhaswt*, "ruler of foreign lands"). The Hyksos were western Semites, who ruled parts of Syria, Palestine and Egypt and who had formed alliances with numerous smaller principalities, probably including the small Hyksos who were known as the Sixteenth Dynasty, and the many city princes like those of Hermopolis and Thebes. The rapid success of the Hyksos was mainly due to their use of horse-drawn chariots, which made them vastly superior to the Egyptian foot soldiers. The most outstanding of the great Hyksos rulers was probably Apophis, whose territory initially extended right into Upper Egypt.

The New Kingdom
(Eighteenth to Twentieth Dynasty, ca. 1550–1070 B.C.)

Again it was a family of Theban princes (Seventeenth Dynasty) who were to succeed in reuniting the country. King Seqenenre Taa II was the first to rise openly against the Hyksos ruler Apophis. His son Kamose continued the struggle but suddenly found himself facing a difficult situation when the Hyksos attempted to take up contact with the Kerma kingdom in Nubia in order to involve the Thebans in a war on two fronts. Kamose succeeded in foiling this plan and penetrating as far as the Hyksos capital Avaris in the eastern delta. But it was left to his brother and successor Ahmosis, the first ruler of the Eighteenth Dynasty and founder of the New Kingdom, to take the city and put the Hyksos to flight. He finally conquered them and around 1550 B.C. united Egypt under his rule. After securing the situation in Nubia and southern Palestine he concentrated on domestic policy, and under Amenophis I the rebuilding of the state was pursued on every level. Binding laws were issued, the calendar reformed and cult regulations laid down. New temples were built throughout the kingdom, and particularly in Thebes, where Amun now finally rose to be the universal godhead, the "King of the gods."

His successor Thutmosis I concentrated on foreign policy. In only his second year on the throne he had to suppress an uprising of Nubian princes, and to deter further unrest after his victorious return he had the corpse of his foe suspended from the bow of the royal vessel. The following year he penetrated far into the south, beyond the fourth Nile cataract, to gain control of trade with central Africa.

Bust of Thutmosis III, Eighteenth Dynasty, ca. 1450 B.C., granodiorite, H. 45.5 cm, Kunsthistorisches Museum, Ägyptisch-Orientalische Sammlung, Vienna

Sphinx of Amenophis III offering wine vessels, Eighteenth Dynasty, ca. 1380 B.C., blue faience, L. 23 cm, The Metropolitan Museum of Art, New York

The Kingdom of Kerma must have finally collapsed as a direct consequence of this military campaign. Only a short time later Thutmosis entered Syria to secure his claims against the powerful Mitanni kingdom there. In Egypt he continued his father-in-law's energetic building activity, and was the first to have his tomb built in the Valley of the Kings.

After the brief reign of Thutmosis II two of the greatest rulers of Egypt came to the throne—Thutmosis III and his step-mother Hatshepsut. She was first instal-led as regent for her stepson who was still under age, but after a few years she assumed the royal status, supported by the priests of Amun. It was now she who decided policy, having proclaimed her legitimization in a legend of her birth and selection. In her terraced temple in Deir el-Bahri two important events are re-corded as well as the legend of her birth— the expedition to Punt to obtain gold and myrrh and the transport and erection of her gigantic obelisks in the temple at Karnak. After her death Thutmosis III continued to rule alone. His successful campaigns, especially in Syria and Palestine, gave Egypt hegemony in the Middle East. At home he strengthened the position of the army and promoted a new elite of officials. He ordered the memory of Hatshepsut to be wiped out throughout the land by having her name removed from the monuments.

Amenophis II and Thutmosis IV were able to maintain Egypt's military presence abroad. The new major power, the Hittites, began to oppress the Mitanni Kingdom, which thereupon sought peaceful coexistence with Egypt. The negotiations were successful and culminated in the marriage of Thutmosis IV to a daughter of the Mitanni king. Amenophis III was even more skillful at diplomacy than his father, making Egypt the center of an extensive trading alliance; art and culture flourished, goods from every corner of the known world reached the royal court and in the workshops the most costly materials were processed. Amenophis III wanted everything superlative, the biggest temples, the finest palaces and the most costly statues were erected to his command, and his program of building and statuary, which extended from the delta to Soleb in Nubia, exceeded anything that had been seen before. The openness of the royal family to foreign ideas and culture, their great interest in scientific discovery and their desire for absolute perfection also appears to have influenced theological discourse towards the end of Amenophis III's reign. New and more abstract interpretations of creation and the course of the sun were evolved, although traditionalists vehemently rejected these. Amenophis IV, the son of Amenophis III and his chief wife Tiye, was

Akhenaten seated, Eighteenth Dynasty, ca. 1340 B.C., dark yellow limestone, H. 64 cm, Musée du Louvre, Paris

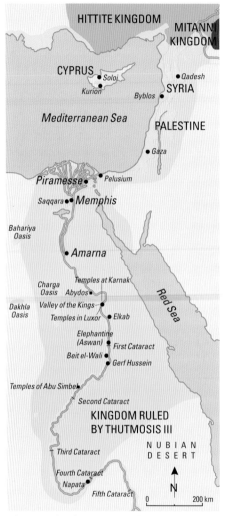

The New Kingdom: Egypt under Thutmosis III

an enthusiastic supporter of these new ideas and developed them into his own religion of the sun. The king changed his name Amenophis ("Amun is content") to Akhenaten ("Beneficial to Aten") and had a huge temple to Aten erected in Karnak, where he was celebrated with his consort Nefertiti as the creative mediator between man and the sun god. When the priests of Amun began to oppose the domination of the new god there was an uprising. Akhenaten left Thebes and founded his capital Akhetaten (now Amarna) in middle Egypt. He ordered the temples of the old gods to be closed and the names and images of the god Amun to be removed. He appointed entirely new priests and officials and set up an administration that was totally dependent on his person.

He had little understanding of Egypt's external problems, and the delicate network of alliances which his father had built up collapsed. Very shortly after his death the child king Tutankhaten was forced to abandon Akhetaten and move to Memphis to reinstate the old gods; he changed his name to Tutankhamun ("the living image of Amun") but died suddenly when he had just reached manhood, and left no heirs.

After a brief interregnum of Ay, "God´s Father," the man who had held the real reins of power during Tutankhamun's reign came to the throne; he was Horemheb, the supreme commander of the army. He succeeded in restoring

Group showing Tutankhamun before the god Amun-Re seated on a throne, Eighteenth Dynasty, ca. 1330 B.C., probably Karnak, granodiorite, H. 220 cm, Musée du Louvre, Paris

stability at home and abroad and instigating urgently needed reforms. He appointed his military companion and vizier Ramesses as his successor, who founded the Nineteenth Dynasty. His son Sety I accelerated the restoration of the temples of the gods throughout the land and the final elimination of the names of all the Amarna rulers he regarded as illegitimate. He set up a new administration center in the eastern delta, which soon became the capital of the Ramesses kingdom under the name of Piramesse. Not only were new temples and palaces built here, huge military camps and weapons workshops were also set up. From Piramesse the Egyptian troops could be mobilized more quickly to protect the trade routes or to hasten to the aid of allies or to exert military pressure to remind them of their obligations under the alliance. A difficult situation arose in the fifth year of Ramesses II's reign, when the land of Amurru transferred its allegiance to the Hittites and the king had to act quickly to secure his claims in Syria. He set out with a huge army (about 20,000 men) to take the fortress of Qadesh, but he was ambushed there by the Hittites and nearly taken prisoner. He was saved as if by a miracle when an elite troop arrived too early, and the Egyptian army was able to withdraw under cover of darkness. On his return to Egypt the king ordered the battle to be celebrated as a great victory, and depicted on temple walls. But sixteen years were to

pass before a peace treaty was finally concluded. Ramesses II ruled for 67 years, during which time he instigated a huge building program. He also brought numerous cult centers up to date by ordering the buildings and statues to bear his name.

Large contingents of troops were always at the ready to suppress uprisings, fulfill obligations under alliances or show enemies abroad the might of the Egyptian army. The sea people were a constant threat; they came from the Aegean region and attacked the coastal towns on the Mediterranean, plundering like pirates. But it was only in the fifth year of Merenptah's reign that they constituted a serious danger to Egypt, when they allied with the Libyans and plundered the Egyptian delta. Although an uprising in Nubia had to be put down at the same time the king

Ramesses II wearing the blue crown, Nineteenth Dynasty, ca. 1275 B.C., Thebes, granite, H. 194 cm, Museo Egizio, Turin

succeeded in obtaining victory on both fronts.

The end of the Nineteenth Dynasty was fraught with disputes over the succession to the throne that caused a crisis within Egypt, and it was only under the second king of the Twentieth Dynasty, Ramesses III, that order was restored. His greatest challenge still came from the sea people, who attacked the delta from both the east and the west, in alliance with the Libyans. Ramesses III won a great battle on land and sea which he ordered to be depicted in extensive relief cycles on the walls of his mortuary temple at Medinet Habu in Western Thebes. Nevertheless, the economic problems multiplied, and the under the last of the Ramesses kings Egypt began to decline rapidly. Power struggles, strikes and unrest broke out. At the end of the Twentieth Dynasty, under Ramesses XI, there was actually civil war, with the Viceroy of Kush in Nubia, Panehsy, fighting the High Priest of Amun, Piankh. Piankh was followed as High Priest of Thebes by his son-in-law Herihor, who rose to be sole ruler after the death of Ramesses XI, with full entitlement, an oracle of Amun/Khonsu having legitimized his position.

Relief showing captured Philistines in procession (a group of the Sea people), Twentieth Dynasty, ca. 1170 B.C., Western Thebes, Medinet Habu, Ramesses III's mortuary temple, first courtyard

The Third Intermediate Period and the Late Period

(Twenty-first to Twenty-fifth Dynasty, 1070–655 B.C.; Twenty-sixth to Thirty-first Dynasty, 664–332 B.C.)

After the end of the New Kingdom a phase of internal conflict began that is known as the Third Intermediate Period. The founder of the Twenty-first Dynasty was Smendes, probably a son of Herihor, the high priest of Amun in Thebes. He moved his capital in the delta from Piramesse to Tanis, having all the representational monuments transported and re-erected in the new metropolis. The

domiciled in Bubastis, and must have been an extremely skillful ruler with a very strong will. After only a short time he succeeded in restoring stability and bringing the Theban priest state directly under his rule. He undertook several campaigns to Palestine and in 925 B.C. also laid siege to Jerusalem. To avoid defeat the city handed over to him the treasures of the palaces and temples. In 756 B.C. the royal family in Bubastis split and two related dynasties, the late Twenty-second and the Twenty-third, ruled simultaneously. Finally the Libyan princes of Heracleopolis, Hermopolis and Sais also declared themselves independent, claiming the title of king. The princes Tefnakhte and Bocchoris (Bakenrenef) of Sais ultimately extended their power to the entire western delta and Memphis, and were later counted as the Twenty-fourth Dynasty.

In Nubia an independent Kushite state had evolved in the middle of the 8th century B.C., its traditions based in part on Egyptian roots. The chief divinity worshiped by these rulers was Amun, and they chose the form of the pyramid for their tombs. King Kashta succeeded in penetrating north as far as Aswan, Pije took Upper Egypt and Shabaqo was finally able to defeat Bocchoris (Bakenrenef), so that the delta princes also recognized

royal tombs were now also set in the vicinity of the great temple of Amun. Nevertheless, the new rulers saw themselves as successors to the Ramesses, and they actually used the name Ramesses as an honorary title. They were related to the priest kings in the divine state of Amun at Thebes, and they probably ruled with mutual consent.

Shoshenq I was the founder of the Twenty-second Dynasty. He came from the warrior nobility in Libya who were

Kushite rule. The kings of the new dynasty, known as the Twenty-fifth, were rich in gold and Egypt experienced an economic upswing. Taharqo in particular had numerous building projects carried out throughout the land. But although the first years of the dynasty were peaceful, catastrophe was not long in coming. The Assyrians attacked Egypt and were supported by the princes in Sais in the war against the Kushites, who finally had to give up Lower Egypt.

After Psametik I had been recognized as ruler in large parts of Egypt, he made himself independent of the Assyrians and founded a new, the Twenty-sixth, Dynasty. This dynasty saw the start of the last great cultural age of the pharaohs, which is known as the Late Period. Subsequently Egypt was involved in the war against the New Babylonian Kingdom as an ally of the Assyrians. Nekau II was able to secure Egypt's old supremacy over Palestine for a short time, but in 605 B.C. he was annihilated by the Babylonian army under King Nebukhadnezar and had to withdraw back to Egypt. Here he concentrated on building up his fleet; he also started a unique project, the construction of a canal from the Red Sea to the Mediterranean. There was renewed confrontation with Nebukhadnezar under King Apries, who supported the uprising of the Jewish and Phoenician towns against the Babylonians. But he was not able to prevent the conquest of Jerusalem, either, and the capture and deportation of the Jews. But it was another conflict that finally caused Aprie's downfall. He fought on the Libyan side against the Greek colony of Kyrene, which was in revolt. After a humiliating defeat with heavy losses the Egyptian army mutinied and

Head of a statue of King Amasis, Twenty-sixth Dynasty, ca. 550 B.C., graywacke, H. 24 cm, Ägyptisches Museum, Staatliche Museen Preussischer Kulturbesitz, Berlin

General Amasis seized power. He succeeded in mediating between the Greeks, the Libyans and the Egyptians, which is no doubt why he is later called a great wise man in Greek records. Under his son Psametik III Egypt again lost its independence when it was conquered by the Persian king Kambyses in 525 B.C. It was made a province of the Persian kingdom and the Persian rulers are known as the Twenty-seventh Dynasty. Only after the death of Darius II did the Libyan ruler Amyrtaios of Sais, the only king of the Twenty-eighth Dynasty, succeed in driving the Persians out of the land. He in turn was overthrown by Nepherites I of Mendes, who founded the Twenty-ninth Dynasty.

Egypt experienced its last cultural upswing under the kings of the Thirtieth Dynasty, who came from Sebennytos in the delta. Art and architecture flourished again particularly under Nectanebo I, and magnificent offerings filled the temples. But only a short time later, in 343 B.C., Egypt was again unable to withstand attack from Persia, and was again made a Persian province (Thirty-first Dynasty). Nectanebo II, the last native pharaoh of Egypt, left the country and fled to Nubia.

Alexander the Great and the Ptolemies
(332-30 B.C.)

Alexander the Great entered Egypt in 332 B.C. after defeating the Persians. He was welcomed as a liberator and had his rule confirmed by an oracle of the god Amun in the oasis of Siwa; later he was revered as a god in Egypt. After his death in Babylon in 323 B.C. his general Ptolemaios, son of Lagos, had the body of the great Macedonian taken finally to Egypt to be buried, but his tomb has never been found.

Ptolemaios first ruled in Egypt in the name of Alexander's successors, Philip III, Arrhidaios and Alexander IV, before crowning himself king in 305/304 B.C. as Ptolemy I Soter. He endeavored to obtain a settlement between the Greek and the Egyptian sections of the population, and the elevation of Sarapis to the new god of the state should be seen in this context, for he is a link between the Egyptian god Osiris-Apis and the Greek gods Zeus and Dionysos. Subsequently two cultures developed side by side, the first in the old Egyptian tradition, as is evident in the great temple buildings of Edfu, Dendera, Kom Ombo and Philae, and the other Hellenistic, to meet the needs of the Greek population. The new capital Alexandria rose to exceptional grandeur, becoming the undisputed cultural center of the Hellenistic world. While the first Ptolemies were still largely able to rely on

Head of Cleopatra VII; ca.30 B.C., marble,
H. 20 cm, Antikensammlung, Staatliche Museen
Preussischer Kulturbesitz, Berlin

keep her throne with the help of Julius Caesar. After his death she bestowed her favors on Mark Anthony, fighting with him against Octavian for dominance of the Roman empire. After their defeat by Octavian, who later became the Emperor Augustus, at the battle of Actium in 31 B.C., Cleopatra and Mark Anthony committed suicide, and Egypt finally became a Roman province. Although many Romans were enthusiastic about Egypt, and Egyptian gods like Isis were revered in many parts of the Roman empire, life for most Egyptians under Roman rule can hardly have been easy. The land on the Nile was exploited as the granary of Rome and its source of raw materials, and it became increasingly impoverished.

the support of the native administration and priests, from the reign of Ptolemy IV there were repeated uprisings and conspiracies; at times the Theban region actually declared independence. Power struggles within the family and assassination conspiracies weakened the ruling family further. The last of these rulers, Cleopatra VII, was finally only able to

Modern Egypt in Facts and Figures

Geography and Population

- Name: Arab Republic of Egypt
- Capital: Cairo
- Official language: Arabic
- National holiday: July 23 (in celebration of the 1952 revolution)
- Currency: 1 Egyptian pound = 100 piasters
- Area: ca. 386,662 sq. miles (1,002,000 sq. km.)
- Topography: Egypt has four different landscape zones, the Nile valley and delta (where ca. 99% of the population live), the Libyan desert in the west (covering ca. 2/3 of the total area), the Arabian desert in the east and Sinai.
- Climate: a desert climate, with a Mediterranean climate on the northern coast.
- Population: ca. 77.5 million (in July 2005). The great majority of the population live in an area of only 13,590 sq. miles (35,200 sq.km.). About 54% of the inhabitants of Egypt live in the Nile delta and Greater Cairo. An estimated 18 million people live in Greater Cairo alone. The average density of population in Cairo is ca. 6,900 people per sq. mile (27,000 per sq.km.).
- Population growth in 2005: 1.78%
- Ethnic groups: Egyptians, Bedouins: 99%, Nubians, Europeans and others: 1%.

Temperatures

	Jan.	Feb.	March	April	May	June	July	Aug.	Sept.	Oct.	Nov.	Dec.
Alexandria °C	18	19	20	23	26	27	28	30	28	27	25	20
Rain days	5	4	3	1	0	0	0	0	1	3	4	5
Cairo °C	19	21	24	28	32	35	35	35	33	30	26	21
Rain days	3	2	1	1	1	0	0	0	0	1	1	2
Luxor/Aswan °C	24	27	29,5	34	40	41,5	42	41,5	39,5	35,5	30	25
Rain days	0	0	0	0	0	0	0	0	0	0	0	0

- Religions: the official religion is Islam; Muslims (mostly Sunnites): 94%, Christians (mostly Copts): 6%.

Egypt since the Revolution (Outline)

July 23, 1952	Coup by the "Free Officers" under General Mohammed Nagib; King Farouk I deposed.
June 6, 1953	Egypt declared a republic.
1954	Gamal Abdel Nasser becomes head of state
1956	The Suez crisis: the nationalization of the Suez canal (in British ownership) results in an attack by Great Britain, France and Israel on Egypt.
1960–1970	Construction of the Aswan dam
1967	Egypt suffers an annihilating defeat by Israel in the Six Days War; Israel occupies the Sinai peninsula.
October 15, 1970	Death of Nasser; Anwar es-Sadat follows him as head of state.
October 6, 1973	Start of the Yom Kippur War when Egypt and Syria launch a surprise attack on Israel; on October 26, 1973 the war is ended after pressure from the major powers.
From 1974	Sadat pursues a policy of opening to the West, encouraging western investment.
November 19, 1977	Sadat visits Israel and starts the peace process between the two countries.
March 26,	Sadat and Begin sign the peace
1979	treaty in Camp David; Sinai is to be returned to Egypt by 1982.
October 6, 1981	Sadat murdered by Islamic fundamentalists; his successor is Mohammed Hosni Mubarak.
1991	Egypt joins in the First Gulf War against Iraq, fighting on the side of the United States.

The Political System and the Administration

- The political structure: Since 1971 Egypt has been a republic with a president as head of state. He appoints both the minister president and the cabinet; he is elected every six years by the chamber of deputies (and his election has to be confirmed in a national referendum); at times of war he is supreme commander of the armed forces.
- The legislature: a chamber of deputies with 454 members; 444 are elected every five years by the people (in a combination of direct elections and proportional representation with an 8% clause), ten members are appointed directly by the head of state. A second chamber acts as advisory organ with 264 members, of whom 88 are appointed by the head of state. Franchise is at the age of 18, voting is obligatory.
- Political parties: since the Multi-Party Law of 1979 the National Democratic Party has been the major party; its leader is President Hosni Mubarak. There are a number of legal opposition parties (e.g. the New Wafd Party, the Socialist Workers Party) and an illegal opposition of Islamic fundamentalist groupings that are gaining in strength.

- The judicature: law courts with four instances on the European model (British common law and the Code Napoléon) taking account of Islamic law.
- The national administration: Egypt is divided into 26 administrative regions and the city of Luxor; the governors of these regions have ministerial rank and are appointed and dismissed by the head of state. The regions in turn are subdivided into districts and municipalities. The local administration on all three levels is composed of elected representatives of the people and executive organs appointed by the government.

The Economy
- Egypt has been pursuing a course of economic stabilization since 1991, combined with fundamental structural reforms. After fighting in the First Gulf War on the side of the anti-Iraq coalition Egypt received massive financial support from the International Monetary Fund (IMF) and extensive debt release by western creditor states. In the 1990s the inflation rate fell and the budget deficit was reduced. The privatization started under Sadat was advanced, as was the improvement of the legislation on commercial enterprises. The general situation has been improved due to higher revenues from tourism and natural gas production. However, the unfavorable unemployment rates threaten the social peace.
- Gross per capita domestic product in 2004: US$ 4,200.
- Economic growth rate in 2004: 4.5%
- Inflation rate in 2004: 9.5%

- Economic sectors: services 49.8%, industry 33%, agriculture 17.2%
- Industry: textiles, foodstuffs, tourism, chemicals, oil, building, cement production, metals extraction and processing. Increase in industrial output in 2004: 2.5%
- Agriculture: only ca. 3.5% of the land is arable; these areas are in the delta and in the Nile valley, which is ca. 621 miles (1,000 km.) long. Intensive irrigation with ground wells is being used in an attempt to obtain more arable land, i.a. in the Kharga and Dechla oases in the Libyan desert (the New Valley Project) and more recently in the Nubian desert near Toshka. The main agricultural products are cotton, rice, sugar cane, maize, wheat, beans, fruit, vegetables; livestock farming with cattle, water buffalo, sheep and goats, and fishing.

Education and Social Structure
- Population: the rapid growth in the population in the 1980s and early 1990s (about 2.5% a year) brought serious economic and social problems, which were exploited, particularly in the last 15 years, by Islamic fundamentalist groups for their purposes.
- For decades the Egyptian government has been propagating birth control, i.a. through a policy of education and the free distribution of contraceptives. State-run family planning centers have been set up all over the country. In the last few years some success appears to have been achieved and the official figure for population growth (estimated) in 2005 is only 1.78%.

- Population structure:
  - 0–14 years old: 33%
  - 16–64 years old: 62.6%
  - over 65: 4.4%
- Social structure: The social structure of the population has changed greatly since the 1952 revolution. Under Nasser a land reform programme was carried out and large parts of the arable land that was mainly in the hands of big landowners were distributed to sections of the population who had been without land.

  The educated middle class were given access to political power. Since Sadat's policy of opening to the west in the 1970s the middle class has grown rapidly, at least in the urban districts.
- Health: since 1952 great efforts have been made to improve the health of the population. Life expectancy has risen strongly since then and infant mortality has been markedly reduced.
- Medical care: the Ministry of Health provides basic health care free of charge for the population, i.a. by operating health centers throughout the country. As well as general hospitals the state also operates specialist and dental clinics.

  However, the health care available in the state-run centers and clinics is often inadequate, mainly due to the shortage of technical equipment and staff.
- Social services: there is very little social security. There has been a state programme of provision for old age since the 1960s, combined with unemployment and invalidity insurance and provision for surviving dependants, but in 1990 only about half the workforce were contributing to this (i.a. state employees).
- Education: great efforts have been made to expand the school system in recent decades, but these have not kept pace with the population growth.

  The public education system consists of five years obligatory elementary schooling, followed by a preparatory school for three years and three more years at secondary school. Pupils then have the possibility of attending vocational school (agricultural, commercial, technical school).
  Admission to one of the 15 universities requires good grades in the centralized school-leaving certificate at secondary school. As well as the universities there are a number of technical colleges.
  Although schooling is obligatory the illiteracy rate among persons over 15 is now 42.3%, for many children from poorer families are never sent to school because the parents have to buy the books and school uniforms themselves. However, 97% of the children visiting the elementary schools, and all public schools are free of charge, but considered to be of low standards.
  Therefore, parents who have the necessary means prefer to send their children to private schools. In the country particularly many children are in the workforce, although child labor is actually illegal.

Internet addresses
- touregypt.net
- egypt.net

Alexandria and the Delta

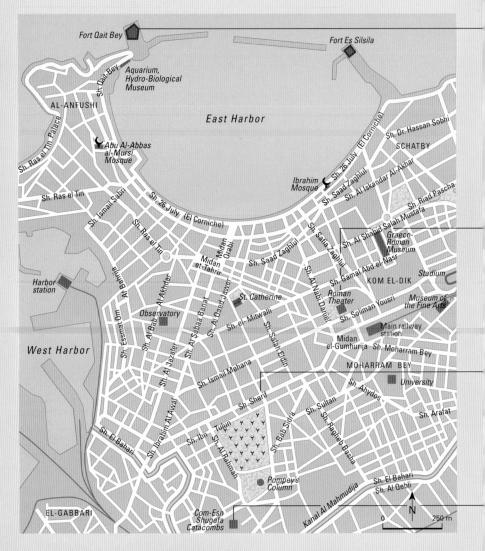

Fort Qait Bey

Fort Es Silsila

Sh. Qait Bey

Aquarium,
Hydro-Biological
Museum

AL-ANFUSHI

East Harbor

Sh. Dr. Hassan Sobhi

SCHATBY

Abu Al-Abbas
al-Mursi
Mosque

Sh. Ras el Tin Palace

Sh. Ismail Sabri

Sh. 26 July (El Corniche)

Ibrahim
Mosque

Sh. 26 July (El Corniche)

Sh. Saad Zaghlul

Sh. Al Iskandar Al Akbar

Sh. Ras el Tin

Sh. Ras el Tin

Sh. 26 July (El Corniche)

Sh. Riad Pascha

Sh. Safia Zaghlul

Sh. Al Shahid Salah Mustafa

Graeco-
Roman
Museum

Midan
Orabi

Sh. Saad Zaghlul

Sh. Gamal Abd el-Nasr

Stadium

Midan
et-Tahrir

Sh. Al Nabi Daniel

KOM EL-DIK

Harbor
station

Sh. Essmat Om

Al Bahira

Sh. Al Bab Al Akhdar

Sh. Al Abbas Banat

Sh. Al Qaed Jawer

Observatory

St. Catherine

Sh. el-Mitwalli

Roman
Theater

Sh. Soliman Yousri

Museum of
the Fine Arts

West Harbor

Sh. Al Jazaier

Sh. Salah Eldin

Main railway
station

Midan
el-Gumhurija

Sh. Moharram Bey

MOHARRAM BEY

Sh. Ismail Mehana

Sh. Ibrahim Al Awal

Sh. Sherif

Sh. Abydos

University

Sh. Arafat

Sh. El Bahari

Sh. Ibn Tulun

Sh. Al Rahmah

Sh. Bab Sidra

Sh. Sultan

Sh. Ragheb Basha

EL-GABBARI

Pompey's
Column

Com-Esh
Shugafa
Catacombs

Kanal Al Mahmudija

Sh. El Bahari

Sh. Al Qebli

N

0   250 m

Fort Qait Bey, p. 51

The theater at
Kom el-Dik, p. 50

Pompey's Column, pp. 48 f.

Kom esh-Shugafa,
vestibule, pp. 44 f.

Alexandria

Since Alexandria was founded in 332/31 B.C. by Alexander the Great "the pearl of the Mediterranean" has been one of the major sites of Egyptian history. After the death of the Macedonian king the city developed under the Ptolemies into the intellectual and cultural center of the entire Hellenistic world. Great scholars lived and worked in the Museion. The great library held the knowledge of antiquity on hundreds of thousands of papyrus scrolls and the lighthouse at Pharos gave warships and trading vessels alike safe entry to the harbor. Cleopatra VII's suicide in 30 B.C. ended Alexandria's great age. The following centuries of Roman occupation were fraught with violent conflicts, which accompanied the slow but sure decline of the city. The Emperor Trajan, for example, (98–117 A.D.) had the Jewish traders driven out, and Caracalla (211–217 A.D.) exacted revenge on the sharp-tongued Alexandrians with a blood bath among the young men. Christianity soon reached the city, and during the 3rd and 4th centuries A.D. the Christians were subject to intense persecution. After the arrival of Islam in 642 the importance of the once great metropolis declined steadily. Today, Alexandria tries to keep up with the glory of its great past.

Previous double page: Luigi Mayer, The Obelisks of Alexandria called "Cleopatra's needles", 1804

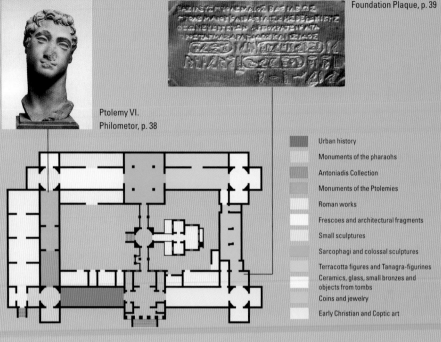

Foundation Plaque, p. 39

Ptolemy VI.
Philometor, p. 38

Urban history

Monuments of the pharaohs

Antoniadis Collection

Monuments of the Ptolemies

Roman works

Frescoes and architectural fragments

Small sculptures

Sarcophagi and colossal sculptures

Terracotta figures and Tanagra-figurines

Ceramics, glass, small bronzes and
objects from tombs

Coins and jewelry

Early Christian and Coptic art

The Graeco-Roman Museum

The museum building to house antiquities of the Graeco-Roman period in Egypt was started in 1891 and it has been extended several times. With nearly 50,000 items it is the largest collection of its kind, and it also includes items from the time of the pharaohs and the Coptic period. As well as 23 rooms of exhibits there is a small court garden containing a selection of more monumental items. Most of the exhibits were found directly in the various excavations in and around Alexandria, but the collection also includes works of art from other sites, if they date from the relevant period. The museum is the recipient of the many chance finds that occur in the historic soil of the city as well. The initial stock was provided by a private patron, John Antoniadis, who bequeathed his collection to the institution at the end of the 19th century, when it had just been founded.

Cast of a cameo
Ptolemaic Period, 3rd century B.C., provenance
unknown stucco, H. 13 cm, W. 16 cm

Only very few of the original and magnificent cameos cut for the court of the
Ptolemies from costly semi-precious stones
(like sardonyx) have survived the ages.
This antique stucco cast of a cameo that
would otherwise be lost is unique. It was
donated to the Museum in 1936 by Fuad I
and it shows the double portrait of Ptolemy
I Soter and his Queen, Berenice I, set side
by side. The features of the founder of the
dynasty, who was deified, are immediately
recognizable by the marked shape of nose
and chin; as well as the chiton and cloak he
wears the ribboned diadem of his royal
rank. Interestingly, the original cameo was
evidently already damaged in antiquity, for
the surrounding relief ground has broken
off. That the cast was made nevertheless is
impressive testimony to the high value
placed on these products of the stone-
cutter's art. However, the marvelous
Cameo is gone by all likelihood.

Head of Arsinoe II
Ptolemaic Period, ca. 270 B.C.,
provenance unknown, marble, H. 24 cm.

Ptolemy VI Philometor
Ptolemaic Period, ca. 150 B.C.,
provenance unknown, marble, H. 41 cm.

Arsinoe II was the sister and consort of Ptolemy II Philadelphos and one of the outstanding women of the Hellenistic age. After her death in 270 B.C. the queen was deified and worshipped in many temples throughout Egypt. Here her head is turned slightly to the left and her eyes are upcast, a sign of her apotheosis ("deification" in Greek). A uraeus was probably set above her brow to accentuate her royal status.

The statues of the Ptolemaic kings in the Egyptian style are highly idealized and can only be identified with certainty from their inscriptions, but their Hellenistic portraits enable them to be identified without difficulty from contemporary portraits on coins. This head of Ptolemy VI combines the formal principles of the landscape style, as it is known, with a somewhat emotional facial expression.

Foundation Plaque

Ptolemaic Period, ca. 210 B.C., Sarapeion, Alexandria, gold, 11 × 5 cm.

The many foundation plaques that were found between 1943 and 1945 under the Ptolemaic wall enclosing the temple compound of the Sarapeion provide important information on the history of the construction of this most famous shrine in Alexandria. The plaques were made in precious metals (gold, silver and bronze) but there are also some in glass, faience and clay. The inscriptions are punched or painted on and they consist of short texts on the foundation. Most of them are in Greek but some are in two languages, Egyptian and Greek. One example bearing the name of Ptolemy III Euergetes I records the building of a temple to Sarapis and a sacred compound. The example illustrated here consists of thin gold leaf and dates from the time of his successor, Ptolemy IV Philopator. Its text records the building of a small shrine in the Sarapeion to the god Harpocrates that was undertaken "on the command" of the gods Isis and Sarapis. "King Ptolemy (beloved of Isis), son of the "gracious divinities," Ptolemy and Queen Berenice, for Harpocrates, upon the command of Osiris-Apis-Sarapis and Isis." This temple to the young god once stood on the eastern side of the Sarapis temple, which in turn was a new building by Ptolemy III, replacing a structure originally built by the founder of the dynasty, Ptolemy I Soter. Burying items in a deep pit, the foundation deposit, under key points (e.g. cornerstones) of temples was customary even under the pharaohs, but the composition of the objects could vary greatly.

Colossal Head of the Emperor Augustus
Roman, ca. 50 A.D., Athribis (delta), marble, H. 79 cm

Like their predecessors, the Ptolemies, the Roman emperors also had their images depicted on the walls of the shrines erected in their names, in the tradition of the Egyptian rulers. Although they ruthlessly exploited the fertility of the land on the Nile, the doctrine of the divine nature of the pharaoh was very welcome to them, as it played into their hands by helping to spread the cult of the emperor. This colossal portrait of Augustus must be seen in this context. It was made only several decades after his death (14 A.D.), and it shows the emperor deified. The top of the head is missing; it was originally a piece attached in stucco, a practice that may be regarded as typical for the rear parts of marble sculptures in Graeco-Roman Egypt. Tiny remnants of color have survived in the hair and eyes, suggesting that the entire statue was originally painted.

Figure of the God Sarapis (detail)
Roman, 1st/2nd century A.D., Faiyum, wood covered in stucco, H. 172 cm

Immediately after he came to the throne Ptolemy I Soter created a god named Sarapis. He combined features of ancient Egyptian and Greek divinities and so idealized the current political situation. The new official god's outer appearance was entirely in the Greek mode, with full flowing hair and beard (like Zeus and

Dionysos). The god Osorapis marked the Egyptian tradition, himself already a composite deity of the gods Osiris and Apis, the sacred bull of Memphis. Both cults of Sarapis and his consort Isis were among the most popular in the whole Roman Empire. The great size of the figure of Sarapis discovered in Faiyum is unique, as is the use of wood as a material. The statue was originally painted over a stucco ground and it shows the god in characteristic form with a full beard and the five strands of hair curling down his brow.

The Lighthouse at Pharos

Under the Ptolemaic kings Alexandria had a number of outstanding institutions, like the Museion with its great library, the grave of Alexander the Great, that has never been discovered, and the Sarapeion, the shrine to the new god of the realm Sarapis. But none of these structures achieved the renown of the lighthouse on the island of Pharos, for this was the latest of the seven wonders of the world in antiquity.

The references to the lighthouse in antiquity certainly express boundless admiration for the work, but they give little concrete information about its architecture, and it is not until the 12th century that a report by an Arab scholar gives a detailed description with the corresponding measurements. The lighthouse may have been ordered by Ptolemy I Soter, and it is presumed to have been completed under his successor Ptolemy II Philadelphos around 280 B.C. The architect of this unique monument, which was larger than any lighthouse subsequently built, is believed to be Sostratos of Knidos. The dedicatory inscription was in huge letters on the front entrance, and according to the version recorded by the Greek satirist Lucian (2nd century A.D.) it read: "Sostratos of Knidos, son of Dexiphanes, (dedicates this lighthouse) to the gods of salvation for the benefit of those who go to sea." The sum of money expended, 800 talents, accorded with the mighty structure, for it was the equivalent of around 45,000 lbs (20,800 kilograms) of silver. But the full height of the tower can only be estimated. It may have been over 420 feet (130 metres). The building material used was "white stone," so probably limestone and marble. The lighthouse had three storeys and it did not stand on the island of Pharos itself but

The harbor with the lighthouse (reconstruction), colored copperplate by J. Emanuel Fischer von Erlach, around 1700

Der von dem Aegyptischen Könige Ptolomæo Philadelpho an der   Le Fameux Phare que Ptolomée Philadelphe Roy d'Egypte

on an outcrop of rock to the east of it. It was surrounded by a rectangular terrace with fortified towers at each of the four corners. A huge cistern was located in the foundations to supply water for general use. The bottom storey was on a square ground plan and extended to a height of around 230 feet (71 metres). The main entrance was on the second storey and could only be reached up a ramp. The next stage consisted of an octagon of around 110 feet (34 metres), with a round structure rising from its platform. This in turn bore a small superstructure with a conical roof crowned with a statue of Zeus. How strong a light was emitted by the fire in the upper part of the Pharos, and how it was directed, remain open questions; probably concave mirrors were used.

St. Mark voyaging to Alexandria (the great lighthouse is on the right), 12th/13th century A.D., mosaic, San Marco, Venice

The Pharos lighthouse stood unharmed for several centuries, until it was almost completely destroyed in a series of violent earthquakes between the 10th and the 14th centuries A.D. The ruins were removed around 1480 by the Mameluke Sultan Qait Bey, who had the fortification named after him built on the same site. In recent years several expeditions by French underwater archaeologists have succeeded in bringing to light numerous monuments and fragments of architecture from the East Harbor, and these include items that appear to be from the lighthouse. The recovery of a colossal royal statue in red granite (the torso weighs 11.4 tonnes) in 1996 was particularly spectacular. It is in the pharaonic style and may possibly be Ptolemy I, donated by his son Ptolemy II Philadelphos. It once stood with another monumental sculpture of his consort (in the form of Isis Pharia) at the ramp leading to the entrance to the lighthouse. Admired by the classical authors it was their later Arab collegues who gave us the true descriptions of the Pharos. The most comprehensive account is owed to Jusuf Ibn esh-Sheikl. He visited Alexandria in 1165 when the lighthouse had already suffered some damage.

Kom esh-Shugafa
Roman, 1st/2nd century A.D.

On the slopes of a hill not far from the ruins of the Sarapeion lies the entrance to the catacombs of Kom esh-Shugafa (Arabic: the hill of fragments), which is the largest and most important burial site of Roman times in Egypt. It is decorated in the mixed Egyptian-Roman style and was discovered in 1900. It consists of three storeys hewn out of the rock, one below the next (the lowest level is in danger of being flooded with ground water). Probably it was once owned by a non-Christian cult community who claimed responsibility for constructing the central section in the 1st century A.D.

View of the Vestibule

A spiral staircase leads from the entrance down into the depths. After reaching the first lower storey with its central rotunda, the visitor finds the triclinium on his left. This is a large room with wide couches where the burial ceremonies were held. Another stairway in the axis leads to the burial chapel with a small vestibule. The façade has a flat, rounded gable supported by two columns decorated with plants. The rear passage to the chapel is flanked by two great snakes, each bearing above its head a round shield with the head of Medusa. Both snakes represent the mysterious Agathos Daimon, the patron saint of Alexandria, assimilated with Serapis.

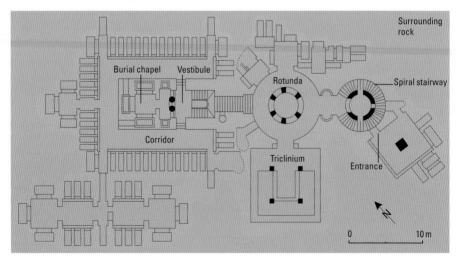

Surrounding rock

Burial chapel   Vestibule

Rotunda

Spiral stairway

Corridor

Triclinium

Entrance

N

0   10 m

Relief in the burial chapel (right niche)

The burial chapel, which is now in danger of being flooded with ground water, has three large niches that contain false sarcophagi. The chests and lids were hewn in sandstone and decorated with elements like garlands, masks and bulls' heads. Sarcophagi of this type, freely worked in hard stone, can be seen in the foreground of the catacombs. All the rear walls of the niches bear high reliefs showing religious scenes on themes derived from the pure old Egyptian tradition. The depiction in the right niche, for example, shows the Roman emperor wearing the double crown of Upper and Lower Egypt and presenting a great necklace to the cult statue of the god Apis, who appears in the form of a bull. The god was native to Memphis and here he stands on a high plinth, wearing a pectoral and with the disc of the sun between his horns. A small sacrifical stand is placed between the ruler and Apis, and on the extreme left the goddess Isis is approaching with great outspread wings. This is a classical temple scene but here, in a private burial chamber, it is largely robbed of its cult significance, appearing only as an image of the general hope for a life after death.

The God Anubis

Beside the passage to the next niche the tomb is watched over by the figure of the god Anubis, his head that of a dog. He appears in the image in the central niche in his classical function as the god of embalmment, where he looks after the mummy of the deceased with Horus and Thoth. Here Anubis stands on a plinth, wearing the armor of a Roman soldier. This is in keeping with the Graeco-Roman imagery, as is his posture, with his head turned slightly to the left and his animals' ears pointing forwards. But the striped headdress and the little sun disc above his head are rudimentary remains of the ancient Egyptian iconography. His left arm is raised, holding a long staff (lance), while his right hand rests on a mighty club. The strap for a sword sheath runs across his breast. This armed character of god Anubis may well have originated in his very ancient function as guardian of the tombs and the whole cemetery.

Pompey's Column
Roman, 292 A.D.

The desolate state of this hill of ruins with the huge column of Pompey gives little indication that the famous Sarapeion once stood here. Under the Ptolemies it was the main temple of Alexandria, but it was destroyed so utterly by the Emperor Theodosius in 391 A.D. during his persecution of the heathen that now not even the ground plan can be traced. According to legend the same emperor is said to have erected the column in memory of the victory of Christianity. But it is more likely that Diocletian—judging by the dedication of 292 A.D. on the base—had the column built as the last part of the old Sarapeion. The column bears a Corinthian capital; it

was worked in red granite and rises to a height of just under 87 feet (27 metres), with a diameter of nearly 9 feet (2.70 metres) and a circumference of nearly 30 feet (9 metres). In 1832, on the occasion of a visit by a European dignitary, 22 people are said to have gathered on the capital and partaken of a meal seated in a circle. The monument owes the name by which it is still known to the early Middle Ages, when the site was believed to be the tomb of the Roman general Pompey, arch rival of Julius Caesar. Around the column various large objects are on display, including two fine royal sphinxes in red granite dating from the early Ptolemaic time; however they were found in the city.

The Theater at Kom el-Dik
Roman, 3rd/4th century A.D.

Many of the ancient buildings in Alexandria have not survived or lie beyond reach under the modern city. Thanks to a detailed description by the Greek historian Strabo (late 1st century B.C.) in the 17th Book of his "Geographica," we do at least have written evidence of major facilities in the old metropolis. But chance played a big role in the discovery of the Kom el-Dik complex. It was not until the old barracks were being demolished, that such interesting founds were made in the ground that the whole site was immediately declared an excavation site. As well as huge baths, a well preserved theater dating from Roman times was discovered in 1964. The rows of seats are arranged in thirteen ranks; they are worked in white imported marble and provided room for about 800 spectators. An outside wall 26 feet high was added later and performances were held into the 7th century A.D. Like other buildings in Alexandria the theater suffered damage from several earthquakes.

Fort Qait Bey
Islamic, 15th century A.D.

On the northern tip of the former island of Pharos, on the spot where the famous lighthouse once stood, stands the mighty fortress of Sultan Qait Bey. After two powerful earthquakes in 1303 and 1326 had finally brought down the lighthouse that dated from antiquity, the remains were used to build this fortress (around 1480). In so strategic a position it could control entry to the great East Harbor, protecting it from any attack. The fortress is in three storeys, and as part of the city's defenses it consists of a square central structure with four round towers at the corners. The whole is surrounded by a massive stone wall that also has several bastion towers. The modern route to the Fort follows in general the old Hepta-stadion, the 1300 m long artificial dam which alluvial deposits have widened beyond recognition over the centuries.

Cleopatra VII—Feminine Power on the Nile

Probably no other queen of Egypt fascinated her contemporaries and posterity as much as the last member of the Ptolemaic dynasty, Cleopatra VII (51–30 B.C.). The many and complex legends that grew up around her were not only the result of political conditions in her time and her eventful life, they were also due to the dramatic circumstances of her death. It is undisputed that Cleopatra was a woman of outstanding intelligence and education. She spoke and wrote several languages, but she was also unscrupulous and driven by lust for power. Although her beauty is praised by writers, this must be seen as something of an exaggeration to judge by her portrait on coins that have

Portrait of Cleopatra VII, ca. 50 B.C., marble, H. 35 cm, Museo Gregoriano Egizio, Vatican

survived. But this slight short-coming was no doubt more than compensated by her strong personality and charm. Cleopatra VII was born in 70/69 B.C.; her father was Ptolemy XII Neos Dionysos, who appointed her and her brother Ptolemy XIII joint rulers in his will. But immediately after ascending the throne (in 51 B.C.) the brother and sister quarrelled fiercely over power and this initially ended with Cleopatra's flight to Syria. But the situation quickly changed when Julius Caesar entered Egypt in July 48 with a small contingent of troops during the Roman civil war. He set up his quarters in the royal palace at Alexandria and declared himself the arbitrator in the disputes over the throne between brother and sister. At his very first encounter with Cleopatra Caesar fell victim to her charms and allowed himself to be made a party to her political aims. He finally emerged victorious from the ensuing hostilities in Alexandria, in the course of which Ptolemy XIII met his death. Cleopatra VII now ruled over Egypt without restriction, and in June 47 she gave birth to Caesar's son, who was named Ptolemy XV Caesarion. Caesar himself had returned to Rome, where Cleopatra followed him the following year. But when Caesar was assassinated (44 B.C.) she immediately returned to Egypt. Her desire to secure the continuance of the Ptolemaic dynasty led the queen to embark upon a new love affair with the man who was then the most powerful commander in the east, Mark Anthony. The couple ruled

Hans Makart, The Death of Cleopatra, 1875/76, oil on canvas, 191 × 254 cm, Neue Galerie, Staatliche Kunstsammlungen, Kassel

over a magnificent court and were revered in a cult like gods—a fit accompaniment to their dream of a great Hellenistic-Egyptian kingdom. But from the year 33 the political climate between Rome and Egypt steadily deteriorated, as Rome refused to accept Mark Anthony's independence. The hostility was fuelled in the background by Octavian, the legitimate heir to the great Caesar. Fearing his own claims were in jeopardy, he actually managed to have Cleopatra declared an enemy of Rome. Open war began in the spring of 31, and ended for Mark Anthony and the queen with a catastrophic defeat at sea in the battle of Actium on September 2 that year. Both were able to escape but they could offer no further resistance to the victorious armies of Octavian, who

later became the Emperor Augustus. When Octavian entered Alexandria on August 1, 30 B.C. Mark Anthony took his own life in dramatic circumstances. The last queen of the Ptolemies followed him a few days later with a poisonous snake bite, having recognized that this time female charms would be of no avail with the Roman conqueror. Nor was she prepared to give Octavian the satisfaction of displaying her as a captive to the mob in Rome in his triumphal procession. After the death of Cleopatra VII her three children by Mark Anthony, Cleopatra Selene, Alexander Helios and Ptolemy Philandelphos, were taken to Rome to be part of the great triumph of Octavian in 29 B.C. Later, Selene was married to King Juba II of Numidia (Libya) and sent to North Africa.

Behbeit el-Hagar

South west of the provincial capital Al-Mansura (in the northern delta) lies Behbeit el-Hagar. It holds the impressive remains of a shrine to the goddess Isis, as can be seen from the names of the location in classical antiquity, Iseum or Isidis Oppidum. The Arabic name for the village, Behbeit, still contains the pharaonic name Hebyt. The temple now lies in ruins but the complex (1170 × 680 feet or 360 × 210 metres) is enclosed by a great wall built of unfired Nile mud tiles, while the temple itself covered an area 260 × 178 feet (80 × 55 metres). The temple building has totally collapsed, probably due to an earthquake, and now the visitor finds only a confusion of granite blocks and other architectural fragments.

The Temple of Isis
Ptolemaic period, 3rd century B.C.

Relief block showing Ptolemy II

The shrine to Isis may well have been erected to replace an older site dating from the Saitic period (Twenty-sixth Dynasty). Nectanebo II of the Thirtieth Dynasty is known to be the first ruler who built in Behbeit, but his building was never completed owing to the Persian invasion in 343 B.C. So it was left to the two early Ptolemaic rulers, Ptolemy II Philadelphos (282–246 B.C.) and his successor Ptolemy III Euergetes I (246–222 B.C.) to decorate the temple with reliefs. They are all in hard stone, including black and red granite, and their quality is outstanding. The ritual shown here depicts Ptolemy II (on the right) handing the god Osiris a pectoral (a decorative breastplate) and a necklace. The god is not shown here in the form of a mummy, he is entirely anthropomorphic, with an Atef crown over his wig.

Wall Fragments in the Sanctuary Area

More recent studies have utilized the great variety and quantity of the surviving fragments of the building, like wall blocks, parts of columns, concave molding and the bases of stairways to reconstruct the ground plan of the shrine. At present, however, there are no plans to rebuild the temple, for that would require the blocks that were removed in the 19th and 20th centuries and are now scattered throughout the world in various collections to be reunited. The temple had a plain façade, behind which stretched a great columned hall with Hathor columns of Aswan granite. Then the axis line led into the barque sanctuary for the main divinities Isis and Osiris; this was enclosed in a wreath of chapels. The most important scenes on the long walls of the sanctuary show the Ptolemaic King (wearing the crown of Upper Egypt) burning incense before the sacred barque of Isis, the "goddess of Hebyt"; her head, with cow's horns and the disc of the sun, has survived here.

The Nile—The Lifeblood of Egypt

Relief: Agriculture with livestock before the tomb owner, tomb of Merj-merj, Saqqara, Eighteenth Dynasty, ca. 1380 B.C., Rijksmuseum van Oudheden, Leiden

The Greek historian Herodotus (5th century B.C.) called the Nile "the father of Egypt," and one must agree that he was right. For it is only the oasis created by the flooding of the Nile with its broad delta that enabled a viable agriculture to evolve and provide food for the people. The Egyptians called their land "Kemet," the black land, in reference to the dark mud, rich in minerals, that was deposited every year when the water retreated after the flood. The Nile floods were a blessing and a curse at once, for they could vary greatly in depth. Depending on the rainfall in the Ethiopian uplands, the level of the floods in Egypt (from August to November) could vary by several metres. If it was too low there would not be enough arable land to feed the people, and if the waters rose too high they caused catastrophic destruction. Egypt's dependence on the Nile, which is the second longest river in the world at 4,160 miles (6,670 km), is also evident in the names given in the texts for the three periods into which the year was divided, the floods, the season of crop sowing and the harvest. The river was worshipped as a god under the name Hapy. He is depicted as a fat man with breasts like a woman, physical features that clearly express the idea of fertility and good care. He often appears on temple reliefs as the bringer of gifts, bearing a plate of offerings in his hands. Among his many additional names Hapy is referred to as the one "flooding the two lands with life-giving water" and even "wet nurse of the whole land" or simply as "the river." The nature and importance of the god was also celebrated in a great hymn from the time of the Middle Kingdom. The high esteem in which the god and his gifts were held is evident in the words "One does not get drunk on silver, and one cannot eat lapis lazuli. But barley is the food of life". Therefore, since the Old Kingdom, in virtually every temple of the country a representation of Hapy could be found, often together with other

Felucca on the Nile at Aswan

fecunity deities. In their myths the Egyptians put the sources of the Nile at the southern frontier of their kingdom, south of Elephantine and not far from the first cataract. The Egyptian guide to Herodotus also referred to this when he told the Greek historian that "the sources of the Nile spring forth amid the hills from a bottomless depth, and one half of the water flows northwards to Egypt while the other flows south to Ethiopia."

Tanis (San el-Hagar)

As one approaches the little village of San el-Hagar in the north eastern delta one can see from afar the huge hills of the ruins of Tanis, called Zoan in the Bible. It was the largest settlement mound of antiquity in Egypt (known as a "kom," an earthen mound over ancient buildings), measuring 5200 × 3900 feet (1600 × 1200 m), and reaching a height of just under 130 feet (40 m). It soon attracted the attention of excavators. Auguste Mariette went to Tanis in 1860, Flinders Petrie followed in 1883/84 and in 1929–1951 the French archaeologist Pierre Montet, who was to succeed in uncovering the tombs of the kings, dug there. A French team is working in Tanis today and no end to their work is in sight. The place was elevated to be the new capital of Egypt at the start of the Twenty-first Dynasty, when the Ramesside capital in Piramesse was abandoned for both political and economic reasons. In the center of the hill lies the great temple of Amun. It is enclosed by a massive brick wall, 1397 × 1200 feet (430 × 370 metres), which was last extended under the Ptolemies. The entrance has a huge gate built by Shoshenq III (Twenty-second Dynasty) and like so many buildings in Tanis it consists of older blocks of granite that were dragged here and fitted together. Behind this, stretches an area full of monuments, statues, obelisks, columns and relief blocks, but the original architecture is almost totally lost.

Colossal figure of Ramesses II, p. 61

Golden mask of Psusennes I, pp. 64 f.

Pectoral of Psusennes' I., p. 64

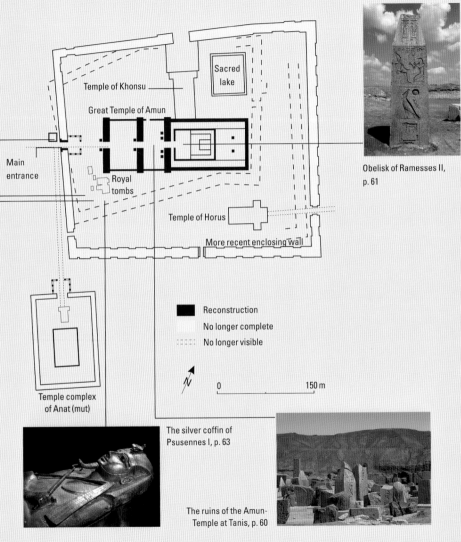

Sacred lake

Temple of Khonsu

Great Temple of Amun

Main entrance

Royal tombs

Temple of Horus

More recent enclosing wall

Obelisk of Ramesses II,
p. 61

Reconstruction

No longer complete

No longer visible

N

0   150 m

Temple complex
of Anat (mut)

The silver coffin of
Psusennes I, p. 63

The ruins of the Amun-
Temple at Tanis, p. 60

The Temple Area
21st/22nd Dynasty, 10th/9th centuries B.C.

When the Tanite rulers took the decision to move their capital further to the north, into the delta, a major problem had to be solved. For the stone quarries for the building material lay far away in Upper Egypt. Consequently, they ordered the buildings and monuments of the Ramesside metropolis to be demolished; these were then taken over a distance of a good 13 miles (20 km), to be re-erected at their new destination. It was a process that must have taken several decades. Even after the political power shifted to other delta cities in the course of the 1st millenium B.C. the tradition of settlement at Tanis persisted right into Greek and Roman times. The main shrine of Amun (ca. 760 feet or 235 m in length) was fitted out with particular elaboration; it had three great pylons before the rear temple building and consisted for the most part of blocks of granite. Four obelisks stood before the third pylon dedicated to Osorkon II alone (Twenty-second Dynasty), with colossal figures from the time of Ramesses the Great.

Colossal Figure of Ramesses II

The long reign of Ramesses II lasted 67 years, from 1279 to 1213 B.C. Among other things it meant that not enough of the statues of the ruler needed for his gigantic building program were available anywhere in the land. Hence numerous statues of earlier kings were removed from shrines in the greater Memphis district as well as from Delta sites and used to adorn the temple buildings. They included original works of the Nineteenth Dynasty like this upper part of a colossal standing figure (12.5 feet or 3.85 m high).

Obelisk of Ramesses II

Although Tanis suffered for many years from the persistent removal of its stones and many individual monuments have found their way into the museums of Cairo and Paris, the great wealth of objects that are still in place do give some idea of the former magnificence of the temple. As well as countless statues, some of which are up to 65 feet (20 m) high, 23 obelisks alone have been discovered. Most of them, like this great fragment (13 feet or 4.20 m high) are of red granite and were once made for the "House of Ramesses" under Ramesses II.

The Tombs of the Kings
Twenty-first/Twenty-second Dynasties,
10th/9th century B.C.

In the south west corner of the temple complex the French archaeologist Pierre Montet found the royal necropolis for the kings of the Twenty-first and Twenty-second Dynasties in 1939. The burial chambers lie close together. They were once underground and no trace had remained of the superstructures that were assumed to have surmounted them. The tombs, and particularly the rich treasure in the tomb of Psusennes I

(Twenty-first Dynasty) can certainly compare with the contents of the tomb of Tutankhamun, with cult vessels of precious stones, magnificent jewelry and not least the golden mask of the king. Psusennes I's consort Mutnodjmet, Pharaoh Amenemope and his general Wendjebauendjed were all buried with Psusennes I. Beside this tomb is the burial chamber of Osorkon II, and slightly to one side the tomb of Shoshenq III. Two more burial chambers remained unfinished. The earth at Tanis may hide more sensations, for great kings of this period, like Shoshenq I, and their tombs have not yet been discovered.

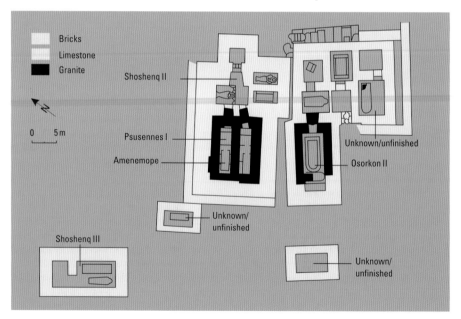

Bricks
Limestone
Granite

N

0   5 m

Shoshenq II

Psusennes I

Amenemope

Unknown/unfinished

Osorkon II

Unknown/
unfinished

Shoshenq III

Unknown/
unfinished

The Silver Coffin of Psusennes I
Twenty-first Dynasty, ca. 1000 B.C., silver, gold,
L. 185 cm, Egyptian Museum, Cairo

As was the custom of the pharaohs of the
New Kingdom, Psusennes I also ordered
himself to be buried in several layers of
coffin. But it was not easy to carry out his
command, for the shortage of stone in the
delta was an unwelcome but indisputable
fact, even for royal tombs. The solution was
pragmatic rather than appropriate to a
pharaoh, for Psusennes used his contacts

with the priest kings of the divine state of
Amun to appropriate a granite sarcophagus of King Merenptah (Nineteenth
Dynasty), whose tomb in the Valley of the
Kings had already been plundered. The
second anthropomorphic coffin of black
granite was also given a new inscription. It
had once held an official of the early
Nineteenth Dynasty. It was in this that the
magnificent silver coffin of the Tanite ruler
was laid and it can be seen as an original
artefact of his time. The changing play of
the metal colors is extremely beautiful.

Pectoral of Psusennes I with heart scarab
Twenty-first Dynasty, ca. 1000 B.C., gold with inlays, H. 10.5 cm, Egyptian Museum, Cairo

The Golden Mask of Psusennes I
Twenty-first Dynasty, ca. 1000 B.C., gold, lapis lazuli, H. 48 cm, Egyptian Museum, Cairo

Montet found many items of jewelry on Psusennes I's mummy, including this magnificent pectoral in the form of a winged scarab (in dark green jasper). The scarab was a powerful symbol of regeneration and recurs on many of the items of jewelry in the tomb. Here it links a Shen ring, the sign of cyclical infinity, with a horizontal cartouche that contains the birth name of Psusennes I. Most of the Tanite gold is suspected to be recycled material from New Kingdom burials.

Whereas only pure face masks were used in the other royal burials at Tanis, the golden mask of Psusennes I completely envelops the head of the deceased ruler, transmitting his features to us in timeless beauty. The king wears the headdress with a rearing uraeus on his forehead, the plaited beard of the divine ruler and a broad necklace adorned with a floral pattern. His eyebrows, eyelids and the plaited beard are inlaid with costly lapis lazuli.

The Mystery of Piramesse

Eyptologists regard it as an accepted fact today that the "City of Ramesses" so often mentioned in the texts of the Nineteenth Dynasty is not the huge hill of ruins at Tanis, it lay further to the south in the eastern delta near the village of Qantir. The controversy lasted for decades until new archaeological finds decided the question. But initially Tanis was believed to be the site of Piramesse ("House of Ramesses"), which the Ramesside rulers made their new capital of Egypt; it is the place mentioned in the Bible where the people of Israel labored. In the last century excavations there revealed numerous figures of the kings and architectural fragments, most of which bore the name of Ramesses II. The French archaeologist Pierre Montet became the most important defender of the Tanis theory, directing the first planned excavations from 1929 on. The overwhelming number of surviving buildings from the Nineteenth and Twentieth Dynasties made him cling all his life firmly to the belief that Tanis was the city of the Ramesside rulers. But doubts were soon expressed, because in contrast to the wealth of monuments it was not possible to trace the architectural history of the New Kingdom in Tanis, while Egyptian archaeologists had found indisputable signs of a great city, with remnants of palaces and temples, at Qantir. Despite these evident signs it was only when an

View of the excavations at Qantir

expedition of Austrian and German scholars undertook extensive excavations from the 1970s in Qantir that certain proof was obtained that this was the most important urban center in the country in the late 2nd millenium B.C. The region of Qantir-Piramesse and the nearby metropolis of the Hyksos kings of Avaris (now Tell ed-Dab'a) covered an area of nearly 11.4 sq. miles (30 sq.km). The huge size of the site, coupled with the difficulty of excavating on arable land, means that progress is only slow, and the explorations are far from being completed even now. But every year brings important new knowledge. So what happened in the course of history between Auaris, Piramesse and Tanis? First the foreign rulers of the Hyksos made their capital Avaris in the eastern delta, ordering monuments of the Middle Kingdom to be transported from the area around Memphis to adorn it. The development was similar in the "City of Ramesses." From then on the rulers of the Nineteenth Dynasty used Avaris as a source, but they used other sources as well. The odyssee ended in Tanis, for when the Ramesside metropolis was abandoned at the end of the Twentieth Dynasty and the kings of the Twenty-first Dynasty decided to make Tanis, till then an almost unimportant town in the extreme east of the delta, their new capital they used Piramesse more or less as a stone quarry, in turn taking many older statues and parts of buildings like columns and obelisks to their new site. These monuments bore Ramesside inscriptions, and this led to the erroneous assumption that Tanis was the famous "House of Ramesses."

Tile bearing the name of Ramesses II, Nineteenth Dynasty, ca. 1250 B.C., Qantir, faience and calcite, H. 26.5 cm, Staatliches Museum Ägyptischer Kunst, Munich

Cairo, Giza and Memphis

Bab al-Futuh,
p. 83

The Egyptian
Museum, p. 88 ff.

The funerary mosque of
Qait Bey, p. 85

Wicker work capital with tree of life, p. 152

Cairo

Cairo has been the living heart of Egypt for over 1000 years. As the capital of the country and the seat of government, it accommodates all the most important Egyptian political, economic, and cultural institutions. It is also the undisputed international center of Sunni Islam. As the largest city on the African continent, with a population estimated at ca. 18 million, Cairo exerts great fascination through its strongly contrasting aspects, combining Islamic traditions with the requirements of the modern age. The city center is threatened daily by the imminent collapse of its traffic system, and the many measures taken to improve the infrastructure, for instance the building of overpasses and a modern subway, have not really succeeded in bringing relief to the Moloch that is Cairo. The first capital on the site dates from the time of Amr Ibn al-As, Caliph Omar's army commander, who founded a city in 641 A.D. in Fustat (now Old Cairo). However, it was destroyed by fire in the year 750 A.D. Over the next 200 years the center of power moved northward twice. The true date of the founding of Cairo was 969 A.D., when the Fatimids conquered Egypt and built a new capital, which they called al-Qahirah (Arab.: the Victorious).

Previous pages: The Desert near Cairo, from: David Roberts, Egypt and Nubia, London 1846–1850

Al-Azhar Mosque
Fatimid period, 10th century

No other mosque in Cairo surpasses al-Azhar, "The Flowering," in tradition and importance. Soon after its foundation in 970 A.D. it became the site of university studies, which have continued there to the present day and on which the fame of the al-Azhar mosque as a center of Islamic scholarship is based. Instruction in the classic subjects, such as theology and Islamic law, was not extended to include modern courses, for instance in medicine, economics, and engineering until 1961. The Fatimid nucleus of the building, which is of the courtyard mosque type, underwent many changes and extensions in the centuries after it was first erected. The main entrance, called the "Barbers' Gate," leads to the western portal of Sultan Qait Bey with its minaret (1469), and thus to the great central courtyard (Arab. *sahn*), 1130–1149, 157 × 105 ft (48 × 32 m). It is surrounded by an elegant colonnade of ogee arches (12th century), its facades lavishly ornamented with alternating stucco rosettes and blind niches.

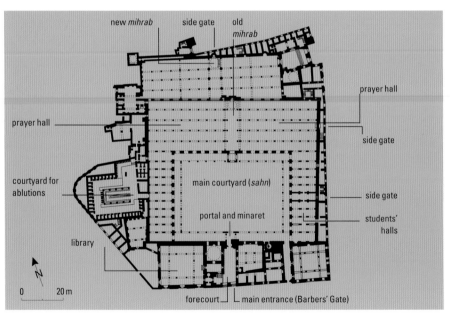

new *mihrab*   side gate   old *mihrab*

prayer hall

prayer hall

side gate

courtyard for ablutions

main courtyard (*sahn*)

side gate

portal and minaret

students' halls

library

0   20 m

N

forecourt   main entrance (Barbers' Gate)

View of the Prayer Hall
Fatimid period, 10th century

Beyond the eastern side of the courtyard lies the great prayer hall, measuring 43,055 ft² (4,000 m²), constructed as a pillared hall with five aisles in the original Fatimid building. The aisles run parallel to the *qibla* wall, facing Mecca. In the 18th century the hall was enlarged by the addition of four more aisles facing east, and a second prayer niche was also added to complement the central *mihrab* of the original building. Many of the marble columns were looted from buildings of classical antiquity and re-used here. This great prayer hall was not only the place where the faithful gathered for Friday prayers, as they still do today, but also served as the main lecture hall. Although it is no longer generally used for that purpose, groups of students being instructed by their teachers can still be seen there today.

Ibn Tulun Mosque
Tulunid period, 9th century

Cairo owes one of its oldest and most beautiful mosques to Ahmed Ibn Tulun, founder of the short-lived Tulunid dynasty. The building, erected in 876–879 A.D., is surrounded by very high outer walls, and on three sides by narrow forecourts 530 ft (162 m) long. The spiral shape of the lower part of the minaret, rising in the northwest forecourt, shows the building's connection with the architectural style of the Abassid mosques of Samarra (Iraq). At the center of the broad inner courtyard, which has sides 300 ft (92 m) long, stands the domed well house, built on a square ground plan. Like the minaret (131 ft, 40 m), it was completely renovated in the late 13th century under Sultan Lagin. The sides of the courtyard are surrounded by pillared arcades with pointed arches, built of red brick faced with stucco. The marble-paneled main prayer niche, the great wooden pulpit (the *minbar*), and the *dikka* (rostrum for the prayer leader) are in front of the prayer hall, which has five aisles.

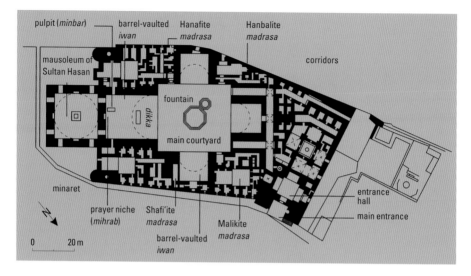

pulpit (*minbar*)   barrel-vaulted   Hanafite   Hanbalite
                     iwan   *madrasa*   *madrasa*

mausoleum of   corridors
Sultan Hasan

                     dikka   fountain

                                main courtyard

minaret   entrance
                                                         hall
prayer niche   Shafi'ite   main entrance
(*mihrab*)   *madrasa*
                              Malikite
            barrel-vaulted   *madrasa*
            iwan

0   20 m

Madrasah Mosque of Sultan Hasan

Mamluk period, 14th century

The mosque built below the citadel by Sultan Hasan (1347–1361) is among the outstanding achievements of Islamic architecture. The fortress-like building is constructed on an irregular pentagonal ground plan (l. 508 ft / 155 m), and covers an area of 85,034 ft² (7,900 m²). The two minarets are of different heights, since the northern minaret collapsed in the 17th century and had to be replaced by a smaller one. The still extant southern minaret reaches the considerable height of 267 ft (81.6 m). The façade, with its tall windows and several rows of stalactite ornamentation, is particularly impressive. The bronze double doors were plundered in 1415 by Sheikh Muaiyad, who used them for his own mosque. The rest of the building consists of an entrance area with several rooms, a central courtyard surrounded by prayer rooms and lecture halls, the main prayer hall, and the mausoleum beyond it, a domed rectangular room, adorned with stalactite ornamentation and surrounded by a calligraphic frieze. Equally unpressive is the metal work in solid gold and silver on its bronze portals. The sultan's catafalque (unused) is at the center of the mausoleum. Hasan was assassinated in the year 1361, and so did not see the inauguration of the mosque a year later.

The Courtyard Complex

The visitor reaches the rectangular courtyard of the Sultan Hasan Mosque by way of a flight of steps leading through the portal, which is 85 ft (26 m) high, then through a domed entrance hall built over a cruciform ground plan, and along a corridor. The courtyard is at the center of this building, which is the "four *iwan*" type of mosque. The four barrel-vaulted rooms (*iwans*) immediately adjoin the four sides of the courtyard, repeating the motif of the cruciform ground plan. Rooms for study, where instruction in the four Sunni schools of law was given as indicated by their names, lay between the *iwans*. The architecture as a whole thus appears square in design from the outside. The fountain for ablutions in the middle of the courtyard has a dome with a gilded calligraphic band of inscriptions running around it.

The Pulpit

The colored marble prayer rostrum (*dikka*), prayer niche (*mihrab*), and pulpit (*minbar*) in the main *iwan* of the Sultan Hasan Mosque are well preserved, and so is the band of inscriptions carved in stucco on the upper part of the walls. The *minbar* consists of an entrance portal with an outward-projecting stepped cornice, decorated with niches. There is a richly ornamented wooden double door at the entrance, and beyond it a steep flight of steps leads up to the pulpit itself, a kind of baldachin crowned by an onion dome on a tall base. As an essential item in the furnishing of a Friday mosque, the *minbar* was placed directly beside the prayer niche, so there was no set number of steps in the stairway leading up to the platform from which the Friday sermon was delivered. A *minbar* of this kind was originally the place where the Caliph himself or his deputy sat.

Muhammad Ali Mosque
Ottoman period (Khedives), 1830–1857

The citadel of Cairo was built under the Ayyubid dynasty between 1176 and 1207, and later extended to become the residence of the Mamluk and Ottoman pashas. Sultan al-Nasir Muhammad I (1294–1340) had a mosque as well as his principal palace built here, and the mosque stands to this day. He also commissioned a great aqueduct to bring water from the Nile and raise it to the citadel by wheel-powered devices. The second great mosque in the citadel was commissioned by Muhammad Ali, the Khedive (viceroy) who reigned in 1805/06–1848. The 42 year-old Pasha of Macedonian origin started the modernization of Egypt. His tremendous mosque was located on the site of the old Sultan's palace, which had been blown up in 1824 when the arsenal exploded. The architect Yusuf "the Bosnian" took his guidelines from the classic Ottoman style, and accordingly his building consists of two slender minarets (h. 269 ft; 80 m), a forecourt with water for ablutions, and the great prayer hall with its mighty main dome and several smaller domes. The walls are clad in alabaster, and the window openings are filled in with thin plates of the same material, hence the building's name of the "Alabaster Mosque." The marble sarcophagus of Muhammad Ali is on the right of the entrance to the domed hall.

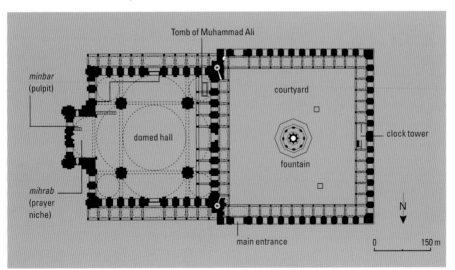

Courtyard with well house

The courtyard of the Alabaster Mosque of Muhammad Ali is surrounded by arcades, roofed with 50 small domes, and has three larger domes over the passageways. The main entrance to the complex is at the eastern corner of the northern arcade, and the entrance to the mosque is in the middle of the eastern arcade. The well for purification (*hanafiya*) is at the center of the courtyard; the projecting edge of its domed roof rests on eight fluted columns. The ornamentation and flower motifs on the well are very reminiscent of the French Empire style. A clock tower, a gift to the Khedive from King Louis Philippe of France (1830–1848), rises in the center of the western arcade.

Domed ceiling of the prayer hall

The ceiling of the prayer hall consists of a huge, lofty dome, 170 ft (52 m) in height, resting on four pillars, with four semi-domes around it, and four more smaller domes over the corners of the hall. The window gallery with its alabaster panes is directly below this domed area, skilfully dividing it, as if by means of a photoelectric beam, from the dark space below, where the walls are covered with alabaster slabs to a height of 36 ft (11 m). The architect Yusuf Bosnak probably took the inspiration of his design from the example of the 16th-century Ottoman architect Sinan.

Bab el-Futuh

Fatimid period, late 11th century

In the late 11th century Vizier Badr al-Jamali had a massive fortress laid out around the residence of al-Qahirah (Cairo) for the Fatimid caliphs. An Armenian master builder from Odessa familiar with the construction of fortifications was engaged as architect. The Armenian erected a mighty structure with rectangular bastions, 60 entrance gates, and rounded battlements along the entire coping of the wall. Although the city wall never had to withstand a siege, only a part of it measuring 1968 ft (600 m) in length has been preserved, along with three gatehouses: the Bab el-Futuh ("Gate of Conquest"), the Bab en-Nasr ("Gate of Victory"), and the Bab Zuwaylah, which was still in use as a place of public execution in the 19th century. The Bab al-Futuh consists of two massive round towers and the gateway between them, with curved flying buttresses and rounded battlements above. The guardrooms also lay above the gateway passage, which is $16^1/_2$ ft (5 m) wide and 20 ft (6.80 m) high, with its original foundations 13 ft (4 m) below the present surface level. The arcades beside the entrance are ornamented with a frieze of radiating lines above the arches.

The Necropolis

The great necropolis, now merged into the modern sea of buildings, lies east of Fatimid al-Qahira at the foot of the Mokattam mountain range. It contains some of the most impressive examples of all Islamic architecture. The northern cemetery is notable for the so-called "caliphs' tombs," meaning the mausoleums of the Burgi Mamluk sultans (1382–1517) and their families. Particularly impressive are the funerary mosques of al-Zahir Barkuk, al-Akhraf Bars Bay, and Qait Bey, with their wealth of architectural decoration. The southern cemetery contains, among other buildings, the tombs of the Bahri Mamluks (1250–1382), and the mausoleums of the great juridical scholar Imam al-Shafii (built 1211) and the family of Khedive Muhammad Ali (19th century).

The Mausoleum and Mosque of Qait Bey

Mamluk period, 1472–1474

This complex is among the finest Islamic buildings in Cairo. It consists of a portal area with a well, a minaret (h. 131 ft; 40 m), the *madrasa* mosque with its four areas arranged in a cruciform pattern around a courtyard (the "four-*iwan*" design), living rooms and maintenance offices, as well as the mausoleum itself and a chamber beside it for the tombs of the sultan's four wives. The dome and minaret are ornamented with filigree arabesque decoration, and the interior too was adorned with valuable incrustations (inlay decoration), and marble floors with intarsia work. Qait Bey's magnificent cenotaph (tomb without a body in it) stands before the prayer niche in the mausoleum, with a reliquary beside it containing the black footprints of the Prophet Muhammad from Mecca.

The Prophet Muhammad

Koran fragment, Irak or Syria, 9th–10th century, parchment with ink and gold illumination, 21.5 x 32.5 cm.
Museum für Islamische Kunst, Staatliche Museen zu Berlin/ I.2211

The Prophet Muhammad was born around 570 A.D. in Mecca. At the age of 25 he married Khadija, a prosperous merchant's widow who bore him several children. As he grew older his mind began to turn to questions of religion, and he had his first visionary experiences of revelation in his 40th year. Finally he felt called by God to convert the Arabs to Islam, that is to say, to a strictly monotheistic religion. However, his mission was rejected in Mecca, where he even encountered outright hostility, and as a result he and his adherents moved to Medina in A.D. 622. Here he formed a community of faith that took political measures in order to achieve its religious aims. A struggle to spread the new religion now began and lasted many years, but in 630 A.D. Muhammad succeeded in entering Mecca. He proclaimed the sacred precinct of the city the center of Islam, and described himself as the "Seal of the Prophets," that is to say, the last of God's prophets, to whom the deity had entrusted the task of leading all mankind to the true faith. After his death in 632 A.D., his immediate successors the caliphs succeeded in conquering the entire southern Mediterranean area, the Near East, Egypt, and later on parts of Spain within only a few decades.

The major articles of faith for every Muslim are the "Five Pillars of Islam." They are the profession of belief in the One God and his messenger Muhammad, the performance of prayer five times a day, the giving of alms, fasting in the month of Ramadan, and pilgrimage to Mecca. The basic of Islam is the Koran. It contains the revelations that the Prophet Muhammad received from God, Islamic doctrine with its ethical concepts, and the Islamic laws. The Koran is divided into 114 suras, which consist of a varying number of verses. Another basic element of Islam is the *sunna*, the handing down of the accurate tradition of the Prophet's deeds and words, understood as commentaries on the Koran. Finally, the *sharia* also plays an important part: it is a catalog of duties drawn up by juridical scholars on the basis of the Koran, the *sunna*, the norms of conduct derived from them, and the traditions generally accepted in the community. In some Islamic states (for instance Iran) the *sharia* is regarded as a binding legal system.

Despite these principles, held in common by all Muslims, Islam is not a homogeneous religion. The various different interpretations of the Koran have led to conflicts, and so have power struggles within Islam. Today, therefore, there are many different Islamic tendencies. The Sunnis and Shiites are the two major Islamic communities, but contain many further schismatic tendencies within themselves.

Prayer niche in the Mosque of Sultan Hasan, colored marble, 14th century, Cairo

The Egyptian Museum

The National Egyptian Museum, which today contains the largest and most important of all collections of Egyptian antiquities, with well over 150,000 objects, lies on busy Midan al-Tahrir ("Freedom Square"). It was built between 1897 and 1901 under the rule of Khedive Abbas Helmi, to plans by the French architect Marcel Dourgnon. The solemn opening ceremony was held on 15 November 1902. This event successfully concluded a long campaign conducted by Auguste Mariette and his successors after the Antiquities Service was founded in 1858, with a view to providing suitable accommodation for the exhibits. (Until recently Mariette's mausoleum stood in the museum garden.) The exhibition rooms are on two floors around a covered inner courtyard. The ground-floor displays are mainly in chronological order, while the upper floor is devoted chiefly to the galleries of treasures from Tutankhamun's tomb and other great archaeological discoveries like the "gold of Tanis." Despite many improvements, the building can no longer meet the needs of a modern museum, and the projected new building in Giza is eagerly awaited.

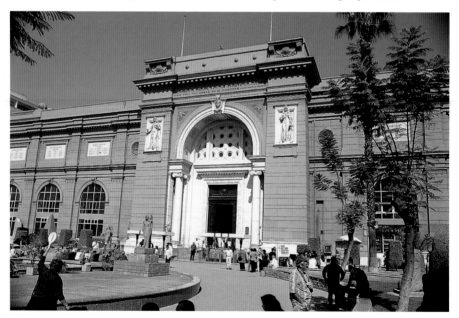

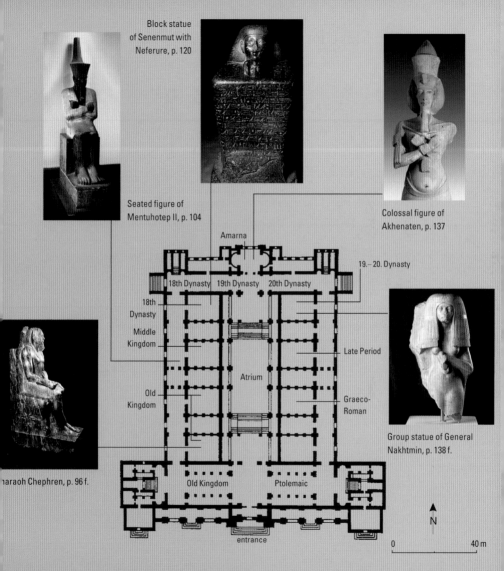

Block statue
of Senenmut with
Neferure, p. 120

Seated figure of
Mentuhotep II, p. 104

Colossal figure of
Akhenaten, p. 137

Amarna

19.– 20. Dynasty

18th Dynasty   19th Dynasty   20th Dynasty

18th
Dynasty

Middle
Kingdom

Late Period

Old
Kingdom

Atrium

Graeco-
Roman

Group statue of General
Nakhtmin, p. 138 f.

haraoh Chephren, p. 96 f.

Old Kingdom   Ptolemaic

N

entrance

0   40 m

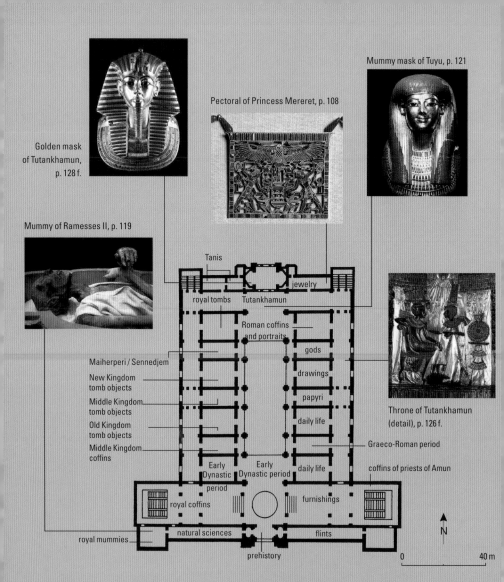

Golden mask of Tutankhamun, p. 128 f.

Pectoral of Princess Mereret, p. 108

Mummy mask of Tuyu, p. 121

Mummy of Ramesses II, p. 119

Tanis

jewelry

royal tombs   Tutankhamun

Roman coffins and portraits

Maiherperi / Sennedjem

New Kingdom tomb objects

Middle Kingdom tomb objects

Old Kingdom tomb objects

Middle Kingdom coffins

gods

drawings

papyri

daily life

Throne of Tutankhamun (detail), p. 126 f.

Early Dynastic period

Early Dynastic period

daily life

Graeco-Roman period

coffins of priests of Amun

royal coffins

furnishings

royal mummies

natural sciences

flints

prehistory

N

0   40 m

Bowl with three-dimensional rim decoration

Predynastic period (Naqada I), 4th millenium B.C.,
Gebelein, painted pottery, H. 11 cm, Diam.19.5 cm

Ceramic items are among the most important artefacts of Egyptian prehistory, and
are indispensable for the dating of archeological finds. This bowl, with its white
painting on a reddish brown ground, is a
typical example from the earlier Naqada
culture (Naqada I). At this time decoration
was usually in the form of geometrical
patterns, but depictions of animals and
plants also occur, and so very occasionally
do three-dimensional appliquéd figures
like the four crocodiles here.

Painted vessel

Predynastic period (Naqada II), 4th millenium B.C.,
pottery, painted, H. 22 cm, Diam.15 cm

During the 4th century B.C. the forms in
which pottery vessels were made and the
variety of their ornamentation developed
constantly. Among the classic types are
vessels with a narrow lip and two broad lug
handles with holes bored into them.
Decorations in the Naqada II period are in
brownish red paint on the light, unpolished pottery ground. Scenic elements are
not yet divided into separate registers, but
are dispersed around the body of the
vessel. This pot shows a group of ostriches,
and above them a rowing boat with a
double cabin. The anchor hangs from the
bows, which are adorned with a palm
frond.

The Narmer Palette

Dynasty 0, ca. 3100 B.C., Hierakonpolis, graywacke, H. 64 cm

In 1894, during excavations in the temple of Horus at Hierakonpolis, a British archaeological team found several depots of discarded cult objects including the magnificent palette of king Narmer from the Protodynastic period (Dynasty 0). The front shows two snake-necked panthers with their necks intertwined. The circular shape in the center symbolizes the solar disk, and the ropes, one taut, one hanging down, by which two men are holding the fabulous animals symbolize the movement of the sun in its course. In the upper register, Narmer is leaving his palace with an escort of standard-bearers to inspect two rows of bound and beheaded enemies. At the bottom of the palette, the ruler is shown as a bull destroying a fortification wall with his horns. The main motif on the palette´s back presents the canonical image of the victorious pharaoh, the so-called "Smiting the Enemies." The king, followed by his sandal-bearer, is shown here wearing the white crown of Upper Egypt. The falcon god Horus appears before him, holding the head of a prisoner on a leash. An integrated sign denoting "land," from which six papyrus reeds are growing, marking Narmer's conquest of the Delta. The top of the palette, on both the back and the front, ends in two cow's heads denoting the archaic sky goddess Bat, flanking the Horus name of the king.

Seated statue of Djoser

Third Dynasty, ca. 2650 B.C., Saqqara, pyramid complex of Djoser, limestone, H. 142 cm

The famous seated figure of King Djoser is the earliest life-size portrait of a ruler yet found in Egypt. Originally it was placed in a small limestone chamber, the *serdab*, directly in front of the north side of the Step pyramid. Two holes at the height of the statue's eyes allowed the dead king to look out at the imperishable stars in the northern sky, according to the beliefs of the time the location of the world beyond the grave. Djoser is seated on a throne resembling a sedan chair, with a back rest and a raised area for his feet. Its front bears the titulary and name of the king (Horus Netjeri-khet, "of divine body"). His figure is enveloped in a long garment, the *sed* festival cloak, from which only the clenched fist of his right arm emerges, held across his chest. His outstretched left hand rests on his left thigh. The king's regalia also includes a wig of strands of hair, partly covered by an archaic version of the *nemes* headcloth with its pointed lappets in front, and the impressive ceremonial beard. The stern expression of the king's face, with its high cheekbones, broad mouth, and moustache, was once emphasized by inlay work of colored materials (e.g. calcite, obsidian) for the eyes and eyebrows. The base from another Statue of Djoser is famous for its front inscription giving us the titles and name of Imhotep, the architect of the Step Pyramid.

Relief panel of Hesyra
Third Dynasty, ca. 2650 B.C., Saqqara, mastaba of Hesy, wood, H. 114 cm

Like the pyramids built for the dead rulers of the Old Kingdom, the mastabas or tomb complexes of officials were subject to architectural development. Their size and structural design reflect the time of their building and the social status of their occupants. Hesy (or Hesyra), who held many high administrative offices under King Djoser, had a huge mud brick-built mastaba built for him to the north of his master's Step pyramid in Saqqara. The main offering chamber is in the form of a long corridor with eleven niches along its west wall. The back of each niche was covered by a tall wooden panel; six panels were still extant at the time of the excavations directed by Auguste Mariette in 1860. They all show the owner of the tomb in various positions and costumes. The athletic figure of Hesy, wearing a wig of many strands and the man's short kilt, stands beneath an area inscribed with his title and name. He holds a scepter of office in his right hand, while his left grasps a staff and several writing implements, including a palette with two paint containers. The powerfully rendered musculature of the figure marks a first peak in the relief art of the Old Kingdom. After the first discovery the location of Hesy's tomb was soon forgotten, and only in 1911/12 accidentally found again by James E. Quibell who then properly eccavated the whole structure.

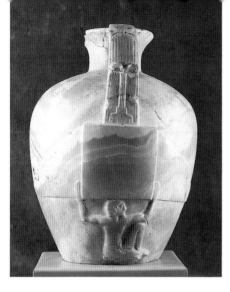

Ceremonial vase
Third Dynasty, ca. 2650 B.C., Saqqara,
Step pyramid of Djoser, calcite, H. 37 cm

Kneeling figure of Hetepdief
Third Dynasty, ca. 2650 B.C., Memphis, red
granite, H. 39 cm

The underground storerooms of the Step pyramid of Djoser contained some 40,000 vessels of all kinds of shapes and made in many varieties of stone, including some very unusual special designs. The subject of the relief decoration of this vase is the ruler's *sed* festival (*hebsed*), that is, the jubilee year of his reign. The kneeling figure of the god Heh ("millions, god of infinity") supports a high rostrum with stairways rising at the sides, and a double *hebsed* pavilion in which the thrones of the Two Lands are depicted. The scarab motif on the upper part of the handle emphasizes the general theme of renewal.

The figure of Hetepdief, on a thin base slab which also gives his title and name, is kneeling on the ground with both hands flat on his knees, in the attitude of prayer. The official, who is wearing a curled wig and an apron, was probably active in the funerary cult of the first three kings of the Second Dynasty, whose Horus names are incised behind his right shoulder. The carving of the body is still clumsy, with an outsize head and almost no neck. Its style marks the figure out as one of the earliest distinguished works of private sculpture; it must date from shortly before the end of the Third Dynasty.

Statuette of King Cheops

Fourth Dynasty, ca. 2560 B.C., Abydos, ivory, H. 7.5 cm

This tiny statuette of Cheops is the only extant portrait of the builder of the Great Pyramid of Giza. The ruler sits enthroned, wearing the red crown of Lower Egypt and a short royal kilt. He holds the scourge in his right hand. Only the lower part of the figurine was initially found during the excavations at Abydos in 1903. The Horus name of Cheops carved on the throne, however, set off a new and intensive (and ultimately successful) search for the head lasting full three weeks.

The Pharaoh Chephren

Fourth Dynasty, ca. 2530 B.C., Giza, valley temple of Chephren, anorthosite gneiss, H. 168 cm

No other statue of a ruler of the Old Kingdom conveys the idea of divine kingship as impressively as this seated figure of Chephren, one of the great masterpieces of Egyptian free-standing sculpture. It unites highly skilled treatment of the material with many complex levels of meaning in its formal construction. Chephren is seated on a high-backed lion throne, and wears the royal headcloth, the short kilt and front panel, and a narrow beard indicating divinity. Both sides of the seat of the throne are ornamented with a combination of motifs showing lotus and papyrus, the emblematic plants of Upper and Lower Egypt. Henceforward, this heraldic representation of the "Union of the Two Lands" was the canonical expression of the existence of a single state. The figure of a falcon, symbol of the sky god Horus, perches on the broad back of the throne, its two wings embracing the ruler's head. The tips of the wings touch the corner points of the side sections and breast lappets of the headcloth, making the figure of the bird an integral part of the statue as a whole. This figure of the "Falcon Chephren" once stood in the pillared hall (center position on the rear wall) of the valley temple of Chephren's pyramid complex at Giza, an eternal manifestation of the divine nature of the king, Horus incarnated on earth.

Triad statue of Mycerinus
Fourth Dynasty, ca. 2500 B.C., Giza, valley temple
of Mycerinus, graywacke, H. 96 cm

In 1907/08, at the very beginning of his
excavations in Giza, G. Andrew Reisner
(Harvard University, Boston) explored the
cult complexes of the pyramid of
Mycerinus. In all, he found four group
statues preserved complete in the ruler's
valley temple, as well as many fragments of
other sculptures of different sizes. Each of
these triads shows the same three persons,
identically arranged: the king, the sky
goddess Hathor, and a deity being the
personification (male or female) of one of
the nomes of Egypt. There is similar consis-
tency in the material used for the works
(graywacke) and the depiction of
Mycerinus wearing the crown of Upper
Egypt. Although Reisner could not find a
single fragment of a triad referring to
Lower Egypt, such works had probably
been originally planned. The king stands at
the center of the group, in front of a tall
back panel, on his right Hathor (with cow's
horns and the disk of the sun), and on his
left the local goddess of the seventh nome
of Upper Egypt (with the emblem of the
nome on her head). The fluid forms of the
two female figures, clearly indicated
beneath their long robes, contrast with the
athletic build of King Mycerinus. The
inscriptions on the base slab mention the
titles and names of Hathor and the king,
and also refer to the offerings for the
funerary cult.

King Userkaf
Fifth Dynasty, ca. 2450 B.C., Abusir, Sun-temple of
Userkaf, graywacke, H. 45 cm

Userkaf, the first ruler of the Fifth Dynasty,
had a temple of the sun built at Abusir,
north of Saqqara, and dedicated it to the
special veneration of the god Re. Found
shortly before excavations there concluded
in 1957, this strongly expressive head was
at first taken for a portrait of the goddess
Neith because of the absence of the ceremonial beard and the crown of Lower
Egypt. However, remnants of colour from a
thin moustache admit no doubt that it is to
be regarded as a portrait of the king.

Rahotep and Nofret
Fourth Dynasty, ca. 2600 B.C., Meidum, limestone, painted, H. 121 and 122 cm

A large brick mastaba was built for Prince Rahotep near the pyramid of his father Snefru, and the two seated figures of the occupant of the tomb and his wife Nofret were found in it in 1871. They are in a state of perfect preservation, and are the finest examples extant of the sculptural art of the early Fourth Dynasty. Rahotep, who as well as holding other offices was High priest of Re in Heliopolis, has his hair cut short and wears a simple linen kilt. Nofret is wearing a sophisticated low-cut robe, a broad collar, and a shoulder-length wig of strands of hair with a diadem.

Standing figure of Ka'aper
Fifth Dynasty, ca. 2470 B.C., Saqqara, sycamore wood, H. 112 cm

When this figure (once painted) was discovered in 1860, the lifelike features of the priest Ka'aper reminded the workers so much of their local mayor that they spontaneously nicknamed him Sheikh el-Beled (Arab.: village mayor). Despite the realistic appearance of the occupant of Kaaper's tomb, the figure is primarily a stock type of private sculpture. His short hair, noticeably stout build, and knee-length kilt represent the figure of a successful and economically prosperous official at the height of his career. Both legs as well as the long staff are modern additions to the statue.

Ipi carried in procession

Sixth Dynasty, ca. 2300 B.C., south Saqqara,
limestone, H. 112 cm

In his official capacity, the steward Ipi is on
his way to the harbor to supervise the
arrival of freight vessels. As befits his position, he is seated in a magnificent litter
with a sun-roof. It is carried by 14 bearers
in all, but only the men on the right-hand
side are visible, while those on the left are
indicated by a double outline along the
shapes of their bodies. The official wears a
curled wig, the short kilt with a starched
front panel, and a panther skin hanging
over his left shoulder. He is holding a short
staff of command in his left hand and a
flail in his right hand. Servants carrying
sunshades accompany the procession at a
run, together with other members of Ipi's
household. The inscriptions between the
bearers are the words of the so-called
"litter song" in which they complain of
their hard, sudorific work.

The Falcon God Horus
Sixth Dynasty, ca. 2300 B.C., Hierakonpolis, gold and obsidian, H. 37.5 cm, 635 g

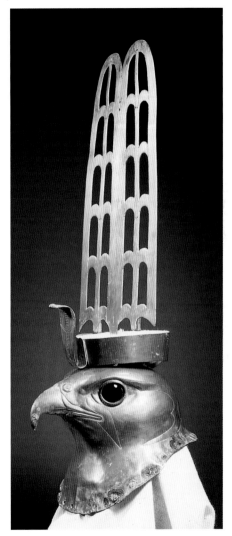

It is very unusual for valuable cult objects made of precious metal to have survived through the ages, since they were constantly being melted down for either legal or illegal purposes. This fine falcon's head, made of chased rolled gold, owes its preservation only to a lucky chance. When the ancient temple of the god Horus in Hierakonpolis (Egypt.: Nekhen) was renovated in the New Kingdom period, various liturgical items were taken out of use and deposited in a pit under the paving of the floor, where they remained in safety until they were discovered in 1897/98 by the British archaeologists James E. Quibell and Frederick W. Green. The former cult statue was made of wood and covered with small copper plates. Only the head was gold, and was fixed in place with bronze and gold nails. The details of the bird's head, portrayed from nature but executed with the minimalist formality of a sculptural work, are extremely well caught. The large eyes consist of an obsidian rod running through the head, with its ends rounded and polished. The ornament on the divine falcon's head is a tall double plumed crown, rising above a ring-shaped, broad diadem with a large *uraeus* (cobra) to the front. Still under discussion is the exact date of the crown´s addition to the basic figure which should be fixed for the early 12th Dynasty of the Middle Kingdom.

Seated figure of Mentuhotep II
Eleventh Dynasty, ca. 2030 B.C., Western Thebes, Deir el-Bahri, temple of Mentuhotep II, sandstone, painted, H. 138 cm

Chance as well as systematic work can be a deciding factor in an archeologist's success. When Howard Carter, later to discover the tomb of Tutankhamun, was riding over the broad forecourt of the mortuary temple of Mentuhotep II in Western Thebes in 1900, the ground caved in under his horse's feet. Since then, the hollow subsequently excavated has been known as Bab el-Hosan (Gate of the Horse). In fact it proved to be the entrance to a long tunnel leading into a chamber under the temple, where a seated figure of the king wrapped in a thin linen cloth was found beside an empty, uninscribed coffin. The entire find indicates that the complex, probably re-using an older building stage, acted as an Osiris tomb. Mentuhotep II sits with his arms crossed on a simple throne consisting of a block without any back rest or inscription. Like the body parts of the statue, it is painted black, the symbolic color of fertility and regeneration. The founder of the Middle Kingdom wears the red crown, the short *sed* festival garment, and a large divine beard. In its self-contained form, its powerfully depicted features, and its forceful corporeality, this portrait marks the beginning of a new tendency in royal free-standing sculpture. This pristine figure was once part of an elaborate series of statues commissioned by Mentuhotep II for his burial complex.

Pillar of Senusret I (detail)

Twelfth Dynasty, ca. 1930 B.C., Karnak, temple of Amun-Re, limestone, H. 434 cm, W. 75 cm

Although the rulers of the early Twelfth Dynasty moved their residential seat north again, to the area around Memphis, they were still anxious to maintain the temples of Upper Egypt. Many new foundations or extensions owed their existence to the intensive building activity under Senusret I in particular. They included the first large temple of Amun in Karnak, built entirely of limestone. The demolition of the Eighteenth Dynasty period left only a few parts of these buildings extant, but they include this monumental pillar, once one of several forming the façade or ambulatory of the central building. Each side of the pillar shows the king embracing one of the most important divinities of the country. The falcon god Horus of Edfu and Amun of Karnak represent the south, and as shown here the creator god Atum of Heliopolis and Ptah of Memphis symbolize the north. Senusret I and Ptah stand together face to face under the roof of a shrine.

The king wears the striped *nemes* headcloth and a short pleated kilt, while the mummy-like figure of the deity is wearing his typical attribute of a close-fitting cap. The clear carving of the large hieroglyphs of the inscriptions complements the stern relief style of this cultic scene to create a dense overall composition. The short text mentions one of the most common epithets of god Ptah, dwelling "south of his walls."

Senusret III at prayer

Twelfth Dynasty, ca. 1860 B.C., Western Thebes, Deir el-Bahri, temple of Mentuhotep II, granodiorite, H. 150 cm

Senusret III had six statues erected in the funerary temple of Mentuhotep II, founder of the Middle Kingdom, in honor of his predecessor. An entirely new development in royal sculpture is the attitude of prayer, with the king's hands placed flat on the apron section of his kilt. The grave but dynamic appearance of the ruler's face is particularly impressive. It has thin features with deep-set eyes under naturally arched brows, clearly marked naso-labial folds, and a narrow-lipped mouth.

The "fish-offering" Dyad of Amenemhat III

Twelfth Dynasty, ca. 1830 B.C., Tanis, granodiorite, H. 160 cm, w. 100 cm

The double statue of Amenemhat III found in Tanis was one of an extremely unusual group of monuments to this king, and probably originally stood in the shrine of the crocodile Sobek at Medinet el-Faiyum. It depicts the ruler twice, showing him with a curious wig of corkscrew curls and an artificial beard. This specific hairstyle conveys an archaic cult action. He is holding an offering plate containing fish, from which lotus plants, another fish, and trapped geese hang down, and he thus embodies the fertility god of the Nile, Hapy. The inscription was secondarily added by Psusennes I (Twenty-first Dynasty).

Pectoral of Princess Mereret

Twelfth Dynasty, ca. 1840 B.C., Dahshur, tomb of Mereret, gold, cornelian, lapis lazuli, amethyst, H. 7.9 cm

As the daughter of Senusret III, Princess Mereret could furnish her tomb using the jewelry produced in the royal workshops. The pectoral shown here has a central inscription with two cartouches giving both the throne names of Mereret's brother King Amenemhat III, who was reigning at this time, and describing him as "the perfect god, lord of the Two Lands and of all foreign lands." The king is depicted on both sides of the pectoral, attacking an Asiatic enemy whom he has seized by the hair in order to strike him with a club. The vulture goddess Nekhbet hovers above this highly symbolic scene. The entire motif is chased on the back of the pectoral too.

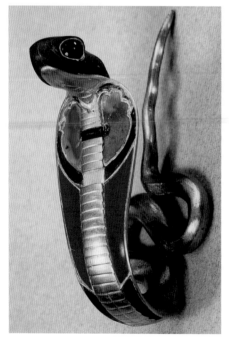

Uraeus serpent of Senusret II

Twelfth Dynasty, ca. 1880 B.C., el-Lahun, pyramid of Senusret II, gold, lapis lazuli, cornelian, feldspar, H. 6.7 cm

Together with the royal crook and flail, the *uraeus* serpent (cobra) was one of the most important symbols of kingship. The king wore its likeness over his forehead to demonstrate his power and his constant readiness to defend the land. The *uraeus* of Senusret II was found in a room beside the burial chamber of his pyramid in el-Lahun in the Faiyum. The site of the find suggests that the jewel had been overlooked by tomb robbers. The body of the snake is worked in gold, with inlaid gemstones of several colors. Two eyelets welded to the coiling tail section served to fasten it to the ruler's headdress (cap or headcloth).

Ka figure of King Hor
Thirteenth Dynasty, ca. 1720 B.C., Dahshur, wood, H. 170 cm; H. of shrine 207 cm

This unique statue was found in a wooden shrine as part of the burial equipment of King Hor, a historically unimportant ruler of the Thirteenth Dynasty whose tomb lay within the enclosure wall north of the "Black Pyramid" of Amenemhat III. The symbol of the so-called *ka* arms above the statue's head show that it is a *ka* figure of the king, an image of the vital force that continues after death. Wearing only a wig of strands of hair and the plaited divine beard, the figure of the *ka* is shown naked and walking forward; its hands no longer hold the king's horizontally carried scepter (right hand) and staff (left hand). Slight remnants of color indicate that the figure was partially gilded. Like the original paint, the gilding was once applied to a thin stucco ground, which immediately disintegrated when the figure was discovered by the French archaeologist J. de Morgan in 1894/95. The narrow burial chamber contained also the coffin of the king with his plundered mummy. Made from high quality imported wood, this masterpiece shows bands of hieroglyphic texts executed in gold foil.

Standing figure of a hippopotamus

Second Intermediate Period, Seventeenth
Dynasty, ca. 1600 B.C., Western Thebes,
Dra Abu'l-Naga, blue faience, H. 11.5 cm

During the Middle Kingdom and the
Second Intermediate Period, tomb objects
consisting of vessels and small figures of
naked women and animals (for instance
hedgehogs, hares, and monkeys) were
often placed in the tombs of the dead.
Hippopotamus figures are particularly
common. There are three basic types,
showing the mighty animal lying, standing, or sitting, with its jaws closed or open
ready to bellow. The blue or green color of
the faience glaze, and the aquatic plants
painted on the figure, not only suggest the
creature's natural habitat but also have a
magical function. The papyrus and lotus,
promising protection and regeneration, are
particularly prominent symbols. Numi-
nous powers were ascribed to hippopotami
from a very early period. On the one hand
they represented untamed nature, and
were regarded as dangerous animals to be
fought, on the other they symbolized fertility, and consequently protecting deities
such as Thoeris appear in the form of a
hippopotamus.

Stela of King Ahmose

Eighteenth Dynasty, ca. 1540
B.C., Abydos, limestone,
H. 225 cm

After emerging victorious from his struggle for liberation against the Hyksos, Pharaoh Ahmose had this stela erected in honor of his dead grandmother Tetisheri. The ruler appears on both sides of the top of the memorial stone beneath the symbol of the winged sun, dedicating a large collection of offerings to the enthroned Tetisheri, who is shown in the regalia of a reigning queen. The wig with its vulture headdress and tall wings, and the flail-like scepter in her hand, are particularly important items. The long text is an account of a conversation between Ahmose and his sister-wife Ahmes-Nefertari, in which he announces that he is setting up a funerary memorial in Abydos to the founding mother of his ruling house. The complex was to comprise a small lake and a garden, as well as a pyramid with a chapel.

Queen Hatshepsut

Eighteenth Dynasty, ca. 1470 B.C., Western
Thebes, Deir el-Bahri, mortuary temple of
Hatshepsut, limestone, painted, H. 61 cm

Hatshepsut, daughter of King Thutmosis I
and wife of her half-brother Thutmosis II,
came to power after her husband's death.
She was intended to act as regent for the
new ruler, her underage stepson Thutmosis III. However, she had herself
crowned queen in the second year of the
reign of Thutmosis III, and henceforward
regarded herself as his coregent. There
seem to have been no open conflicts
between her and Thutmosis III during
their reign of almost two decades, for they
had themselves depicted together, for
instance making offerings to the gods.
Only after her death toward the end of her
stepson's long reign was Hatshepsut's
name as ruler and her pictorial representation effaced from her memorials, even in
her mortuary temple at Deir el-Bahri. The
fragment of a face shown belongs to one of
the colossal statues on the upper terrace of
her temple in front of the pillars of the
façade. These "Osiride pillars" show the
queen in the person of a god, that is, in the
shape of a mummy with the divine beard.
They also wear one or other of the crowns
of the Two Lands, in this case the double
crown (only a remnant of the crown of
Lower Egypt is preserved), proving that the
statue to which the face belonged stood on
the northern side of the terrace.

Kneeling figure of Thutmosis III

Eighteenth Dynasty, ca. 1450 B.C., Western
Thebes, Deir el-Medineh, marble, H. 26.5 cm

This small royal figure was found in 1912
among rubble by the western encircling
wall of the temple of Hathor at Deir el-
Medineh. It shows Thutmosis III offering
wine, a popular type of royal sculpture in
the New Kingdom. The ruler kneels on the
ground, holding a globular vessel in each
hand for presentation to the deity. Worth
mentioning is the material, marble, which
was rarely used for sculpture.

Seated figure of Queen Isis

Eighteenth Dynasty, ca. 1450 B.C., Karnak, temple of Amun-Re, granodiorite, H. 98.5 cm

This statue of Queen Isis was set up in the royal temple at Karnak by her son Thutmosis III, as indicated by the inscription on the left of the throne: "He did this in memory of his mother, the Queen Mother Isis, justified." The queen is wearing an ankle-length robe with shoulder straps, a wide collar, and a long plaited wig. The two *uraeus* symbols of Upper and Lower Egypt rise from her forehead. All that has been preserved of the tall feathered crown (probably made of precious metal) is the gilded lower section.

The Hathor Chapel of Thutmosis III

Eighteenth Dynasty, ca. 1430 B.C., Western Thebes, Deir el-Bahri, painted sandstone, H. 225 cm

When Thutmosis III closed down the cult in the mortuary temple of Hatshepsut in Deir el-Bahri with the established veneration of Hathor there, he not only built a temple of his own above the adjacent temple of Mentuhotep II, but also added a new rock-cut chapel in honor of Hathor. It was his successor Amenophis II, who then added the monumental cult image of the cow goddess Hathor with the figure of the king. This statue almost entirely fills the little grotto with its well-preserved frescoes (showing Thutmosis III offering to the gods).

The Royal Mummies of the New Kingdom

In the 19th century, when modern archaeologists embarked on excavations in Egypt, and European countries became interested in acquiring objects of Pharaonic culture for their museums, another "professional group," one with a tradition thousands of years old behind it, began to flourish again. These professionals were tomb robbers, and the great necropolis of Western Thebes was among the main sites of their illegal activities. Probably in the summer of 1871, members of the old-established Abd el-Rasul family of tomb raiders discovered the entrance to a funerary complex south of the valley of Deir el-Bahri. When they had climbed down into the access shaft, which was twelve meters deep, the two brothers Ahmed and Hussein could hardly believe their eyes. Dozens of coffins and boxes containing *shabti* figurines (see p. 434 f.), statuettes, and many papyri were stored in the adjoining corridor. It was a positive goldmine, and called for careful exploitation. But despite the family's skillful sales strategy, after a while the authorities realized that more and more objects from royal burials were circulating in the art trade of Cairo and Europe. In 1881 therefore, the Frenchman Gaston Maspero, who was director general of the Antiquities Service at the time, went to Upper Egypt to look into the matter. He was soon

G. Maspero and companions at the entrance to the Cachette of the royal mummies, Western Thebes, valley of Deir el-Bahri

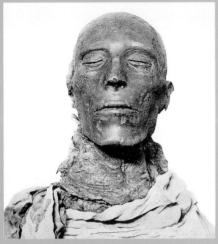

Head of the mummy of Sety I after unwrapping, Nineteenth Dynasty, ca. 1280 B.C., Egyptian Museum, Cairo

Reburial inscription from the coffin of Ramesses II, Twenty-first Dynasty, ca. 1060 B.C., Egyptian Museum, Cairo

able to identify the prime suspects, but the Abd el-Rasuls denied any part in what had been going on, and even a search of their houses brought no result. Maspero handed the brothers over to the Mudir of Kena as the authority responsible. Several months under arrest, and methods of interrogation which were anything but gentle, belatedly took effect. The eldest brother, Muhammad, finally gave the secret away, and in July that year he led a commission set up by the Khedive (the regent in Cairo) to the hiding place in Deir el-Bahri, the famous "*cachette*" of New Kingdom royal mummies. Maspero was officially represented by his colleague Emil Brugsch, who later described his first impression thus: "I collected

all my senses , and immediately saw, by the light of my torch, that the coffins were those of royal personages. (…) On entering the last chamber I found an even larger collection of coffins standing by the wall or lying on the ground. Their gold leaf covering and polished surfaces reflected my excited countenance as clearly as if I were about to look into the faces of my own ancestors." But Emil Brugsch could not afford to indulge in further meditations of this kind, for the rumour of a huge treasure spread among the local population, and the archeologist feared raids on it. Consequently he took urgent action: he had the contents of the mummies' hiding place cleared within 48 hours, put them on board a steamship, and sent

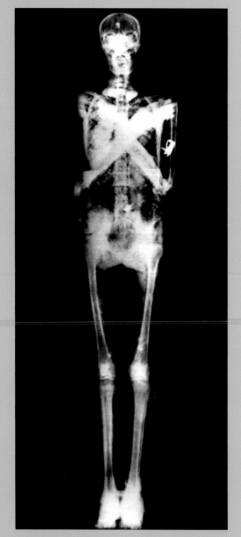

X-ray photograph of the mummy of Sety I

them to Cairo. It is credibly reported that in many places men hurried down to the banks of the river as the ship passed by, to fire a salute in honor of the dead rulers of Egypt.

The discovery in a single tomb complex of over 40 mummies of rulers, queens, and members of the families of the Theban High priests, together with almost 6000 items of funerary objects, raised many questions. Maspero's answer was long considered definitive. In his opinion the royal graves had been raided by organized bands of robbers, and at a later date priests of a pious turn of mind had taken what remained to a place of safety and then rewrapped the mummies. However, the results of recent research suggest that this was not exactly what happened. After the death of Ramesses XI in 1070/69 B.C., the country finally split into two power blocs. In the north, the rulers reigned as kings in Tanis, while Upper Egypt was under the control of the priesthood of Amun in Thebes. Conflicts in the nature of civil war had already broken out under the last Ramessides, with the general and high priest Piankhi opposing the viceroy of Nubia, Panehsy. In view of the country's disastrous economic situation, new sources of finance had to be found, and Piankhi resorted to previously unthinkable methods: he ordered two necropolis scribes to track down royal and private tombs in Western Thebes and then plunder them. His successors in office also helped themselves to the gold of the Pharaohs. The royal mummies, stripped of all their valuable funerary equipment, were first placed in various temporary depots, and finally a great many of them were brought to Deir el-Bahri. They included the mortal remains of such great rulers as Sety I and Ramesses II. It was not until the beginning of the Twenty-second Dynasty (ca. 930 B.C.) that the mummies were to find their final resting place in the family vault of the high priest Pinodjem II. Once rediscovered, they underwent many investigations to determine their causes of death and the disorders from which they had suffered in life. Particularly spectacular were the results of radiological testing of all the royal mummies a few years ago. The well-preserved mummy of Ramesses II was subjected to extensive examination by over 100 specialists at the Musée de l'Homme in Paris from September 1976 to May 1977. Among the results of the tests on him was the curious fact that the pharaoh, who died in old age, must originally have had red hair. Using the most sophisticated technology, the mummy of Tutankhamun was recently checked again. Result: the young king was not murdered, but died from an infection caused by a broken leg.

Mummy of Ramesses II, Nineteenth Dynasty, 1213 B.C., Egyptian Museum, Cairo

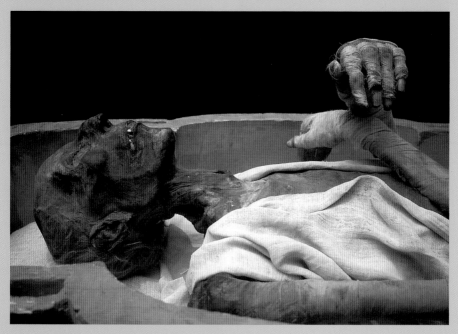

Block statue of Senenmut with Neferure

Eighteenth Dynasty, ca. 1470 B.C., Karnak, temple of Amun-Re, granodiorite, H. 130 cm

For many years Senenmut was one of the most influential officials at the court of Hatshepsut, enjoying the particular confidence of the queen herself. He was chief steward, government spokesman, and tutor of the queen's daughter Neferure. As overseer of all building works he was responsible for the employment of crafts-

men, artists, and architects, and thus for the building of Hatshepsut's terraced temple at Deir el-Bahri. At the height of his career, Senenmut held almost 80 official and honorary titles. It is surprising how many memorials to this man and contemporary mentions of him are still extant; we know of well over 20 statues, several of them new types of sculpture, many other depictions of him, mentions of his name on inscriptions in tombs and temples, and a practice drawing portraying him on an ostracon (sherd used as writing material). Some time after the death of the crown princess in the 11th year of her mother's reign, however, Senenmut fell out of favor; we can only speculate on the reason, but there may have been a conflict of loyalties toward the two regents Hatshepsut and Thutmosis III. As a direct result of his fall, the royal favorite's tomb and many other monuments were destroyed. Senenmut had particularly favored statues showing him as royal tutor with the crown princess Neferure. This group includes figures in which he is squatting with his legs drawn up ("cuboid" or "block" statues), with only the head of the little princess visible, as if he had wrapped her tightly in his robe. Neferure's youthfulness is indicated by the sidelock on her cap of hair (she has the *uraeus* on her brow), and by her gesture in licking her index finger. Senenmut himself wears a wig of slightly wavy strands of hair, leaving both his ears free. His face features the typical Thutmoside style.

Mummy mask of Tuyu

Eighteenth Dynasty, ca. 1380 B.C., Western Thebes, Valley of the Kings (KV 46), gilded cartonnage, H. 40 cm

As the parents of Queen Tiye, Yuya and Tuyu had the unusual privilege of permission to build their tomb in the Valley of the Kings. The tomb furnishings and coffins were brought to light almost intact in 1905. The finds included Tuyu's elegant mummy mask, made of gilded cartonnage. The eyes, eyebrows, and cosmetic markings were made of inlaid gemstones and glass paste; the colored opaque glass known as "liquid stone" was considered especially valuable. The remnants of a thin linen cloth remain on the wig.

Queen Tiye

Eighteenth Dynasty, ca. 1360 B.C., Serabit el-Khadim, temple of Hathor, green steatite, H. 7.2 cm

Tiye, wife of Amenophis III, was one of the most powerful queens in the New Kingdom. This is probably the reason why her characteristic idealized portrait was so individual. Several of its features are clearly visible in the head found by A. Petric in 1904 at Serabit el-Khadim, including the full-lipped mouth with its downturned corners. Here the queen wears a curled wig, two cobras over her forehead as symbols of Uto and Nekhbet, the goddesses of Upper and Lower Egypt, and the base of a crown bearing the cartouche of her name.

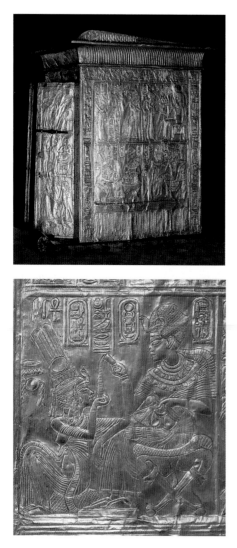

Statue shrine of Tutankhamun (with detail)
Eighteenth Dynasty, ca. 1325 B.C., Western
Thebes, Valley of the Kings (KV 62), gilded wood
and silver, H. 50.5 cm

This small shrine was found in the antechamber to the tomb of Tutankhamun,
still with the statue's ebony pedestal
(H. 25 cm) and a chain with pendant in
the form of the serpent goddess Weret-
heqau, suckling the young ruler in front of
her. The solid gold statuette of the king was
missing. The shrine, covered with a thin
layer of gold leaf, has a domed lid with a
cavetto cornice and is mounted on a sleigh
covered by sheets of silver. All the decorations were imprinted into the gold leaf over
a linen-wrapped layer of plaster, and then
chased. The front of the roof and the lintel
are adorned with winged solar disks. There
are 16 pictorial areas arranged over the
walls of the shrine and the two wings of
the door, showing Tutankhamun and his
wife Ankhesenamen. It is noticeable that
in most of the scenes the queen is tending
her husband: clothing him, anointing him,
and giving him offerings. In this she is
imitating the actions which the king
himself performs before the gods. One of
the scenes shows the king sitting on a valuable folding chair; he has just received a
bouquet of flowers from his wife, who
squats on the floor in front of him. In
return, he is pouring wine into her cupped
hand, a motif known to us from similar
depictions in the private tombs of Amarna.

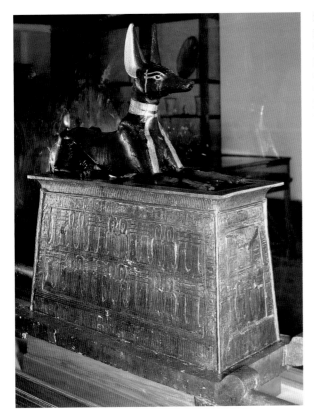

The god Anubis
Eighteenth Dynasty, ca. 1325 B.C., Western Thebes, Valley of the Kings (KV 62), varnished and gilded wood, H. 118 cm, L. 270 cm

The figure of the god Anubis, lying on a portable shrine mounted on bars for carrying it, was probably taken to the tomb in Tutankhamun's funeral procession, and then placed directly at the transitional point between the treasure chamber and the burial chamber. It was intended to protect the contents of these chambers, such as the canopic shrine with the jars for the internal organs. A piece of royal linen with a weaver's mark showing that it dates from the seventh year of King Akhenaten's reign was wrapped around the body of the jackal god, which was also adorned with a scarf and a garland of flowers. The figure itself is lacquered black, and the insides of the attentively pricked ears, the collar, and the scarf below it are gilded. The eyes are inlaid with gold, obsidian and quartz, the claws of the paws with silver. The ornamentation of the shrine, which has a cavetto cornice, was incised and gilded. It consists of alternating pairs of *djed* pillars (the symbol of Osiris) and *tyt* knots (the symbol of Isis). The surrounding inscriptions gives the names and titles of the king. Howard Carter found several faience amulets, two alabaster bowls, and eight pectorals inside the shrine.

The "Painted box" of Tutankhamun

Eighteenth Dynasty, ca. 1325 B.C., Western Thebes, Valley of the Kings (KV 62), painted wood, H. 44 cm, L. 61 cm

This unique chest, adorned with minutely detailed paintings of war and hunting scenes, stood in front of the walled-up entrance to Tutankhamun's burial chamber. The lid is divided along its length into two areas, one showing the ruler hunting lions in his chariot, the other depicts the hunting of various desert animals (ibex, gazelles, hyenas, wild asses and ostriches). The two long sides of the chest are devoted to scenes of war; one side shows a battle against the Nubians, the other a battle against the Syrians. While the king and his retinue press forward in well-ordered ranks, on foot and in chariots, their enemies are in full chaotic flight. The details of the separate motifs are astonishingly lifelike, for instance showing the pharaoh's dogs biting the enemies' heads or hands, and the horses pulling the fallen Syrian war chariot desperately trying to free themselves. A canonical theme is depicted on both narrow sides of the chest: two sphinxes, representing the king, are shown trampling down the enemy. Equally formally presented, for all the individuality of the detail, are the depictions of the two major themes—war and hunting. They stand for the victory of the Egyptian pharaoh over his country's physical enemies, and metaphorically for defence against all the dangerous forces of the disorderly world as symbolized by the wild animals of the desert. The heraldic character of the scenes is clear from the obvious fact that such a young boy of Tutankhamun's age could hardly have taken part in those events. The burial of the king yielded altogether six complete but dismantled chariots. At least two of them were highly embellished and identified as "state chariots" for ceremonial use.

Royal statuette on a barque

Eighteenth Dynasty, ca. 1325 B.C., Western Thebes, Valley of the Kings (KV 62), gilded wood, bronze, H. 69.4 cm

The treasure chamber of the tomb contained several sealed shrines holding in all 32 figures of kings and gods made of gilded wood. The seven royal statuettes show Tutankhamun in the simple attitudes of a man walking forward, standing on a leopard, or in a papyrus boat, as in the figure shown here. The pharaoh wears the crown of Lower Egypt, a pleated kilt with apron, and sandals. He has his right hand raised to throw a harpoon, and holds a coil of rope, the harpoon line in his left hand. The background to this motif is the theme of the hippopotamus hunt, understood on a mythical level as a struggle against the forces of chaos.

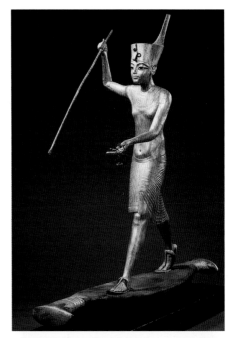

Name pectoral with winged scarab

Eighteenth Dynasty, ca. 1325 B.C., Western Thebes, Valley of the Kings (KV 62), gold and gemstones, H. 9 cm

Close examination of this pectoral shows that it is not merely an image of the sun god in the form of a beetle, but an artistic representation of the king's throne name Nebkheperure, "Re is the lord of manifestations," which is made up of the symbols of the solar disk, the scarab, the basket, and the three markings known as plural lines. This piece of jewelry was probably worn by the young pharaoh on his coronation day.

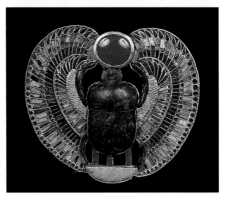

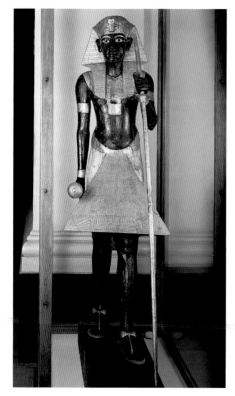

clothing and insignia are gilded, the bodies of the figures are covered with black resin, black being the color of fertility and regeneration. The two figures differ from each other only in the fact that one wears the *nemes* headcloth and the other a bagwig. There is also one final mystery about these figures: on the underside of the king's projecting apron a wooden dowel is visible below the gilding, closing either a knot hole or a hidden hollow space to hold a roll of papyrus.

Throne of Tutankhamun (detail)

Eighteenth Dynasty, ca. 1325 B.C., Western Thebes, Valley of the Kings (KV 62), gilded wood, silver, gemstones, glass paste, H. of throne 102 cm

The famous throne of Tutankhamun also seems to have been used at an early stage in the ruler's lifetime. Parts of the inscriptions refer to his original name of King Tutankhaten ("living image of the Aten"). It was only later, leaving the city of Akhenaten (Amarna) for good, that he changed the last element in the name to "-amun." The king is depicted enthroned inside the back of the throne itself, being anointed like a god by his wife Ankhesenpaaten or Ankhesenamen. The scene is played out beneath the protecting rays of the Aten, the divine symbol of the heretic pharaoh Akhenaten in Amarna. The bodies and wigs are inlaid with faience and glass paste, the garments with silver and semi-precious stones such as lapis lazuli.

Statue of Tutankhamun

Eighteenth Dynasty, ca. 1325 B.C., Western Thebes, Valley of the Kings (KV 62), gilded wood, resin, and bronze, H. 192 cm

The walled-up entrance to the burial chamber was flanked by two wooden figures of the king holding a club and a staff of honor. While all the elements of his

Golden coffin of Tutankhamun

Eighteenth Dynasty, ca. 1325 B.C., Western Thebes, Valley of the Kings (KV 62), gold, gemstones, and glass paste, L. 187 cm, 110.4 kg

The mummy of Tutankhamun lay in an anthropoid coffin of solid gold, which was inside two further coffins made of gilded wood. The whole ensemble was placed in a rectangular stone sarcophagus, itself surrounded by four wooden shrines of different designs. The innermost, golden coffin shows the dead king with the *nemes* headcloth, the national symbols of the vulture and cobra over his forehead, a divine beard as worn in the next world, and the crook and flail in his hands. The body is protec-

tively embraced by the outstretched vulture wings of the tutelary goddesses Uto and Nekhbet. The king wears a richly inlaid collar and bracelets.

Golden mask of Tutankhamun

Eighteenth Dynasty, ca. 1325 B.C., Western Thebes, Valley of the Kings (KV 62), gold, gemstones, and glass paste, H. 54 cm, 11 kg

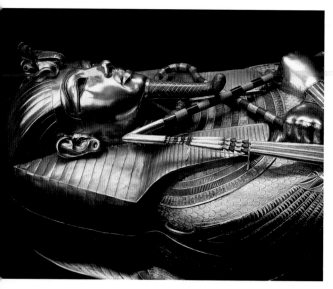

The head and chest of the mummy of Tutankhamun were covered by a golden mask showing the king with youthfully idealized features. The timeless beauty of this portrait has made such a lasting impression on the modern world that to many people it not only appears the awe-inspiring quintessence of ancient Egyptian art, but is familiar—and often misused—as an advertising medium. The mask was richly inlaid with semiprecious stones and glass paste, providing impressive color contrasts, particularly between the gold and the dark blue stripes of the *nemes* headcloth. There is an engraved text on the back of the mask: Chapter 151b of the *Book of the Dead*, which identifies for protection different parts of the mask with the corresponding members of several gods.

Jean-François Champollion and the Hieroglyphs

The script of the ancient Egyptians has fascinated people to the present day. Over a long period the variety and form of the characters led to widely varying attempts to interpret them, for after the closing of the last ancient Egyptian temples in the 5th and 6th centuries A.D. all understanding of their function was lost. Later attempts to decipher the script were at first impeded by a basic error of interpretation which assumed that every sign had a sacred meaning. The Greek philosopher Plotinus (3rd century A.D.), for instance, thought that each hieroglyph conveyed a complex idea, and the Jesuit Athanasius Kircher (1602–1680) believed that the hieroglyphs were symbols "allowing insight into (…) great concepts and profound secrets."

However, all this was changed by the discovery in 1799 of a stone bearing inscriptions in the city of Rosetta, to the east of Alexandria (the stone is now in the British Museum, London). It contained the text of a priestly decree dating from the ninth year of the reign of King Ptolemy V (196 B.C.), written in three versions: one hieroglyphic, one Demotic (the abbre-

The Rosetta Stone, Ptolemaic period, 196 B.C., grey granite, H. 114 cm, The British Museum, London

Léon Cogniet (1794–1880), portrait of Jean-François Champollion, 1831, oil on canvas, 73.5 × 60 cm, Musée du Louvre, Paris

131

viated ancient Egyptian script), and one Greek. Since it was possible to read and understand the Greek text, the first step was to try to establish the names of places and people by comparing it with the hieroglyphic and Demotic versions. There was now intense competition to decipher the hieroglyphs between the Englishman Thomas Young, the Swede David Akerblad, and the Frenchman Sylvestre de Sacy. However, the correct approach was discovered by another man, Jean-François Champollion (1790–1832). Even as a child Champollion had been fascinated by Egypt, and at the age of 13 he was studying several Oriental languages as well as Latin and Greek. Later he also learned Coptic, the final stage in the development of the ancient Egyptian language. He was appointed assistant professor of ancient history at Grenoble University when he was only 19, but soon had to give up this post for political reasons. In 1821 he went to Paris to join his elder brother, who was private secretary there to Bon Joseph Dacier, a philologist specializing in ancient languages. Champollion now bent his mind to the intensive study of a copy of the Rosetta Stone, and finally found the key to the basic structure of hieroglyphic script, that is to say, he realized that it was a combination of phonetic and ideographic characters. He gave an account of his first successful attempts to decipher the script in a letter of September 27, 1822 to Monsieur Dacier. He had deduced the first alphabetical phonetic values from the writing of the name of the king, Ptolemy, which was marked out in the hieroglyphic part of the text by being placed inside an oval frame, the cartouche. He transferred the phonetic value of the Greek characters to their hieroglyphic equivalents, and thus established their phonetic significance. Then he checked his system by examining the written names of other Ptolemaic and Roman rulers and queens. Once he had found the key, and with the aid of his excellent knowledge of Coptic, Champollion succeeded in reading and understanding other texts as well. He tried to decipher as many written sources as possible, and in 1824 received permission to study the ancient Egyptian objects in the Drovetti Collection in Turin (today the Museo

Jean-François Champollion, hieroglyphs from his grammar of ancient Egyptian, 1836, Paris

Egizio). In 1828/29 he and a team of artists traveled to Egypt and Nubia, where they copied as many inscriptions as possible, thus convincing even the last sceptics of the validity of his interpretations.

The Egyptian language has of course changed considerably over the millennia, but it is possible to trace a continuity of vocabulary and certain grammatical constructions. Today we divide the language into five different stages, overlapping in time: Old and Middle Egyptian, Late Egyptian, Demotic, and Coptic. The oldest written documents date from the late 4th millenium B.C., and the latest linguistic stage, Coptic, is still used today as a liturgical language in the Orthodox church of Egypt.

From as early as the Old Kingdom period, there were two forms of script: hieroglyphic and hieratic. The latter script was principally used by the administration, and could be inscribed on a wide range of different surfaces with brushes and ink. In order to speed up the act of writing,

The Egyptian "alphabet" with all the single-consonant signs

Sign	Sound	Object	Sign	Sound	Object
	ꜣ (a)	Vulture		e (h)	Wick
	j (i, y)	Reed leaf		ḫ (ch, as in "loch")	Ball of string
	y (y, y)	Reed leaves		i (h, soft as in huge)	Animal belly
	o (a)	Arm		z (s, voiced)	Door bolt
	w (u, w)	Chick		s (s, unvoiced)	Cloth
	b (b)	Leg		u (sh, as in "ship")	Pool
	p (p)	Stool		q (q, as in "queen")	Slope of hill
	f (f)	Horned viper		k (k, as in "kit")	Basket
	m (m)	Owl		g (g, as in "get")	Jar stand
	m (m)	unknown		t (t)	Bread
	n (n)	Water		c (tj as in "tune")	Tethering Rope
	r (r, l)	Mouth		d (d)	Hand
	h (h)	Reed shelter		v (dj, as in "judge")	Cobra

133

the hieroglyphic characters were greatly simplified in hieratic script, or several might be joined together in what are known as ligatures. However, hieroglyphs were used for religious and state purposes, and could be carved on stone in either low or high relief or painted.

Ancient Egyptian writing consists of a combination of ideographic and phonetic signs. The most frequently used hieroglyphs are the so-called single-consonant signs, which form a kind of alphabet. There are also two-consonant and three-consonant signs, which may be accompanied by single-consonant signs as an aid to reading. Ideograms often appear at the ends of verbs and nouns, pointing up the nature of a term. Verbs of movement, for instance, are denoted by the hieroglyph of the "running leg," nouns by a "seated woman" or "seated man" (depending on gender), and abstract terms by a "book scroll." A few signs have a symbolical meaning and stand for a single term; they include the sign of the "solar disk," which can stand for the sun god. The arrangement of hieroglyphs is determined by functional and esthetic factors, and consequently the size of the signs varies, as does their position in relation to each other. The direction of writing can be to the left or more rarely to the right, but is also found in columnar form, running from top to bottom. Over the centuries the number, form, and execution of both the hieratic and the hieroglyphic characters changed, and in the 1st millenium B.C.

Chest (detail): pair of cartouches with the birth name and throne name of Tutankhamun, Eighteenth Dynasty, ca. 1325 B.C., painted wood, Egyptian Museum, Cairo

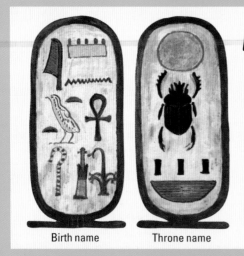

Tut-ankh-Amun heka-Iunu-skhemai
Tutankhamun, Lord of southern Heliopolis (= Thebes)

Neb-kheperu-Re
Re is the lord of manifestations

Birth name   Throne name

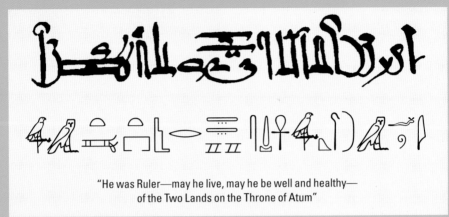

"He was Ruler—may he live, may he be well and healthy—
of the Two Lands on the Throne of Atum"

Papyrus Harris I: line in hieratic script, and conversion into hieroglyphs, Twentieth Dynasty, ca. 1150 B.C., The British Museum, London

another script came into use, and is described as Demotic, the term also employed for the developmental stage which the language reached at the same time. Demotic is a kind of abbreviated writing in which the original hieroglyphic basic form can often hardly be recognized.

Although the ancient Egyptian system of writing is not easy to learn, it does convey the variety and high degree of abstraction of the language's expressive possibilities and the quality of the literature. The diversity of texts is impressive. They contain beside administrative facts, religious and political statements, court records, didactic and scientific materials, tales, poetry, letters and much more. Some of the tales were so popular that students used them for writing exercises. Despite the complexity of the system, almost everything was written down, so that today the Egyptians often seem closer to us than the people of other ancient civilizations.

In the Graeco-Roman epoch, Greek increasingly replaced Egyptian as the language of administration, and Greek script became more important; later on, with the addition of a few extra characters, it was also used to write the Egyptian language in its final stage of development, known to us now as Coptic. There were various different dialects of Coptic; Saitic was the one used for standardized bible translations and as literary language. It was replaced in the 8th/9th century A.D. by the lower Egyptian dialect Bohairic. After the conquest of the country by the Prophet Muhammad there was an even greater change, for Arabic now superseded both the Egyptian language and the Coptic script connected with it.

Queen Nefertiti
Eighteenth Dynasty, ca. 1340 B.C., Tell el-Amarna, brown quartzite, H. 35.5 cm

This unfinished masterpiece was found in 1932 in the ancient craftsmen's quarter of Tell el-Amarna. Undoubtedly the features are those of the idealized portrait of Queen Nefertiti. The head was made as part of a composite figure to be assembled from several components and made of different materials. The sculptor's guide lines are still clearly visible, but the head is very close to completion. The missing ears could be proof of a close fitting wig (of faience) once planned to be attached.

Canopic jar of a queen
Eighteenth Dynasty, ca. 1345 B.C., Western Thebes, Valley of the Kings (KV 55), calcite, H. 38.3 cm

When Tomb Number 55 in the Valley of the Kings was discovered in 1907, it was found to contain a large quantity of different objects, all from Amarna, which were re-used here. They included a set of canopic jars with lids in the shape of the heads of queens or princesses; a hole for a royal *uraeus* to be fixed in place had been bored later. Although the inscriptions on the jars were almost entirely chiselled away on purpose, a few years ago the name of the original owner was successful established; she was an early secondary wife of Akhenaten called Kiya.

Colossal statue of Akhenaten

Eighteenth Dynasty, ca. 1350 B.C., Eastern Karnak,
Aten temple, sandstone, H. 4.10 m

Shortly after he came to the throne,
Amenophis IV began to encourage a new
idea of religion which had developed in the
last years of his father's reign. At the center
of this religious system was the sun god
and his omnipotent power. Amenophis IV,
who changed his name to Akhenaten,
regarded himself and his wife Nefertiti as
divine beings who acquired creative force
from the sun god, the Aten. In order to
express this new religious concept the
pharaoh had a mighty temple (covering an
area of 426 × 656 ft; 130 × 200 m) built
east of Karnak and dedicated to the Aten.
Colossal statues of the king (height over
16.5 ft; 5 m) were set up in front of the
pillars in a large courtyard, showing him as
a very unusual figure. The proportions of
the statues, which are only partially
preserved, convey an impression of physical extremes. The arms and legs are very
long, the head, neck and chest slender, the
belly and thighs extremely plump. The
long, thin face also diverges from any norm
and seems to be made up of opposites: the
eyes are narrow, the nose long, the mouth
full-lipped, and the chin round and rece-
ding. The king wears the double crown
above the *khat* headcloth, the *uraeus*, and a
royal beard. His arms are crossed, and he is
holding his crook and flail. To his body
several double cartouches with the name-
formula of the Aten were attached.

Group statue of General Nakhtmin

Eighteenth Dynasty, ca. 1320 B.C., crystalline
limestone, H. 34 cm and 85 cm

These two large fragments once belonged
to a statuary group sharing a backing slab.
Both the subjects were depicted standing,
with the woman embracing the man on
her right in the traditional fashion. Despite
the severe damage the group has suffered,
its high quality is evident even today, and is
reflected not only in the detail of the
clothing and wigs but also in the fine
modeling and estheticism of the faces. The
noticeable, almost sensuous corporeality of
the female figure is also clearly in the sculptural tradition of Amarna. Only slight
remnants of painting around the eyes and
mouth can still be seen. The inscriptions on
the backing slab give Nakhtmin's names
and titles. He apparently held the rank of
an army general, but is also described as a
king's son. As the inscription breaks off at
this point, we can only speculate that
Nakhtmin may have been a son of Ay, who
occupied the pharaonic throne for a few
years as successor to Tutankhamun. The
flail visible to the right of his head, a sign of
honor, also underlines his important position. The name of the woman who stood

beside him has not been
preserved, but the gesture
of embrace clearly indicates
a relationship suggesting
that she can only be his wife
or mother. Another stat-
uary group of Nakhtmin
mentions his mother, a
"chantress of Isis" called Iui.
However, it is more likely
that the female figure in
this group, now in Cairo,
represents the high-ranking
military officer's wife. As a
son of King Ay, Nakhtmin´s
monuments suffered a
similar fate, which is very
recognizable by the inten-
tional damage done to both
faces of this group statue.

Sphinx of Ramesses II

Nineteenth Dynasty, ca. 1260 B.C., Karnak, temple of Amun-Re, hard sandstone, H. 18 cm, L. 37 cm

The royal statuary type of the sphinx was known from the Old Kingdom onward; it shows the ruler in the form of a crouching lion with a human head. As well as this classic form, the New Kingdom produced, with increasing frequency, special types showing the sphinx in a context of action. Instead of animal paws, this sphinx figure of Ramesses II has human hands in which it holds an offering vessel with a lid shaped like a ram's head. Such vessels, described as Amun vases and originally probably made of precious metal, were among the liturgical utensils (often presented as royal gifts for the New Year's feast) kept in every temple of Amun. Reliefs show us that small stone sphinxes were placed on projections flanking temple doorways, in order to emphasize the role of the ruler as the supreme head of the cult.

Bust of Ramesses II
Nineteenth Dynasty, ca. 1275 B.C., Tanis,
granodiorite, H. 80 cm

Queen Meritamun
Nineteenth Dynasty, ca. 1250 B.C., Western
Thebes, chapel near Ramesseum, painted
limestone, H. 75 cm

This bust of Ramesses II belonged to a life-size statue of the ruler enthroned, showing him with youthful features shortly after the beginning of his reign. Originally displayed in Piramesse, the figure was moved to the new capital city of Tanis at the beginning of the Twenty-first Dynasty. Ramesses II is wearing a curled wig with a diadem and the *uraeus* serpent, and is holding the *heka* scepter in his right hand.

Stylistic and iconographic comparisons allow us to identify this figure, once known as the "White Queen," as the daughter of Ramesses II, Meritamun, who rose to the rank of "Great Royal Wife" after the death of her mother Nefertari. The queen is wearing a wig of many small curls, depicted in detail, and the large base of a crown consisting of *uraeus* serpents, as well as a diadem with the double *uraeus* over her forehead.

The Zagazig treasure

Nineteenth Dynasty, ca. 1200 B.C., Tell Basta (Zagazig), silver pitcher: H. 16.5 cm, golden pitcher: H. 11.2 cm

During roadworks carried out in 1906 near the town of Zagazig in the eastern Delta, two associated hoards of treasure were found in the precincts of the ancient temple of Bubastis. They consist of a number of fine vessels made of precious metal. The first find included a silver pitcher with a rolled gold rim and a handle shaped like a goat rearing up. The rounded body of the pitcher is decorated with chased leaf motifs, and its shoulder bears a line of inscription. Two delicately executed sequences of scenes adorn the tall neck of the vessel, arranged in two registers one above the other. The upper register bears Middle Near Eastern motifs showing desert creatures, fabulous animals, and stylized plants; the lower contains the two typically Egyptian scenes of fishing and bird-catching. The second hoard included a golden pitcher, its rounded body completely covered with decoration chased in the metal and reminiscent of corn kernels. The neck is engraved with four rows of floral ornamentation.

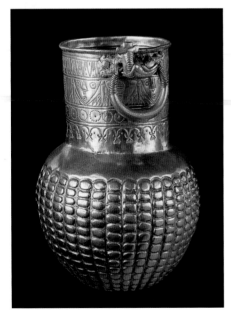

Standing figure of Mentuemhat

Twenty-fifth Dynasty, ca. 670 B.C., Karnak, temple of Amun-Re, granodiorite, H. 137 cm

The figure of Mentuemhat, governor of Upper Egypt, mayor of Thebes, and Fourth Priest of Amun, depicted in a walking position, was discovered in the famous "cachette," the hidden deposit of statues in the temple of Karnak. It shows this high-ranking official in an attitude and wearing a costume usual in Egypt from the time of the pyramids onward, indicating that he was a prominent traditional conservative. On the other hand, his extremely energetic features have been strongly influenced by the contemporary royal images of the Twenty-fifth Dynasty. He flourished professionally at the time of the Kushite ruler Taharqo (690–664 B.C.), who ruled an empire reaching to the Mediterranean from his residence at Napata (Sudan). After repeated invasions, the Assyrians under their king Assurbanipal succeeded in reaching Thebes and plundering the city in 656. Since Taharqa had withdrawn, Mentuemhat was the *de facto* ruler of Upper Egypt, and at the center of political events. He was able to continue his career after the final expulsion of the Kushites from Egypt, and was confirmed in office by Psametik I (664–610 B.C.), the founder of the Twenty-sixth Dynasty. When he died in 548 B.C., he was laid to rest in one of the largest tombs ever built in the Theban necropolis.

Modern Egyptian Painting

Abdel Ghaffar Shedid

Yusef Kamil, The Conversation, *oil on canvas, Museum of Modern Egyptian Art, Cairo*

In 1908 the Academy of Visual Arts, the first art academy in Egypt, was founded in Cairo by Prince Yusef Kamal. Its teaching methods and the structure of its study courses were on the French and Italian models; students were trained by classical academic rules, which meant that only the works of Greek and Roman antiquity and subsequent European stylistic tendencies were used as examples and teaching models. The director and teachers at the Academy were Europeans, particularly French and Italians, and the entire art world of the country at the time was strongly influenced by foreign painters, who had been brought into the country in the middle of the 19th century by Sultan Muhammad Ali, and then by the francophile Prince Yusef Kamil, to decorate palaces in the style of the French Baroque and Rococo. The upper social classes and aristocracy of Egypt took their esthetic guidelines from these late Orientalists, and from impressionists, eclecticists, and exponents of Art Noveau. Among the people of the country as a whole, however, Egyptian calligraphers and painters who produced such purely ornamental works as decorative pages for the Koran were popular. A naïve folk art existed side by side with these trends. Society was still influenced by the Islamic prohibition on the depiction of images, although it was no longer implemented with such a heavy hand as before. At the end of the 19th century, attitudes towards the pictorial depiction of objects began to change, not least because the well-known Imam Muhammad Abdu gave it as his opinion that pictures had an important function in scholarship, and stated that the representation of objects did not have an injurious influence on religion and faith. Modern painting rapidly began to develop. Egyptian students went abroad to study at academies in Italy and France, and as early as 1910 presented their works to the public in their first exhibition. These artists were particularly strongly influenced by contemporary French art, but added new touches with great stylistic confidence and set out along paths of their own. Among them were artists such as Yusef Kamil, Ahmed Sabri, Muhammad Nagi, and Raghib Ayyad, who are now regarded throughout the Arab world as classic Modernists, and whose works are in great demand. Yusef Kamil (1891–1971) represents the Impressionist school in Egypt, but in his subjects and style moves away from the academic teaching he had received in Italy. His favorite themes are street scenes from the Old Town of Cairo and life in the city's suburbs, which were still in the nature of villages. His snapshot-like pictures are spontaneous and lively, and unlike the European impressionists he emphasized the strength of the sunlight and the intense play of color by adding black accents. His powerfully spare and lively brushstrokes are very striking. His pupils Kamil Mustafa, Muhammad Sabri, Sabri Ragheb, and Hosni Banani remained faithful to this style. Ahmed Sabri (1889–1955) specialized in still lifes, and above all in portraits of a very intense nature. He studied abroad in Paris, where he learned from the impressionists in particular. A warm color palette, calm and harmonious composition, and a distinctive style of brushstroke are characteristic features of his works, which are constructed very well and with fine craftsmanship. Similar work was produced by Muhammad Hassan (1892–1961), Ahmed Sabri's pupil Hussein Picar (born 1913), and Abdel Aziz Dervish. Muhammad Nagi (1881–1956) was

Mahmoud Said, The City, *oil on canvas, Museum of Modern Egyptian Art, Cairo*

another exponent of Egyptian portrait painting. He also painted legendary subjects and village scenes. In his late work he shows himself inspired by the strict style of composition in ancient Egyptian painting and reliefs, and experiments, for instance, with the division of the pictorial area into strips or registers. His studio at the foot of the pyramids, containing an exhibition of his works, is now one of the major museums of classic modernism in Cairo. Raghib Ayyad (1892–1983) was another portrait painter, and also chose pictorial motifs from Egyptian folklore. He devoted whole series of his works to peasants and the poor. He wanted to create a national form of art, and tried to do so in compositions using ideas from ancient Egyptian and Coptic painting.

Abd el Hadi el Gazar, Wedding, *pen and ink drawing on paper, Museum of the Academy of Art, Cairo*

In 1935 the poet Georges Henein founded the "Art and Freedom" group in Cairo, with the aim of making fruitful use of expressionism, cubism, and surrealism in Egyptian art. Members of this group expressly opposed the persecution in National Socialist Germany of the "degenerate" artists who followed those stylistic tendencies. Painters as Kamel Telmisany, Ramses Younan and Fouad Kamel joined the movement. Mahmoud Said (1897–1964) went his own way; this self-taught artist developed a distinctive style of painting, using strongly three-dimensional forms and intense colors. His subjects are nudes, animals, views of the Nile with its feluccas, scenes from everyday life, and a series of "Egyptian Women." A museum in Alexandria is devoted to his work. Outstanding figures in the art world of the 1940s and 1950s were Seif Wanli (1906–1979) and his brother Adham Wanli (1904–1961), who may both be considered Expressionistic in the handling of their subjects and compositions. Seif Wanli's series showing folk dancers and dance ensembles, both foreign and Egyptian, are well known.

After the Egyptian revolution of 1952 a number of artists organized themselves into groups and associations, which still form the base for an Egyptian movement in an artistic landscape previously more noted for individualists. The earlier works in particular of members of these artistic groups express a mood of national self-assurance, articulated in the intensive reworking and reformulation of their subject matter, as well as in techniques of Egyptian culture, both ancient Egyptian and Islamic, employed through over 5000 years. They established connections with Egyptian folklore, either in its colorful naïve painting or its extremely varied and very attractively shaped everyday ceramic utensils, its traditional costumes, and so on, and they also had recourse to the wealth of picturesque subjects available: the Old Town of Cairo, genre scenes from the lives of ordinary people, Egyptian desert and Nile landscapes, and the festivals and ceremonies of popular belief. A second main tendency is the Islamic art of

Kamal el Sarrag, The Letter S, *oil on canvas, Museum of the Academy of Art, Cairo*

Egypt, which by comparison is formally rather strict and notable for its ornamentation, particularly in the practice of calligraphy, which has a long tradition behind it and is very skilfully executed. Another artistic tradition derives from the omnipresent works of ancient Egyptian art—painting, sculpture, and architecture—bringing the early advanced civilization of the country before our eyes in all its stylistic and technical perfection. One of the first overriding concerns of this generation of artists was to take elements from these three great cultural movements and rework them, either purely formally, in terms of content, or from the technical aspect. In the 1960s a group of artists practised a popular type of pictorial art, using motifs from folklore and employing a style reminiscent of a kind of magical realism. The link with European art is thus established in terms of

Abdel Ghaffar Shedid, Stones, *oil on canvas, in the possession of the artist*

form, but the subjects come from Egyptian folklore, concentrating on themes concealed behind human behavior and the unconscious, the fantasy world of legends, sagas, magic, and popular belief. The artists also saw their subjects in sociological terms, bringing the viewer face to face with the misery of the lower classes and the ignorance of the population. Representatives of this group are Abd el Hadi el Gazar (1925–1966) and Hamed Nada (1924–1992). This folkloric tendency is also represented by Sayed Abdel Rassoul and a strong group of women painters: Taheya Halim, Effat Naghi, Gazbeya Sirry, and Inji Efflatoun. Related to this movement is the painting of Hamed Abdallah (1917–1985), who was the first to incorporate characters from Arabic script into his large compositions. The development of the work of Salah Taher (born 1911) begins with a rather impressionistic stylization of his pictorial figures and moving on to abstraction. Samir Rafi (born 1926) has pursued an objective surrealist path, with an underlying mood of pessimism. In the 1980s works of art turned considerably more strongly to international trends as a result of increased communication with western and eastern European and American artists. In the work of this generation of artists the pupils of Hussein Picar and Abdel Aziz Darvish— Zacharia el Zeni, Kamal el Sarrag, and Abdel Ghaffar Shedid—traditional, realistic, neo-expressionistic, and surrealist tendencies all emerge. Purely abstract art is represented by Farouk Hosni and Ahmed Fouad Selim. Mounir Kanaan (1920–2000) also composed works with strongly contrasting areas of color, experimenting with collages and coloured, structured card. At present there are also, of course, artists who exploit the new media, turning to video installations and making use of computers.

Modern painting, and the visual arts in general, attract a great deal of attention in Egypt. In the big cities of Cairo and Alexandria many private galleries and international biennales and triennales offer a broad range of exhibitions. Recent years have seen the opening of several small museums, which concentrate in particular on programs featuring the classic Modernists and contemporary art. These museums include the Mohammed Nagi Studio Museum, the Mahmoud Said Museum in Alexandria, the collections of the country's art academies and, above all, the Museum of Modern Egyptian Art in Cairo, which stands opposite the new opera house.

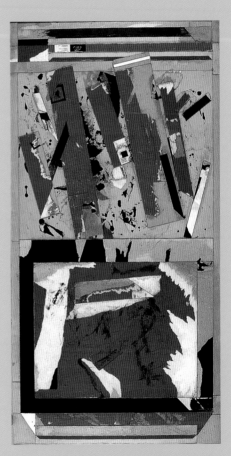

Mounir Kanaan, Composition, *card collage, the artist's estate*

Old Cairo

The part of the city now known as Old Cairo consists of the Coptic quarter of Qasr el-Shama ("Fortress of the Candle") and the city of Fustat, founded in the 7th century as the capital of Egypt. The Coptic quarter was built inside the walls of the Roman fortress of Babylon, erected in the 1st century A.D. and renovated in the Byzantine period. The oldest churches were founded here in the 4th to 5th centuries, but were repeatedly destroyed later, so that most of the present buildings are no earlier than the 10th to 11th centuries. el-Moallaqa, the "hanging church," rises above the southern tower of the fortress in the south of the quarter. It is dedicated to the Virgin Mary, and for some time was the seat of the Patriarch of Alexandria. The oldest churches in the north are those of Sts. Sergius and Bacchus, St. Barbara, and St. George. The former church of St. Michael was converted to a synagogue in the 12th century, and is today called either after the Chief Rabbi of Jerusalem, Ben Ezra, who commissioned the conversion, or after the prophet Elijah, who is said to have appeared here.

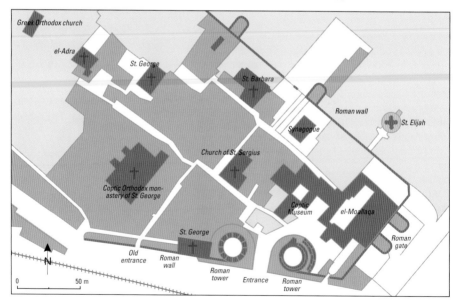

The Coptic Museum

The Coptic Museum, founded in 1908 by Marcus Simaika Pasha, contains the largest collection of Coptic monuments in the world. The building surrounds an inner courtyard, and has been equipped over the years with doors, windows, ceilings, and floors from nearby houses and churches. Its exhibits include all kinds of architectural sculptures from churches and monasteries (apses, friezes, and capitals), funerary stelae and figures, items of wood, ivory, and metalwork, frescos and icons, as well as many kinds of textiles going back to the period of late antiquity. Particularly notable is the Museum's extensive archive of manuscripts, including the Gnostic codices of Nag Hammadi (4th/5th centuries), invaluable to the history of early Christianity.

Frieze with cross and fronds of leaves
5th/6th century A.D., Saqqara, monastery of St. Jeremiah, limestone, H. ca. 35 cm

The monastery of St. Jeremiah was built in Saqqara in the 4th century A.D., near the Unas causeway, and destroyed by the Arabs around 960 A.D. Even today the ruins are still impressive, but most of the decorated blocks of masonry have been moved to the Coptic Museum. Recently, researchers from the DAI (the German Archeological Institute in Cairo) have studied the monastery again. The frieze shown here has a characteristic motif, consisting of a cross with guilloche decoration and trefoil acanthus leaves in the angles between the arms. It is surrounded by a large circular band in four segments connected by curving knots. Fronds of leaves flank the cross to right and left.

Large wickerwork capital
6th century A.D., Alexandria, marble, H. 83 cm

This large rectangular capital is covered with deeply carved basket-weave ornamentation, rising above a floral band with leaf and loop motifs. Each of the sides has a large, square pictorial area with a highly stylized floral motif which goes back to ancient Egyptian principles of design in its clear, symmetrical organization. Similar capitals are also known outside Egypt (for instance in San Vitale, Ravenna). The capital was obviously hollowed out to be used for some other purpose later; it may, for instance, have acted as a font. The material also indicates the value of the capital, since marble had to be imported from abroad. But most likely the stone block originated from a building of Graeco-Roman times and was later recut into its present form.

Pages from the Nag Hammadi Codices
Late 4th century A.D., found at Nag Hammadi, papyrus, H. 28.2 cm

The famous Nag Hammadi Codices were found in 1945 in a jar at the foot of the Djebel el-Taref. However, it was several years before anyone realized that this was a find of Gnostic scriptures and thus an international sensation. Something was known from the sermons and letters of the early church leaders about the "harmful influence" of the Gnostics, whose view of the world was pessimistic and who saw salvation as recognition of our origin in an immaterial world of light, but hardly any original texts had previously been found. The double page shows the title of the apocryphal book of St. John, placed at the end of the text in the usual way.

The Ascension of Christ
6th/7th century A.D., Bawit, monastery of St. Apollo,
fresco on plaster ground, H. of niche 2.20 m

The monastery of Bawit, situated between Hermopolis and Asiut in Middle Egypt, is well known for its fine frescos, including this famous niche painting. Jesus is shown enthroned in a mandorla; his right hand is raised in blessing, and his left hand holds an open book containing the word "holy" repeated three times. He is surrounded by the four apocalyptic creatures (man, eagle, lion, and bull), and by the archangels Michael (left) and Gabriel (right). The Virgin Mary sits enthroned in the lower part of the fresco with the Christ Child, who is holding a scroll. The twelve apostles and two local saints stand to left and right of her, all with halos and holding books under their left arms. Furthermore, the name of each disciple is clearly written in Coptic above the figures. St. Peter, on the right of the Virgin, also carries his attribute of the key, and St. Paul, on the extreme left, a long staff with a cross on top of it. The niche is bordered by a frame containing medallion busts.

The el-Moallaqa Church

5th/6th century A.D.

The church of the Virgin Mary was constructed above the two 59-ft (18-m) towers of the southern gateway of the fortress of Babylon, replacing a small older building of the 4th century. Since there is a view from it down to the Roman complex, the building soon became known as the "hanging" church, el-Moallaqa. The original church, which had three aisles and was built in the 5th/6th century, was destroyed in the 9th century and the remains converted into a mosque. The Patriarch Alexander had it restored in the 10th century, and from the 11th to the 14th century it was even in use as the seat of the patriarchate. None the less, the church was subjected to repeated attacks, for instance by the Crusaders in 1168 and the Mamluks in 1259 and 1280. The last major rebuilding took place in the 18th and 19th centuries, when the church was extended by the addition of a fourth aisle. Today it consists of a narthex, the main four-aisle layout, and three sanctuaries dedicated to the Virgin Mary (center), John the Baptist (right), and St. George (left). Two stairways descend from the northern part of the outer aisles, one leading to an underground area used by the priests and deacons as a shelter and place of prayer in time of danger, the other to a way of escape.

The chapel adjoining the main building is dedicated to the Ethiopian saint Takla-Hajmanot. During restoration work in 1984, 14th-century frescos were discovered here. Since the church holds relics of several saints, including St. Theodosius and St. Damiana, it is still a place of pilgrimage today. A number of the church's valuable manuscripts, icons, and works of art in wood, however, are no longer here but in the Coptic Museum where overall conditions are to the object's advantage.

Interior with pulpit

Inside the church, the visitor's eye falls on two rows of eight columns dividing the nave from the side aisles. Three more columns, spanned by arches, appear to stand in the middle of the building. They lie on the axis of the wall separating the sanctuaries of the Virgin Mary and St. George, and thus mark the dividing line between the old nave and the northern aisle in the old three-aisle basilica. The pulpit, described as an "ambo," dates from the 11th century. It rises on 15 slender columns, and is made of colored marble. The sanctuaries are divided from the body of the church by a tall iconostasis of the 12th/11th century. It is made of cedar and ebony, and ornamented with geometrical patterns and ivory inlay work. Icons are fitted into the upper part of this screen, showing Christ with the Virgin Mary, the archangels Michael and Gabriel, and Sts. Peter, Paul, and John the Baptist. At the right-hand aisle is situated the chapel of Takla Hajmanot (saint, 13th C.).

Giza

It was probably the construction problems encountered by his father Snefru in Dahshur that made King Cheops look for a new site for his own pyramid. He found it on a plateau 131 ft (40 m) high on the border of the Libyan desert, today some 8 miles (12 km) from the center of Cairo. Since the time of the Fourth Dynasty the pyramids of Cheops, Chephren, and Mycerinus in Giza have not only borne witness to one of the greatest architectural achievements in the history of mankind, they have also stood, and still do, for pharaonic culture as a whole. Our admiration is aroused by the way in which the technical problems in the building of these mighty complexes were overcome, and is increased yet further by the logistical challenges involved. Besides the pyramid itself, the appropriate cult structures had to be erected, and the mastaba tombs of high-ranking officials also called for a huge labor force. In the course of time, Giza saw the rise of a whole necropolis with the Great Pyramid at its center. The pyramid exerted a magical fascination from an early date, attracting scholars and archeologists as well as adventurers and dreamers of every kind. Several archeological teams have worked intensively in Giza since the end of the 19th century, notable among them those led by Hermann Junker for the Academy of Vienna, and by George A. Reisner (until 1942) of Harvard University, Boston.

The Pyramid of Cheops, p. 158 f.

The Western cemetery of Giza, p. 162 f.

The solar barque of Cheops, p. 174 f.

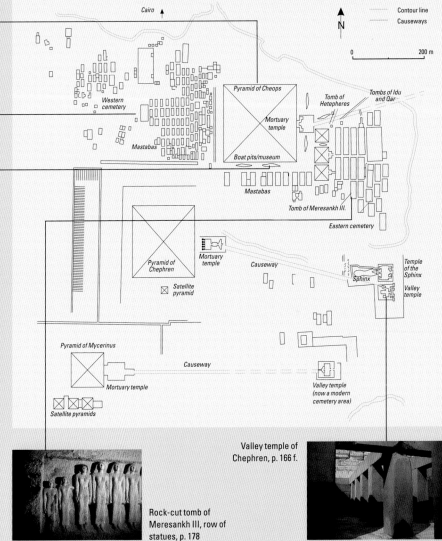

Cairo ↑

N

| | Contour line |
| | Causeways |

0   200 m

Western
cemetery

Pyramid of Cheops

Mortuary
temple

Tomb of
Hetepheres

Tombs of Idu
and Qar

Mastabas

Boat pits/museum

Mastabas

Tomb of Meresankh III.

Eastern cemetery

Pyramid of
Chephren

Mortuary
temple

Causeway

Satellite
pyramid

Sphinx

Temple
of the
Sphinx

Valley
temple

Pyramid of Mycerinus

Mortuary temple

Causeway

Satellite pyramids

Valley temple
(now a modern
cemetery area)

Valley temple of
Chephren, p. 166 f.

Rock-cut tomb of
Meresankh III, row of
statues, p. 178

The Pyramid of Cheops
Fourth Dynasty, ca. 2560 B.C.

The largest pyramid ever built in Egypt was known as "the horizon of Cheops." This building, astonishing in the precision of its execution, rightly heads the list of the seven wonders of the ancient world. It is 760 ft (230.38 m) square, and the sides diverge from the average length only by a maximum $4^{1}/_{4}$ in (11 cm). At the top of the structure, the divergence is a mere $^{3}/_{4}$ in

(2.1 cm). The pyramid of Cheops originally rose to a height of 479 ft (146.6 m), but the top and the pyramidion capping it are now missing, entailing a loss in height of some 32 ft (10 m). Apart from some small remnants, the facing blocks of white limestone from the quarries of Tura on the eastern bank of the river are also now missing. For the main part of the masonry, the builders of the time used 2.5 million blocks of local numulithic limestone, each weighing 2.5 tonnes, rising above one another in 210 courses. The northern entrance now used is a tomb robbers' passageway from the caliphate period, situated slightly below the original point of access. After about 124½ ft (38 m), a narrow corridor leads into the Great Gallery, from which a horizontal passage branches off into a burial chamber from the first phase of building. At the far end of the Great Gallery a short passage then leads to the final burial chamber, where the empty sarcophagus of the ruler still stands. Unlike the pyramid, the cult buildings on the eastern side are poorly preserved. Little

remains of the mortuary temple except the black basalt paving of the courtyard. Three smaller pyramids for the queens rise directly beside the main pyramid. Huge boat pits were dug on both sides of the mortuary temple and at the start of the causeway (now destroyed) to the valley temple. Two more pits on the southern side of the pyramid still contained the dismantled mortuary boats of Cheops, one of which has been reassembled and is exhibited where it was found, in a special museum building over the old boat pit.

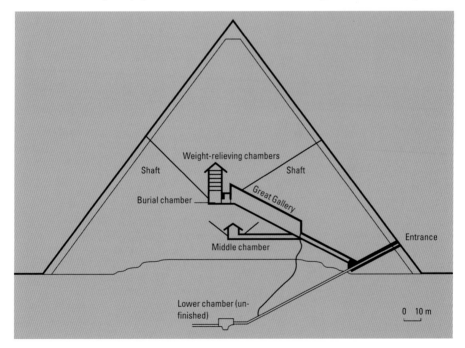

The Great Gallery

Leading diagonally upward, this monumental gallery is 154 ft (47 m) long, and 27 ft (8.5 m) high. It ceiling was designed as a narrowing corbel vault (the last room ever built in this style) in seven courses, roofed at the top with horizontally laid stone slabs. The enormous dimension of the hall are explained by the fact that the stone blocks (some 25 of them) required to close the lower part of the corridor after the king was laid to rest were stacked here. Small lateral niches on the walls mark the places which supported massive wooden beams to position these blocks and prevent them from slipping prematurely out of place.

The Portcullis System in the Pyramid of Cheops

A short passageway only 4 ft (1.10 m) high begins at the end of the Great Gallery, and leads into a long chamber containing three granite slabs poised to drop and seal off access. The burial chamber lies beyond them. Since the building of the Bent Pyramid of Snefru, a device consisting of three stone slabs placed one after another had been part of the design; the idea was to block the corridor to the burial chamber and protect the dead ruler's resting place. However, even this obstacle could not ultimately foil tomb robbers: they either went around the stone slabs or chiseled a way through them.

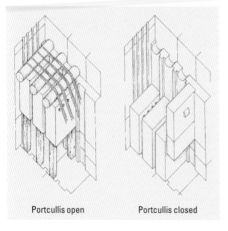

Portcullis open   Portcullis closed

The Burial Chamber

The burial chamber in the pyramid of Cheops, measuring 33 × 17 ft (10.50 × 5.20 m) is a good 138 ft (42 m) above ground level, and was built entirely of red granite. The nine mighty monolithic slabs of the ceiling alone have a span of 17½ ft (5.5 m), and each weighs between 30 and 40 tonnes. The ruler's lidless stone sarcophagus (7 ft; 2.30 m long), which once contained other interior coffins and the mummy, stands not quite centrally in the room. It must have been brought in during the building work, since it would not have fitted along any of the corridors. The two narrow shafts leading out of the north and south walls were not to provide ventilation, but had a symbolic function: they were to ensure that the pharaoh's transfigured spirit could rise to the stars. Five weight-relieving chambers (still accessible) with a gabled (saddle) roof over them were built above the burial chamber; modern calculations have shown that this was a rather excessive measure to relieve the huge weight of the stone. Quarry inscriptions bearing the name of Cheops have been found on the blocks of masonry in the weight-relieving chambers, and prove for certain that he was the king for whom the pyramid was intended.

The Western Cemetery at Giza

Fourth Dynasty, ca 2580–2460 B.C.

The layout of the pyramid complex as a whole reflected the social hierarchy of the country, which was expected to be maintained as before in the next world. In line with the divine position of the kings the pyramids, as royal tombs, tower above all other buildings. The queens' pyramids are considerably more modest in size. Court officials had themselves buried in their mastaba tombs around the pyramid of Cheops. At the time of Cheops and Chephren, burial in the various sections of the cemetery followed a clearly organized plan. The eastern area, near the pyramid of Cheops, was reserved for members of the royal family, while the courtiers were assigned to the western cemetery. However, the grid-like pattern of the tombs was to a great extent impaired by the annexes and additional structures built on to them in the late Old Kingdom period. The superstructure of a large mastaba (cf. drawing of reconstruction below) consisted of limestone blocks with faced, slightly sloping outer sides. A cult chapel with an offerings dish lay in front of its eastern side; the shafts to the underground burial chamber led down from the main superstructure. It was in the core area of the western cemetery that Hermann Junker carried out most of his excavations; he was extremely successful there between 1912 and 1929, working on behalf of both the Academy of Sciences and the Kunsthistorisches Museum in Vienna.

The Pyramid of Chephren
Fourth Dynasty, ca 2530 B.C.

King Chephren had his pyramid built in Giza at a diagonal angle to the building erected by Cheops. Because it is on a higher site it looks larger, but with a height of 470 ft (143.5 m) it is in fact rather smaller than the pyramid of Cheops. The limestone facing of the complex, which has lower courses of red granite, is well preserved, particularly at the top. Architecturally the equal of its great predecessor, its internal layout is entirely different but very simple. Two entrances, dating from different phases of the building, lead to two downward-sloping passages, which finally unite in a single main entrance running horizontally into the burial chamber. The chamber itself measures 46 × 16½ ft (14.1 × 5 m), and has a gabled roof. In modern times, the first man to enter it was the Italian adventurer Giovanni Belzoni in march 1818 (wall inscription of the burial chamber). He found the king's empty granite sarcophagus let into the floor. The small amount of space used inside the pyramid, by comparison with the pyramid of Cheops, led to speculation that there were further chambers inside, but radiological investigation produced no results.

The Mortuary Temple of Chephren

Fourth Dynasty, ca 2530 B.C.

Although the characteristic ensemble of the religious sites associated with pyramids appeared as early as the time of Snefru, comprising a valley temple, a causeway, and a mortuary (pyramid) temple, the fully developed design does not appear until the time of the Giza complexes. However, an individual plan for the separate buildings was devised for every Fourth-Dynasty-ruler. Only from the Fifth Dynasty onward

was the plan for the buildings and the spatial program more extensively standardized, and it remained obligatory until the end of the Old Kingdom. The core walls of the pyramid temple of Chephren (361 × 183 1/2 ft; 111 × 56 m) still emerge from the rock, stripped of their former facing of granite and limestone blocks, so that the (supposed) depictions on the walls are also lost. The large courtyard complex where twelve colossal figures of the king once stood in front of pillars can easily be made out. At the back of the courtyard, five deep sanctuary rooms for Chephren's cult barques lie side by side.

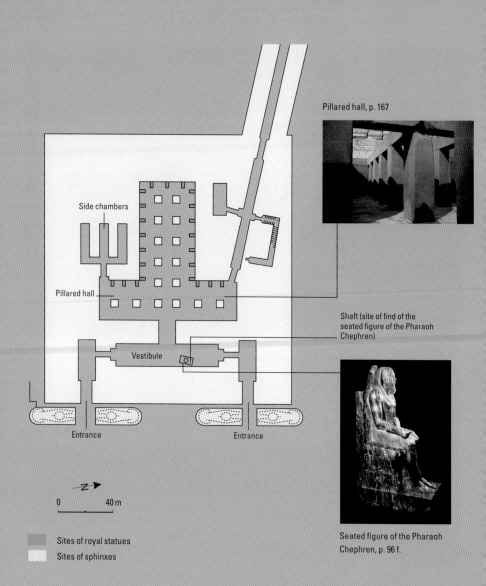

Pillared hall, p. 167

Side chambers

Pillared hall

Vestibule

Shaft (site of find of the
seated figure of the Pharaoh
Chephren)

Entrance

Entrance

0   40 m

Sites of royal statues

Sites of sphinxes

Seated figure of the Pharaoh
Chephren, p. 96 f.

The Valley Temple of Chephren

Fourth Dynasty, ca 2530 B.C.

With the Great Sphinx, the valley temple of Chephren (147 × 147 ft; 45 × 45 m) is the best preserved sacred building of the Old Kingdom. The immensely heavy granite blocks facing the walls are particularly impressive for the smooth technique whereby they fit together. Two symmetrical gateways lead from the eastern façade to the entrance chambers, each of which has a tall niche providing access to a transept. From here, a passage leads to the central part of the building, the T-shaped pillared hall. 16 monolithic granite pillars with mighty architraves once supported the ceiling of this hall. The floor was paved with calcite slabs, and 23 cult images of Chephren (made of gneiss, basalt, and calcite) originally stood along the walls. Traces left in the paving indicate their sites. One of them was the famous seated figure of the "Falcon Chephren" (see p. 96 f.), found in 1860 by A. Mariette dumped in a shaft in the vestibule with other statues of the king. The French excavator was completely stunned: "...one of them... might be thought to have come from the hand of the sculptor only yesterday."

The Great Sphinx
Fourth Dynasty, ca 2530 B.C.

The figure of the Great Sphinx was worked from a rocky outcrop. The colossal sculpture (240 × 65¹/₂ ft; 73.5 × 20 m) of Chephren faces east, and show the classic combination of the body of a recumbent lion with the pharaoh's head. The ruler wears the striped *nemes* headcloth, and has a *uraeus* worn flat on his forehead. Regarded as an image of the god-king at the time of its creation, the sphinx was thought later, in the New Kingdom period, to be a figure of the sun god Horemakhet, "Horus in the horizon." In the reign of Amenophis II (Eighteenth Dynasty) a small brick temple was erected to the left of this manifestation of the god, while the monumental building in front of the sphinx's paws, known as the Harmachis temple, dates back to the 4th Dynasty. Vandalism, wind, and weather, as well as a rise in the groundwater level, have done the monument visible damage, and it has recently proved necessary to begin a comprehensive program of restoration.

The "Sphinx Stela" of Thutmosis IV
Eighteenth Dynasty, ca 1390 B.C.

In the Eighteenth Dynasty period Thutmosis IV had a monumental red granite stela (H. 3.60 m, 11¹/₂ ft.) placed between the

front paws of the Great Sphinx; it is also known as the "Dream stela." In its text the pharaoh says that while he was still a prince he once stopped to rest beside the Sphinx, and dreamed that the god promised him the kingship of Egypt if he would free the divine image from the sand. Naturally the stela was not set up until after he came to the throne, in order to emphasize the divine choice of his person. In the upper part of the monument, Thutmosis IV is shown beneath the symbol of the winged solar disk making offerings to a representation of the Sphinx on both sides.

The Pyramid of Mycerinus
Fourth Dynasty, ca 2500 B.C.

The modest height of the pyramid of Mycerinus, which formerly reached 216$\frac{1}{2}$ ft (66 m), may have been a consequence of the demands made on the country's economic resources over decades by the mighty buildings of the pharaoh's predecessors. Despite his quite long reign of almost 30 years, the cult buildings of the pyramid could not be fully completed either; in addition they were partly built of mud bricks. Excavations at the beginning of the 20th century by a team from Harvard University, Boston, brought to light many statues of the king, including the famous triads (p, 98/99) from the valley temple. Access to the burial chamber, which was cut into the rock and clad with granite, is along a simple corridor with an anteroom and three stone portcullis devices. The mighty basalt sarcophagus still stood in the burial chamber in 1837, but sank in the Bay of Biscay with the ship carrying it when it was being taken to the British Museum in London.

Entrance to the Pyramid of Mycerinus

While Cheops had his pyramid entirely faced with fine limestone from the Tura quarries, the lower courses of the pyramid of Chephren were red granite. This new approach became even more marked in the building erected for Mycerinus, where the lower 16 courses were faced with granite blocks. Limestone was still preferred as the facing material for the upper courses: it provided a clear color contrast in the outer appearance of the pyramid, and it was probably no coincidence that red and white were also the colors of the two parts of the country: red stood for Lower Egypt, white for Upper Egypt. The granite blocks are neatly smoothed off only at the entrance area on the north side of the pyramid, which is slightly above ground level. In the Twenty-sixth Dynasty an inscription was added here, referring to restoration measures undertaken on what was already a venerable building at the time.

Success and Disaster—the Building of the Pyramids

The positively superhuman monumentality of the great pyramids has not only impressed posterity ever since classical antiquity but has repeatedly raised the question of their function and the way in which they were built. To this day, however, they are also the subject of speculation and the wildest of assumptions. Some claim that extra-terrestrials built them thousands of years ago, or think that the sarcophagus of Cheops is a measure of capacity, or suspect the existence of further undiscovered chambers behind the stone blocking a shaft which has in fact been examined by a robot device in the Great Pyramid of Giza: the imagination seems to know no bounds where pyramids are concerned. An apt nickname still given to these so-called experts today was coined in the 1920s by the German architectural historian Ludwig Borchardt, who called them "pyramidiots."

Those seriously interested in the building of the pyramids must look at the architectural data if credible theories are to be put forward, for unfortunately the Egyptian sources themselves have nothing to say on the subject. No papyrus scroll of architectural drawings exists, no account of the technique or logistics involved has come down to us. In the Third and early Fourth Dynasties "step pyramids" were built, constructed from a series of inward-sloping courses of relatively small blocks placed around a core structure. They could thus hardly exceed a certain height. The outstanding example of this method of building, and at the same time the earliest pyramid still extant, is the complex laid out by Djoser (2665–2645 B.C.) in Saqqara. The change from the step pyramid to the pyramid proper took place under King

Reconstruction of ramps possibly used in pyramid building

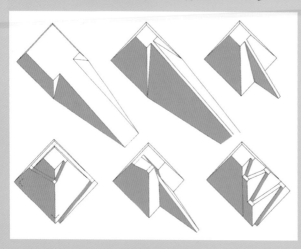

Snefru (2614–2597 B.C.), the predecessor of Cheops. His building in Meidum began as a step pyramid and was extended to become a classic pyramid during the last phase of building. The first great disaster also falls into Snefru's reign. The plan for another and even larger building in Dahshur (H. 450 ft; 137.5 m) failed, since the foundations were not strong enough for the huge weight, and spectacular damage occurred. Structures to prop the building up and flatten the angle of inclination in its upper part did not work, and it has been known since then as the Bent Pyramid. The king ordered another pyramid known as the Red Pyramid to be built in Dahshur, and it was here that he was finally laid to rest.

The Giza complexes represent the unsurpassed high point of pyramid building. The mighty limestone blocks were laid in horizontal courses, and the facing blocks for the exterior, consisting of very high-quality stone, were built in at the same time. The cap of the pyramid, the pyramidion, was probably also taken up from course to course as work progressed, so that it could finally be fitted to crown the whole work without any problems. It has often been suggested that the pyramidion was gilded, but this is unlikely. While the mass of blocks for the lower third of the body of the building was moved with the aid of many ramps, there is still controversy about the technique used for building the rest of it. Some kind of levering system must have been used to move the stones. Solving logistical problems on such a huge building site would have been bound up with questions of technical execution, for not only did the site premises providing for several

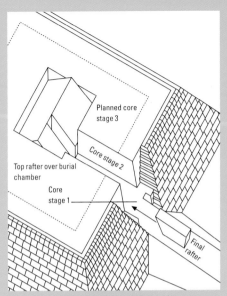

Section of a pyramid of the Fifth/Sixth Dynasty (Old Kingdom), with its burial chamber

thousand workers (their quarters and tombs have recently been found) have to be supplied and organized, the transportation of stones and work in the stone quarries also required careful coordination. The results speak volumes for the skill of the ancient architects and their administrative staffs. Despite centuries of experience, even the pyramid builders of the Twelfth Dynasty (Middle Kingdom) were not immune against surprises. In much the same way as with Snefru's Bent Pyramid, Amenemhat III had to abandon his building in Dahshur because of irreversible damage and construct another pyramid in Hawara instead.

The Solar Barque of Cheops
Fourth Dynasty, ca 2560 B.C.

In 1954, yet another sensational find was made in the necropolis area of Giza, already far from lacking in major discoveries. While work was in progress directly in front of the south side of the pyramid of Cheops, the Egyptian Antiquities Service came upon two boat pits which still had their original contents. When the eastern pit (L. 101½ ft; 31 m) was opened, a boat dismantled into 1224 separate parts came to light. The second boat still lies in its pit, but a photographic probe in 1987 confirmed its exis-

tence. The excellent state of preservation of the Lebanese cedar wood after more than 4500 years is due to the plaster mortar, which hermetically sealed the joints between the 41 huge limestone blocks covering the pit, each of them weighing some 20 tonnes, and prevented damp and injurious insects from endangering the timber. Recovering the parts of the boat and then reconstructing it represented a great challenge, and it was over 20 years before the work came to a successful conclusion. Today the great barque of Cheops can be seen in a museum specially built for it over the place where it was found. The elegantly curving vessel is 141 ft (43 m) long, and the finials at bow and stern are shaped like lotus flowers. The planks of which the boat is made have been lashed together with strong ropes, using a special technique, so that no nails or other metal pins had to be used. Brief written indications of their order of arrangement were found inside the planks. The huge planks making up the keel (L. 75½ ft; 23 m) alone weigh over 4 tonnes. Twelve great oars with lance-shaped blades were also found, the longest of them intended for use as a rudder. The cabin, measuring 7 ft × 29½ ft (2.50 × 9 m), was situated under a canopy of delicate tentpole columns, and was in two parts. There was an open tent in the prow for the captain of the boat. The Cheops-ships are the largest ever found, but the religious concept behind them was in place at the latest by the First Dynasty (ca. 2900 B.C.).

Tomb of Qar (G 7101)

Sixth Dynasty, ca 2260 B.C.

Depictions of the funerary ritual

Even after the rulers of the Fifth Dynasty and their pyramids had moved to Saqqara and Abusir, the mortuary cult for their Fourth-Dynasty predecessors continued at Giza. Performance of the cult for the dead was in the hands of a specially appointed priesthood. The small tomb complex of Qar is only a few meters from the pyramid temple of Cheops in the eastern cemetery. According to the inscriptions in his tomb, he officiated in the cult of Chephren and Mycerinus at the time of Pepy I. After going down a flight of steps the visitor enters the courtyard, roofed over in modern times, which has walls bearing extremely interesting reliefs. To the right of the entrance, a rectangular building with two symmetrical access ways is depicted; this is the "tent of purification," a temporary structure made of lightweight material which was probably used for washing the corpse during the rituals of embalming and interment. Its precise location in the necropolis precincts is still a source of controversy.

Tomb of Idu (G 7102)

Sixth Dynasty, ca 2260 B.C.

False door with tomb owner

The official Idu also had his tomb laid out in the eastern cemetery, close to the mastaba of his father Qar. The narrow cult chamber contains six standing figures of the occupant of the tomb carved from the rock in niches along its east wall (on the left). The red color of the wall is intended to imitate hard stone. The inscriptions inform us that Idu was active in the administration of Pepy I's pyramid city. Small-scale scenes on the inner wall of the entrance again depict the funerary ritual. They show the coffin being taken in procession on a sleigh pulled by oxen as it leaves the embalming hall, the transportation of the coffin, the tent of purification, and the coffin's journey by boat

under a shrine. Particularly striking is the design of the false door (right-hand wall) with a small offering table in front of it. Its lower half is occupied by the three-dimensional head and torso of the official, with his arms stretched out and his hands upturned to claim and receive offerings.

Rock-cut tomb of Meresankh III (G 7530-7540)

Fourth Dynasty, ca 2510 B.C.

Row of statues, the queen with her daughter

Further to the south of the eastern cemetery, a tomb complex consisting of three chambers hewn out of the rock was built for Queen Meresankh III. The daughter of Prince Kawab, a son of Cheops, she died at the relatively advanced age of over 50 in the reign of Mycerinus, and interestingly it was her mother, Queen Hetepheres II, who had the tomb built. An inscription in the intrados of the entrance mentions the name of the owner, the day of her death, and the day of her interment, those two events being over 270 days apart. The first main chamber has an unusual relief on the wall, showing Meresankh wearing a panther skin over her long robe, the chief priest Nebemakhet, and Queen Hetepheres in front of them. The queen is wearing a dress with pointed shoulder sections and has a blonde hairstyle, probably to be interpreted as a fine hairnet of gold filigree. The chamber on the right contains an impressive row of statues carved from the rock; there are no inscriptions, but they must be of the two queens and further royal daughters. They all wear the ankle-length woman's robe and shoulder-length wigs. There are further items of free-standing sculpture in the entrance chamber: six small figures of scribes in three wall niches, probably a secondary addition, who should be regarded as part of the mortuary cult of Meresankh.

During the excavations, carried out by a team from Harvard University, the queen's black granite sarcophagus (ornamented with a depiction of the palace façade) was also found, and it was possible to establish that it had originally been made for her mother. Although the tomb had been robbed, there were still bones and a skull inside it. Those remains let us determine the height of the queen at the time of her death at just 5 ft. (1.54 m).

An Archeologist Takes a Stand—
Interview with Dr. Zahi Hawass

Seated figure of the dwarf Pernyankhu, Fourth Dynasty, ca. 2500 B.C., Giza, western cemetery, basalt, H. 48 cm, Egyptian Museum, Cairo

The Egyptologist Dr. Zahi Hawass leads as Secretary General Egypt´s Supreme Council of Antiquities. Responsible for the vast number of ancient monuments and all related museums of the country he serves in addition as Director of the Giza Pyramids Excavations. We spoke with Dr. Hawass in his office in Giza (2001).

Publisher: Whose examples influenced you and perhaps helped to determine your choice of career?

Hawass: First of all my father, who taught me the principles of honor and dignity in my youth. While I was studying for my doctorate in the United States (University of Pennsylvania) I was able to turn for advice to the Egyptian ambassador of the time, who is now one of my closest friends. And in my professional career as an Egyptologist and archeologist I owe much to the former President of the Antiquities Service, late Dr. Gamal Mokhtar.

Publisher: What excavations are you planning to carry out in the immediate future?

Hawass: Our next project is to continue excavations in Giza south of the pyramid of Mycerinus. However, I shall pay particular attention to the investigations of the section of the cemetery where the tombs of the builders of the pyramids were found; this work has been in progress since 1990. Last year we established the presence of tombs there with a very unusual and unique appearance. Some are pyramid-shaped and some have a kind of causeway running up the slope, in imitation of the royal buildings in Giza. Another major project will be to continue the excavations in Bahariya, where I shall concentrate on the sites of the Twenty-sixth Dynasty. Last May (2000) I uncovered the tomb of the oasis governor, Djed-Khonsu-iuef-ankh, and I hope to find the tombs of his family as well.

Publisher: Could you tell us a little bit more about the significance of the tombs of the pyramid builders at Giza?

Hawass: With pleasure. There was no telling what to expect when we started this excavation ca. 1 km (0.6 m) southeast of the Great Sphinx. To our surprise we discovered a whole necropolis with over 600 tombs so far, located on two levels. The upper tombs (around 40) are larger, more elaborated and belonged to persons of higher professional status, like a "Superintendent of Works" or "Overseers of masonary". The majority of the tombs can be attributed to the workmen and builders of the pyramids. Of more modest size they were made primarily of unfired mudbricks. Beside small mastabas, we found vault tombs and even tombs with circular structures and cupolas.

Publisher: Are there plans to recover the second mortuary boat from the pyramid of Cheops in the near future, and what is your opinion of the present boat museum in Giza?

Hawass: At the moment a Japanese team is working in Giza. Its members have installed a roof over the boat pit containing the second vessel to protect it, and they are also working to counter any damage by harmful insects inside the pit. But before anyone can contemplate bringing the boat to light, the Japanese have to ensure that governmental financing is available to support the project. On the Egyptian side it has been decided to accommodate both boats in a new museum building on the road to the Faiyum.

However, I don't expect the project to be realized within the next decade. As for the present boat museum in Giza, it is architecturally not very attractive, and it definitely was not a good idea to build it right in front of the southern side of the Great Pyramid. So we will do all we can to help the Japanese plan to come to fruition.

Publisher: When will the mystery of the blocked air shaft in the pyramid of Cheops be solved?

Hawass: Well, first I have to say that the question of the so-called "door" in this shaft in the

The Egyptian archeologist Dr. Zahi Hawass

Great Pyramid is certainly not going to be solved like something out of a Hollywood movie. When the Egyptian Antiquities Service and Mr. Gantenbrinck investigated the shaft with the aid of a robot device, I am afraid that some problems and misunderstandings arose. So we have decided to clarify the matter by adopting a scientific approach. A new remote-controlled mobile device is being developed to introduce a miniature camera underneath the block of stone, so that we can see what lies beyond it. I am sure everyone will be satisfied with this project—scholars and adherents of the esoteric movement alike. In my view, however, and for technical architectural reasons, the block is not a door at all, just a stone that was left behind in the shaft. [This investigation was launched already in 2001 under worldwide TV-audience. Behind the blockade just a small empty space was located. Red.]

Publisher: What is the present state of conservation of the Great Sphinx of Giza?

Hawass: Restoration work on the Sphinx was concluded, in close collaboration with international colleagues, in less than ten years. The closing ceremony was held in 1998 in the presence of President Mohamed H. Mubarak. But in spite of all the improvements to the condition of this world-famous monument, we must continue to keep a careful eye on it. We know that the old stone is very vulnerable, and even the bedrock further from the surface is not in an ideal condition. A committee has been set up to ensure that the oldest "patient" in the world gets the best possible care in future.

Publisher: Could you explain to us the Giza plateau project you have proposed?

Hawass: To combine the necessary protection of our monuments with the demands of modern tourism is a matter very close to my heart. I am firmly convinced that well-organized management of the entire archeological field is necessary. We have decided on a rotation system at Giza: when one pyramid or tomb is opened, others are closed. In addition, there is to be a protection zone free of all tourist activities around the whole necropolis. We shall also establish daily quotas for

The oasis of Bahariya, view of a tomb complex in the Roman cemetery, with several mummy chambers, 1st century A.D.

access to the individual monuments, for instance not exceeding 300 visitors a day to the pyramid of Cheops. We ought to think about limiting numbers of visitors to other well-known sites too, so as not to put their future at risk. I would argue for the complete closure of the tomb complex of Queen Nefertari in Western Thebes, and long-term control of the numbers of tourists visiting the tombs of Tutankhamun and Sety I. I have addressed UNESCO in Paris on these issues already.

Publisher: When will the new National Museum in Giza be finished?

Hawass: In view of the huge volume of investment necessary for this new building, it will be a little while yet before work on it even begins. In my opinion the museum should be specially reserved for the treasures from Tutankhamun's tomb, comprising all the objects found there, some 5000 of them, and for the royal mummies. Such a building would not just relieve the burden on the old Egyptian Museum but also offer tourists a new and very attractive site to visit. As for its interior organization and the presentation of the exhibits, I can imagine that the Anthropological Museum in Mexico City might serve as a model. However, due to the absolute priority and importance of this project we will see an international architecture competition for the design of the new "Grand Museum of Egypt" very soon. [This competition took place, and the results were published by the Egyptian Ministry of Culture in 2003. Red.]

Publisher: How are your excavation projects in the oasis of Bahriya going?

Hawass: After our excavation of seven more group interments, comprising 102 mummies in

Mummy mask of a man, late 1st century A.D., oasis of Bahriya, Roman cemetery, gilded cartonnage, H. 74 cm, Oasis of Bahariya Museum

all, we shall curtail our work on the "Valley of the Golden Mummies" to some extent in the next few years. I would particularly like to find the tomb complexes of the upper social classes in Bahariya, and concentrate on studying the everyday life of the oasis dwellers in the Graeco-Roman period. All the mummies so far discovered will stay *in situ*, except for six of the finest examples, which will be exhibited with their gilded facial masks in a new local museum, to satisfy the extraordinary interest taken in them by the public. However, the tombs themselves will remain closed in future.

Memphis

"Sic transit gloria mundi"—the present situation of the ancient capital of Egypt could hardly be put more cogently, for very little of the former glory of the metropolis remains. A few colossal royal statues, the great alabaster sphinx, the embalming house of the Apis bulls, and the remains of the great temple of Ptah can still be seen among palm groves near the village of Mitrahina, some 12½ miles (20 km) south of Cairo. Founded as a royal citadel in the Early Dynastic period, Memphis rose to become the undisputed center of the country under the Old Kingdom. It lay on the dividing line between Upper and Lower Egypt, was the formal capital of the first nome of Lower Egypt, and was also known as "the balance of the Two Lands." The Greek name Memphis derives from Men-nefer-Pepi, the name of the pyramid town and the pyramid of Pepy I (6th Dynasty) at Saqqara. The turbulent history of the city continued into the 12th/13th centuries A.D., when Memphis finally fell victim to intensive plundering of its stone for buildings in Cairo. Modern excavations in the old city area still take place, but now have to contend with a groundwater level much higher than in the past, and with increasing settlement of the area.

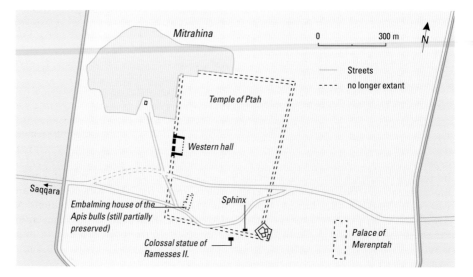

The Temple of Ptah
Nineteenth Dynasty, ca 1250 B.C.

Western hall

The creator god Ptah was venerated as the patron deity of Memphis. With the lion-headed goddess Sekhmet and the lotus-flower god Nefertem, he was a member of the city's sacred triad. The temple of Ptah was once one of the largest temple complexes in Egypt, but it was so totally destroyed that not even its ground plan can now be made out. Only the mighty western hall built by Ramesses II can to some extent be reconstructed. It marked the western entrance to the temple precinct, inside which there was a pylon, and beyond the pylon a hypostyle hall with 16 papyrus columns arranged in four rows at the center, and surrounded by lower columns. The temple itself, over 186 ft (300 m) in length, adjoined the hall to the east, and it seems likely that all the major rulers from the Old Kingdom onward turned their minds to making additions. As late as the Ptolemaic period the entire precinct was surrounded by a gigantic trapezoid enclosure wall, maximum measurements 2067 × 1574 ft (630 × 480 m).

The "Alabaster Sphinx"
Eighteenth Dynasty, ca 1420 B.C.

The mighty proportions of the temple of Ptah called for comparably impressive sculptural ornamentation of the pylons and courtyard layouts. The garden of monuments at Memphis contains the colossal calcite figure of a sphinx found in 1912 by the famous archeologist W. M. Flinders Petrie not far from its present location. The severe damage to the right side is the result of the long-term effect of groundwater. The ruler's head is enveloped in a royal head-cloth with the *uraeus* on his forehead, while a plaited divine beard rolled up at the end is attached to the chin. Since there is no inscription on either the breast or the tall plinth, the sphinx can be dated only by stylistic criteria, which suggest that Amenophis II (Eighteenth Dynasty) was the pharaoh concerned. In spite of its monumental size and weight (28 × 14 ft; 8.70 × 4.70 m; 80 tonnes) the sphinx was probably one of a pair which would originally have flanked the axis of the temple in the courtyard or at one of the entrances. As other statues found in Memphis, the sphinx shows some severe water damage too.

Colossal figure of Ramesses II
Nineteenth Dynasty, ca 1250 B.C.

A whole series of colossal statues of the pharaoh, using different kinds of stone, came into being at the time of the intensive building activity in and around the temple of Ptah under Ramesses II. Finally uncovered in 1888, although it had been known to exist since earlier in the 19th century, this standing statue of the ruler (H. formerly 43 ft; 13.50 m) now lies on its back in a modern building constructed to protect it. It is made of a dense variety of limestone,

and its high quality suggests that it must have been among the finest works of freestanding sculpture of the time of Ramesses II. The king wears the headcloth, with a partly destroyed double crown and the ceremonial beard. A dagger with two falcon's heads on the handle is stuck into the belt of his finely pleated kilt, and there is a pectoral on the breast with the symbol of the ruler's name. Queen Bint-Anat is depicted in relief on the material bridging the space between the legs (the feet and base of the statue have broken off). Originally, this figure probably stood at the southern entrance of the temple of Ptah.

Triad of Ramesses II with Ptah and Sekhmet

Nineteenth Dynasty, ca 1250 B.C.

In his lifetime, Ramesses II frequently had his divine nature as ruler expressed in free-standing sculpture through statuary groups showing him identical in size with various deities. This triad of red granite (H. ca. 11 ft; 3.80 m) combines him with Ptah and Sekhmet, the two chief divinities of Memphis. However, the king does not assume the role of the youthful god Nefertem, but appears as a god himself with a solar disk above his basin-shaped wig.

Embalming House of the Apis bulls

22nd Dynasty, ca 930 B.C. /
Late period, 6th–4th century B.C.

The precinct of the temple of Ptah once contained the principal sanctuary for the Apis bull in which the animal, honored as divine, was also kept. While no archeological remains of this building have yet been found, the embalming house (the most recent unit of it) attached to it has been discovered. It consists of several rooms with calcite embalming tables of different sizes, one of which can be dated to the Twenty-sixth Dynasty by the name of King Nekau II. After the death of an Apis bull, the animal's body was mummified here and then interred in the Serapeum at Saqqara.

The Pharaoh's Chief Minister—The Vizier

"Vizier" is the term used for the official at the head of the Egyptian administrative hierarchy; there are records of the existence of the office itself from the early Old Kingdom to the time of the Thirtieth Dynasty. Besides bearing a specific title, viziers from the Middle Kingdom period onward also wore a special official costume, consisting of a long kilt reaching up to the armpits and fastened round the neck by straps. The responsibilities of viziers were extremely comprehensive. Directly appointed by the ruler—or dismissed by him if they did not give satisfaction—they had to account to no one but their royal masters. During the Eighteenth Dynasty, at the time of Thutmosis III, the office was divided, so that there were two viziers in office at the same time: the vizier of Upper Egypt and his Lower Egyptian colleague, based respectively in Thebes and Memphis (and temporarily in Piramesse, the capital of the Ramessides) during the Nineteenth and Twentieth Dynasties. The broad spectrum of the vizier's duties was regulated by a detailed set of rules, some New Kingdom versions of which are preserved in tomb inscriptions. The high demands of the office, leading to the appointment of the most trusted and recognized candidates, are impressively outlined by

Tomb relief of Ptahemhat (detail); the two viziers behind General Horemheb (right), Eighteenth Dynasty, ca. 1330 B.C., painted limestone, W. 128 cm, Ägyptisches Museum, Staatliche Museen Preussischer Kulturbesitz, Berlin

the king in his speech inducting the chosen official, as in the case of Thutmosis III speaking of the vizier Rekhmire: "Consider now the vizier! See, it is not a comfortable office! See, it is bitter as gall." Rekhmire is then warned: "It is evil in the sight of God if a man goes over to one side (i.e. is partisan). This is the doctrine. You shall act accordingly and treat all alike, the known and the unknown, those close to you and those far from you." Circumspection and the ability to assert oneself are also required: "Do not act blindly against a man, like a thunderstorm! When there is cause for anger, then you may be angry. For the great man who is feared is great indeed. See, it is the virtue of a great man that he practices *maat* (justice)." Many paragraphs then specify the powers of the vizier, the most important among them being supreme legal authority

Kneeling figure of the vizier Paser in official costume, Nineteenth Dynasty, ca. 1270 B.C., Karnak, temple of Amun; granodiorite, H. 108 cm, Egyptian Museum, Cairo

and the business of the state administration. The manner in which files are to be kept is also set out, and so is the order of business for official meetings. The vizier has to be well informed about everything in the land in order to make his decisions. "Any official—from the highest to the lowest—shall enter into the vizier's hall to consult together. (…) He sends the mayors and village elders to the fields at harvest time. He appoints the police chief in the hall of the royal house. He appoints the man who listens to the mayors and village elders, and travels in his name to Upper and Lower Egypt. All things are reported to him."

From Saqqara to Faiyum

Saqqara

Beside the cemetery area of Western Thebes, Saqqara is the most extensive mortuary town in Egypt, and it is known to have been used from the Early Dynastic period (First/Second Dynasties) right into the time of the Ptolemies, indeed, down into the Christian era with the construction of the monastery of St. Jeremiah in the 5th century A.D. As the main necropolis for Memphis the area extends over four and a half miles (seven km) in a north/south direction, along the edge of the western desert. In keeping with the political situation of the country, Saqqara experienced its greatest age during the Old Kingdom, with the Step Pyramid of King Djoser as the outstanding feature of the whole burial field. Around its complex are more pyramids, with the mastabas of the officials and courtiers from the Third to the Sixth Dynasties. Further to the north animal cemeteries of the Late Period were hewn out of the rocky ground, and close by the slope of the desert plateau are the impressive brick tombs of the first two dynasties. The subterranean burial chambers for the Apis bulls were also created in Saqqara, as were tombs in the New Kingdom cemetery section near the Unas Pyramid. Some of the kings of the late Old Kingdom chose to have their pyramids set up in South Saqqara.

Previous double page: The pyramid complex of King Djoser in Saqqara

The Unas Pyramid, pp. 206 ff.

The Step Pyramid of King Djoser, pp. 197 ff.

The Small Chapel Court, p. 199

Mastaba of Ptahhotep, hunting birds and
fishermen's games, pp. 218 f.

Mastaba of Ti,
cattle being
slaughtered,
p. 213

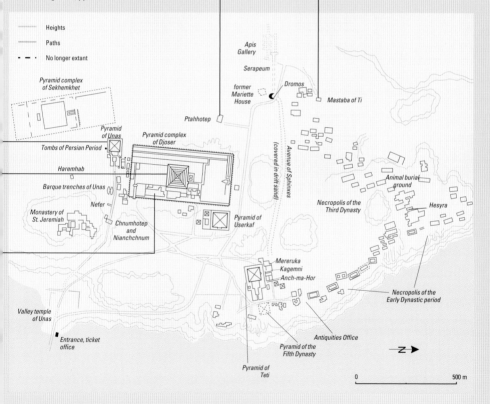

Heights

Paths

No longer extant

Apis
Gallery

Serapeum

former
Mariette
House

Dromos

Mastaba of Ti

Pyramid complex
of Sekhemhet

Ptahhotep

Avenue of Sphinxes

(covered in drift sand)

Pyramid
of Unas

Tombs of Persian Period

Pyramid complex
of Djoser

Animal burial
ground

Haremhab

Barque trenches of Unas

Nefer

Monastery of
St. Jeremiah

Chnumhotep
and
Nianchchnum

Pyramid of
Userkaf

Necropolis of the
Third Dynasty

Hesyra

Mereruka
Kagemni
Anch-ma-Hor

Necropolis of the
Early Dynastic period

Valley temple
of Unas

Entrance, ticket
office

Antiquities Office

N

Pyramid of the
Fifth Dynasty

Pyramid of
Teti

0   500 m

The Pyramid Complex of Djoser

Third Dynasty, ca 2650 B.C.

The great burial district of King Djoser forms the lonely peak in the development of the royal burial sites of the early 3rd millenium B.C., which combine elements of the Upper and Lower Egyptian traditions. The various structures around the pyramid were the first sacral buildings in stone, and they offered the deceased pharaoh lasting proof of his life after death. With the exception of his tomb and the mortuary temple, which was the burial place and cult center, the other buildings were executed as façades only, they define their function but are not incorporated in any concrete sequences of action. This concept of a residence in the afterlife that would be used for eternity evolved in several building phases like the pyramid itself, it was not an inspired original design by Imhotep, although as site manager he directed most of the project. It was only later that he was seen as the inventor of building in dressed stone, a wise man who came to be revered as a god. Despite intensive efforts the search for Imhotep's tomb, which was certainly located to the north of the Step Pyramid, has so far been unsuccessful. Not only was the achievement of Djoser's brilliant official to live in the minds of those who came after him for thousands of years, the building itself was regarded as particularly admirable in the late period. The reliefs in the false door niches of the south tomb, for example, served as models for similar scenes in the Palace of King Apries (Twenty-sixth Dynasty) at Memphis.

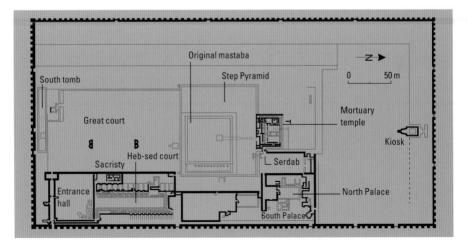

The Step Pyramid

The Step Pyramid of King Djoser was the first monumental building in stone in the history of mankind. It stands on the northern end of the great court. Originally the tomb was intended to be a huge mastaba in stone, but it then underwent several extensions. Only later was the building changed into a structure in four steps; these were then extended again until the pyramidal form was finally reached in the sixth stage, at a height of nearly 200 feet (60 m).

The pyramid is built of relatively small blocks of stone and these were then covered in Tura limestone, while the stepped structure was retained. The entrance to the tomb of King Djoser is on the north side, near the mortuary temple, where the small chamber of statues (Serdab) containing the celebrated seated figure of the king (cf. p. 93) was revealed. The subterranean chambers (down to a depth of 100 feet or 32 m), including the burial chamber of the king in red granite, are labyrinthine; the storerooms alone held ten thousands of stone vessels.

The Great Enclosure Wall

The entire areal of the pyramid (1771 × 900 ft or 545 × 278 m) is enclosed by a mighty wall built of blocks of limestone and subdivided by niches. It is 32 ft (10.5 m) high and also subdivided by 14 false gateways; the only real entrance is in the south east corner. This gateway leads into a long colonnade that was once roofed; ribbed engaged columns were used here, imitating bundles of reeds. The roof beams in the entrance corridor and a wing of the door that has been opened, as well as a roof tile, illustrate the principle of blind and "dummy" architecture, for the earlier models in wood have been translated into the new material, stone here.

The "Palace of the South"

To the east of the pyramid stand two false buildings each with its own court. They are known as the "Palace of the South" and the "Palace of the North," and they represent the idea of the dualism of Egypt. Their external form is modeled on the cult chapels of prehistoric times. The façades are covered with four slender fluted half-columns, the inside two of which flank the entrance (behind are only small corridor-like rooms. The entrance zone of the "Palace of the South" has been reconstructed and it has a decorative band directly above the door with pointed elements known as the "Kheker frieze."

The Heb-Sed Court

The small Heb-sed courtyard is one of the finest individual sites in the cult precinct. Originally it was accessible down a long passage leading from the entrance. In its present form the court and the chapels flanking it are the life's work of the French archaeologist Jean-Philippe Lauer, who has been studying the Djoser complex since the 1930s and is directing the reconstruction work. His findings have greatly furthered our knowledge and understanding of these buildings, which bear no relief decorations or inscriptions that might assist their interpretation. In their two different basic types the chapels, that are in blind (or "dummy") architecture, are modeled on the canonical shrines of Upper and Lower Egypt. Together here as regional shrines of the gods they symbolize the entire country, and so offer the deceased pharaoh a kind of cult stage for the eternal celebration of his jubilee as ruler (Egyptian "Heb-Sed"). However, the rites of the Sed festival were actually performed in the king's palace in Memphis. Unfortunately, nothing is known about these facilities.

The South Tomb

The South Tomb, named after its position in the burial compound, is in the shape of a mastaba with a vaulted roof. On the court side it has an extension, the outer wall of which is subdivided by shallow niches, while the top is crowned with a magnificent frieze of uraeae. The function of this second tomb was a subject of controversy for a long time, but it is probably right to see it as the mythical burial place required for the Sed festival and intended for the regeneration of the ruler. Together with the great court before the pyramid, which is the fictive location of the cult ceremonies and the small Heb-Sed court with its chapels for the gods, the South Tomb was one of the essential structures in this major royal festival.

King Djoser performing the Sed-festival

Like the genuine tomb of King Djoser under his pyramid the South Tomb also has a burial chamber in red granite; it lies at the foot of a deep shaft. As in the actual tomb some of the surrounding chambers were given particular prominence by covering the walls with small turquoise faience tiles. These little vertical tiles were attached to the wall with mortar between stone strips. They were additionally held in place with a thin string made of vegetable fibres that ran through little eyes on the back of the tiles. The carpet-patterned structure of the walls which this created in this palace of eternity is interrupted by niches designed like false doors with raised reliefs on their rear walls. The depictions show King Djoser performing the various ceremonies in the Sed festival, although it remains an open question whether the ruler ever actually had to perform this ritual. But the image remained in use right down to Greek and Roman times (in temple reliefs) as a highly effective symbol of the physical power of the pharaoh. On the outer frame of the niches the king's titles are inscribed. The name Djoser was not used in his own time, he was known by his Horus-name as Netjeri-khet ("divine in body").

Auguste Mariette in Saqqara

Auguste Mariette (1821–1881) with a new found statue group in Saqqara, print, 1893

himself can hardly have imagined the spectacular success he was to have the very next year. For his requests to purchase met with little response from the Coptic patriarchs, and he does not appear to have taken the matter further. Instead, he went to Saqqara. When he saw the head of a sphinx protruding out of the sand there he remembered a passage in the work of the Greek geographer Strabo (1st century A.D.), who mentions that "there is a temple of Sarapis in Memphis, in a place that is so sandy that the winds heap up huge quantities of sand, under which we saw sphinxes, some half buried, others with only the head projecting, and one may surmise that a visit to this temple would not be without risk if one were to be surprised by a sudden gust of wind." Without obtaining an official permit from the authorities Mariette started digging here at the start of November 1851. He told his workmen to follow the avenue of the sphinxes, where on average they had to clear drift sand over thirty feet (10 m) high. A few days later they did indeed find the entrance to the Serapeum, the subterra-

The huge necropolis at Saqqara is inseparably linked with the name of a man who was one of the great founders of Egyptian archaeology in the 19th century, Auguste Mariette (1821–1881). Thanks to his outstanding achievements as an excavator he was appointed the first director of the Antiquities Service in 1858, and in 1863 he opened the Egyptian Museum in Cairo in the Boulaq district. He was sent to Egypt by the Louvre in 1850 to buy Coptic manuscripts, and he

nean chambers where the sacred Apis bulls were buried. So Mariette had first found the structures from the latest phase of building in the site as a whole, the great gallery more than 950 feet (300 m) long that was created in the late period (Twenty-sixth Dynasty) and remained in use until the late Ptolemaic age. In the chambers on both sides of the corridor stood mighty stone sarcophagi, each of the 24 examples weighing between 60 and 70 tonnes. But the excavators were disappointed to see that grave robbers of ancient times had certainly been before them.

In spring 1852 Mariette found another, if smaller, gallery dating from the Nineteenth Dynasty and the oldest individual tombs of the early New Kingdom which date back to the time of Amenophis III. Here the French archaeologist did find a bull's tomb that was still intact, with two wooden coffins. It still contained valuable items, including a fine pectoral bearing the name of Ramesses II. It was clear evidence of the munificence with which the Apis bulls were buried. The large number of archaeological items bearing his name let us believe that the Apis tombs recieved special care by Prince Khaemwaset, son of Ramesses II and High Priest of Ptah in Memphis. In this capacity he had an undeniable "professional interest" in the cult of the Apis who served as living manifestation or "herald" of Memphis' main god. After long negotiations Mariette was allowed to keep his finds, nearly 6000 individual objects, which came into the Louvre in 1852/53. They include a monumental figure of an Apis bull dating from the Thirtieth Dynasty from the temple buildings dedicated to the god above ground, and some large canopic urns from a number of Apis vaults of the Eighteenth Dynasty (from Amenophis III and Tutankhamun). The many stelas (from the New Kingdom) are of particular importance for the cult tradition; they bear information on the date of death and age of an Apis bull.

Pectoral bearing the throne name of Ramesses II, Nineteenth Dynasty, ca. 1250 B.C., Serapeum, Saqqara, gold with colored inlay, H. 13.5 cm, Musée du Louvre, Paris

The Serapeum
Late Period and Ptolemaic Period,
7th–1st century B.C.

Further to the east, behind the Djoser pyramid, lies the entrance to the Serapeum, the subterranean galleries where the sacred Apis bulls were interred. Its discovery is one of the pioneering achievements of 19th century archaeology (1851), but most of the remnants of the superstructures have since been reclaimed by the desert sand. In the district around Memphis the cult of Apis can be traced back to Early Dynastic times by inscriptions, but the earliest individual burial in Saqqara dates from the time of Amenophis III (Eighteenth Dynasty). Today visitors to the Serapeum can see the great

gallery of the Twenty-sixth Dynasty, that was enlarged further under the Ptolemies. Immediately at the entrance a great number of niches can be made out in the rocks. They once held stelae bearing texts that are important sources of information on the dates when the Serapeum was used. The chambers that held the interred bulls then lead off on both sides of the main entrance (one can walk in for over 220 yards (200 m). Immediately after reaching the main gallery one can see on the left the niche containing the oldest sarcophagus to have survived. It is of red granite, and its inscription bears the date of the Twenty-sixth Dynasty. In a side corridor (see ground plan) one sarcophagus was left unfinished, and this may have been the last intended interment of an Apis bull, in the 1st century B.C.

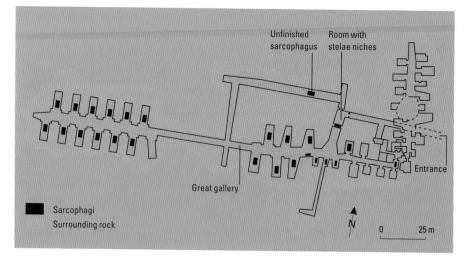

Unfinished sarcophagus

Room with stelae niches

Great gallery

Entrance

■ Sarcophagi
Surrounding rock

N

0   25 m

A Demolished Sarcophagus
Ptolemaic period, 3rd/2nd century B.C.

According to Herodotus a bull had to have certain markings on his hide (e.g. the image of a vulture on the back) to be declared an Apis bull. After his enthronement the animal was kept near the temple complex of Ptah as a kind of "herald" of the god of Memphis. After death, an Apis bull was embalmed like a human being and then taken in solemn procession to the Serapeum. From the time of Psametik I the bulls were interred in huge stone sarcophagi, which can weigh up to 70 tonnes. The value of the items in gold and precious stones interred with the mummy have attracted grave robbers since the Roman times.

A Late Beauty
Ptolemaic period, 2nd/1st century B.C.

Right at the end of the great gallery stands what is probably the finest sarcophagus in the Serapeum. Worked in black, highly polished granite it is decorated with a façade resembling a palace in a sgraffito technique, with inscriptions. The saddleback lid was only pushed back far enough by the robbers to enable them to reach the golden face mask of the mummy and other valuable items. The elaborate method of interment of the Osiris-Apis bulls underlines their importance. Simply transporting a sarcophagus of this weight was an achievement in itself.

The Unas Pyramid
Fifth Dynasty, ca. 2340 B.C.

The Processional Route (Causeway) and Entrance Gate to the Mortuary Temple

In the immediate vicinity of the south side of the Djoser complex King Unas, the last ruler of the Fifth Dynasty, had his pyramid built. Now largely robbed of its facing it looks more like a great heap of rubble over 139 feet (43 m) high. Nevertheless, the south side bears on its exterior an inscription of several lines dating from the Nineteenth Dynasty, in which Prince Khaemwaset records that he restored the building (as he did with other pyramids) upon the instructions of his father Ramesses II.

A causeway over 760 yards (700 m) long had to be built from the valley temple, that is now almost totally destroyed but which once stood on the edge of the fertile land, to the mortuary temple before the eastern side of the pyramid. Part of this causeway has been reconstructed, showing that the ascent was roofed with huge blocks of limestone, the only light entering through a thin slit in the roof. Very little has remained of the elaborate relief decoration on the inside walls.

The Burial Chamber

In the Fifth Dynasty an ideal arrangement was evolved for the chambers inside the pyramids, and it was used here, too. The entrance is on ground level outside the pyramid in the north, and a short corridor leads obliquely downwards from this to a little vestibule. On the other side of this the corridor levels. After passing the facility for three portcullises the visitor enters the antechamber to the burial chamber, which branches off to the right. The great basalt sarcophagus of the ruler still stands here under a saddleback roof adorned with stars. These two rooms, like the end of the corridor, originally bore religious texts arranged in columns, known as the Pyramid Texts. Opposite the burial chamber a room with three niches is situated to house the Ka-statues of the King.

The Pyramid Texts

Since the time of Unas religious texts with blue hieroglyphs have covered the walls of the inner chambers of a pyramid of the Old Kingdom. The texts were composed before the late Fifth Dynasty, and from then on every king made an individual selection out of the full repertoire for his tomb. The texts sublimated and assisted the deceased ruler, and also discussed his existence in the afterlife in the community of the gods. Views differ on how the texts were used. Were they, or parts of them, recited by the priests during the burial rites, or, as powerful pronouncements in the immediate vicinity of the dead king, were they only available to him?

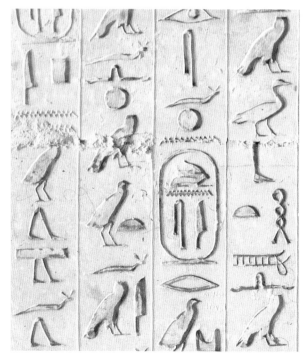

The Pharaoh—God and Man

The name pharaoh (Egyptian: *per-aa*—"Great house") was used for the royal palace in the earliest times, until in the New Kingdom it came to be used for the ruler himself. As "god on earth" the king was at the head of the state, ruling by divine will. The institution of a kingdom bound to religious rites and observances remained a principle of the dogma to the end of ancient Egyptian culture, although it underwent

many changes. It was in any case so attractive that all foreign rulers of the country, like the Kushites in the Twenty-fifth Dynasty, the Ptolemies and the Roman emperors, adopted the pharaonic tradition. Generally the throne was hereditary, the eldest son following his deceased father. The actual assumption of power and the ascent of the throne could be performed on any day in the year, but the coronation ceremonies were held on a date that promised particular good fortune. In the New Kingdom this was often when there was a new moon. During these events the new pharaoh was handed the insignia, like the crook and flail and his crowns. Of equal importance was his investiture with his many titles and their proclamation. The king had five titles or names: the Horus name, the Two-Ladies name (referring to the goddesses of Upper and Lower Egypt), the Golden Horus name (referring to the sun), the throne name, composed upon his ascent to the throne, and his own birth name. Only the last two, incorporating the titles "King of Upper and Lower Egypt" and "Son of the Sun," were set in oval rings known as cartouches. All the names had religious or political significance: Tutankhamun means "living image of the (god) Amun,"

Throne seat (back) from a statue of Chephren, "The Unification of the Two Lands," Fourth Dynasty, ca. 2500 B.C., Giza, Basalt, H. 108 cm, Egyptian Museum, Cairo and Amenophis (Amunhotep) means "Amun is content." In the official dogma the ruler, as representative of the gods on earth, had to ensure that the "maat," the principle of divine world order, was properly observed. This was done in the temple cult, which the king had to perform as the supreme priest, although the actual rites were generally performed by the appointed priests. Similarly, the ruling pharaoh was accorded power over all the known world; his triumph over the enemies of his kingdom is described in the temple reliefs, where we see him smiting his foes. The personality of the pharaoh largely disappeared behind his official role, and there are scarcely any surviving records that might permit an assessment of the individual human being. The official pronouncements and depictions reflect his divine status and the dogma did not permit of any weak points.

Tomb stela of King Djet bearing his Horus name, First Dynasty, ca. 2900 B.C., Abydos, limestone, H. 143 cm, Musée du Louvre, Paris

The Mastaba of Ti

Fifth Dynasty, ca. 2400 B.C.

East of the Serapeum lies the mastaba of the official Ti, and this was one of the great discoveries by Auguste Mariette during his excavations in Saqqara in 1860. The official bore the title of Supreme Court Hairdresser, and he also held numerous offices in the administration of two pyramid compounds and four temples to the sun god during the Fifth Dynasty. No doubt Ti owed this wealth of offices to his personal relations to the ruler, which also brought him the rank of "unique friend to the king." The rich remuneration from his many offices enabled him to order a representative burial place, and assure himself of the services of the best artists in the royal workshops. The mastaba once stood above ground, but it is now half-covered in desert drift sand. One enters through a little vestibule leading to the great court of the complex that is enclosed by a colonnade. The shaft leading down to the subterranean burial chamber is also in this court. A narrow corridor leads out of the

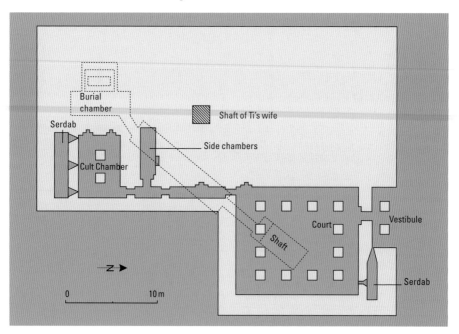

Burial chamber

Serdab

Cult Chamber

Shaft of Ti's wife

Side chambers

Shaft

Court

Vestibule

Serdab

N ▶

0   10 m

south west corner past the store chamber to the cult chapel, the most important room in the complex. While the west wall is filled with two false doors for the sacrificial cult small eye slits in the south wall betray the Serdab behind, where Auguste Mariette found an over-lifesize standing figure of Ti (a copy in the tomb).

Slaughtering Cattle

The offering cult for the deceased owner of the tomb was laid down during his lifetime in written instructions on his burial place. It included natural produce from the deceased's estates, which the priests would bear on the offering table and place before the false door. But of course the physical performance of the offering rites was limited in time, and only the depiction had the magical reality that could offer a guarantee of eternity. Scenes showing cattle being (ritually) slaughtered were among the canonical images of this thematic complex, as a sufficient supply of pieces of meat was an essential element in the offering ritual. In Ti's tomb we see an ox already slaughtered, lying tethered on the ground. One of his front legs is just being cut off. On each side of the relief a big bowl bearing the blood that has been collected is being taken away while another butcher is sharpening his firestone knife with a whetstone. The short inscriptions above the scene comment on the different actions.

Cattle being Driven through a Ford (with detail)

As an agricultural land Egypt was dependent on the prosperity and productivity of its farmers, and it is hardly surprising that the depictions in the tombs devote much space to peasant life. The aim was not to embellish the walls with genre scenes illustrating rural life, but to provide an ideal picture of reality that would be available to the official in eternity. A famous scene in Ti's tomb is in the cult chamber immediately to the right of the entrance. A herd of cattle is returning home from the fields and being driven through a ford. The farmer in front has slung a little calf over his shoulders to bring it safely to the opposite bank. The little animal is looking back fearfully at its mother, who is bellowing for her young with head raised. A small detail, but a great artistic achievement by bringing this dense psychological moment into life. Equally precise observation of nature is evident in the artist's effort to indicate the refraction of light in the strip of water by painting the legs of the men and beasts without contours. The man bearing the calf was one of the individual motifs in the repertoire of scenes that was used in other tombs as well.

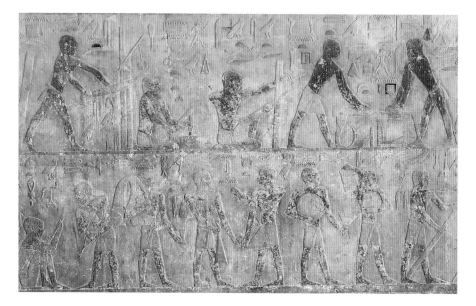

Carpenters at Work

As well as the agricultural scenes the reliefs
also show craftsmen at work, as here on
the southern wall of the cult chamber,
where carpenters are depicted doing
various jobs. On the extreme left one sees a
great plank of wood being sawn, then
come two men seated, knocking in nails
and sawing planks. Finally two men are
polishing a wooden bed. The lower frieze
shows tradesmen in a village market; the
depiction of a man crouching (extreme
left, lower frieze) drilling a cylinder seal is
unique.

The Procession of the Domaines

The deceased's endeavour to retain the
official position he had achieved and
secure his social position in the afterlife
through the reliefs in the tomb applied to
his material prosperity as well. In the
lowest frieze on the north wall Ti ordered a
long train of serving girls to be shown,
each personifying one of his estates. Each
of the estates is named, and each name is
combined with Ti's own name. Altogether
108 estates supplying produce are listed in
his tomb, and quite a number of them
were located far away from Memphis.

The Mastaba of Ptahhotep

Fifth Dynasty, ca. 2350 B.C.

Catching Birds and Fishermen's Games

Somewhat later in the Fifth Dynasty than the mastaba of Ti, the vizier Ptahhotep had his tomb built in Saqqara; it was also used to inter his father Akhethoptep. Despite the official's high position, the decorations in the tomb had to remain unfinished, and only the two cult chambers have relief cycles. But although they are of high quality it cannot be denied that the absolute peak of relief art in the Old Kingdom was reached in the reliefs in Ti's tomb and had already past by this date. The compositions are broader and flatter, and the figures have gained in volume. The entrance to the tomb opens into a long room where the unfinished pictures give a good impression of the method of working. On the right one then enters an undecorated hall with pillars, from which the cruciform cult room of Akhethotep branches off on the right, while the south side gives access to the sacrificial chamber of Ptahhotep through a small vestibule. On the west wall the owner of the tomb is seen before a dining table, between two great false doors. Provision for Ptahhotep in the cult is the concern here, but the opposite wall is decorated with scenes of rural life. In the top band of the section illustrated here we see papyrus boats being made, in particular the ropes being tightened around the bundles of plants. The main

scene beneath this is of bird netting. While the first team are already hard at work following a sign from their leader the second group are still waiting for the command to draw the net. The lower scene is full of dynamic action. It shows a fisher-

men's game in which four papyrus boats and their crews are taking part. The aim is to thrust the opponents into the water using long poles. On the extreme left the artist of the tomb is crouching in a boat and just being offered a drink. His name and title are given: "Niankhptah, Chief Sculptor." Although not a unique scene, we can very seldom name the person behind the art. Indeed, the man here most probably was the supervisor of the work and not the artist "on the chisel."

A Desert Hunt

The east wall of the cult chamber also contains in its upper section a depiction of a desert landscape with hunting scenes. The undulating ground illustrates the topography, which is enriched with scattered plants in relief or wall painting. In one highly realistic and precisely observed scene a

lioness is shown attacking a cow by biting its mouth and nose to cause the animal to suffocate. The death throes of the prey are as carefully observed as is the fatal bite from the great cat. The cow is resisting her imminent demise with all his strength and releasing a powerful jet of muck.

The Mastaba of Mereruka
Sixth Dynasty, ca. 2300 B.C.

The Hippopotamus Hunt

The mastaba of Mereruka (or Meri) was discovered 1892 by J. de Morgan and stands only a short distance from the pyramid of King Teti, the first ruler of the Sixth Dynasty. Mereruka acted as vizier to Teti and he was also married to one of the pharaoh's daughters. This burial complex has 32 rooms, making it the largest tomb (surface with almost 1,000 sq. m.) ever made in the Old Kingdom, as befitted

the highest official in the state. While the greater majority of the rooms were for Mereruka, the northern extension behind the main cult chamber was assigned to his son; his wife was also allotted several chambers. In the very first room behind the entrance, both the south and the north wall bear large reliefs showing the owner of the tomb hunting in a papyrus thicket. A secondary scene is perhaps the most impressive image of a hippopotamus hunt created in the Old Kingdom. Two boats and their crews have hemmed in three of the huge river creatures, who are threatening the hunters with the mighty teeth in their great open jaws. But the successful outcome of the hunters' adventure is already apparent, for the harpoons have found their target and the prey can be pulled in with the ropes. The idyllic depiction of the water plants contrasts with the dangerous hunting scene, for the plants stand peacefully, inhabited by frogs and grasshoppers.

The Cult Chamber

By far the biggest room in the mastaba is the cult chamber, which has six pillars arranged in two rows. A huge stone ring set in the floor was probably used to tie up sacrificial animals. The visitor's gaze will be caught immediately upon entering the room by the high niche set in the north wall and which contains the cult figure of the tomb owner. A short flight of steps leads up to the figure, stopping before the sacrificial table. The door hinges have survived, showing that the doors to the niche were only opened for the performance of the offering rituals, to enable the vizier to take part in the rites of provision. This is a highly unusual arrangement, in other cases the cult statues of the owners of the tombs were placed in separate, inaccessible chambers known as Serdabs.

Metal Working

The growing differentiation and sophistication of the crafts during the Old Kingdom also led to the expansion of the relief program in contemporary tombs. A particularly informative scene showing the various stages of metal casting is from the Mereruka complex. Two groups of metal workers are squatting on the ground around the melting pot in the center, increasing the inflow of oxygen by blowing down long pipes in order to raise the fire to the temperature needed. The molten metal is then poured into molds, while one workman regulates the flow and its speed with a little rod. A scribe (left) made a note on the established weight of the metal ingots. On the extreme right (not in this illustration) the metal block is then hammered to prepare it for further working.

Market Gardening

Without very intensive irrigation of the arable land adequate harvest yields could never have been obtained in Egypt. But although the Nile flooded the land every year, smaller market gardens, like those used to grow vegetables, needed a constant supply of water. The necessary quantity had to be brought from reservoirs or directly from the river. This rare depiction in the tomb of Mereruka shows one of these fields with irrigation channels arranged in a grid and the edges of the fields planted with bushes as protection against wind and drift sand. Several farm workers, wearing only a simple loin cloth, have shouldered a yoke and are carrying water in two round clay vessels to water the plants. Because all kinds of greens and vegetables were an essential part of the daily diet, proper care of those gardens and fields was indispensable.

Tombs of Nefer and Kahay
Fifth Dynasty, ca. 2400 B.C.

The Owner of the Tomb

When the long causeway to the Unas Pyramid was being built some mastaba tombs that were already standing had to be removed, or they then stood directly beside the outer wall of the royal processional route. One of them was the modest rock tomb of Nefer and Kahay, both of whom directed the singers at the royal court. Behind the south wall of the cult chamber lies the Serdab for the cult figures, whose existence is only indicated by three horizontal slits in the wall for the incense that was always used here. The over-life size figure of Nefer, who is followed by his brothers, leans on a staff of his rank to receive the diverse offerings. At the foot of the owner of the tomb sits his wife, smelling a lotus flower; she is also receiving offerings.

Rural Life

No doubt the two court choristers could not employ the great artists of their time to decorate their tomb, but the reliefs are vivid and the paintings are well preserved, with many surprising details. They prove that, although the basic themes were always the same, each tomb was ultimately given an individual pictorial decoration. The selection and range of the images depended on the space available, and the size of the mortuary complex generally denoted the social rank of the owner. The two upper panels in this illustration are linked by a thicket of tall papyrus plants, in which water birds (including herons) and butterflies have settled. Three workmen arre gathering papyrus stems that are being used immediately in the adjacent scene to build boats. Beneath, a shepherd is directing his little herd of cattle across a ford. Colleagues are engaged in livestock farming. Beside them lies a cow, tethered to the ground and chewing the cud, while another is just being watered. The main theme of the lower band is bird netting. Behind the great net with its rich catch

stands a farmer bearing over his shoulder a staff with the rolled draw rope and two wooden posts. He is followed by two more men who are carrying off the dead birds.

Fishing and Goat Herds

The classical pictorial repertoire of the Old Kingdom tombs also included scenes of fishing, and various methods are shown. Here we have two groups of fishermen standing on the river bank energetically hauling in a huge net by the draw ropes. The fish they have caught are shown so true to nature that they can easily be identified. The register above is a pastoral scene with herds of goats grazing. Some of the animals are eating the leaves of the low, bushy trees, watched by shepherds, while on the left of the image a goat is just being slaughtered. A field foreman (upper register, extreme left) is handing a written report on the action to the owner of the tomb. Although the small-sited pictures each some artistic quality, they impress by the vivid postures of all individual persons shown.

The Mastaba of Niankhkhhnum and Khnumhotep
Fifth Dynasty, ca. 2400 B.C.

Where the reconstructed section of Unas' processional route now ends stands the great double mastaba of two owners, Niankhkhhnum and Khnumhotep. Presumably they were brothers, and they both served at court as supervisors of the royal manicurists. They also officiated as priests of the god Re in the special temple to the sun god of Pharaoh Niuserre. Whereas tombs generally fit into one of two catego- ries, and are either cut into the rock or in the form of a walled mastaba, this one combines both forms in its specific topographical situation. For while the cult chamber was initially cut into the outcrop of rock, a mastaba was added later with sloping walls of limestone blocks. When King Unas had his processional route (causeway) built a few decades later the projecting mastaba had to be removed. The stones from the demolition found their way into the foundations of the causeway, where they were discovered during excavations, so enabling the mastaba to be reconstructed to the fullest extend.

Inside the Workshops

Fitting his tomb out as extensively as possible was one of the central tasks of an official, beside building the tomb itself, his "house for eternity." A large part of his private and official income was used for this, as according to Egyptian beliefs it was the only way he could secure the existence in the afterlife which he desired. For this reason the wall decorations often include depictions of the production processes for the various objects with which the tomb was provided. Here we see two painters working on a box which is most likely a container for statues. One of the artists is standing and applying the paint with a brush while his colleague is sitting on a block, utterly absorbed in the same task.

He has stuck another brush behind his left ear. Both painters hold a shell in their other hand which serves as a palette, and more of these are shown on their containers behind the man on the left. In the register beneath several men are busy melting metal, blowing more oxygen into the melting pot through long tubes. At the bottom great collars are being made, as the inscription tells us: "The necklace knotters of the mortuary foundation knotting the collars." Further left a complete collar is inspected by two workers, and then (not shown) "washed" with cosmetic oils.

The Mastaba of Mehu

Sixth Dynasty, ca. 2330 B.C.

The Procession of Offering-Bearers

Before the south wall of the Djoser complex stands one of the most beautiful
tombs in Saqqara, the mastaba of Mehu.
The original polychrome painting in particular still radiates some of the old lumi-
nosity of the reliefs. Both the long walls of
the cult chamber have depictions of a
seemingly endless procession of men bearing offerings, set on a deep blue ground.
They are bringing the produce (e.g.
poultry) from the vizier's estates, for in
addition to his office as vizier Mehu also
held the important offices of director of the
granaries and of the two treasuries.

The False Door in the Cult Chamber

As the interface between life on earth and
the hereafter the false door in a tomb was
the most important place in the cult for the
supply of the deceased with material offerings. The false door in Mehu's tomb is in
the classical style with a cavetto cornice
above, but is painted dark red to imitate
more precious granite. Above the narrow
slit of the door the vizier is shown seated at
the dining table. The inscription in yellow
painted hieroglyphs contains the offering
formula to Osiris and Anubis and the titles
and names of the official. Beneath each
pair of columns stands an image of Mehu.
In addition, a strip of pictures runs up the
wall on each side of the door, showing
images of vessels for offerings.

Dahshur

Only a few miles south of Saqqara stretches the important and extensive pyramid field of Dahshur (opened to the public in 1996). Immediately on the edge of the fertile land lie the brick buildings of three rulers of the Twelfth Dynasty: in the north the building of Senusret III, in the middle the site of Amenemhet II and further south the Black Pyramid of Amenemhet III. Further into the desert King Snefru, founder of the Fourth Dynasty, had two huge stone pyramids built, one known as the Bent Pyramid in the south and the Red Pyramid about 2 km (¹/₄ m) further north.

The Bent Pyramid
Fourth Dynasty, ca. 2590 B.C.

After Snefru had to abandon his first pyramid construction in Meidum, he moved the royal necropolis to Dahshur and began building an even larger pyramid, which is now known as the "Bent Pyramid" owing to its characteristic shape. Considerable settlement of the stone while the building work was in progress caused the angle of inclination to be changed halfway up and reduced to a good 44°. The

flatter angle meant that the pyramid only reached a height of just under 340 feet (105 m) with sides 614 ft (189 m) long. It was the first real pyramid, but when designing it the architects neglected to test the load-bearing capacity of the foundations. For the facing, large sections of which have survived, fine limestone from the Tura quarries was used. Another special feature of the Bent Pyramid is that it has two entrances, one on the north side and one on the west side. They lead to two separate sets of chambers with corbelled roofs on different levels. But deep cracks appeared inside this pyramid as well, and it could not be used for the king's interment.

The Offering Chapel

The overall concept for the cult buildings around the Bent Pyramid used the classical division into the valley temple (or lower temple), the causeway and the small mortuary temple, but their individual designs mark the end of a tradition which was to be abandoned at the Red Pyramid. As in Meidum, a small sanctuary was set directly before the east side with a vestibule and an open court in which the main offering place was set. It was flanked with two monumental limestone stelae, ca. 9 m high, now in the Egyptian Museum in Cairo. They bore the titles of Snefru and an image of him robed for the *Sed* Festival.

The Red Pyramid
Fourth Dynasty, ca. 2580 B.C.

The impossibility of using the Bent Pyramid owing to the massive faults in the building necessitated the construction of another tomb for Pharaoh Snefru. This made him the builder of three pyramids altogether and so the greatest builder in the Old Kingdom. The Red Pyramid owes its name to a reddish coloring of the blocks used for the core construction. Despite the huge length of the sides, that are more than 700 ft (220 m) long and only exceeded by the Great Pyramid of Cheops, the building only rises to a height of about 340 ft (104 m), as the angle of inclination was kept to 43° right from the start, to avoid the problems encountered with the Bent Pyramid. The entrance is on the north side, and it leads into a simple system of rooms with two antechambers and the ensuing burial chamber. Of the cult complex to the east only the mortuary temple, which is badly damaged, has been excavated, and so far no trace of the causeway or the valley temple has been found. The pyramidion, the pyramid tip, has been restored and placed in the mortuary temple.

The Black Pyramid of Amenemhet III
Twelfth Dynasty, ca. 1820 B.C.

The rulers of the later Twelfth Dynasty chose sun-dried mud bricks as building material for their pyramids, and it is the dark color of these that has given Amenemhet III's complex its name. In the matter of security for the royal burial places no further reliance was placed on the huge stone masses of the Old Kingdom, and these builders preferred to rely on a veritable labyrinth of corridors and chambers. But when the protecting casing of limestone had gone Amenemhet III's building began to weather, and now it stands in the landscape like a tower crowned with a huge mass of rubble. With a height of over 250 ft (78 m) and sides over 340 ft (105 m) long it was once the largest building in the Middle Kingdom. However, it suffered a similar fate to the Bent Pyramid of Snefru, for the ground did not prove strong enough here either. Considerable faults developed, necessitating the cessation of all work, and the granite sarcophagus of the king, that was already installed, remained empty.

Artists and Workmen

Who were the sculptors of the great figures of the pharaohs, who made the thousands of reliefs on the temple walls, and who executed the wonderful paintings in the countless burial sites? Can we regard them as artists in the western sense, or should they be seen rather as highly qualified artisans? Only rarely do the depictions include the master and give his title and name, and only in absolutely exceptional cases can one identify an artist's signature. From the time of the Old Kingdom wall paintings in tombs showing the craftsmen at work are very frequent. But all the men remain anonymous members of their professional group, they are not conceived as individuals.

Only one source has survived on the theoretical bases of Egyptian art, it is the famous "self-portrayal" of an ancient Egyptian artist on a stela of the early Middle Kingdom (Eleventh Dynasty, time of Mentuhotep II, stela of Irtjsen of Abydos and now in the Musée du Louvre, Paris). A longer passage in the text contains a list of the specialized knowledge an artist needed. It included a knowledge of the models in the pattern books, command of the canon of proportions with their measurements, the techniques of working in sculpture, relief and painting, and knowledge of the many motifs and how to extract and mix the colors and

Work on a Colossal Figure of Thutmosis III, Eighteenth Dynasty, ca. 1450 B.C., tomb of Rekhmire, Western Thebes

mediums. Only when he knew the right way to depict images in the round or on a flat surface could an artist create a finished work that would have a true and powerful effect in the functional environment of a tomb or a cult building. For only a statue or scene that was executed "correctly" in the ancient Egyptian sense could fulfill its purpose in the cult and guarantee the desired reality in the afterlife. The strict set of rules that the artist had to observe was particularly evident in the depiction of the human body. This had to conform to a prefixed canon of proportions in which the relations of the measurements of the individual parts of the body to each other were defined. Hence they could be scaled as required, that is, the size could be varied to need. As a result an ancient Egyptian work is immediately recognizable as such, even by the unpractised eye of the modern viewer; at the same time the impression may arise that Egyptian art underwent no phases of development. Far from it! In typology, iconography and especially styles major differences are evident in the course of the long history of the country. It is equally correct to say that at all times, as well as the great mass of well trained craftsmen, great artists were able to exploit their potential to the full within these rules, and they have left works that may be counted among the peaks of world art. However, at first the raw material, e.g. stones, had to be provided in the necessary quantities. The continuous setting up of quarries and their proper management – including logistics and transportation – was therefore a demanding task, entrusted only to the most experienced officials or members of the royal family.

Naos stela of the sculptor Bak, Eighteenth Dynasty, ca. 1340 B.C., quartzite, H. 63.5 cm, Ägyptisches Museum, SMPK, Berlin

Meidum

Far from the Nile, in the direction of the eastern entrance to the Faiyum, lies the necropolis of Meidum with the Step Pyramid, as it is called, as its outstanding feature. In the immediate vicinity of the pyramid, senior officials of the early Fourth Dynasty had large mastaba tombs erected, which were excavated in the 19th century by Auguste Mariette and Flinders Petrie. They include the famous sites of Prince Rahotep (see pp. 100f.) and Nefermaat.

The Pyramid of Snefru
Fourth Dynasty, ca. 2590 B.C.

The pyramid of Meidum is exactly on the borderline between the building traditions of the Third and Fourth Dynasties. It was planned by King Snefru as a solid step pyramid (299 feet or 92 m high), but it was to have a better technique of setting the blocks of limestone than Djoser's work in

Saqqara. The core building underwent several extensions or enlargements as the steps were laid and this is easily visible today from the sequence of smooth and rough zones in the masonry. Probably only after this work was finished did the idea evolve of achieving the geometric shape of a genuine pyramid by filling in the steps. The evident instability of such a structure is plain from the huge quantities of rubble and stones that lie around the foot of the pyramid like a wreath. From the entrance on the north side one descends a corridor into the burial chamber. The east side of the pyramid has a modest offering chapel consisting of a two-chamber construction with no decoration. Behind this rise two monumental stelae, but no royal name is mentioned (H. 13 feet or 4.20 m). They mark the offering place. In the rooms, near the main entrance, hieratic inscriptions left by visitors from the time of the New Kingdom show that Snefru was venerated after his death.

Papyrus—The Paper of Kings

Harvesting Papyrus, Fifth Dynasty, ca. 2450 B.C., tomb of Nefer, Saqqara

The papyrus reed (Latin: Cyperus papyrus) was put to a wide variety of uses by the ancient Egyptians. It grew everywhere, particularly in the marshes of the delta. The stalks grow to twelve feet high and the plant is so characteristic of this part of the country that it was chosen as a plant for the coat-of-arms of Lower Egypt. The stalks were used to make boats, baskets and mats, while the fibres made ropes and the roots were actually eaten as vegetables. But incontestably the plant reached its greatest importance when it was processed to make a substance to take writing. Some papyrus sheets are known already from the First Dynasty, although it bears no writing. The oldest written documents of any quantity on papyrus are the so-called "Abusir Papyri," administration records of the royal mortuary temple of the Fifth Dynasty. The Greek name "papyros" probably derives from the Egyptian "pa-en-per-aa" (belonging to the Pharaoh), an indication that under the Ptolemies the export trade in the writing material, which was costly and in great demand, was controlled by the king. Papyrus plants no longer grow wild in Egypt today, because the marshlands they need have been drained. Although there are no ancient Egyptian depictions of the production of papyrus the method can easily be reconstructed by studying the originals. First the freshly gathered stalks, that are triangular in profile, were peeled and cut into lengths of about 16 inches (40 cm). The pith thus exposed was cut into thin strips which were then laid on a flat bed in horizontal, slightly overlapping rows. A second layer was set in vertical rows. Pressure was then exerted, and this squeezed out the juice, which contained starch and stuck the two layers together. When the sheet was dry it was smoothed with a polishing stone and the edges were straightened. For longer writings (e.g. a copy of a "Book of the Dead") several sheets could be stuck together, as required, creating the classical papyrus scroll. Records show that in the 20th dynasty of the New Kingdom a standard scroll consisted of twenty sheets stuck together. Royal papyri, like the "Papyrus Harris I" (now in the British Museum, London) were over 120 feet (40 m) in length.

Papyrus was so costly a material that on principle it was only used for important documents. Nevertheless, there were not only differences in format but also in color, which could vary from light yellow to dark brown, and in the quality of the fibre structure. Each papyrus scroll was sealed and, if it was to be kept in the archives, put into a case, to be kept in a relatively small chest with other scrolls. Yet, the content of a given storage chest for Papyri was indicated either by writing a note on the container itself or by a fixed little plaque (made of faience or other materials) serving as a kind of "ex libris."

The great demand for papyrus under the pharaohs could no doubt only be met by organized manufactories and these were controlled by the king. The central administration's offices alone must have needed literally countless scrolls.

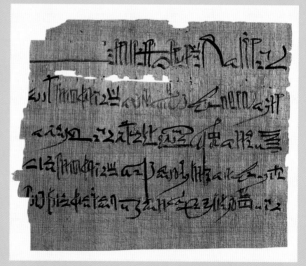

Letter from the High Priest Menkheperre, Twenty-first Dynasty, ca. 1050 B.C., papyrus, H. 18 cm, Musée du Louvre, Paris

The Faiyum

About 56 miles (90 km) south of Cairo, the great Oasis of Faiyum stretches along a valley in the Libyan Desert. But as it extends for 40 miles (65 km) along its east-west axis, calling this an oasis is to give a false impression. Moreover, the Faiyum is linked to the Nile valley through the tributary of Bahr Jussuf (the Joseph's canal), which starts at Deirut in Middle Egypt, then runs for 186 miles (300 km) parallel to the great river, to empty into Lake Karun (Birket el-Qarun). This is now 148 feet (45 m) below sea level, and has lost much of the area it covered in ancient times through evaporation and silting. Even in the late Paleolithic age (ca. 8000 B.C.) the fringe areas of the Faiyum were populated by hunters and gatherers. Under the pharaohs extensive thickets of reeds and papyrus were characteristic of this marshy landscape, the arable potential of which was first utilized by the rulers of the

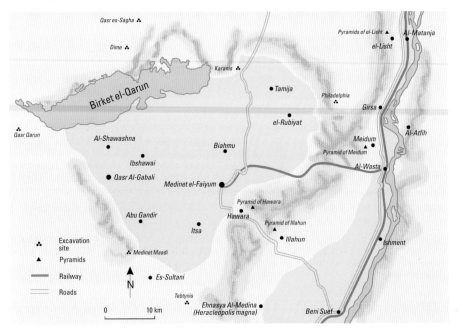

Twelfth Dynasty. Under Amenemhet II (around 1830 B.C.) a major irrigation project was successfully completed to win land in the Faiyum by constructing a whole system of canals and dams. This king set up a shrine at Mit Fares to the crocodile god Sobek, who was the main divinity worshipped in the Faiyum. It was near what is now the provincial capital Medinet el-Faiyum. Amenemhet III also built more temples, and was ultimately so associated with the Faiyum that he was venerated as a local saint in later times. The region only again became the focus of attention in the Ptolemaic period, when Ptolemy II increased the yields of the arable areas further by intensive drainage. The old capital Shedet was renamed Krokodilopolis and a broadly based settlement policy led to numerous new local settlements.

The Pyramid of Hawara
Twelfth Dynasty, ca. 1830 B.C.

Faults in the building on the Dahshur site forced Amenemhet III to build a new burial pyramid and the site he chose was Hawara to the south east of the Faiyum. The pyramid once reached a height of 333 feet (105 m), and was built on the skeletal principle to give greater stability. The stone ribs were set in star formation and the spaces between were filled in with great mud bricks; finally the surface was faced with limestone plates. The now badly damaged mortuary temple became famous for its architecture, the "Labyrinth," which according to a description by the Greek historian Strabo (1st century B.C.) consisted of 1500 rooms on two storeys.

Karanis (Kom Aushim)

Graeco-Roman period, 3rd century B.C. /
4th century B.C.

At the northern entrance to the Faiyum,
directly on the desert road to Giza stretches
the extensive settlement of Karanis. It
experienced its peak in the 2nd and 3rd
centuries B.C. Numerous objects of everyday use found here give a richly varied
picture of life in the town, some of the
dwellings of which are still well preserved.
Of particular interest are more than 5000
papyrus fragments and ostraca that provide information on business life in Roman
Egypt. Several limestone shrines were dedicated to a local version of Sobek, and to
Sarapis and Zeus-Ammon as well.

The Temple of Qasr es-Sagha

Twelfth Dynasty, ca. 1800 B.C.

On a hill far into the desert north of Lake
Karun stands the temple of Qasr es-Sagha.
It dates from the late Twelfth Dynasty and
has walls consisting of huge limestone
blocks. The central entrance leads into a
narrow room set crossway (68 feet or 21 m
wide), with seven chapels on its rear wall
arranged one beside the next. Like the
entire temple they were left unfinished
without any depictions or inscriptions. So
what divinities were worshipped here
must remain an open question, although
they will almost certainly have included
the great gods of Faiyum at this time—
Sobek, Renenutet and Horus.

Mummy Portraits—Images from the Desert Sand

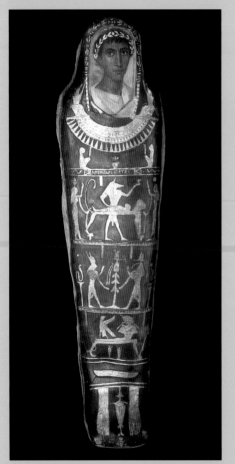

Roman rule under the Emperor Augustus marked the start of a new period of history for the land on the Nile, and it also brought the slow but final farewell to the pharaonic tradition. Politically Egypt played no further role, its prosperity was exploited by Rome and cultural achievements like the hieroglyphic system were only cultivated and understood by the priests in the great temples. But an innovation was introduced in the burial practices that were of such significance in Egypt, and this represented a successful synthesis between the old mummification practices and elements of Roman art. It was the custom of attaching a wooden panel above the mummy's head bearing a portrait of the deceased, and incorporating this mummy portrait, as they are called, in the bandages or casing. The earliest examples are from the time of the Emperor Tiberius (14–37 A.D.), and the custom continued to be practised for around 300 years, during the time of the Roman emperors. Although mummy portraits have been found all over Egypt, the great oasis of Faiyum was the main center, which is why these painted panels are also sometimes called Faiyum portraits. The two most important sites in the Faiyum where they

Mummy of Artemidorus with portrait,
ca. 100 A.D., Hawara, wood, painted and gilded,
Mummy: L. 167 cm, The British Museum,
London

have been found are the cemeteries of el-Rubayat and Hawara. The excavations by the British archaeologist W. M. Flinders Petrie (1853–1942) deserve special attention, for he was the founding father of all archaeology and scholarly methods of excavation in Egypt. He went to Hawara in the winter of 1888/89 intending to explore the pyramid of Amenemhet III of the late Twelfth Dynasty and its mortuary temple with the famous labyrinth. The search for the entrance to the pyramid proved more difficult than Petrie had expected, and he had to employ some of his workmen elsewhere. They very soon found a Roman burial site containing dozens of mummies with portraits, many only laid in flat graves. A second expedition in 1911/12 took Petrie back to Hawara, where he was able to excavate another 70 mummies. His precise notes and observations on the conditions under which the finds were made have been of immense value to other scholars in this field. Most of the mummy portraits are in the encaustic (melted wax) technique, but use of tempera has also been observed. Many of the panels were made while the subject was alive; they were then cut to size after his or her death and incorporated in the mummy wrappings. The portraits of both men and women can be dated best from their hair styles, which largely followed the urban Roman fashions. The main reason for introducing portraits into the mortuary cult, so giving the mummy a degree of individualization hitherto unknown, was probably that the portraits raised the status in a way that certain social classes regarded as essential. In their variety and their good state of preservation the Egyptian mummy portraits are

Mummy portrait of a woman, 2nd century A.D., Hawara, wood, painted, H. 43.7 cm, Royal Scottish Museum, Edinburgh

among the best examples of painting we possess from Roman times. Finally, even though a good deal of the original number of all mummy portraits may have survived, it is to remember that only a small percentage of the Roman burials were provided with them.

From Beni Hassan to Hermopolis

Beni Hassan

The collapse of the Old Kingdom at the end of the Sixth Dynasty spelled the end of Egypt's first centralized state which broke down into smaller, regional powers. In the ensuing period, the newfound independence of local potentates led them to construct entire cemeteries in their own nomes or regions. During the Eleventh and Twelfth Dynasties the nomarchs of the 16th Upper Egyptian "Gazelle" nome built their rock tombs on the east bank of the Nile. The paintings in these tombs are among the most outstanding examples of Ancient Egyptian art. A total of 39 tombs

were hewn out of the rock half-way up a mountain range where they generally took the form of a single chamber with a cult niche. Several of these tombs are undecorated. While the older tombs (Eleventh Dynasty) have plain entrances, the façades of later structures were elaborately decorated with double columns and a portico (see illustration bottom).

Previous pages: Caravan of Semites in the tomb of Khnumhotep in Beni Hassan, from: Richard Lepsius, "Monuments of Egypt and Ethiopia," Berlin 1849–1859

Tomb of Kheti (No. 17)
Twelfth Dynasty, ca. 1960 B.C.

The nomarch Kheti bore the title "Great Leader of the Gazelle Nome in its Entirety." The hall-like room (c. 39 × 52 ft; 12 × 16 m) with its gently vaulted ceiling is divided at the rear of the cult chamber by two rows of columns. Of the tomb's six lotus stem columns two have survived with most of their original paintwork. The stems and buds of these columns were copied as closely as possible from nature. The thin bands of the architraves were continued down the walls to become slightly projecting pilasters. Particularly remarkable are the depictions of a desert hunting scene with nets (north wall, left), different kinds of bird traps and the groups of wrestlers which can be seen in several registers on the rear wall.

Tomb of Baket (No. 15)

Twelfth Dynasty, ca. 1980 B.C.

Girls juggling

Baket, another nomarch, had a tomb very similar to that of his son Kheti. In the case of the father however the large room (41 × 54 ft; 12.5 × 16.5 m) was divided by only two lotus stem columns (now destroyed). In the southwest corner is a small wall niche which once contained a sacrificial table, and in front of this is the main shaft (c. 98 ft/ 30 m deep) leading down to the burial chamber. The tomb's varied pictorial program reaches its peak on the east wall with a depiction of 220 pairs of wrestlers. These paintings reveal the artist's fondness for portraying complex movement, as does another famous depiction on the north wall in which three female acrobats can be seen juggling balls. The girls are shown wearing wigs with extended braids and they are clad in calf-length robes.

Tomb of Amenemhet (No. 2)
Twelfth Dynasty, ca. 1920 B.C.

Groups of wrestlers

The tomb of Amenemhet is without doubt one of the finest in Beni Hassan. The cult chamber is organized by four rows of 16-sided, finely fluted columns. Its main axis is oriented towards a large statue niche in the eastern wall containing a seated image of Ameni (an abbreviated name of the tomb owner) with figures of his wife and mother. The central vault of the ceiling features a mat pattern while the entrance (doorway) is decorated with a long biographical inscription recounting this nomarch's various military activities. It dates from the 43rd year of the reign of Senusret. I.

As in the older tombs of Baket and Kheti, a generous area of space was given to images of wrestlers. These pictures are located on the east wall and are therefore accorded a prominent position around the statue niche. The dynamism of the wrestlers' movements is particularly well depicted, and not a single one of the 59 pairs of figures is repeated. Variations in the brightness of color used for the bodies helps to distinguish and define the contours of the figures. Linked to these wrestling scenes are further registers depicting the battle for a fortress; the connection thus created between these two scenes implies that the wrestlers were the nomarch's own troops.

Tomb of Khnumhotep (No. 3)

Twelfth Dynasty, ca. 1880 B.C.

The funerary architecture and wall paintings of Beni Hassan reach their final peak in the tomb of Khnumhotep. This tomb-owner held high office under Amenemhet II and Senusret II as "Mayor of Menat-Khufu" (Wetnurse of Cheops) on the east bank of the Nile; at the same time he also bore the title of a "Principal of the Eastern Desert." Just a few years after the death of Khnumhotep, Senusret III. abolished the nomarchs' privileges in favor of a stronger central administration, and building in the central Egyptian Cemeteries came to a standstill. Massive architraves divide the large cult chamber into three sections with vaulted ceilings. The central statue niche (east wall) is framed by inscriptions and flanked on the adjoining walls by a pair of large-scale figures, a composition which had already been used in the Old Kingdom. Representing Khnumhotep, each of these figures stands in a barque hunting quarry in a papyrus thicket. On the left he prepares to hurl a throwing stick at waterfowl while on the right he impales two Nile perch on his harpoon. Directly over the statue niche (see illustration bottom) the tomb-owner is pictured snaring birds with a fowling net. As befits the dignity of his office, Khnumhotep is shown seated on a stool behind a protective reed wall where he pulls tight a net full of prey. The birds have been painted with such care that their individual species can all be identified—as is the case in a famous image of a hoopoe, for example. Two figures are shown following the mayor: his oldest son, Nakht, and the site manager of the tomb, Baket. The base of all walls is covered by the extensive biography of Khnumhotep.

Caravan of Semites

Probably the most famous painting from the tombs of Beni Hassan can be found underneath a great desert hunting scene on the north wall of Khnumhotep's tomb. It shows a small caravan of Semitic traders being led before Khnumhotep by his chief hunter, who hands the mayor a document recording the date of this event: "Year 6 of His Majesty, the Horus, Unifier of the Two Lands of Upper and Lower Egypt, Kha-Kheper-Re (the throne name of Senusret II); the number of Aamu (inhabitants of the Eastern Desert) brought by the son of Khnumhotep in the matter of cosmetics, numbers 37." Among the duties Khnumhotep had to discharge in his function as "Principal of the Eastern Desert" was the conduct of foreign trade. The leader of the caravan is depicted at its head together with an ibex; he bows before Khnumhotep (out of the picture to the right) and holds a small crook in his hand. An inscription refers to him as "Leader of the foreigners, Ibsha." This latter expression (Egyptian: heka chaswt) ultimately led to the term Hyksos, used to refer to the foreign rulers of Egypt in the Second Intermediate Period (Fifteenth Dynasty). The hairstyles, beards and richly patterned robes also all point to the Ibsha as being members of a Semitic tribe. Rendered with similar attention to detail are the calf-length dresses worn by a group of four women in the middle of the procession who all wear white ribbons as part of their elaborate hairstyles. The shape of their leather ankle boots is further evidence of their membership of a Bedouin tribe from the Eastern Desert. The importance of this unique scene unfortunately doesn't protect it against a misled conservation project on the paintings of Beni Hassan.

Priests performing rites for the mortuary cult

The southern wall of the tomb of Khnumhotep is devoted to depictions of the mortuary cult and the provision of his material needs. Arranged in two small registers, the rites are being carried out by several priests who represent different professional classes. Firstly, one of the funerary priests offers a libation of water; he is followed by a Sem priest, clad in a leopard skin, and a lector priest with a papyrus scroll in his left hand. The kneeling group at the bottom also includes three lector priests with the diagonal sash typical of their office. At the far right another priest is seen walking away after completion of the rites; he sweeps the ground with a broom-like object thereby restoring the cult purity of the room.

The Mystery of the Mummies

God Anubis looking after the mummy of the deceased, 19th Dynasty, ca. 1250 B.C., Western Thebes, Deir el-Medineh, Tomb of Sennedjem

The ancient Egyptians believed the preservation of the human body after death to be absolutely essential to their continued existence in the hereafter. While the spiritual components of the deceased passed over into the kingdom of the dead, the body remained in its tomb in this world. The corpse was bound to earthly life and represented a connection to the living who provided for the dead by carrying out cult rites. In order to counter the decomposition of the corpse various methods of embalming were practiced. In prehistoric times it was sufficient to mummify the body in the hot, dry desert sands. During the Old Kingdom the first artificial methods began to be used, although it is not until the Middle Kingdom that embalming proper began. This first involved extracting the brains of the deceased with a long hook and filling the empty cavity of the skull with hot oils and resins. Then, the chest and abdomen were opened and the innards of the deceased removed. Only the heart (or a heart-scarab) was reinserted; the other parts were washed by the embalmer, treated with natron salts and placed in four canopic jars. The corpse itself was also laid in dry natron in order to remove any trace of bodily fluids before it was anointed with oils and the body cavities filled with aromatic herbs and a wide range of other substances.

Later, pitch or bitumen was used as an additional preservative and it is from the Arabic word for bitumen that the term mummy is derived. Ultimately, however, the excellent state of preservation of many mummies is due to Egypt's arid climate. While the effort invested in mummification depended to a large extent on the financial position of the deceased and his or her family, the techniques involved underwent a number of changes over time (for example in the types of bandages or material used to fill the cavities). Until the end of the 19th century investigations of mummies tended to resemble rather haphazard attempts at unpacking luggage. This state of affairs only changed after the discovery of X-rays (1895), which were considered much more effective for researching mummies. Without having to intervene in the body directly, information could now be obtained as to the dead person's sex, age and state of health. Today, computer tomography (CT) or even more recent technology is frequently used to generate very thin cross-sectional images and this data allows for a three dimensional reconstruction of the body. Recently DNA analysis of samples from mummies has begun, although this method has yet to prove its full potential.

In 1920, long before any such procedures were thought of, an excavation team from the Metropolitan Museum in New York stumbled across the modest but completely intact tomb of

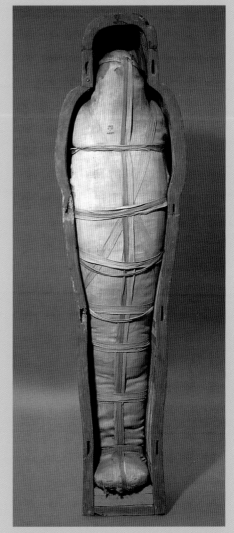

Coffin with mummy in its bandages, Twenty-first Dynasty, ca. 1000 B.C., Western Thebes, L. 183 cm, The British Museum, London

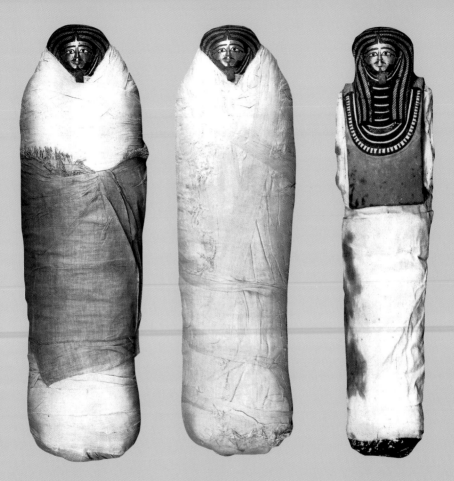

Wah in the cliffs south of Deir el-Bahri; the complex dated from the very late Eleventh Dynasty / Early Twelfth Dynasty. The mummy of this slightly built official, who died approximately 30, was elaborately bandaged and is among the oldest mummies to be found in such a good state of preservation. When the archaeologists removed the bandages in 1939 they calculated that a total of 448.5 sq yds (375 m²) of linen had been used to wrap the corpse (the

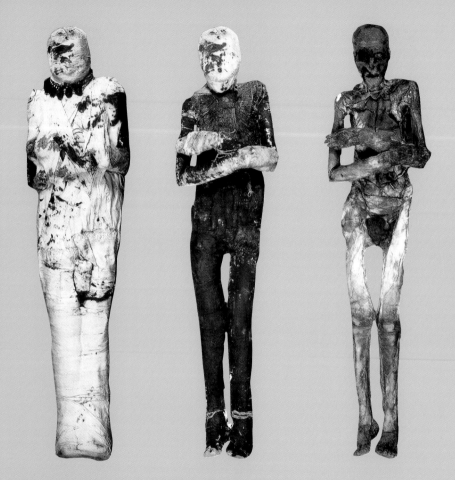

longest single piece of material measured over 27 yds; 25 m). Along with various necklaces, two magnificent silver scarabs (one bears an inscription of golden inlaid hieroglyphs) were discovered in the mummy's bandages.

Mummy of Wah (various stages of unwrapping), Early Twelfth Dynasty, ca. 1970 B.C., Western Thebes, Tomb of Wah, The Metropolitan Museum of Art, New York (20.3.203)

Tell el-Amarna

King Akhenaten called his new capital Akhetaten, "Horizon of the Aten," and ordered it to be built in a broad valley basin on the eastern bank of the Nile; today, the site lies around 9 miles (15 km) south of the modern town of Mellawi. At the start of his reign the king had resided in Thebes as Amenophis IV. He soon changed his name to Akhenaten, however, and founded several temples to the east of Karnak in honor of the god Aten. The State dogma he propounded was of one supreme god, the sun disc Aten, with the king as his sole messenger, and these new teachings sparked a search for a place previously unburdened by other cult uses. The semi-circular plain of Tell el-Amarna met this criterion perfectly. In the fifth year of his reign, Akhenaten ordered the founding of a new city on the site and probably moved there with his court just a year later. On what was now sacred soil the urban atmosphere appropriate to a royal center had necessarily to be produced in record time. Massive temples to Aten and various palace buildings were laid out parallel to the Nile on the so-called Royal Road while residential areas were built around the city center. Officials were allocated rock tombs as a sign of royal favor; many were left unfinished and have never been used for burial. In 1891 the demolished tomb of Akhenaten was found in a wadi some 7.5 miles east of the city in the desert.

The North Palace, p. 266

Small Temple of Aten, p. 264 f.

Bust of Queen Nefertiti, p. 272

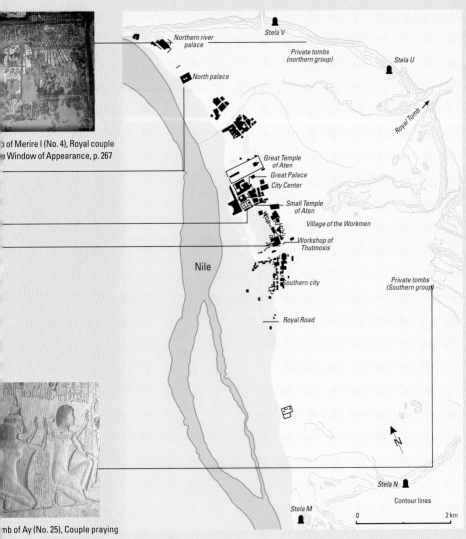

Stela V

Northern river palace

Private tombs (northern group)

Stela U

North palace

Royal Tomb

of Merire I (No. 4), Royal couple
e Window of Appearance, p. 267

Great Temple of Aten
Great Palace
City Center

Small Temple of Aten

Village of the Workmen

Workshop of Thutmosis

Nile

Southern city

Private tombs (Southern group)

Royal Road

mb of Ay (No. 25), Couple praying
d Great Hymn, p. 267

N

Stela N

Contour lines

Stela M

0   2 km

Tell el-Amarna   **263**

The Temples of Aten
Eighteenth Dynasty, ca. 1345 B.C.

The visitor who today looks at the areas formerly occupied by temples in the central city of Akhetaten will scarcely be able to conceal his disappointment. A few squat remnants of mud brick walls and the occasional base of a stone column are all that remain of this once glorious complex. After the city was finally abandoned under Tutankhamun the systematic demolition of all the stone structures built by the heretic king began in the early Nineteenth Dynasty.

The great stone blocks freed up in this way were used for the buildings of other pharaohs. Ramesses II, for example, used around 1500 of them for the foundations of his temples in the city of Hermopolis which lay on the opposite, western, bank of the Nile. After its complete destruction, Akhetaten was never resettled so that beneath its sands archaeologists have been able to reveal how the original Eighteenth Dynasty city must have looked. Together with depictions of the temples in private tombs, the surviving ground plans have provided sufficient information to enable these places of worship to be reconstructed.

The so-called Great Temple of Aten was situated in an enormous precinct (832 × 295 yds, 760 × 270 m) to the east on the Royal Road and encompassed two temples separated by more than 380 yds (350 m). A few hundred yards to the south lay the Small Temple of Aten whose girdle walls feature projections like bastions (see p. 264) and which perhaps served as sites for the royal mortuary cult. Spatial divisions are provided by three pairs of pylons and in the first courtyard there is a great high altar surrounded by 108 smaller altar pediments. This series of open courtyards with large numbers of altars for the god's cult is the most outstanding characteristic of Amarna religious architecture.

The Royal Family

Eighteenth Dynasty, ca. 1345 B.C., Wall painting on plaster, 165 × 40 cm, Ashmolean Museum, Oxford

All the palaces in Amarna—the Great Palace, North Palace and River Palace—originally had extensive paintings on their walls and floors although only a few examples of these have survived. This fragment (from the King´s House, belonging to a royal compound opposite the Great Palace) pictured above shows two of the younger princesses seated at the feet of the royal couple in a domestic scene typical of Amarna art. Their older sisters are shown between Akhenaten and Nefertiti.

The North Palace

Eighteenth Dynasty, ca. 1345 B.C.

The large number of palaces in Akhetaten raise the question as to which of them served as a home for Akhenaten and his family. The vast complex of the central palace west of the Royal Road (ca. 1794 sq yds; 1500 m²), which was joined by a bridge to the royal buildings on the other side of the thoroughfare, seems to have been used for purely representative purposes. The remains of the North Palace are better preserved; they feature two great courtyards and a lake leading on to covered and pillared halls and a throne room all of which lie along a central axis. To the sides of the building are areas which were largely devoted to functional uses. This relatively modest building however has more the character of a ceremonial palace and was therefore probably not the king's home. The River Palace in the far north of the city is more likely to have served this purpose; although it has never been fully excavated, it was equipped with all the features necessary for permanent residence.

Tomb of Merire I (No. 4)

Eighteenth Dynasty, ca. 1340 B.C.

Royal couple at the Window of Appearance

A total of 25 tombs belonging to court officials were hewn from the rock in the hills surrounding Amarna. Their reliefs are fundamentally different from those of private tombs in Thebes in that they all focus on the king and his family. This scene from the tomb of Merire I, High Priest of Aten, shows Akhenaten at the Window of Appearance, conferring the gold of honor on Merire and his entourage.

Tomb of Ay (No. 25)

Eighteenth Dynasty, ca. 1340 B.C.

Married couple worshipping

Known as "The God's Father," Ay was one of the most influential officials at the Amarna court. The hall of his tomb was to have been supported by 24 papyrus columns but the work was never completed beyond the left half of the room. In spite of this, the tomb has yielded up one of the great jewels of world poetry: "The Great Hymn to Aten," a poem which deals in an ecstatic way with the creation of all beings by the god Aten. On the right wall of the entrance passageway is a relief depicting Ay kneeling with his wife Tiya, wetnurse to Queen Nefertiti, as they raise their arms in a gesture of worship and prayer.

Boundary stela A

Eighteenth Dynasty, ca. 1345 B.C.

Boundary stela S

Eighteenth Dynasty, ca. 1345 B.C.

The decree founding the new capital was recorded on 14 (15) huge rock stelae which encircled the city and also served as boundary stones. Eleven (twelve) often inaccessible stones mark the city boundary in the eastern range of hills while three others were positioned on the western bank of the Nile at Tuna el-Gebel, including the so-called boundary stela A. Statues of Akhenaten and Nefertiti (sometimes of their daughters too) were often added to the inscriptions; here they can be seen with outstretched arms bringing offerings.

The use of boundary stones to provide a visual marker for fields or even for provinces (nomes) was known before the Amarna period, but the definition of an urban area with rock stelae can only be understood in terms of particular cultic and topographical considerations. In the text of two (three) of the stelae, the so-called "early declaration" of his 5th year of reign, Akhenaten expressly makes a kind of public announcement concerning the choice of location which, he claims, was determined by the god Aten and did not allow for an alternative: "(…) At this place shall I found Akhetaten for my father Aten. Neither to the north, south, east or west shall I build Akhetaten." The remote but still vulnerable location of the boundary stelae (up to 29.5 feet; 9 m high) has unfortunately exposed them to both erosion and vandalism. Many of them have been damaged in recent decades as is the case of a large fragment of Stela S (see red frame in illustration, right) which is today in Boston (Museum of Fine Arts, 1992.18). When this stela was first published around 1910 the fragment was still in its original position in the upper field. It shows the two oldest daughters of the king, Meritaten and Maketaten, each holding a sistrum and helping their parents make sacrifices under the rays of the sun disc, Aten.

The Workshop of the Sculptor Thutmosis

The far-reaching political changes which occurred intermittently throughout Egypt's long history represent a window onto the past and offer excellent archeological potential for modern scholars. The tasks of a royal residence or a necropolis demanded that, when a move was being contemplated, the officials in charge should make a decision about the quality of the items they took with them. Objects regarded as superfluous were left behind—such as the famous "Papyri of Abusir," administrative documents of the mortuary priesthood at the eponymous Fifth-Dynasty pyramid complexes situated between Giza and Saqqara.

These documents had become obsolete after the royal cemetery was transferred back to

Reconstruction of House P 47.2, Eighteenth Dynasty, ca. 1340 B.C., Tell el-Amarna

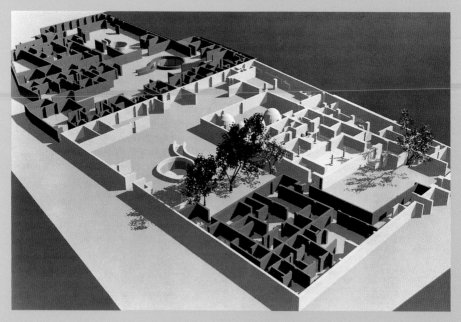

Saqqara under the last rulers of the dynasty.

The case of Akhetaten, the newly founded capital of Akhenaten in Middle Egypt, is more complex. Shortly after the death of the so-called heretic king, an entire city was abandoned, never again to be inhabited. Although the city-dwellers—whether they were officials, priests or tradesmen—took their personal property with them, specifically religious objects were left behind as were, of course, houses, workshops and other functional buildings. The extirpation of Akhenaten's memory and the Aten-centered faith he had propagated meant that not only were his palaces and places of worship ultimately demolished in the Nineteenth Dynasty, most of the royal statuary was also destroyed. It is only due to luck that the many images of Akhenaten and his family from the workshop of Thutmosis escaped the persecution of the pharaoh's successors.

It is also possible that they were just not considered important enough; most of them were bozzettos or components of statues and as such either had no official character or were not yet conse-

King Akhenaten, Eighteenth Dynasty, ca. 1340 B.C., Tell el-Amarna, plaster, H. 26 cm, Agyptisches Museum, Staatliche Museen Preußischer Kulturbesitz, Berlin

crated for religious purposes. In the course of a normal change of government these pieces would usually have been disposed of because sculptural work would now be reserved for depictions of the new king. When the chief sculptor, Thutmosis, left his vast complex of workshops however, he did not bother to take this trouble, preferring to leave the now useless and ideologically embarrassing images of his dead master to their fate. This "negative choice," combined with the fact that the city was never resettled, provided the German archeologist Ludwig Borchardt with a dramatic discovery. In December 1912, in room 19 house 47.2 (the site's sober grid reference), he unearthed the "Workshop of Thutmosis," the establishment of the most trusted sculptor in Amarna.

Magnificent portrait busts and other statue parts of the royal family—mainly of Nefertiti and the princesses—came to light in quick succession. They were generally made from yellowish to red-brown quartzite, the preferred material for royal sculptures during the Amarna period. Alongside completed works were others whose unfinished state documented the artist's

Bust of Queen Nefertiti, Eighteenth Dynasty, ca. 1340 B.C., Tell el-Amarna, painted limestone, H. 50 cm, Agyptisches Museum, Staatliche Museen Preußischer Kulturbesitz, Berlin

Head of a princess, Eighteenth Dynasty, ca. 1340 B.C., Tell el-Amarna, quartzite, H. 21 cm, Agyptisches Museum, Staatliche Museen Preußischer Kulturbesitz, Berlin

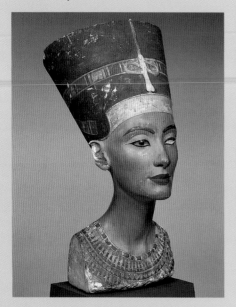 

working processes. All the sculptures in stone were made for so-called composite figures which meant that the head and extremities were inserted into an existing body made from a different type of stone. Other details, such as the crown, could be made separately from faience, pâte de verre or even precious metals and these gave the statues an indefinable air of divine majesty. Also of great interest were 20 model heads made from gypsum plaster; which included portraits of Akhenaten and Nefertiti as well as images of officials and their wives. One of the heads is claimed to be that of Ay, *eminence grise* at the Amarna court and later king (1323–1319 B.C.). Only after intensive investigations was it revealed that the plaster heads were in fact casts produced from clay models. They were kept in the studio and used as templates for manufacturing other statues.

The most magnificent of all the workshop finds is, without doubt, the world famous painted limestone bust of Queen Nefertiti. The harmonious features of the queen's face speak of a timeless ideal of beauty and bear no traces of the expressive images of the early Amarna period. She wears a high crown with diadem and *uraeus*—the so-called bonnet of Nefertiti—as well as a multi-rowed collar of stylized flowers. The left eye of the piece is missing, a flaw which emphasizes the character of the bust as a sculptor´s model. Efforts by the German archeologists to locate the missing eye were ultimately unsuccessful: it had, in fact, never been inserted in the first place. Already Borchardt had reached this conclusion when he wrote that "no trace of an adhesive can be detected in the hollow of the eye; also the back-

Hands from a royal group statue, Eighteenth Dynasty, ca. 1340 B.C., Tell el-Amarna, quartzite, H. 9 cm, Agyptisches Museum, Staatliche Museen Preußischer Kulturbesitz, Berlin

ground is smooth and has not been carved in any way to receive an inlay." When the finds were officially distributed in 1913 by the Egyptian authorities, the Nefertiti bust went to the Berlin businessman, James Simon, who had financed the excavations of the German Oriental Society in Amarna. Simon gifted the piece to the Prussian state in 1920. Since then, the bust of Nefertiti has become a treasured icon for the culture of ancient Egypt, a position she shares only with the Pyramids in Giza and the boy-king Tutankhamun.

Hermopolis and Tuna el-Gebel

Capital of the 15th Upper Egyptian "Hare" nome, the city of Hermopolis lies some 186 miles (300 km) south of Cairo on the west bank of the Nile. While the Arabic name Ashmunein is reflected in the ancient Egyptian place name of "Chemenu," the word Hermopolis refers to the Greek god Hermes, who was believed to be the equivalent of the local deity, Thoth. Hermopolis was an important religious center and home to the eight primeval gods of the Egyptian pantheon. In antiquity the great temple to Thoth from the 4th century B.C. stood in the center of the city. Still in existence at the start of the 20th century it has all but disappeared today save for a few insignificant remains. The same is true of a pylon built under Amenemhet II from the Twelfth Dynasty and buildings from the era of Ramesses II. Outside the walls are the most important remains from the Graeco-Roman settlements with streets from the 1st—2nd centuries A.D. and parts of a peripteral temple from the reign of Ptolemy III. The Christian 5th century basilica was erected over this purely Greek place of worship. From Hermopolis the road runs west for 6 miles (10 km) before reaching Tuna el-Gebel, the cemetery of Hermopolis. The main sight of interest there is the tomb chapel of Petosiris (4th century B.C.) with the surrounding necropolis and extensive Ibis catacombs.

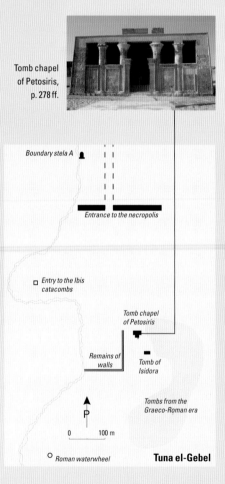

Tomb chapel of Petosiris, p. 278 ff.

Boundary stela A

Entrance to the necropolis

Entry to the Ibis catacombs

Tomb chapel of Petosiris

Remains of walls

Tomb of Isidora

Tombs from the Graeco-Roman era

0   100 m

Roman waterwheel

Tuna el-Gebel

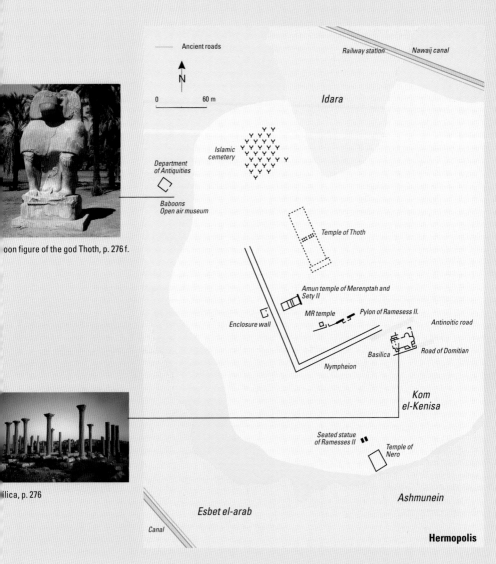

Ancient roads

N

0   60 m

Railway station   Nawaij canal

Idara

Islamic cemetery

Department of Antiquities

Baboons
Open air museum

Temple of Thoth

oon figure of the god Thoth, p. 276 f.

Amun temple of Merenptah and Sety II

MR temple   Pylon of Ramesess II.

Enclosure wall

Antinoitic road

Basilica   Road of Domitian

Nympheion

Kom
el-Kenisa

lica, p. 276

Seated statue of Ramesses II   Temple of Nero

Ashmunein

Esbet el-arab

Canal

Hermopolis

The Basilica
Coptic, 5th century

Baboon Figure of Thoth
Eighteenth Dynasty, ca. 1380 B.C.

The gigantic basilica of Hermopolis which gave its name to nearby Kom el-Kenisa (Hill of the Church) is among the largest (around 213 feet; 65 m long) of the churches built in early Christian Egypt. Constructed between 410 and 440 A.D., it was dedicated to the Virgin Mary. Although the walls have largely been destroyed, a number of red granite columns have been re-erected. These columns once divided the church into three sections and lined the apses at the sides.

Fragments from originally eight colossal baboon figures made of brown quartzite were salvaged from the foundations of the Ptolemaic Thoth temple; they had been donated to the court of the temple during the reign of Amenophis III, reflecting the epithet of Thoth as "Lord of the Ogdoad." Each of the figures weighs over 35 tons and has a height of some 15 feet (4.5 m). In spite of their huge size, the characteristics of these sacred animals have been perfectly rendered.

Tomb Chapel of Petosiris
Late 4th century B.C.

The history of the Tuna al-Gebel necropolis begins in the New Kingdom, although the character of the area is determined by its Greek and Roman buildings. The most splendid of the tombs was built by the High priest of Thoth in Hermopolis, Petosiris, shortly before the beginning of Ptolemaic rule in Egypt. Designed as a typical family tomb both the occupant's father, Nes-Shu, and brother, Djed-Djehuti-iuef-ankh, were interred here. The tomb's superstructure is in the form of a small temple with a columned façade; the scenes carved on the partitions depict Petosiris making sacrifices. The tomb is famed for the mixed Greek and Egyptian styles of its images. Reliefs in the portico featuring agricultural scenes and depictions of artisans emphasize the Greek component, while the religious motifs of the adjoining chapel with its four pillars are entirely derived from the Egyptian tradition. Although the tomb was already plundered in antiquity, the French archeologists who excavated the tomb in 1920 were still able to make an astonishing find by unearthing Petosiris's wooden inner coffin which is remarkable for its glass-inlaid hieroglyphic text.

Metal workers

The depictions on the walls of the tomb's portico show a thorough knowledge of ancient Egyptian subject matter, some of which dates back to the Old Kingdom. These include agricultural scenes on the left wall—such as plowing, threshing, harvesting flax and grain—and the scenes of mustering cattle and wine-making from the right wall. The stylistic execution of the work and its iconographic details however were borrowed from contemporary styles influenced by the Greeks—an aspect which may be remarked in the clothes and bodies of those depicted. The inward facing partitions are devoted to depictions of tradesmen; the two eastern partitions include scenes of carpenters at work while on the western side there are scenes of metal workers. Under the gaze of a foreman, three goldsmiths are shown seated on the ground applying chased patterns to various vessels. While one of them works the rim of a tall vase, his colleagues decorate an animal-headed rhyton and double rhyton (drinking vessels); these were not typical of Egypt but were most likely of Achaemenid origin. Worthwhile to mention is the fact that those elaborate vessels were produced at a time (ca. 340 / 300 B.C.) when the real poltical power, the Persian Empire, behind the use of such foreign designs was already gone.

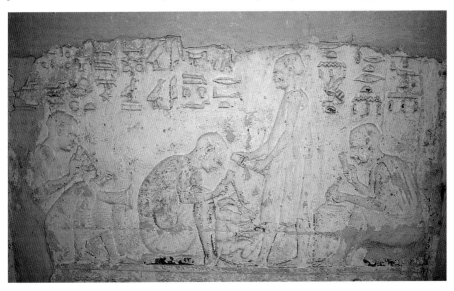

Wine production

Probably because the climate was so favorable in those regions, the wine growing areas of Egypt were traditionally located in the Delta and oases. Wine had been known since predynastic times when it was introduced into the country from the Syria-Palestine area. As a luxury good, wine was reserved for kings and high-ranking officials. The many depictions of wine production in tombs, particularly from the time of the New Kingdom onwards, are further evidence of the great esteem enjoyed by this beverage. In the tomb of Petosiris, one of the registers on the right-hand side wall is also devoted to this theme. After harvesting the grapes are shown being brought to a great stone press in which four men trample the fruit. The juice flows out a spout into a great vat before it is poured into jugs and amphorae. Finally, an exact record is made of the wine production before it is then delivered to the administrators of the estates.

The Ibis Catacombs

Lateperiod/Ptolemaic period, 6th–1st century B.C.

A short distance from the tomb of Petosiris the visitor can descend, through an unremarkable entrance, to the subterranean galleries of the animal cemetery. This complicated network of corridors and chambers once served as a place of both veneration and burial for hamadryad baboons and ibis—animals sacred to Thoth, the god of wisdom. The mummified remains of ibis were frequently brought to the site in simple terracotta jars, hundreds of which were then stacked on top of each other in a rock chamber; painted wooden coffins and small limestone sarcophagi were also often used to hold the corpses. The early Ptolemaic kings built several cult chambers with reliefs and sacrificial altars in the galleries, and these are presently being investigated by a team of archeologists from Munich, Germany.

The Scarab

The dung beetle, the sacred scarab, was thought by the Egyptians to be one of the forms in which the sun-god manifested himself. Just as the scarab rolled a ball of dung, for example, the Guides to the Netherworld depict the god as a beetle rolling the sun disc out of the Earth every morning, thus becoming reborn. The Egyptians held that the beetle was spontaneously generated out of the earth and this belief, together with the shape of the dung ball, led to a conceptual relationship being established between the beetle and the sun. The character

Scarab belonging to estate manager Wah, Eleventh Dynasty, ca. 1970 B.C., Western Thebes, Tomb of Wah, silver and gold (inscription), L. 3.8 cm, The Metropolitan Museum of Art, New York

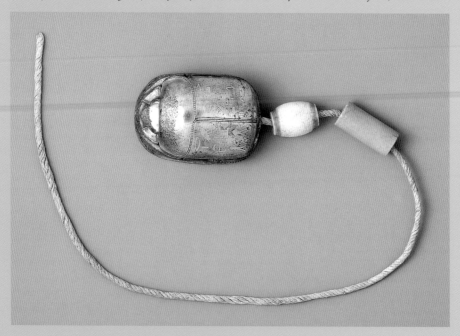

of a scarab in Egyptian script also indicates this notion of cyclical renewal: the character was read as "kheper" and meant "to become, to be transformed."

Scarab-shaped amulets therefore possessed great significance throughout Egyptian history. There were both beetle-shaped varieties, held to be rejuvenating and bearers of good fortune simply because of their appearance, and others with smooth undersides which bore inscriptions. From the Middle Kingdom some scarabs were provided with a royal name. The name engraved on the scarab generally had a religious meaning which, together with the power of the king, was thought to have a beneficial effect on the wearer. Not only the names of living kings were so used: the names of deceased kings were thought to be particularly effective. From the time of the New Kingdom the role of the scarab as a lucky charm and protective device was reinforced by short spells or a combination of characters in which the name of the god Amun-Re, written in its various forms, played an especially important role. Scarabs with the names of private individuals come to us mainly from the Middle Kingdom when they generally served as seals—though they might also be given as presents. Although the seal and amulet scarabs are generally small in size there were two other types which were on a larger scale. These are the heart scarabs, inscribed with chapter 30 B from the *Book of the Dead* in order to protect the deceased from being judged harshly in the afterlife; and the commemorative scarabs which were issued (especially by Amenophis III) to mark important events. For this king we learn about a royal hunt of wild

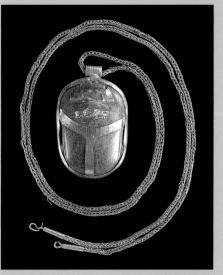

Heart scarab of General Djehuti with gold chain, Eighteenth Dynasty, ca. 1450 B.C., Saqqara, gold and nephrite, L. 8.3 cm, Rijksmuseum van Oudheden, Leiden

bulls and lions, his marriage with Queen Tiye as well as the construction of a large lake at Western Thebes. Scarabs were not only worn by both the living and the dead in Egypt, they were also exported abroad as protective amulets. Demand was so great that manufacturing sites were set up throughout the Mediterranean. Scarabs made in these places had the same external appearance as the Egyptian type but the inscriptions on their undersides are no longer legible and should be seen merely as attempts to imitate the magic of Egyptian characters.

Dendera Dec. 7th 1838

Abydos and Dendera

Abydos

One of the most important religious centers of the country, the necropolis of Abydos—capital of the eighth Upper Egyptian nome—lies around 9 miles (15 km) south of the modern city of Balyana. From the days of the Old Kingdom this was a place of worship for Osiris, the god of death and vegetation. Later, he became one of the local holy trinity along with his wife, Isis, and son, Horus. Almost all periods in Egyptian history are represented in Abydos by important monuments. In the middle of the desert near Umm al-Qaab (Arab., "Mother of Pots") the royal tombs of the Early Dynastic period (Dynasty 0 – Second Dynasties) were built; in recent years their architecture has again been the subject of investigations by scholars from the German Archeological Institute in Cairo. To the northeast in the gigantic cemetery lie the ruins of the great temple of Osiris on the Kom el-Sultan, once the cult center of Abydos. The two early Ramesside temples however, represent the real glory of Abydos's architecture. Built under Sety I. and his son Ramesses II during the Nineteenth Dynasty these well-preserved structures are unique for the intensity of color of their decorative reliefs.

Previous pages: The Hathor Temple of Dendera, David Roberts, from: "Egypt and Nubia," London 1846–1850

The Osireion, p. 293

The Osiris Myth, p. 292

Erecting the Djed pillar, p. 290

Temple of Sety I, view of the second hypostyle hall, p. 288

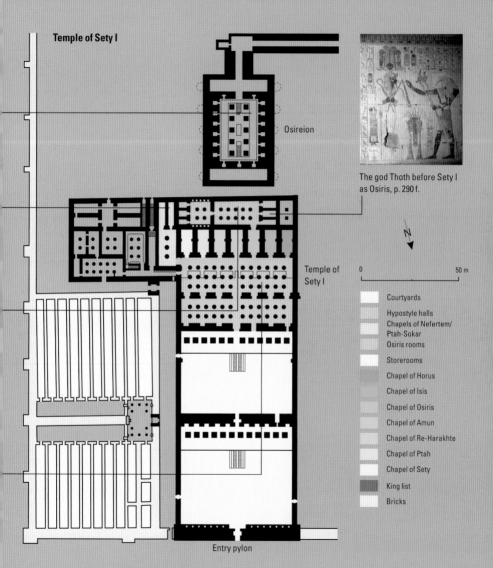

Temple of Sety I

Osireion

The god Thoth before Sety I
as Osiris, p. 290 f.

as Osiris, p. 290 f.

N

Temple of
Sety I

0   50 m

Courtyards

Hypostyle halls
Chapels of Nefertem/
Ptah-Sokar
Osiris rooms

Storerooms

Chapel of Horus

Chapel of Isis

Chapel of Osiris

Chapel of Amun

Chapel of Re-Harakhte

Chapel of Ptah

Chapel of Sety

King list

Bricks

Entry pylon

Temple of Sety I
Nineteenth Dynasty, ca. 1280 B.C.

The temple of Sety I occupies a prominent position in the religious buildings of the New Kingdom because of its unique architecture and the high quality of its reliefs. After passing through two great courtyards, the visitor is confronted by the pillared façade of the temple which provides access to both the adjoining hypostyle halls. One

of the peculiar features of the layout is the series of seven slightly elevated sanctuaries behind the halls which are dedicated to the local deities Osiris, Isis and Horus, the imperial gods Amun-Re, Re-Horakhty and Ptah as well as the deified-king Sety I. Of these, only the Osiris sanctuary has an opening to the rear which leads on to the rooms where the mysteries of the god were celebrated. In the southern part of the temple is the corridor with the famous "King List of Abydos" containing almost all the cartouches of royal names from Menes to Sety I himself. From here another elongated room leads off via a staircase to the Osireion directly behind the temple. The decoration was done under Ramesses II including some unusual scenes such as: the King lassoos a wild bull together with his then Crown prince, Amunherkhepeshef.

View of the second hypostyle hall

Originally the temple façade had seven entrances corresponding to the number of sanctuaries. With the exception of the central entrance, these were walled up under Ramesses II who also completed the courtyards and the first hypostyle hall (170 × 36 ft; 52 × 11 m) which he ornamented with reliefs. A total of 24 papyrus bud columns flank the main cult axes and this pattern is also repeated in the second hypostyle hall. From here, short ramps lead up to the level of the sanctuaries supported by a row of twelve columns.

The Ritual for the Cult Image

The seven elevated sanctuaries of the Sety temple were equipped with high vaulted ceilings and divided into two sections by projecting pilasters. The rear walls each have a double false door (except the Osiris chapel) while the depictions on the other walls have retained the most complete pictorial version of the "Daily Temple Ritual." In 36 individual scenes the process which took place every morning and evening in the inner sanctum where the image of the god was housed is precisely depicted. The reliefs show the king himself taking part in the ceremony though in reality it was the High Priest of the temple who fulfilled this role. He entered the sanctuary, lit a torch and burned incense before opening the shrine and taking out the divine image (most probably a figure of solid gold with a

height of 1 Royal cubit, 52.5 cm) which was then purified by anointing it with oils, applying cosmetics and attiring it in the finest vestments (illustration with cult image of Amun). After completion of these tasks the requirements of the god could then be catered for anew. Finally the priest left the room, taking care to brush away his footprints in the sand with a broom, and locked the double doors to the sanctuary.

Erecting the Djed pillar

Concepts of the afterlife in Egypt from the end of the 3rd millennium B.C. were closely associated with the lord of death, Osiris, whose burial place was held to be in Abydos. It was therefore the ambition of many people to participate in the annual resurrection mysteries of the god. Not everyone could be buried in the sacred necropolis of Abydos however; a solution to this problem was to donate at least a memorial stone (stela) or cenotaph to the site. This secured active participation by the donor in the public part of the mystery play which consisted of a procession by the god through the cemetery, ending at the temple on the Kom el-Sultan. The secret rites in the temple were the subject of some of the

pictorial program in the rooms behind the Osiris sanctuary. The scene of the "erection of the Djed pillar," which Sety I raises up with the assistance of the goddess Isis, was connected with the theme of resurrection. This event was based on an ancient Memphitic fertility rite although the pillar itself was considered the central cult fetish of Osiris.

The god Thoth before Sety I as Osiris

To the right of the pillared Osiris hall behind the god's sanctuary are three small chapels dedicated to the divine family of Abydos. The central room houses large-scale cult scenes depicting the Osiris king, Sety I, in association with various gods; the paintwork of these images is conspicuously well-preserved. At the right the Ibis-headed god, Thoth, advances and proffers the *ankh* sign to the mummy-shaped figure of the king. He also carries two long heraldic staffs with plants symbolizing the Two Lands (papyrus and lotus); the two patron goddesses (snakes for Uto and Nekhbet) of Upper and Lower Egypt entwine and crown these symbols of authority. A short inscription between the figures (to the right of the offering tables) clearly states: "To your face I confer the power of life, and the two staffs of the goddesses before your perfect countenance." Behind the Osiris-figure of Sety I an emblematic name configuration is represented. It shows a standard with the king´s Horus name on top, holding a long staff as symbol of the royal *Ka* in one hand.

The Osirian myth

In the southern wing of the temple a small hall was constructed for the Memphite gods Nefertem and Ptah-Sokar who, as youthful sun god and chthonic god of death respectively, were associated with the regenerative aspects of Osiris. This explains the two depictions in the right-hand chamber at the rear which were taken from the myth of Osiris. The mummy of the god lies on a bier while Isis and Horus approach from opposite sides. The sister and bride of Osiris, Isis, appears also in the form of a falcon lowering herself onto his erect penis—a scene representing the posthumous conception of Horus, who was to grow up in the marshes of the Delta before avenging the death of his father. A three dimensional sculpture made from black granite of this scene stood from the Late period era in one of the royal tombs of Umm el-Qaab where it became the center of a popular pilgrimage to Abydos.

The Osireion

Nineteenth Dynasty, ca. 1280 B.C.

This gigantic cenotaph was laid out directly behind the temple of Sety I and marked the mythical tomb of Osiris. In the center of this false tomb or cenotaph—the largest ever built—lies an artificial island surrounded by a moat on which stand two rows of five enormous granite pillars each weighing 55 tons. Water was channeled through a subterranean pipeline which is still functioning today. Two square depressions on the island—mythologically the first land in the primeral waters—mark the site of the sarcophagus and a canopic chest. Though now open, the complex was originally covered over and probably sealed off under an earthen mound, planted with bushes as a symbol of creation. The real entrance to the cenotaph lies to the north outside the great enclosure walls. Some 32 feet (10 m) under the ground a 420 foot (128 m) long corridor (with texts and scenes from the *Book of Gates*) leads to an antechamber where the passageway to the main building leads off at an angle.

Temple of Ramesses II
Nineteenth Dynasty, ca. 1270 B.C.

While work was proceeding on his father's complex, Ramesses II built his own temple of limestone somewhat to the north on the edge of the desert. The upper section of the wall has disappeared into the local lime kilns and even the entrance pylon today no longer exists; this is an especially regrettable loss as their reliefs were superb and featured well-preserved paintwork. The external walls bear very fine depictions of the Battle of Qadesh while the walls in the second courtyard are decorated with long offering processions. Adjacent to this are two smaller pillared halls flanked by side chambers. The sanctuary encompasses three rooms dedicated to the Osirian trinity. The central inner sanctum of Osiris houses a statue group made from darkgrey granite; its five figures depict the divine family of Osiris, Isis and Horus as well as the deified kings Sety I and Ramesses II. The rear wall still presents in fragmentary condition a false-door (made from calcite) decorated with the figures of Osiris.

Clothing store

Pictorial context and room function formed an inseparable whole in ancient Egypt; architectural ornamentation and accompanying texts therefore allow conclusions to be drawn about the meaning of a given room. On the southern side of the second hypostyle hall, the first chamber retains a large-scale scene in its lowest register which indicates that the room was used as the temple's clothing store. At the far left Ramesses II sacrifices a jar of ointment and offers a libation of water. The small proces-

sion in front of him is received at the right by the Ibis-headed god, Thoth, with the two lector priests at the front each presenting a *menat*, an ornamental cult device worn across the chest by a goddess. There then follow four priests bearing a large chest on poles with a frieze of uraeus snakes around the top; the chest itself is protected by a baldachin. The short inscription below explains the event: "Transport of clothing to the inner sanctum." Chests containing clothes (for use in the "Daily Temple Ritual") were once placed on the stone benches which ran around this room.

Gold—the Flesh of the Gods

In antiquity, Egypt was considered the land of gold as this precious metal was one of the most important items used in foreign trade. Gold was indispensable within the country as well, however, and was used for furnishing royal palaces and temples. The Egyptians distinguished between two types of gold with, presumably, the same value: these were "nebu" and "djam" or electrum, an alloy of gold and silver which was probably also produced artificially. Gold was the same color as the sun and did not corrode. Like the sun, therefore, it was considered a guarantee of never-ending renewal and the material from which the flesh of the gods themselves was made. For this reason the cult figures in temple sanctuaries had to be made wholly or partly of gold, as were the masks and finger and toe caps of the royal mummies. Hardly anything remains of the golden figures of the gods, though the famous treasure of King Tutankhamun (1333–1323 B.C.) is proof of the magnificent gold trappings in royal tombs of the New Kingdom. Only small quantities of gold were available for private use; instead, yellow paint was often used in the hope that it would have the same regenerative effect.

The enormous demand for gold could not be satisfied by the mines of the Eastern desert and so at an early stage the Egyptians began to exploit sources of the metal in Nubia. Particularly during the New Kingdom (ca. 1550–1070) when Egypt ruled all of Nubia, vast quantities of gold must have been transported to Egypt, word of which reached the country's neighbors. The king of the Mitanni, Tushratta, wrote to Amenophis III for example with a request for gold: "May my brother send me in very great quantities that has not been worked, and may my brother send me much more gold than he did to my father. In my brother's country gold is as plentiful as dirt…"

Bowl belonging to General Djehuti, Eighteenth Dynasty, ca. 1450 B.C., Saqqara, gold, Dia. 17.9 cm, Musée du Louvre, Paris

Nevertheless, the actual quantities mined are still a matter for debate. The annals of Thutmosis III state that not more than 300 kg of gold were provided annually by Nubia; if local production were added the total would come to around 600–700 kg per year. At the same time, however, there are sources which speak of 15000 kg of gold being donated to the temple of Amun in Karnak. Gold was generally made into rings or ingots for transport and gold dust placed in small bags. The metal was worked in a variety of techniques including filigree, inlay, granulation and gilding. The tips of obelisks were clad in gold and sometimes even parts of the shaft as is evident from the biography of the treasurer Djehuti who was in charge of the transportation and gilding of two massive obelisks belonging to Queen Hatshepsut (1479–1458/57 B.C.) in Karnak. Other architectural components might also be elaborately ornamented with gold. Amenophis III claimed of his mortuary temple in Western Thebes: "(…) the place (temple) of my father's (Amun's) rest for each of his festivals, magnificently furnished in sandstone, its length clad in gold, its floors ornamented in silver, its doors also in gold (…)." From the time of Ramesses IV (ca. 1150 B.C.) a papyrus with the oldest geological map has survived, documenting a gold-mining settlement in the Wadi Hammamat. Gold was also used to produce jewelry, cult objects and items for display as well as awards. This last category includes the famous gold of honor, often a collar with multiple rows of gold beads which the king conferred on deserving officials. The golden bowl of General Djehuti (illustration left) might also have been such an item.

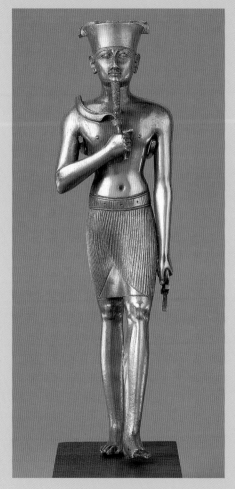

Statuette of the god Amun, Twenty-first Dynasty, ca. 1000 B.C., gold, H. 17.5 cm, The Metropolitan Museum of Art, New York

Dendera

Like other respected cult sites the temples of Dendera, the capital of the sixth Upper Egyptian nome, have a long architectural tradition. Even under Cheops a temple in honor of Hathor, the divine matriarch and royal goddess who took the shape of a cow, was said to have stood in the old town of Iunu. The earliest tangible archeological remains however date from the Middle Kingdom and include a small chapel of Mentuhotep II which was dismantled and now stands in the Egyptian Museum in Cairo. According to inscriptions, the holy site was extended during the brilliant Eighteenth Dynasty under Thutmosis III, and Amenophis III donated a figure of the Nile god, Hapy, worked in precious metals. The gigantic building which still stands today dates from the Graeco-Roman era. It is situated in the center of a large precinct (318 × 306 yds; 291 m × 280 m) and features the obligatory enclosure wall of mud brick. Begun under the late Ptolemaic kings (probably Ptolemy XII) two building phases under the Romans followed. The Emperor Tiberius undertook the building of the great pronaos while Nero's stone enclosure wall did not progress beyond the first row of stones. The elaborate decorative program was still being worked on in the second century A.D. Other structures were also built in front of and to the side of the temple, including the Roman mammisi, dedicated to Ihy, god of music.

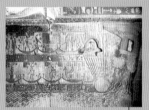

Ceiling of the pronaos, p. 302

Relief on an inter-columnar slab of the Roman mammisi, p. 304 f.

Roman mammisi, p. 304

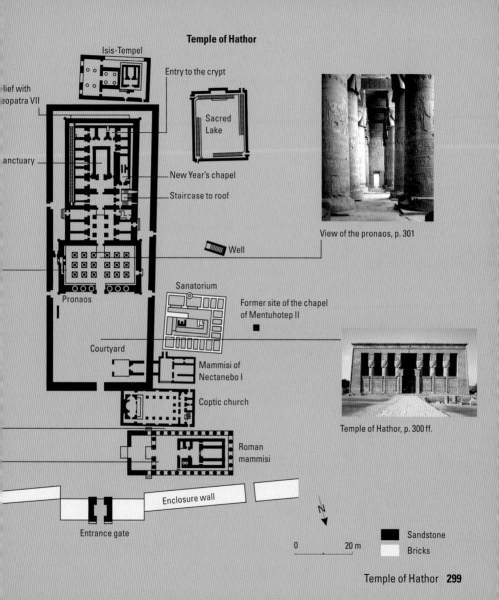

Temple of Hathor

Isis-Tempel

...lief with ...eopatra VII

Entry to the crypt

Sacred Lake

...anctuary

New Year's chapel

Staircase to roof

Pronaos

Well

View of the pronaos, p. 301

Sanatorium

Former site of the chapel of Mentuhotep II

Courtyard

Mammisi of Nectanebo I

Coptic church

Temple of Hathor, p. 300 ff.

Roman mammisi

Enclosure wall

Entrance gate

N

0   20 m

Sandstone

Bricks

The Temple of Hathor

Graeco-Roman period, 2nd/1st century B.C.–
2nd century A.D.

Today the sacred precincts of Dendera are entered through a mighty and imposing gateway; because the planned courtyard with entry pylon was never built, the start of the temple (88 × 38 yds; 81 × 35 m) is marked by the monumental façade of the great hypostyle hall. A veritable forest of 24 Hathor columns supports a ceiling ornamented with astronomical depictions.

Behind the pronaos, the main building begins with another pillared hall, the so-called Hall of Appearance. Continuing along this axis there are a further two rooms until one finally attains the great barque sanctuary. Like its counterpart in Edfu it is surrounded by a ring of chapels from which access to the crypts can be gained. To the right of the sanctuary are the stairway to the roof and the New Year chapel whose courtyard is decorated with long lists of offerings. Two unique scenes on the rear exterior wall feature Cleopatra VII with Caesarion, her son by Julius Caesar.

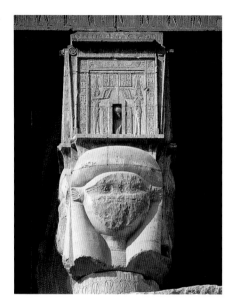

Hathor capital

View of the Pronaos

When Auguste Mariette began excavating the deeply buried temple in 1859 he discovered that the paintwork on its walls was still in a relatively good state of preservation. Today only a few faded traces of this once magnificent decorative scheme remain—such as here on a capital of the pronaos columns. The face of the goddess Hathor appears on all four sides with her characteristic attributes of cows' ears and braided wig. Above her head is a naos with side spirals symbolizing the goddess's horns. The mutilated faces of the capital is the work of Christian iconoclasts.

At the time of the Middle Kingdom a type of column first appeared which continued to be used until the Roman era: this was the Hathor or Sistrum column, and it featured mainly in buildings sacred to the goddess Hathor. The most gigantic specimens are without doubt those in the pronaos in Dendera where their sheer scale means they bear almost no resemblance to the sistrum from which they derive. This rattle-like instrument played such a dominant role in the cult of Hathor that her temple became known as the "House of the Sistrum."

Ceiling painting in the Pronaos

The notion that a temple was a reflection of the cosmos itself meant that their ceilings became seen as the canopy of heaven. From the time of the New Kingdom this comparison was usually rendered by using astronomical imagery which, especially in the case of Dendera's buildings from the Greek and Roman era, brought entire heavenly landscapes to life. The architraves of the pronaos pictured here divide the ceiling into seven sections with the most

interesting images being located in the two segments at the very sides. Here, the viewer is able to recognize the attenuated body of the goddess of heaven, Nut, who swallowed the sun every evening only to give birth to it every morning in an eternally recurring cycle. The sun's rays are seen to fall upon the holy site of Dendera, symbolized by the head of Hathor. Below the body of Nut the figures of personified stars travel in their barques across the firmament; they include Isis-Sothis (Sirius) in the form of a reclining cow.

The roof

Building on the roof was not just confined to the temples of later periods, but nowhere are these structures better preserved than in Dendera. Two separate staircases lead from the interior onto the roof, the reliefs on their walls showing a long procession of priests carrying a diverse array of cult objects. Their destination was a small kiosk in the southwest corner of the roof where the cult images were ritually reunited with the sun. Once this rite was completed, the images, now magically recharged with vital forces, were taken down again into the crypts. Two Osiris shrines, where the resurrection of the god was celebrated, were also situated on the roof.

The crypts

The crypts of the temple lie in the massive outer walls, some of them reaching down as far as the foundations. Their entrance-ways were once blocked off by stone slabs, and the cult images and other objects stored there only left their gloomy abode on special occasions like the important New Year´s festival. On the walls of the crypts were depictions of those objects, forming the temple treasure, and the size of these, as well as the material from which they were made, were recorded in accompanying inscriptions. A figure of this falcon with its carefully observed plumage was among the crypts' 162 cult images.

The Roman Mammisi
Roman period, 1st century A.D.

In front of the temple, and to the right of the gate as one enters, there stand a number of buildings: the so-called "sanatorium" (sacred baths for temple visitors), the mammisi of Nectanebo I (Thirtieth Dynasty), a Coptic church (5th century A.D.) and, closest to the entry gate, the mammisi from the Roman empire. A peripteral temple—that is, one surrounded by a single row of columns—the mammisi was built under Nero and its decorations were still being worked on in the second century A.D. Depictions on the walls of the inner sanctum show the birth of the god-child, Ihy, in a series of images based on models from the New Kingdom. The external columns of the building are connected by high partition walls (intercolumnar slabs) which feature what must be the finest reliefs of their era in Egypt. Surrounded by a torus molding and crowned by a cavetto cornice with a frieze of *uraeus* snakes, this illustration shows the Emperor Trajan wearing the crown of Lower Egypt and making cult offerings to the goddess Hathor who is shown suckling her son Ihy.

Priests—The Servants of God

Block figure of the High Priest Rama, Nineteenth Dynasty, ca. 1210 B.C., Karnak, Temple of Amun, limestone, H. 105 cm, Egyptian Museum, Cairo

Observing the cult of the gods, the king and the deceased was a crucial part of everyday life in Ancient Egypt. Only the pharaoh was permitted to have direct contact with the gods, so that in temples throughout the country it was the king who was depicted performing the offering rituals. In reality, however, it was the temple priests who attended to the routines of the cult. So-called Wab priests were employed for the more menial tasks while the actual cult practices were the responsibility of the priesthood proper. Since the Old Kingdom, priests were organized into rotating shifts or phyles (Greek equivalent of the Egyptian "sa" or "watch") and were led by high priests who came from the upper echelons of the official class. There were also professional priests who had received a specialized education. They included the so-called lector priests who read out the ritual instructions and who knew all the necessary regulations and spells; for this reason they were also attributed with magical and healing powers. Farmers and artisans as well as administrative and security personnel were also employed, and it was they who tended to the supply, equipment and general order of the temple.

The daily routines of the cult had a prescribed order such as purifying the temple with incense and holy water, preparing and dedicating the offering tables, and carrying out the actions of the "Daily Temple Ritual.".

In the course of the latter the precious image

Papyrus of Hunefer (Book of the Dead): priests before the mummy and tomb, Nineteenth Dynasty, ca. 1280 B.C., painted papyrus, H. 39 cm, The British Museum, London

of the god was taken from its shrine, purified, clothed, anointed and painted with cosmetics before being decorated with jewelry and various insignia. There were also numerous processions and festivals during which the cult image left the sanctuary in a barque in order to be transported either up onto the roof, into the outer courtyard or to another temple. On the occasion of great festival processions music was also performed with female singers and dancers playing a particular role. Other priestly functions could also be performed by women—the Divine Adoratrice of Amun, for example, was one of the most important political offices in the Twenty-fifth and Twenty-sixth Dynasties.

Selected dignitaries also benefited from the temple cult in addition to the gods and king. They were permitted to set up statues or stelae in the areas of the temple, a privilege which was an honor—and ensured that they profited from the offerings made there. For the cemeteries, it was the duty of the relatives of the deceased to attend to their burial and funerary cult. Soon, however, this task was taken over by professional mortuary priests who carried out rituals and made offerings on certain religious holidays.

Thebes (Luxor)

Thebes (Luxor)

After modest beginnings as a provincial city in the fourth Upper Egyptian nome, Thebes—the ancient town of "Waset"—rose to become the most brilliant metropolis in Egypt. It first became the focus of political power in the early Middle Kingdom under Mentuhotep II (Eleventh Dynasty) who chose Thebes as his official residence in the course of reuniting the country. The city achieved its fullest flowering however in the Eighteenth Dynasty of the New Kingdom. For over 250 years great pharaohs such as Thutmosis III ruled from Thebes over a vast empire which stretched from the southernmost reaches of Nubia to the borders of Syria-Palestine. To honor the imperial god of Amun-Re a gigantic temple city arose in Karnak. On the west bank of the river the rulers erected their mortuary temples and had themselves buried in the famous Valley of the Kings. Even after the Ramesside era when the court was moved to Piramesse in the eastern delta, Thebes still remained the most important religious center in the country. Early in the first millennium B.C., the rulers of the Twenty-first Dynasty established a theocracy dedicated to Amun in Thebes, which was to come to prominence once again under the "black" Pharaohs of the Twenty-fifth Dynasty.

Previous pages: View over the ruins of the Karnak Temple

The Great Hypostyle Hall, p 336 f.

Obelisk of Hatshepsut, p. 340

Pharaoh Senusret III, p. 325

Courtyard of Ramesses II, p. 316

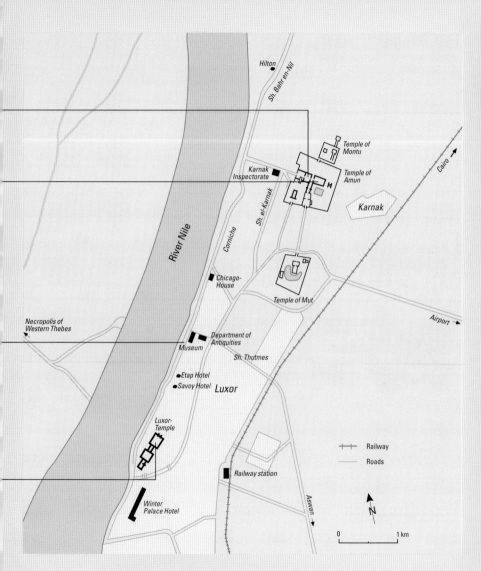

Hilton

Sh. Bahr en-Nil

River Nile

Cairo

Temple of
Montu

Karnak
Inspectorate

Temple of
Amun

Karnak

Corniche

Sh. el-Karnak

Chicago-
House

Temple of Mut

Airport

Necropolis of
Western Thebes

Department of
Antiquities

Museum

Sh. Thutmes

Etap Hotel

Savoy Hotel

Luxor

Luxor-
Temple

Railway

Roads

Railway station

Aswan

Winter
Palace Hotel

N

0   1 km

The Temple of Luxor
Eighteenth/Nineteenth Dynasties,
ca. 1380–1250 B.C.

The temple of Luxor stretches out through the center of the modern city of the same name on the eastern bank of the Nile. This place of worship was founded by two of the greatest rulers of the New Kingdom. While the temple, courtyard and great entry colonnade at the rear were planned under Amenophis III, Ramesses II in the Nineteenth Dynasty extended this struc-ture to the north to include another court-yard and a vast pylon so that the temple achieves a total length of over 273 yds (250 m). Remarkably, this Ramesside addi-tion was built at a slight angle to the previous axis, probably in order to enclose an older way station within the courtyard. The temple of Luxor was long regarded as the "Harim" of the imperial god, Amun. New investigations have revealed a much more complex picture. Two aspects stand out. Every year during the Opet Festival ("The Beautiful Feast of Opet") a proces-sion was held in which the cult images of

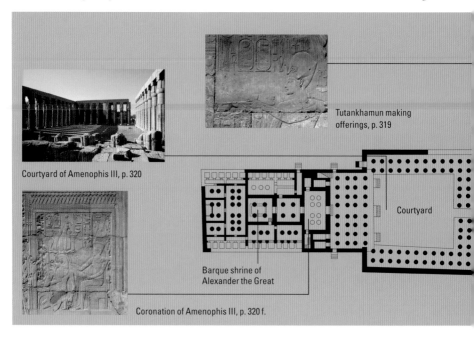

Tutankhamun making offerings, p. 319

Courtyard of Amenophis III, p. 320

Courtyard

Barque shrine of Alexander the Great

Coronation of Amenophis III, p. 320 f.

the Theban trinity of Amun, Mut and Khonsu were paraded from Karnak to Luxor Temple (name: "opet of the South") in their sacred barques.

After the barque of Amun only was carried into the central sanctuary, the secret rites of cosmic regeneration were performed there as well as in the side rooms. This cyclical repetition of creation by Amun was the most important function of the whole temple, which was therefore also known as the "Place of the First Time." Luxor's temple was also important for the royal cult because it provided a monu-mental stage on which the ruler could be raised to the level of the gods. The focus of this ritual, which took place before the king or a particular cult figure, was the unifica-tion of the monarch with his *ka*. It was only in this way that the ruling pharaoh could achieve the status of a divine creature who held office by virtue of being the "Image of Amun." It is in this context that depictions on the walls of two rooms to the east of the barque sanctuary should be seen: in a long series of individual pictures (as earlier for Queen Hatshepsut) they deal with the divine origin (birth legend) of the king.

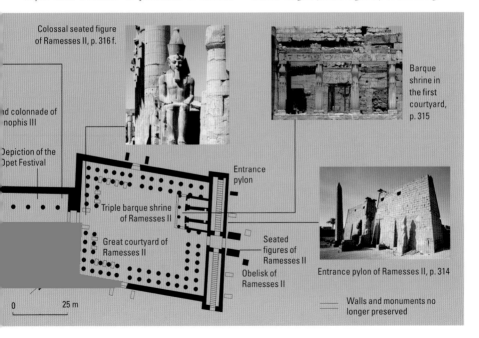

Colossal seated figure of Ramesses II, p. 316 f.

Barque shrine in the first courtyard, p. 315

...d colonnade of ...nophis III

...epiction of the ...pet Festival

Triple barque shrine of Ramesses II

Great courtyard of Ramesses II

Entrance pylon

Seated figures of Ramesses II

Obelisk of Ramesses II

Entrance pylon of Ramesses II, p. 314

0   25 m

Walls and monuments no longer preserved

Entrance pylon of Ramesses II
Nineteenth Dynasty, ca. 1270 B.C.

In the first years of his reign Ramesses II had already ordered the extension of the temple in Luxor. A massive pylon (W. 213 ft, 65 m) has since sealed off the temple to the north. Two narrow niches can still be seen in the walls of the pylon towers and these mark the place where great flagposts once towered over the building. The colossal seated figures at the entrance (H. 46 ft, 14 m) as well as another standing figure of Ramesses II are remnants of the pylon's original sculptural decoration. Up until 1836, two obelisks of red granite also rested in their original positions. The western monolith, however, was transported to France as a gift of state and is today a feature of the Place de la Concorde where it stands shrouded in automobile fumes. In front of the temple an avenue of sphinxes (original pavement) stretches away for 1.5 miles (2.5 km), connecting Luxor with the imperial temple at Karnak. The sphinxes themselves however are replacements from the era of Nectanebo I. (Thirtieth Dynasty).

Barque shrine in the first courtyard
Eighteenth Dynasty, ca. 1470 B.C.

In the northwestern corner of the Ramesside courtyard directly behind the pylon tower lies a tripartite barque shrine for the Theban family of gods, Amun, Mut and Khonsu. Some of its architectural elements derive from the reigns of Hatshepsut (1479–1458/59 B.C.) and Thutmosis III. Originally this small structure stood in the area around the Luxor temple and formed the last way station for the processional barques of the Opet fest-

ival. The façade features four papyrus bud columns of red granite with ribbed shafts spaced at regular intervals. When new inscriptions were being carved to appropriate them in the name of Ramesses II, the workmen made a minor error: they forgot to eliminate the feminine ending of one word—there is therefore no doubt that the columns should in fact be attributed to Hatshepsut. The execution of the column shafts also indicates an earlier provenance; in the Eighteenth Dynasty they were made to imitate stem bundles of papyrus plants.

Courtyard of Ramesses II
Nineteenth Dynasty, ca. 1270 B.C.

The great courtyard (187 × 167 ft; 57 × 51 m) which extends behind the pylon has a colonnade with two rows of 74 papyrus bud columns. In the southern part of the courtyard standing figures of the pharaoh were placed between the columns.

Although the slightly smaller examples wearing the nemes headdress are original work from the reign of Ramesses II, the others were taken from a building by Amenophis III and were appropriated by providing them with new inscriptions.

Colossal seated figure of Ramesses II
Nineteenth Dynasty, ca. 1270 B.C.

Two colossal granite figures of Ramesses II flank the entrance to the great colonnade in the first courtyard just as they do at the main portal of the pylon. Most likely both gigantic statues had been planned on the very same spot already for Amenophis III, but came into existence only some decades later under Ramesses II. The youthful ruler is seated on a simple block throne with a high footplate and his hands are stretched out on his knees. He wears the finely pleated royal kilt, a headdress with double crown and *uraeus* snake as well as a ceremonial beard. The features of the monarch are marked by a gentle smile and a prominent nose. It is an idealized royal portrait whose timeless air of serenity expresses the character of the office bearer rather than the individual. Beside the right leg of the king is the tiny figure of his chief wife at the time, Queen Nefertari. This statue (23.6 ft, 7.2 m) embodies a particular aspect of the divinity of Ramesses the Great, manifested in the two proper names carved on his shoulders: the statue bears the title Ra-en-hekau, "Sun of the foreign rulers."

The Opet Festival (Detail)
Eighteenth Dynasty, ca. 1330 B.C.

The last phase of Amenophis III's building was a monumental entry colonnade consisting of seven pairs of papyriform columns which was built in front of his courtyard. The wall reliefs in this gigantic space, however, were only added in the late Eighteenth Dynasty under Tutankhamun and Horemheb. Their subject matter is the Opet Festival, the western wall featuring the procession of divine barques southwards from Karnak to Luxor (about 2 km, 1¹/₄ miles) with the eastern wall depicting the return journey of the Theban triad—Amun, Mut, Khonsu—to the temples at Karnak. In the beginning the festival, celebrated in the second month of the inundation season of Akhet, lasted some 11 days but in the course of the New Kingdom this period became as long as 27 days. Both legs of the procession were made on water (certainly by the time of Tutankhamun) with the smaller barques of the gods first loaded onto large river boats before being towed over the Nile by teams of men. The festive atmosphere of the event is conveyed in this image from the western wall by the accompanying groups of soldiers, dancers, singers and musicians.

Opet Festival: Tutankhamun making offerings
Eighteenth Dynasty, ca. 1330 B.C.

Before the processional barques with the cult images of Amun, Mut and Khonsu left their home temples in Karnak, the king performed an offering ritual to the gods. These actions, carried out here by Tutankhamun, were depicted on the short north wall of the grand colonnade. His face leaves no doubt as to his identity, even if the two cartouches were later overwritten (usurped) by Horemheb. The king wears the Blue Crown (Egyptian: khepresh) with *uraeus* and a broad ceremonial collar. In his left hand Tutankhamun holds an elaborate incense burner and offers the gift of fragrance to the gods. It was only after this sacrificial ceremony was over that the portable barques were taken from their pedestals, placed on the shoulders of priests and brought to the great quay near the temple. There, the great river boats were waiting for their precious cargo.

Courtyard of Amenophis III
Eighteenth Dynasty, ca. 1370 B.C.

Coronation of Amenophis III
Eighteenth Dynasty, ca. 1370 B.C.

The great festival courtyard of Amenophis III (170 × 151 ft; 52 × 46 m) was built during a second phase of construction and became an integral part of the Luxor temple's theological concept. It was here that the ruler revealed himself to his courtiers after observing the rites of his apotheosis in the inner temple. A veritable thicket of double rows of papyrus bud columns surrounds the courtyard on three sides, an impressive symbol of the ideas of creation and regeneration which in ancient Egypt were always associated with this plant.

On the main axis of the temple and behind the great hall of pillars with its 32 papyrus columns lies a room, the southern wall of which depicts the ritual of the coronation. Here, as in other related scenes, Amenophis III kneels in a shrine before the enthroned figure of Amun-Re who lays his hand on the composite crown of the king. As proof that he has attained divine status, the rams' horns of Amun curl around the ears of the monarch. His regalia is completed by a heka scepter (crook) which Amenophis III holds in his right hand.

Ramesses II and the Battle of Qadesh

There is no doubt that Ramesses II (1279–1213 B.C.) was one of the very greatest of Egyptian rulers, and even today his name still seems to represent the power and majesty of the pharaohs. During his 67-year reign he was active as a great builder but he also achieved stability for Egypt both at home and abroad. The first years of his reign, however, were characterized by constant friction, especially with the empire of the Hittites.

Probably the most famous clash between these two great powers took place at the fortress of Qadesh on the Orontes in Central Syria in the fifth year of the king's reign—a battle which both the Egyptians and the Hittites claimed as a victory. Ramesses II had marched with four divisions (20 000 men) to the Orontes to drive the Hittites out of the Egyptians' sphere of interest in order to further the foreign policies of his father, Sety I.

Ramesses II at the Battle of Qadesh, Nineteenth Dynasty, ca. 1250 B.C., Temple of Luxor, first pylon

He crossed the river with the "Amun" division in order to establish his camp to the west of Qadesh. Taken in by a Hittite trick, Ramesses advanced with part of his army but was attacked by the charioteers of King Muwatallis who had been waiting close by with 37 000 infantrymen and 2500 chariots. The Amun division was surrounded and the "Re" division which tried to rescue them was virtually wiped out. Two other Egyptian divisions were situated too far to the south to be able to intervene. Ramesses II's situation looked hopeless when, miraculously, a unit of elite Egyptian troops which had been expected to march along the coast and attack from the west suddenly arrived on the scene. They broke through the ranks of the besieging army, rescuing the king and enabling the survivors to flee. The Hittites chose not to pursue them, probably because it was getting dark. Indeed, instead of imposing one final battle on what was by now a stabilized, but shaken Egyptian army, the Hittites retreated. Ramesses II was therefore able to return unmolested to Egypt and there celebrate his alleged victory over the Hittites. The significance of this battle for the king must have been enormous and he interpreted the timely appearance of his crack troops as the direct intervention of the god Amun. This probably explains why the king insisted on his desperate situation at Qadesh and his so-called victory there being constantly represented in art. In the "Poem" on the battle of Qadesh he is characterized in effusive words as a triumphant hero: "…My soldiers came to praise me: Hail o good warrior, firm of heart, you have saved your soldiers, your chariotry, you are Amun´s son." Although Ramesses II embarked on other campaigns over the years, he always tried to avoid a confrontation with the Hittites. Sixteen years after the battle on the Orontes, the first known peace treaty of ancient times was signed. It was later strengthened by two diplomatic marriages between the king and Hittite princesses.

The "Poem" on the Battle of Qadesh, Nineteenth Dynasty, ca. 1200 B.C., papyrus, H. 20.5 cm, Musée du Louvre, Paris

The Luxor Museum

After a long period of planning, the Luxor Museum finally opened its doors in 1976. Situated directly on the banks of the river, the exemplary presentation of its exhibits makes it one of the finest museum buildings in Egypt. Two floors of exhibits mainly highlight monuments from the greater Theban area. On the ground floor a gallery has been reserved for the more than 20 royal statues found in the "cachette" of the Temple of Luxor.

Amenophis II as archer

Eighteenth Dynasty, ca. 1410 B.C., Temple of Amun-Re, Karnak, red granite, W. 234 cm

The depiction on this relief slab, which was once part of a gatehouse built by Amenophis II in the main temple of Amun at Karnak, shows the monarch as an archer. He is seen charging ahead at full gallop in his chariot, firing an arrow at a target post sheathed in copper. Underneath is another copper plate riddled with arrows thus demonstrating the superhuman strength of this royal warrior.

Pharaoh Senusret III
Twelfth Dynasty, ca. 1860 B.C., Temple of Amun-Re, Karnak, red granite, H. 80 cm

Colossal head of Amenophis III
Eighteenth Dynasty, ca. 1370 B.C., mortuary temple of the king, Western Thebes, red granite, H. 215 cm

Originally this head belonged to an outsized standing figure of the king which, together with its counterpart, probably flanked a portal in the Middle Kingdom temple at Karnak. Senusret III wears the double crown of Upper and Lower Egypt and a high supporting pillar rises up behind him. The expressive features of the monarch's face can be counted among the most outstanding achievements of ancient Egyptian portraiture.

Amenophis III built what was probably the greatest mortuary temple of any ruler of the New Kingdom in the necropolis at Thebes. Between the columns in the courtyard of this complex stood colossal figures of the king from which this head bearing the crown of Upper Egypt was taken. The characteristic physiognomy of the ruler is defined by his almond shaped eyes, the broad bands of his eyelids and the full mouth with sharply contured lips.

Amenophis III and the god Sobek
Eighteenth Dynasty, ca. 1360 B.C., Temple of
Sobek, Dahamsha, calcite, H. 256.5 cm

In 1967 canal workers chanced upon this
magnificent statue group of Amenophis III
with the crocodile god Sobek while digging
at the bottom of a shaft south of Luxor.
Along with other finds it proves the significance of the ancient site of Sumenu as an
important cult center in the Eighteenth
Dynasty. The enthroned deity confers the
symbol of life (e.g. ankh) on the monarch
who stands next to him, the king's hands
resting on his kilt in a gesture of prayer.
The broken snout of the god was probably
restored in the course of re-inscribing the
statue for Ramesses II.

Standing figure of Thutmosis III
Eighteenth Dynasty, ca. 1450 B.C., Temple of
Amun-Re, Karnak, greywacke, H. 90.5 cm

This image of Thutmosis III was discovered
in 1904 in the famous "cachette" at Karnak
together with over 800 stone statues and
about 18 000 bronze figures. The greatest
warrior of the Eighteenth Dynasty is
shown here wearing the three-part royal
kilt, a *nemes* headdress and long ceremonial
beard. The almost mannered elegance of
this figure is considerably heightened by
the superbly polished surface of the stone.
The statue probably once stood together
with others of the same material in the
festival temple (Akh-menu) of the King.

Amenophis, son of Hapu
Eighteenth Dynasty, ca. 1370 B.C., Temple of
Amun-Re, Karnak, granodiorite, H. 130.5 cm

Temple wall of Akhenaten (detail)
Eighteenth Dynasty, ca. 1350 B.C., Aten temple,
Karnak, painted sandstone, 2.97 x 17.2 m

As personal advisor to Amenophis III the
official Amenophis enjoyed the highest
level of protection and this also allowed
him to erect a number of statues in the
temple at Karnak. This scribal figure shows
Amenophis seated on the ground with
crossed legs and a papyrus scroll spread out
across his kilt. The statue interceded for
visitors to the temple who had special
request and wishes, a function which is
explained by the inscription on the pedestal: "Come to me that I may convey to
Amun-Re in Karnak all that is told to me."

In the east of the Amun temple Amenophis
IV, Akhenaten, built several temples for
Aten, his new state god. When the older
Amun cult was restored in the late
Eighteenth Dynasty, these structures were
demolished and their stones later used
as fill for foundations and pylons. These
blocks, found in the ninth pylon of
Horemheb, were reconstructed to form a
temple wall. The left-hand side shows the
king bringing offerings under the rays of
the sun-disc Aten, while on the right
temple storerooms and workshops are
pictured.

The Temple City of Karnak

Where today thousands of tourists stand in awestruck silence at Karnak's gargantuan architecture there once beat the religious heart of ancient Egypt. The entire temple complex was formed from three independent precincts, each of which was enclosed by walls of unfired mud bricks. At the center lay the gigantic Amun temple which covered an area of well over 100 ha (247 acres). It was adjoined immediately to the north by the smaller precinct of Month, the old local deity of Thebes. The other neighboring temple of the goddess Mut was built to the south of the Amun temple, and the two were connected by an avenue of sphinxes. The network of processional roads on the Theban east bank alone covered several miles and was flanked by almost 1300 statues of sphinxes. Archeologists have shown that Karnak's 2000 year architectural history began in the early Middle Kingdom and stretched into the Graeco-Roman period. Its intrinsic scale was established by the enormous building programs initiated by the monarchs of the New Kingdom. Almost all the pharaohs of this era left their mark on the imperial temple of Amun in order to honor their divine father Amun-Re, "King of the Gods."

The complex has two axes, the main one running in an east-west direction from the inner sanctum to the first pylon. The side axis, the cult route to the precinct of Mut, starts at the fourth pylon and runs south through pylons seven to ten with their courtyards. Within the walls of the Amun precinct stands a series of other shrines and chapels including a temple for the moon god Khonsu from the Twentieth/Twenty-first Dynasties and the small temple to Ptah at the northern enclosure wall whose core was built during the reign of Thutmosis III. The same king built a temple for the sun cult directly outside the eastern enclosure wall of the main temple; a single obelisk (H. 101 ft, 30.7 m) stood at its center but since 1587 this has decorated the St John in Lateran Square in Rome. The continual expansion of the Amun temple necessarily meant the demolition of older buildings. The stone from these buildings was then recycled (see p. 329) and provides the basis for our knowledge of temples in the Middle Kingdom and early Eighteenth Dynasty; these include such shining examples of architecture as Senusret I's "White Chapel" and the great barque shrine of Hatshepsut, the "Red Chapel." Ever since Auguste Mariette excavated at Karnak in 1858 investigations at the site have largely been carried out by French scholars. Responsibility for the main archaeological work and conservation effort has been exercised by the *Centre Franco-Egyptien* since 1967.

The Great Hypostyle Hall in Karnak
Painted lithography from David Roberts' "Egypt and Nubia," London 1846–1850

Pictures from the 19th century record how the Great Hypostyle Hall then looked with its growing piles of rubble, toppled columns and collapsed architraves. Extensive damage to the foundations finally led to the deafening collapse of this famous building on October 3, 1899. Decades were to pass before it was reconstructed.

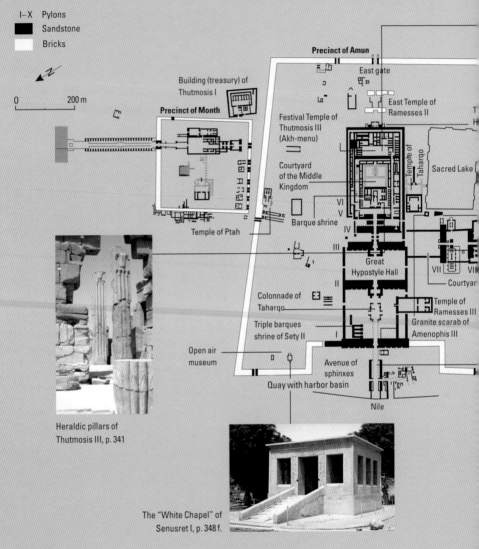

I–X Pylons

Sandstone

Bricks

Precinct of Amun

East gate

Building (treasury) of
Thutmosis I

Precinct of Month

East Temple of
Ramesses II

Festival Temple of
Thutmosis III
(Akh-menu)

T
H

0   200 m

Temple of Taharqo

Sacred Lake

Courtyard
of the Middle
Kingdom

VI
V

IV

Barque shrine

Temple of Ptah

III

VII   VI

Great
Hypostyle Hall

Courtyar

II

Colonnade of
Taharqo

Temple of
Ramesses III

Granite scarab of
Amenophis III

Triple barques
shrine of Sety II

I

Open air
museum

Avenue of
sphinxes

Quay with harbor basin

Nile

Heraldic pillars of
Thutmosis III, p. 341

The "White Chapel" of
Senusret I, p. 348 f.

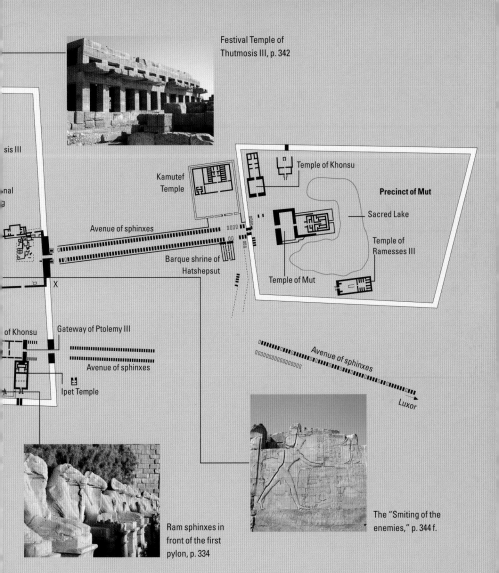

Festival Temple of
Thutmosis III, p. 342

sis III

...nal
...g

Kamutef
Temple

Temple of Khonsu

Precinct of Mut

Avenue of sphinxes

Sacred Lake

Barque shrine of
Hatshepsut

Temple of
Ramesses III

X

Temple of Mut

of Khonsu

Gateway of Ptolemy III

Avenue of sphinxes

Avenue of sphinxes

Luxor

Ipet Temple

The "Smiting of the
enemies," p. 344 f.

Ram sphinxes in
front of the first
pylon, p. 334

Ram sphinxes at the first pylon
Nineteenth Dynasty, ca. 1250 B.C.

The architectural history of the Amun temple began with a building by Senusret I. in the courtyard of the Middle Kingdom (now destroyed) before advancing westwards. The first pylon, dating from the Thirtieth Dynasty, was the last monumental structure (W. 370 ft, 113 m) to be built along this axis although it was never completed. The largest gateway ever built, this pylon interrupted a long avenue of sphinxes which originally led from the second pylon of Horemheb to the quay of the temple (with its great harbor basin and canal connecting it to the Nile) and which was probably laid out under Ramesses II. Mounted on high pedestals on both sides of the cobbled processional avenue are the figures of so-called cryos sphinxes combining the body of a lion with the head of a ram, the sacred animal of Amun. Royal statuettes held between the paws of each sphinx symbolize the favor and protection shown by the god.

Colossal figure at the second pylon
Nineteenth Dynasty, ca. 1250 B.C.

The great courtyard behind the first pylon (south tower with remains of the brick construction ramp) is occupied by a number of buildings from a variety of eras. The center is dominated by the gigantic pillared kiosk of King Taharqo of the Twenty-fifth Dynasty. Of the ten 69 ft (21 m) high papyrus columns which supported this structure, only one still stands. It must have been at the time of this construction work that the avenue of sphinxes was blocked off and the individual figures at the sides of the courtyard were put in storage. This courtyard was constructed during the Twenty-second Dynasty under Sheshonq I when the area in front of the second pylon was enclosed by a colonnade. Behind the north tower of the first pylon is the tripartite barque shrine of Sety II while the temple of Ramesses III is integrated into the ensemble on the southern side of the courtyard and at right angles to the main axis. A colossal standing figure (H. 36 ft, 11 m) in red granite has been re-erected at the gate of the second pylon; its fragments were discovered in 1954. The king is shown wearing a headdress with the double crown and a short loincloth. His hands, crossed on his chest, hold the crook and flail of his office; a small figure of a queen stands at his feet. Although the inscriptions indicate the owner as being the priest-king Pinudjem I (Twenty-first Dynasty) the colossus may well have been carved in the Ramesside era.

The Great Hypostyle Hall
Nineteenth Dynasty, ca. 1290–1260 B.C.

At the time of the completion of the second pylon (under Horemheb), plans may had already begun for the largest ever hypostyle hall in Egyptian architectural history to be constructed between Horemheb's pylon and the third pylon of Amemophis III. Realized and completed under the early Ramesside rulers Sety I and his son Ramesses II, this gargantuan structure covers an area of over 6458 sq yds (5400 m²) and is occupied by a total of 134 papyrus columns. Three elevated central aisles are supported by two rows each with six papyrus columns featuring wide bell-shaped capitals (H. 69 ft, 21 m, diam. 11.5 ft, 3.50 m) while, for the 14 smaller side aisles, papyrus bud columns (height 43 ft, 13 m) were used. The height difference between the aisles of this basilican structure was bridged by stone grids which cast light onto the main processional route below while the broad aisles to the sides remained in a gloomy twilight. The massive sandstone columns were composed of a series of drums and set atop these were great square stone blocks (abacus) on which rested the architraves. These architraves weigh up to 70 tons and have retained fragments of their original paintwork. Both the columns and the walls are richly illustrated and the different periods in which each component was erected can be determined from the prevailing style of the relief. Sety I commissioned a raised relief for the northern part of the hall while the southern part,

under Ramesses II, was decorated with sunken reliefs. These show the monarch bringing offerings to the gods of Thebes, extracts from the coronation and the departure of the processional barques. The external walls, on the other hand, record the military campaigns of both these Nineteenth Dynasty kings with battles in Syria and Palestine from the first years of the reign of Sety I being shown in particular detail on the north wall. Weathering and earthquakes have taken their toll on the structure over the years and the appearance of the hypostyle hall today is the result of decades of careful restoration work.

Sacred Lake
Eighteenth Dynasty, ca. 1450 B.C.

To the south of the inner temple precinct is the sacred lake of Karnak with the soaring obelisks from the reigns of Thutmosis I and Hatshepsut nearby; measuring 393 ft × 252 ft (120 m × 77 m) it is the largest lake at any temple in Egypt. Laid out under Thutmosis III, the lake was extended still further in the Twenty-fifth Dynasty. In antiquity this enormous basin was provided with water by a canal cut through from the Nile though today the lake is supplied by ground water. A number of stairways lead down to the lake which was initially used for the lustration rituals of the priesthood and as a reservoir for the libations used in cult ceremonies. Ritual boat journeys also took place here as we are told in a Karnak text: "My majesty built a lake that the divine body (the king) might be rowed in everlasting labor in order to journey across the waters on his great feast days at the New Year." Various functional structures were discovered in the area around the lake including a pen for keeping fowl. Along with the ram, the goose was another animal sacred to the imperial god Amun and sloping covered walkways provided these birds with direct access to the water. At the northwestern corner of the lake a colossal red granite scarab from the reign of Amenophis III was erected and a short distance away lies part of a toppled obelisk from Queen Hatshepsut.

Obelisk of Queen Hatshepsut
Eighteenth Dynasty, ca. 1464 B.C.

Continuing in the spirit of the building work carried out by her father, Thutmosis I, Hatshepsut constructed a number of monuments in Karnak. Together with a new barque sanctuary, the "Red Chapel," two of the most important contributions from this self-confident female pharaoh were the massive twin obelisks erected between the fourth and fifth pylons. Only the northern obelisk still stands—its counterpart later collapsed and was stored with the upper part at the sacred lake. The erection of these stone monoliths (97 ft, 29.5 m) was such an extraordinary event that it was documented on several of the queen's other monuments. A depiction on the "Red Chapel" mentioned above, for example, celebrates its dedication to the god Amun in the following words: "His Majesty had two great obelisks erected for his father Amun-Re before the glorious hypostyle hall, cladding them in gold in great quantities." In reality it was only the pyramidion, the point of the obelisk, which was gilded and decorated with a coronation scene. All four sides of the shaft have long titular columns and the upper third of the obelisk is noticeably weathered and discolored. When Thutmosis III came to power he blotted out any reference to Hatshepsut and had both obelisks enclosed up to roof height; it is only in this protected area that the red granite has retained its original color.

Heraldic pillars of Thutmosis III
Eighteenth Dynasty, ca. 1450 B.C.

Thutmosis III was among the greatest of Karnak's builders. During his reign he built the seventh pylon on the south axis, the festival temple of the king in the east of the Amun precinct, and a barque sanctuary which replaced that of Hatshepsut. He also donated numerous obelisks, colossal figures, and other cult items in honor of Amun of Ipet-sut—as Karnak was known in ancient times. In the Hall of Annals in front of the main façade of the central barque sanctuary Thutmosis III put up two great symbolic pillars being that way united with the record of his military campaigns. These so-called heraldic pillars in red granite (H. 22.2 ft, 6.77 m) are a unique embodiment of the ideas underpinning Egyptian national unity. One side of each pillar is decorated in high relief with plants, each surmounted by a flower, symbolizing the two lands of Egypt. To the north (here at the left) was the Lower Egyptian papyrus, while to the south (right) stood the lily of Upper Egypt. The enduring power of the pillars' symbolism assured their survival when the sanctuary was rebuilt towards the end of the 4th century B.C. by Phillipos Arrhidaios, a half-brother of Alexander the Great, and they have survived to this day. Both pillars have suffered greatly from the effects of salt-laden groundwater which causes the granite to crumble from the bottom up. Karnak is not unique in this respect; sadly,

this threat to temple architecture has become more serious since the construction of the high dam at Aswan.

Festival Temple of Thutmosis III
Eighteenth Dynasty, ca. 1450 B.C.

Thutmosis III built his Festival temple, the Akh-menu, to the east behind the courtyard of the Middle Kingdom and within the enclosure wall of the central Amun temple. This extraordinary building lies at right angles to the old main axis and could only be entered from the southeast corner. The central festival hall (144 × 53 ft; 44 × 16 m), formed like a basilica, is an architectural rarity. Two rows each with ten gigantic columns (colors in bright condition) like tent poles support the high central aisle giving the hall the appearance of a ceremonial pavilion. As a "House of Millions of Years" the Akh-menu (Egyptian: "Most Splendid of Monuments") was entirely devoted to the royal cult and it was here that the regeneration rites of the king's coronation and jubilees were celebrated. Even Alexander the Great sought to secure this guarantee of power for himself and he had the walls of one of the rooms decorated with reliefs of his own.

The "Botanical Garden"
Eighteenth Dynasty, ca. 1450 B.C.

From the great central hall of the Akh-menu a passageway on the eastern side leads through three successive rooms, the last of which has on its north wall a door situated well above the level of the floor. Through this doorway a small hall can be reached whose roof is supported by four papyrus columns. Depictions of animals and plants in relief decorate the still standing lower parts of the wall and these have given the room its somewhat erroneous name of "The Botanical Garden." Despite the detailed and most extensive depictions of leaves and flowers—which must have had an even more intense appearance with their original paint-work—the room does not indicate that Thutmosis III took a great deal of interest in nature. Rather, these images of flora and fauna express creation beliefs which were given literary form 100 years later in Akhenaten's "Great Hymn" to the Aten.

The "Smiting of the Enemies"
Eighteenth Dynasty, ca. 1450 B.C.

One of the classical images used to symbolize the enemy was the "Smiting of the Enemies" by the reigning king and Thutmosis III employed this type of triumphal depiction on the west tower of the seventh pylon (width 207 ft, 63.2 m) he built in Karnak. With his outstretched left arm the king holds a horde of Asiatic prisoners, who raise their hands and beg for mercy, while preparing to dispatch them with his mace. The monarch wears the Red Crown of Lower Egypt and the three-part pleated kilt with a bull's tail.

The eighth pylon
Eighteenth Dynasty, ca. 1470 B.C.

The southern side axis of the Amun temple had already been laid out under Senusret I (early Twelfth Dynasty) although archeologists still know little about its buildings. The cult route in the direction of the temple of Mut began to be the subject of monumental building work with the construction of Hatshepsut's eighth pylon. There were once six (today only four) colossal seated figures in front of the southern façade, which were dedicated to the queen, her co-regent Thutmosis III, as well as deceased predecessors of the royal house.

The temple of Khonsu
Twentieth Dynasty, ca. 1170 B.C.

In the southwest corner of the Amun precinct a temple was built for the moon god Khonsu, the son of the Theban family of deities, in the late Ramesside era. This well preserved structure was begun by Ramesses III but its decoration was only completed under his successors, Ramesses IV and Ramesses XI, and the later king Herihor. Behind the entrance pylon (W. 105 ft, 32 m; four flag posts) stretches a pillared courtyard with an elevated hall to the rear followed by a hypostyle hall situated at right angles. In this highly compressed spatial structure, there then follows a barque sanctuary before the cult image room with its side chapels is attained at the very rear. During the Twenty-ninth Dynasty a kiosk-like addition was built at the rear wall of the temple; this was connected with the inner sanctum by an opening in the wall (now blocked up) and was probably used by the priests for conveying oracles.

Temple of Ptah: Imhotep and Amenophis
Eighteenth Dynasty, ca. 1450 B.C.

The temple of the creator god of Memphis, Ptah, is reached through the northern gate of the Great Hypostyle Hall. The core of this modest temple was built under Thutmosis III though the path through the gate and the entrance are both from the Ptolemaic era. Other additions are as late as the Roman times. Behind the courtyard and the tiny portico with its two 16-sided columns lie the sanctuary rooms, the central chapel of which still houses the headless seated image of the god. The impressive lighting effects developed for the cult statue in ancient times are revealed when the door (a modern addition) is closed. A standing figure of Sekhmet in the side chapel to the right however was probably relocated from elsewhere. The most interesting individual scene in the temple, executed in low relief, is situated on the rear outer wall. Two officials, who were worshipped as demigods in their own right in the Graeco-Roman period, are shown behind Ptah and Hathor. The first of these is Imhotep, King Djoser's architect from the Third Dynasty, who wears a tight-fitting cap and carries a scepter and ankh symbol; a short inscription characterizes him as "Son of Ptah." He is followed by Amenophis, son of Hapu, in the Eighteenth Dynasty a wise counselor and outstanding figure at the court of his king, Amenophis III. Amenophis, the official, wears a chest high robe and carries a writing implements in his right hand. A shrine-like structure of wood was placed in front of the relief and served visitors to the temple as a place for personal prayer. Suppliants would seek the active assistance of these two divine officials in order to realize their requests and desires.

Open Air Museum

The "White Chapel" of Senusret I
Twelfth Dynasty, ca. 1925 B.C.

Karnak's open air museum was opened in 1987 in the northwest corner of the great enclosure wall (Thirtieth Dynasty) and is to be reached by proceeding through the north gate of the first courtyard. Here, important monuments illustrating the architectural history of the Amun temple are exhibited or have been reconstructed. Among these are the famous barque sanctuaries of Senusret I and Hatshepsut, a calcite chapel of Amenophis I and, the most recent addition, an entire temple wall from the reign of Thutmosis IV.

Named after the material from which it was built—white limestone—this small way station (21.5 ft × 21.5 ft, 6.5 m × 6.5 m) was constructed on the occasion of the *Sed* festival for Senusret I. Its original location is unknown though it is thought to have stood in front of what is now the fourth pylon. Two ramps with low balustrades lead up to a platform, enclosed by 16 pillars, which contained the barque pedestal. In the Eighteenth Dynasty the kiosk was demolished and its stone blocks used as foundations for the third pylon.

Senusret I among the gods
Twelfth Dynasty, ca. 1925 B.C.

As the only complete building from the Middle Kingdom in Karnak the architecture of the "White Chapel" has attracted considerable admiration for its balance and harmony. The rich reliefs on its pillars also make it one the most outstanding examples of this art form from the Twelfth Dynasty. In a complex network of relationships the pillars' 60 individual scenes are thematically interconnected down the vertical axis, the ritual activities depicted being directed towards the god Amun in his two chief forms. These show the "First of the Gods" in his classical form wearing a tall plumed crown and as an ithyphallic fertility god known in the inscriptions as Kamutef (Egyptian: "Bull of his Mother"). On the broader corner pillars are images showing the king being led into the temple. One of these depicts the god of creation, Atum of Heliopolis (illustration top) presenting Senusret I to Amun in his Kamutef form, and in the other the king is accompanied by the falcon-headed god, Month (illustration, bottom). A list on the upper zone of the pediment (r. and l. outer wall) is particularly interesting as it lists all 42 nomes of Egypt with their main gods and cult centers. The measure of length of each nome is provided so that by simple addition the size of the entire country may be calculated. This could be a strong hint of a comprehensive reform by Senusret I to strengthen his new central administration.

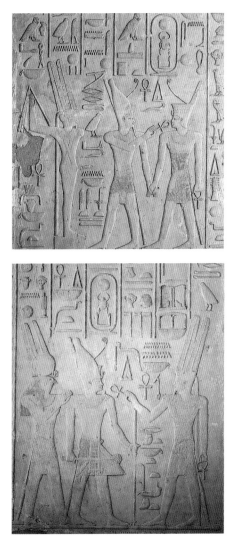

The "Red Chapel" of Hatshepsut
Eighteenth Dynasty, ca. 1460 B.C.

Like Senusret I's "White Chapel," the "Red Chapel" takes its name from the stone used to build it, a reddish brown quartzite. The only color variation is at the base of the walls (niched pattern, the "palace-façade") where black granite was used. Known as the "Seat of the Heart of Amun" and dating from the 16/17th year of the reign of Hatshepsut, this monumental barque sanctuary (L.49 ft, 15 m) stood for only a short period in Karnak. Thutmosis III had it pulled down to make way for his own building work. After a long period in storage the stones were finally used by Amenophis III for the foundations of the third pylon which today is badly damaged. Around two thirds of the original material, over 300 blocks, were rescued from this pylon by French archeologists. The detailed pictorial program is largely concerned with offering scenes, the coronation ritual and the great Theban festivals (Beautiful Feast of the Desert Valley, Opet Festival).

The sacred barque of Amun-Re
Eighteenth Dynasty, ca. 1460 B.C.

The "Red Chapel" houses the oldest known representation of the Opet Festival, and this provides valuable clues as to the form taken by processional events in the reign of Hatshepsut. Between Luxor and the temple of Karnak there stood six small way stations in which the barques were rested after being borne on the shoulders of priests and accompanied by the monarch and her youthful co-regent Thutmosis III. The appearance of both pharaohs in public might also have helped prevent them from engaging in the disputes which, some modern historians believe, marked their reign. Here, the sacred barque is pictured on its pedestal together with the poles used to carry it; it can be identified by the rams' heads at the bow and stern. A short inscription names the chapel and indicates its numerical position on the route. The processional image of the god was situated on the barque within a shrine which in turn was covered in a shroud. So-called Osiride pillars of the queen flank the entrance to the building and Hatshepsut is seen approaching from the side making offerings of incense. Her figure is that of a male pharaoh; it is only elements of Hatshepsut's accompanying titulature that indicate without any doubt her real gender.

"Alabaster Shrine" of Amenophis I
Eighteenth Dynasty, ca. 1505 B.C.

Amenophis I, second ruler of the Eighteenth Dynasty, added a series of other buildings and chapels to the temple complex of the Middle Kingdom. This barque shrine (H. 177 inches, 450 cm) of fine-grained calcite was dedicated to Amun and originally boasted wooden doors with bands of precious metals. The dedicatory text to the ruler on both sides of the entranceway refers to this by stating: "… he (the king) made it as a monument to his father, Amun, the lord of the throne of the two lands: he made for him a shrine (with the name) "Amun endures in monuments" from calcite-alabaster from Hatnub (a quarry in middle Egypt), the doors covered in metal plates of black copper, the reliefs furnished in gold… ." The reliefs in the narrow interior space show the ruler making offerings, the face of Amenophis I being executed in the manner of a portrait. On the outer walls of the shrine some scenes were finished only by Thutmosis I.

Temple wall of Thutmosis IV (details)
Eighteenth Dynasty, ca. 1390 B.C.

Thutmosis IV's new buildings in Karnak concentrated on a courtyard and its gateway situated in front of the fourth pylon. His successor, Amenophis III, demolished these buildings however in the course of constructing the third pylon. Two long registers on a wall recently reconstructed in the open air museum show the king taking part in various cult activities—for example, with the local Theban god Month—but they also picture a procession of elaborately festooned sacrificial cattle. The speed with which the individual blocks were re-used meant that the original colors of these exquisite high reliefs were preserved surprisingly well.

Obelisks—The Needles of the Pharaohs

Along with the sphinx and the pyramid the obelisk is considered the most typical symbol of Ancient Egypt. Strictly speaking, obelisks are tall four-sided pillars with points in the shape of pyramids, and these were sometimes clad in gold in order to reflect the sun's rays. Obelisks were royal monuments to the sun-god whose main cult site in Heliopolis also featured a towering natural stone monument representing the god's first appearance out of the primeval flood waters at the creation of the world. The oldest masonry obelisks were made in the Fifth Dynasty as central points for the so-called sun-temples built on the western edge of the desert at Abu Ghurob/Abusir. A short time later the first monolithic obelisks appeared; they were erected in temple precincts though smaller scale versions were also used in private tombs. In the Middle and New Kingdoms monarchs erected gigantic obelisks in and around the imperial temples. Spectacular evidence for these efforts is provided by the obelisks of queen Hatshepsut (1479–1458/57 B.C.) which she dedicated to her divine father Amun-Re. Measuring almost 91 ft (30 m) in height and weighing 323 tons these monuments were carved in granite quarries near Aswan and brought by ship to Karnak.

The whole undertaking must have been quite extraordinary because it was not only recorded

Obelisk of Senusret I in Heliopolis, Twelfth Dynasty, ca. 1950 B.C., red granite, H. 20.40 m

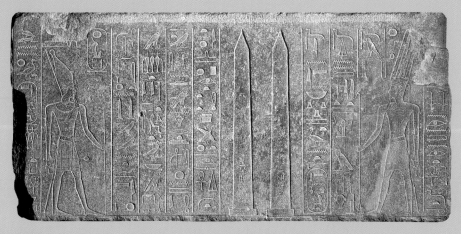

Block from the "Red Chapel": Hatshepsut donates two obelisks to the god Amun-Re, Eighteenth Dynasty, ca. 1460 B.C., Temple of Amun, Karnak, quartzite, H. 60 cm, Open Air Museum, Karnak

in the biographies of the officials in charge of the operation, the queen herself had the transport of the obelisks depicted on the lowest terrace of her mortuary temple in Deir el-Bahri. On the base of the northern obelisk the time taken for their production and transportation is given as seven months, and it is frequently stated that their upper halves were clad in gold. The work involved in quarrying these obelisks—using only tools of dolorite—and their transportation were masterpieces of technical achievement. So too was the erection of these gigantic monoliths, an exercise requiring the use of ramps of mud brick and various scaffolding devices whose precise appearance is still a matter for conjecture. The mightiest obelisk ever planned was to have measured 128 ft (42 m) but the stone developed a flaw while still in the quarry at Aswan and it was never completed. Roman emperors were also fascinated by obelisks and had 13 of them taken to Rome. Among these was the largest ever made by Thutmosis III from Karnak. From an inscription added by his grandson Thutmosis IV we know that this behemoth—it weighed 446 tons (455 tonnes) and measured almost 105 ft (32 m)—remained on its side for almost 35 years after it arrived at the temple before finally being erected. Despite all holiness, Karnak was in reality an everlasting construction site. In the 4th century A.D. it was carried away on the orders of Constantine I before being taken to Rome by his son, Constantine II, where it still stands on the St John in Lateran Square. Later, obelisks were taken to other cities around the globe such as Istanbul, London, New York and Paris.

The Necropolis of Western Thebes

Western Thebes

The necropolis of Thebes stretches over several kilometers down the western bank of the Nile. The extensive cemetery area was laid out as early as the 3rd millennium, beginning with some brick mastabas of the Old Kingdom. During the Eleventh Dynasty the Theban ruling house had its members interred in the cemetery of its native city; the funerary complex of Mentuhotep II in the valley of Deir el-Bahri is the oldest monumental building in the necropolis. However, in line with the political and religious importance of Thebes during the New Kingdom, its rise to the status of the largest necropolis in the country really came in the Eighteenth Dynasty. Until the end of the Twentieth Dynasty, a desert valley to one side of the city was used as the traditional burial place of all the kings, who had their great mortuary temples built on the borders of the fertile land. In these temples, known as "Houses of Millions of Years," the cult of the dead ruler was combined with worship of the national god Amun-Re of Karnak. Once a year, at the "Beautiful Feast of the Desert Valley," Amun and the deities Mut and Khonsu visited the gods of the Theban western bank in a great boat procession which from the Nineteenth Dynasty onward ended in the complex of the reigning king.

Previous pages: Western Thebes, view of the valley of Deir el-Bahri

Tomb of Horemheb (KV 57): Horemheb brings offerings to the god Osiris, p. 392 f.

Tomb of Sennefer (TT 96), The Purification, p. 423 ff.

Medinet Habu, Ramesses III hunting wild bulls, p. 375

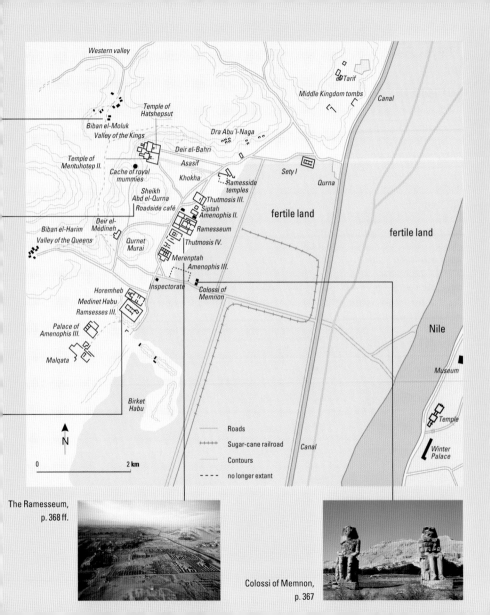

Western valley

el-Tarif

Middle Kingdom tombs

Canal

Temple of
Hatshepsut

Biban el-Moluk
Valley of the Kings

Dra Abu 'l-Naga

Deir el-Bahri

Temple of
Mentuhotep II.

Cache of royal
mummies

Asasif

Sety I

Qurna

Khokha

Ramesside
temples

Sheikh
Abd el-Qurna

Thutmosis III.

Roadside café

Siptah
Amenophis II.

fertile land

fertile land

Deir el-
Medineh

Biban el-Harim

Ramesseum

Valley of the Queens

Qurnet
Murai

Thutmosis IV.

Merenptah

Nile

Amenophis III.

Inspectorate

Colossi of
Memnon

Horemheb

Medinet Habu

Museum

Ramsesses III.

Palace of
Amenophis III.

Temple

Malqata

Winter
Palace

Birket
Habu

N

0   2 km

Roads

+++++   Sugar-cane railroad

Contours

Canal

- - -   no longer extant

The Ramesseum,
p. 368 ff.

Colossi of Memnon,
p. 367

The Theban Mortuary Temples

Temple of Mentuhotep II
Eleventh Dynasty, ca. 2020 B.C.

The complex built for Mentuhotep II in the valley of Deir el-Bahri was of a generally innovative character, but was still the traditional combination of mortuary temple and monumental tomb. A causeway (W. 150 ft; 46 m) measuring 3936 ft (1200 m) ran from the former building in the valley to the temple, where it led into a great forecourt, with a temple garden containing a plantation of trees and standing statues of the king. At the front of the courtyard area, a depression in the ground marks the place giving access to the king's second, Osiride tomb. This entrance is known as the Bab el-Hosan (Arab. "Gate of the Horse.") The main building, reached along a ramp, is set on a high terrace and surrounded on all sides by an ambulatory of octagonal pillars. It was crowned by a structure resembling a mastaba (possibly also planted with trees; see drawing), probably representing the idea of the primeval mound. The area behind the temple building, with its courtyard, pillared hall, and sanctuary was reserved for the cult of the deified king and god Amun. From here a tunnel 492 ft (150 m) long leads into the rock, and the burial chamber of Mentuhotep II lies at the end of it.

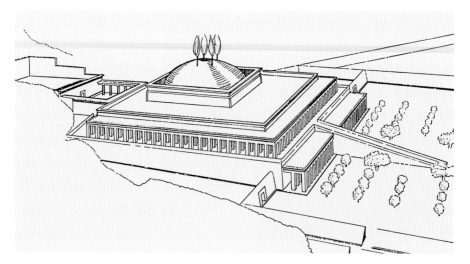

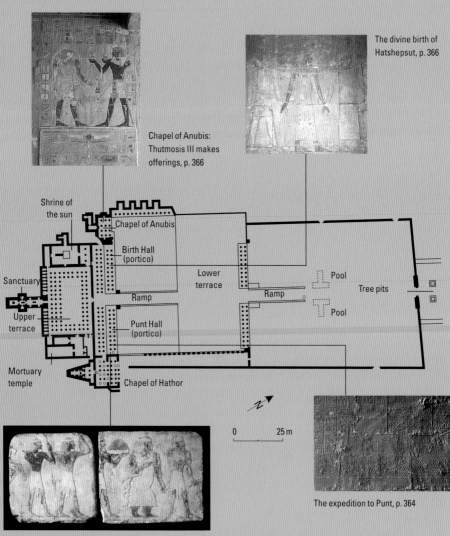

The divine birth of
Hatshepsut, p. 366

Chapel of Anubis:
Thutmosis III makes
offerings, p. 366

Shrine of
the sun

Chapel of Anubis

Birth Hall
(portico)

Lower
terrace

Pool

Tree pits

Sanctuary

Ramp

Ramp

Pool

Upper
terrace

Punt Hall
(portico)

Mortuary
temple

Chapel of Hathor

0   25 m

The ruler of Punt and his wife, p. 365

The expedition to Punt, p. 364

The Mortuary Temple of Hatshepsut

Eighteenth Dynasty, ca. 1470 B.C.

Queen Hatshepsut had her mortuary temple, one of the most individual achievements of Egyptian sacred architecture, built next to the temple of Mentuhotep II (Eleventh Dynasty) in front of the steep rocks of the western mountain range. The limestone building consists of a broad courtyard with two terraces adjoining it, one after the other. Their façades consist of open pillared halls, each divided in two by the ramps giving access. The side sanctuaries of Anubis (to the north) and Hathor (to the south) were built on to the lower terrace, which contains the Birth Hall (northern portico) and the Punt Hall (southern portico), while the temple itself is on the upper level. A broad court lined with columns lies beyond a façade with monumental pillars showing Osiride statues of the queen. Beyond this court the visitor enters the barque sanctuary and the cult image chambers of Amun-Re and Hatshepsut. A shrine with open court for the solar cult and a chapel for the mortuary offerings of the queen and her father Thutmosis I are also located at the upper terrace.

The Expedition to Punt

The reliefs in the southern hall on the lower terrace are devoted entirely to the great trade expedition to the land of Punt ordered by Queen Hatshepsut in the ninth year of her reign. Although there are written accounts of trade missions to the African interior from the Old Kingdom onward, this is the only extant pictorial version of such an expedition. The Egyptians, in five ships commanded by the chancellor Nehesi, first sailed along the western coast of the Red Sea, and then set out overland to reach their journey's end in the north of what is now Eritrea. Besides such classic natural products of the regions as gold, ebony, ivory, and the skins of big cats, they were particularly interested in importing the highly prized incense resin so essential to the rituals of worship in the many temples of Egypt. In addition, the ships took on board a cargo of myrrh trees with their roots in containers; according to the inscriptions, 31 of these trees survived the long journey back to Thebes. However, any attempt to naturalize them in the temple garden at Karnak would have failed because of the climate.

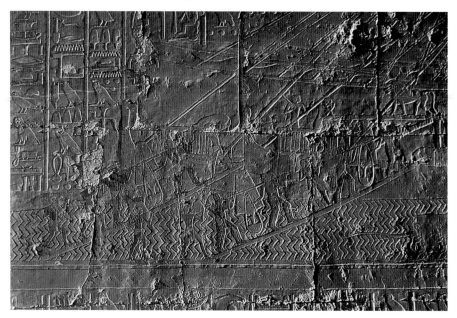

King and Queen of Punt

The Egyptian expeditionary team, headed by its envoy, is received by the King of Punt and his wife. This African ruler, "the great one of Punt," has a normal figure and a long, pointed beard, and wears a short kilt with a dagger in the belt. The figure of the extremely obese Queen Ati, however, was so unusual that the picture precisely catches the symptoms of her sickness, with the pronounced curvature of her spine and the overhanging fatty tissue. Her wavy hair ends in a plait and is held back with a wide band. The woman's jewelry consists of a necklace of large gold disks and pairs of anklets and bracelets. Even in the Ramesside period, the picture of Ati so fascinated an artist in Deir el-Medineh that he made a rough sketch of her figure on an ostracon (a splinter of lime-stone). A member of the expedition may have brought first-hand knowledge of the queen's appearance back to Thebes and thus made its original representation possible. Anyhow, the outrageous figure of Ati spiked the minds of the Egyptians as much as the desire to give Hatshepsut full credit for the great success by launching the Punt expedition. The ruler and his wife are followed by their servants, who are bringing gifts to send to the Egyptian court in Thebes: natural products presented on flat dishes or carried in baskets on the shoulders of retainers. The still extant blocks of stone bearing this unique depiction were once stolen, and were lost for a considerable time. After they had fortunately been recovered they were given to the museum in Cairo, and the temple now contains only not very well executed plaster casts.

The divine "birth" of Hatshepsut

The northern hall of the first terrace contains the great cycle of reliefs illustrating the divine descent of Hatshepsut, the oldest known pictorial version of the myth of the divine inception of the rulers of Egypt. The course of the story begins with the decision of the national god Amun to create a new ruler, continues by showing the queen mother Ahmose (center) accompanied during the process of birth by the gods Khnum and the frog-headed Heket, and ends with the ram-headed creator god of Elephantine making the royal child and its *ka* on his potter's wheel.

The Anubis chapel: Thutmosis III making offerings

A separate chapel for the god Anubis was built on the northern side of the Birth hall. It consists of a broad forecourt with twelve columns, and the cult chambers cut out of the rock. While the depiction of Hatshepshut has been effaced from the walls here, as everywhere else in the temple, a scene remains over the right-hand niche of the pillared court which impressively demonstrates the high quality of the relief art of the time, and is equally impressive in the lavish color of its painting. It shows Thutmosis III making an offering of wine to the falcon-headed sun god Re-Horakhty, whose cult image probably once stood in the niche. A comperable niche on the opposite wall held the figure of Amun-Re.

The Colossi of Memnon

Eighteenth Dynasty, ca. 1370 B.C.

The mortuary temple complex of Amenophis III in Thebes, the largest single temple ever build in Egypt, was the crown of his extraordinary architectural achievements. Nothing now remains of that monumental structure (surrounding wall 2296 × 1804 ft; 700 × 550 m), which has been almost entirely destroyed by earthquakes and stone robbery, apart from the two gigantic seated figures of the ruler known as the Colossi of Memnon. Each worked from a single monolithic quartzite block, they reach a height of some 59 ft (18 m). The figures owe their name to a natural phenomenon. An earthquake in the year 27 B.C. severely damaged the northern colossus, and it subsequently began to "sing" in the morning. These sounds, probably caused by the difference between the daytime and night-time temperature, causing particles of stone to splinter off, were interpreted in antiquity as the lament of the goddess Eos for her son Memnon, who fell at the siege of Troy. When the Roman emperor Septimius Severus had the figure restored in A.D. 199, it fell silent again for ever.

The Ramesseum
Nineteenth Dynasty, ca. 1260 B.C.

Only a short time after Ramesses II came to the throne, work began on his great mortuary temple, the Ramesseum. The temple itself and an extensive complex of storerooms with barrel vaulting, some of it well preserved, occupy a surface area of roughly 161,548 ft² (15,000 m²). Beyond the mighty pylon at the entrance (W. 216 ft; 68 m), the first in mortuary temple architecture to be built of sandstone, lie two courtyards containing several colossal figures of the ruler. Three parallel ramps then lead from the second courtyard to the elevated temple building, and the visitor reaches the great hypostyle hall. In its basilical style of building, with 48 papyrus columns in all, it reflects the hypostyle hall of the temple of Karnak. The following room has a ceiling with depictions of astronomical subjects, and there are pictures of the barque procession on the east wall. Next is the space of the so-called offering hall. However, the sanctuary area itself has been completely destroyed.

"Ramesses, the Sun of Foreign Sovereigns"

One of the largest colossal figures of the deified Ramesses, to which this name was given, rose south of the ramp leading up from the first courtyard to the second pylon. The enormous remains of this seated statue still fascinate us today. It once reached a height of over 60 ft (18 m), and weighed more than 1000 tonnes. The individual measurements of the carefully worked gigantic statue are impressive too: for instance, the breadth of the chest is 23 ft (7 m), the circumference of an arm $17\frac{1}{2}$ ft (5.30 m), and the middle finger is 3 ft (1 m) long. Described and admired in classical antiquity by the historian Diodorus (1st century B.C.), this figure acquired international fame as Ozymandias (a Greek corruption of the king's throne name User-Maat-Re) in Percy Bysshe Shelley's sonnet of 1817. A much smaller statue of the queen mother Tuya seems to have stood in the northern half of the courtyard, but only a number of fragments have been found.

Osiride pillars in the second courtyard

Large pillared figures are known to be used in the sacred architecture from the Old Kingdom period, but not until the New Kingdom is there evidence of their use in the design of a courtyard ambulatory. The pillars are joined to the statues rising behind them, but have no supporting function like similar figures in Greek architecture. Because of the mummiform execution of the bodies and the crossed arms with hands holding the crook and flail, they are usually termed "Osiride pillars."

View into the Hypostyle Hall

An architectural design was created for the construction of Ramesses II which differed markedly from that of his father Sety I, the first in the series of Ramesside mortuary temples in the northern part of Western Thebes. One of the new elements was the great hypostyle hall. Its powerful and at the same time harmonious spatial effect, with the central aisle only slightly raised, was mentioned by Jean-François Champollion in a letter: "As for great monuments, the Ramesseum is perhaps the finest and most beautiful in Thebes."

The Battle of Qadesh

Ramesses II had the dramatic events of the famous Battle of Qadesh against the Hittites in 1275 B.C. represented in detail in his mortuary temple (name: "House of Millions of Years United with Thebes"), in order to lend his triumph an eternal character in the eyes of the gods. A complete version was given on the inside of the first pylon, and a further series of pictures adorns the section of the eastern wall still standing in the second courtyard. The tumult of battle is evident in a scene of chaotic disorder, with the bodies of enemies transfixed by arrows and their war chariots toppled, while Hittite chariots, carrying three men each, are driving up in the lower register (left-hand picture).

They are shown to be Hittites not only by their clothing but in particular by the octagonal shields that are part of their arms and armor. Large-scale battle pictures which may cover whole temple walls were a Nineteenth-Dynasty innovation, and the narrative nature of the pictorial composition is an inheritance from the Amarna period. The detailed depiction of the course of the battle includes certain less important parts of the action. The warriors in front are reaching their hands down to comrades who have fallen into the water to save them from drowning, and rows of Hittite infantry armed with spears can be seen standing on the bank of the river Orontes where the fortress of Qadesh lay (right-hand picture).

Medinet Habu

The Mortuary Temple of Ramesses III
Twentieth Dynasty, ca. 1170 B.C.

The temple of Medinet Habu in the south of Western Thebes is the best preserved mortuary temple in the whole necropolis. The mighty brick wall around it (1033 × 672 ft; 315 × 205 m) also surrounds two other complexes: the Eighteenth-Dynasty "Small Temple" (Hatshepsut/Thutmosis III), and in the southeast the funerary chapels of three God's Wives of Amun from the Late period. The entrance to the whole temple precinct is marked on the eastern side by a fortress-like building known as the "High Gate." From here, the eye falls on the first pylon of the mortuary temple of Ramesses III, which has a ground plan largely following that of the Ramesseum. The entrance pylon is followed by two courtyards; the first, in the south, adjoining a large cult palace. However, the temple beyond, containing various hypostyle halls and the barque sanctuary, is not so well preserved. Extensive premises for domestic and administrative purposes surround the temple, showing that Medinet Habu was the seat of the Theban administration at this time.

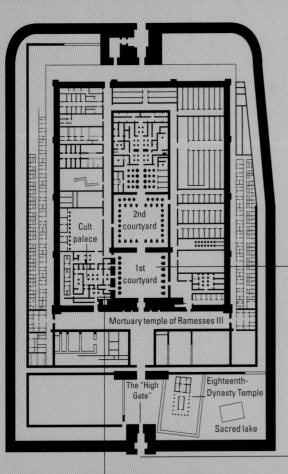

Cult
palace

2nd
courtyard

1st
courtyard

Mortuary temple of Ramesses III

The "High
Gate"

Eighteenth-
Dynasty Temple

Sacred lake

View of the first courtyard, p. 376

The "High Gate" of Medinet Habu,
p. 374 f.

Ramesses III hunting
wild bulls, p. 375

0   50 m

The "High Gate" of Medinet Habu

This monumental gate (H. 62 ft; 19 m) is of an unusual design for Egyptian temple architecture, and was probably influenced by Middle Eastern fortress buildings. Two towers crowned with battlements and the adjoining masonry flank the entrance; they are linked by a double upper story only behind the façade. The ruler could stay for short periods in the inhabitable interior rooms; some reliefs show scenes of his private life with the ladies of his harem. Probably here the reported assassination attempt against Ramesses III took place.

Ramesses III hunting wild bulls

The western wall of the southern pylon tower, visible outside the courtyard, bears two large hunting scenes which are among the finest of the genre in the dynamism of their pictorial construction. The lower relief shows Ramesses III killing three wild bulls on the outskirts of the Delta marshes. Transfixed by arrows, the animals are collapsing in their death throes or falling under the king's chariot. Below the royal team, the accompanying retinue is hurrying up, headed by several princes who are taking an active part in the hunt.

View into the first courtyard

The subject matter of the reliefs in the first courtyard (108 × 137 ft; 33 × 42 m) concentrates on depicting Ramesses III's victories over the Libyans and the Sea Peoples. The two battles against the allied tribes of the so-called Sea Peoples (including the Peleset normally identified with the Biblical Philistines) in the eighth year of his reign were important events in international politics. An account is given in inscriptions on the second pylon at the western side of the courtyard, and pictorial depictions of both the land and the sea battles were placed on the northern exterior wall of the temple. The construction of the courtyard includes a set of seven Osiride statues of the king on the right-hand (northern) side. Free-standing additions of hieroglyph signs to the crowns and shoulders of the figures make them intol stone cryptograms of the throne name of Ramesses III: User-Maat-Re merj-Amun ("Strong in *maat* is Re, the Chosen One of Amun"). The Window of Appearance pierces the wall on the opposite side of the courtyard, beyond the papyrus columns, and together with two lateral gates joins the courtyard and the cult palace.

Counting the dead enemies (detail)

The extensive depictions of war in the mortuary temple of Ramesses III continue into the second courtyard, which has preserved an interestingly detailed scene from one of the Libyan campaigns on its southern wall. In the presence of the two viziers (right) the ruler is informed of the exact number of enemies killed. The count of the dead considered necessary was carried out in an unconventional if effective manner: the right hand and genitals were cut off every fallen soldier, and recorded by an army scribe.

The cult palace of Medinet Habu

During the excavations carried out by the Oriental Institute of Chicago from 1926 onward the royal cult palace was uncovered, and its lower courses of masonry reconstructed (using modern bricks). It is level with the first courtyard on the southern side of the temple, linked to it by the Window of Appearance. This was where the ruler showed himself to the officials assembled in the courtyard on the occasion of an important ceremony, the "Giving of the Gold of Honor," awarded to deserving members of the administration. The palace itself had a large throneroom with palm tree columns, a bedroom, and a bathroom (and lavatory), as well as several subsidiary apartments for the members of the pharaoh's family.

The Valley of the Kings

The rise of Thebes to become the capital of the country obliged the rulers of the early Eighteenth Dynasty to find a new cemetery area for their tomb complexes. The choice fell on a desert valley in the western mountain range of Thebes, about five kilometres from the Nile, where all the pharaohs of the New Kingdom after Thutmosis I were interred. Only the heretic king Akhenaten, who left Thebes for good, was buried in a tomb near his new capital at Amarna. In view of the nature of this site it was decided to abandon the tradition of pyramid burial, for even the mightiest pile of stones could not have guaranteed the security of the royal mummies. Instead, a rock-cut tomb in the remote wadi seemed the ideal way to meet the requirements of secrecy and security, as the much-quoted statement of an official in his own autobiographical funerary inscription shows: "(…) I saw how the rock-cut tomb of His Majesty (Thutmosis I) was dug in a lonely place; no one saw it, no one heard it." But shortly after the end of the New Kingdom all the tombs were robbed, and only a lucky chance allowed the modest complex of Tutankhamun's tomb to survive the millennia. During the Eighteenth Dynasty an official personally appointed by the ruler was responsible for the work at the royal tomb, while the same tasks were carried out in the Ramesside period by whichever vizier was in office at the time.

Tomb of Thutmosis III (KV 34)

Eighteenth Dynasty, ca. 1450 B.C.

The Wadi Biban el-Moluk, the Valley of the Kings, divides into two arms, the eastern one containing the central area with most of the tombs. The western part of the valley was used as a burial place only by Amenophis III and Ay. The interior of the valley offered particularly good conditions at the foot of its rock formations for digging out tombs in concealed situations and filling them in again after the interment. The care taken in choosing the site of a tomb for the dead ruler is impressively demonstrated by the tomb of Thutmosis III, where the entrance is through a small crack in the rock above ground level which can be reached today only by climbing a modern iron ladder. The tomb was discovered in 1898 by the French archeologist Victor Loret, and has the right-angled axial turn typical complexes of the Thutmoside period. Steep stairways lead through a large antechamber to the decorated burial chamber, which has a star-decorated ceiling supported on two pillars, and is the last of its kind constructed on an oval ground plan.

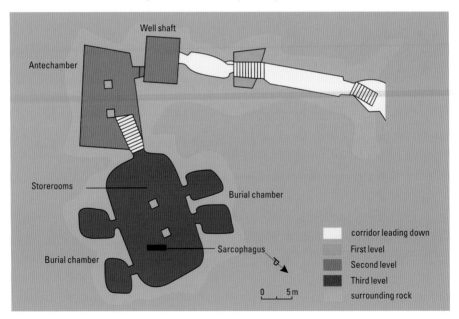

Well shaft

Antechamber

Storerooms

Burial chamber

Burial chamber

Sarcophagus

corridor leading down
First level
Second level
Third level
surrounding rock

0   5 m

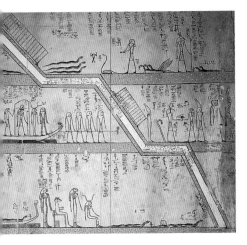

The *Amduat*: the Fourth Hour of the Night

The walls of the burial chamber bear the oldest complete version of the *Amduat*, originally entitled "The Writing of the Hidden Chamber." This funerary text describes the voyage of the sun god in his barque through the twelve hours of the night. The textual and pictorial areas are still arranged here to match the points of the compass. That is why some hours with texts and pictures were condensed beyond elegance. The fourth hour of the night is therefore placed directly by the entrance to the burial chamber. The route taken by the barque traces a zigzag course through the sandy desert regions of Rosetjau, the land of Sokar, the Memphite god of the dead, and is also towed along an underground watercourse (central register).

The suckling of Thutmosis III

Not only the walls but also the two pillars in the burial chamber are decorated. The sketch-like style of the pictures is striking. In the upper register, Thutmosis III and his mother Isis are rowing in a barque, while in the lower register he is being suckled by a tree goddess, "his mother Isis," as the brief inscription explains. The identical names of the king's physical and divine mothers reinforce the theme of maternal care for eternity. In addition, the pharaoh is followed by three wives and one daughter.

Burial chamber: the Twelfth Hour of the Night of the *Amduat*

The king's cartouche-shaped stone sarcophagus, made of brownish-red quartzite and the central item of his former tomb equipment, still stands at the back of the burial chamber. Many fragments of these magnificent objects, robbed of their gold plating, have been found in the four small side chambers. However, the mummy of Thutmosis III had already been found a few years earlier in the famous cache of royal mummies at Deir el-Bahari. The foot end of the sarcophagus points to the twelfth hour of the night (on the northeast wall), in which the sun is reborn. The middle register shows the ram-headed god traveling in his barque and transforming himself, in the body of a mighty primeval divine snake, into the figure of a scarab (right) which is raised to the eastern horizon by the outspread arms of the god of the air Shu. At this point the god begins his twelve-hour journey through the day before going down into the underworld again in the west. The idea of the dead ruler's participation in this eternal cycle was an important part of his guarantee of life beyond the tomb.

Tomb of Amenophis II (KV 35)

Eighteenth Dynasty, ca. 1410 B.C.

The tomb of Amenophis II was cut from the soft limestone of the western mountain range of Thebes, in a rather less well concealed position than the complex of his father Thutmosis III. It follows much the same ground plan, but there are some differences of detail. The burial chamber was now designed as a rectangular room, with six pillars ornamented with scenes showing the pharaoh in front of the gods, while the floor was sunk considerably lower at the back of the room. This was where the king's magnificent quartzite sarcophagus, still containing the mummy of Amenophis II, was found when the tomb was discovered in 1898. The kneeling goddesses Isis (at the foot) and Nephthys (at the head) are shown on the narrower sides of the sarcophagus. Besides fragments of the original tomb equipment, nine more royal mummies, brought here later for safety, were found in one of the four small side chambers. A complete version of the *Amduat* adorns the walls of the burial chamber. The anteroom, on the other hand, remained undecorated, as did the deep shaft complex leading to it and now known as the tomb robbers' shaft.

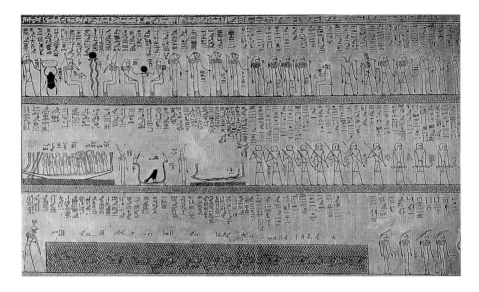

The *Amduat*: the Tenth Hour of the Night

Once again the solar barque is depicted in the middle register. Ahead of it appear the god Sokar, shown as a falcon over the body of a double-headed snake; Osiris as a falcon-headed snake; and the sun god's armed guards. The lower register shows a stretch of water with the figures of drowned men drifting in it. The god Horus, standing on the bank, is leading them to a blessed existence in the next world even though they have not been buried, since their corpses have been lost. The idea was to avert the danger which threatened even the king of accidental death by drowning in the river.

Amenophis II before the goddess Hathor

Large-scale scenes showing the king with various gods appear for the first time on the pillars of the burial chamber in the tomb of Amenophis II. The style of depiction used on the walls was abandoned in favour of a more conventional manner for these scenes. The sparing use of flesh tint is a striking feature. The selection is limited to three deities: Osiris, the god of the dead; Anubis, as the god of necropolises and embalming; and Hathor, here giving Amenophis II an *ankh* symbol, standing for the breath of life. Some mistakes in the inscriptions lead surprisingly to the conclusion that no professional scribes were here at work.

Howard Carter and the Golden Pharaoh

When the men working for the British archeologist Howard Carter came upon a flight of steps in the rock in the Valley of the Kings on November 4, 1922, Carter could not guess that he was about to make one of the greatest discoveries in the history of archeology. He had already spent five seasons investigating the debris of millennia in the valley on behalf of Lord Carnarvon, who was financing his team, but without success. Carter based his firm belief in the presence of the tomb complex of Tutankhamun, a king of whom very little was previously known, on a find made in 1907 by the American businessman Theodore M. Davis,

Tomb of Tutankhamun (KV 62), Eighteenth Dynasty, ca. 1325 B.C., Western Thebes, Valley of the Kings

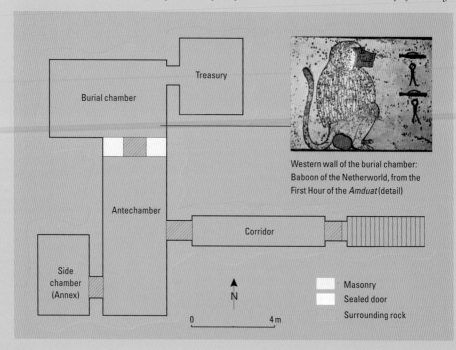

Western wall of the burial chamber:
Baboon of the Netherworld, from the
First Hour of the *Amduat* (detail)

who held the concession to excavate in the area at that time. Pots, remnants of fabric, a floral collar, a seal bearing the name of Tutankhamun, and other items had come to light in a small chamber in the ground. Although the real significance of these very diverse objects was not at first obvious, they were a clear indication that the person of Tutankhamun had some link with the Valley of the Kings. As yet, however, Carter did not dream of finding an almost complete royal tomb, the only such tomb to have survived the millennia. At the end of 1922 he turned

Howard Carter examines the golden coffin of Tutankhamun, still resting inside the middle coffin (time of excavation, 1924)

his attention to a small area very close to the entrance of the tomb complex of Ramesses VI. It transpired that when the workers of antiquity were digging out that tomb they had dumped all the spoil on top of the entrance to the tomb of Tutankhamun, thus hiding it from the eyes of potential tomb robbers at the end of the New Kingdom. On the afternoon of the day of Carter's great discovery, the steps were already sufficiently uncovered for him to see the seal on the entrance to the tomb, which was still blocked up. But he could not make out any name. Drawing on all his powers of self-control, he told his men to stop work and sent a telegram to Carnarvon, who was in England at the time: "At last have made wonderful discovery in Valley; a magnificent tomb with seals intact; re-covered same for your arrival; congratulations." Barely

Seal impressions from the wall of the entrance to the tomb; right, the official seal of the necropolis

Northern wall of the burial chamber: on the right King Ay, Tutankhamun's successor, wearing a leopard skin, comes before the Osiris figure of the king and performs the ritual of the opening of the mouth. On the left, Tutankhamun is greeted by the goddess of the sky, Nut, with the njnj gesture.

two weeks later Lord Carnarvon arrived in Luxor, and within a few days the two Englishmen were standing at the end of the corridor, which had now been cleared, facing another blocked passageway. The suspense must have been unbearable when Carter made a small opening in the stonework, shone a candle through it, and stood there in silence. Finally Carnarvon, who was standing behind him, asked: "Can you see anything?" The answer was short and momentous: "Yes, wonderful things." The finds brought to light in the years that followed kept the world of archeology in a state of amazement. Objects never seen before emerged from the darkness of the tomb: all the riches of a royal burial of the New Kingdom crammed together in only four rooms. Bringing the extensive treasures of the tomb to the light of day was a difficult task, and beyond the capacity of Carter's team on its own. Fortunately he could call on the help of experts from the Metropolitan Museum of New York

Eastern wall of the burial chamber: the shrine containing the mummy of the dead ruler is drawn to the interment by twelve high-ranking courtiers, including the two bald-headed viziers of Upper and Lower Egypt, and General Horemheb (nearest to the shrine).

expedition which was also working in Western Thebes at the time. Its members included the photographer Harry Burton, to whom we owe a photographic record of the excavations which is a model of its kind. When Carnarvon died of an infection in 1923 the entire responsibility for the operation rested on Carter's shoulders. It was to be ten years before all the objects had been taken to the Egyptian Museum in Cairo, after first undergoing provisional conservation treatment on the site. The length of time was due not only to the magnitude of the operation, but also to the fact that Carter was constantly at loggerheads with the press and the Egyptian authorities. Some of the work even had to be brought to a halt. Although according to the wording of the license Carnarvon had a claim to a share of the finds, it was decided that the treasure of Tutankhamun's tomb should be kept in Egypt intact. However, Carnarvon's heir, his daughter Evelyn, received financial compensation for the enormous expense entailed.

Tomb of Thutmosis IV (KV 43)

Eighteenth Dynasty, ca. 1390 B.C.

Although the walls and pillars in the tomb of Thutmosis IV had been fully smoothed to take decoration, it was never added. Only the shaft room and the anteroom to the burial chamber were ornamented with paintings before the interment. In fact we quite often find that a king's funerary complex was not completed when he died, even though his reign had been of some length. One can only speculate on the reasons for delays in preparing the royal tomb. Here, the rapidly executed scenes of gods and goddesses were placed against a golden yellow background for the first time, and the individual figures were then completely colored in. Each of the gods of the dead—Osiris, Anubis, and Hathor—is holding an *ankh* symbol before the face of Thutmosis IV. His burial underwent a restoration in Year 8 of Horemheb as we learn from a short walltext in the antechamber.

The Sarcophagus of Thutmosis IV

When Howard Carter discovered the funerary complex of Thutmosis IV in 1903, he found the king's gigantic quartzite sarcophagus (L. 9½ ft; 300 cm; W. 5¼ ft; 160 cm) standing in its traditional place in the burial chamber. The choice of quartzite as the material for the royal sarcophagi of the early Eighteenth Dynasty was based on its close connection with the cult of the sun, since it had come from the stone quarries of Heliopolis, the ancient city of the sun god.

The decorative pattern follows an established canon, with an increased number of texts because of the size of the sarcophagus. The two protective goddesses Nephthys and Isis stand at the head and foot of the sarcophagus, their arms spread wide, while four more deities are portrayed on each of the long sides, including the tutelary canopic gods Amset, Hapy, Qebehsenuef, and Duamutef. The hieroglyphs painted in yellow and the restrained polychromy of the figures form a lively contrast with the background color of the sarcophagus.

Tomb of Horemheb (KV 57)

Eighteenth Dynasty, ca. 1300 B.C.

A new type of ground plan was introduced in the tomb of Horemheb, the last ruler of the Eighteenth Dynasty, and on the whole was to remain standard throughout the following Ramesside period. The characteristic axial turn in the design of earlier royal tombs was abandoned, and replaced by a two-part system of corridors with a displaced axis. In this division, the sun god Re-Horakhty presided over the upper part of the tomb, and Osiris, the god of the dead, over the lower part. The burial place of Horemheb was discovered in 1908 by archeologists working for the American businessman Theodore M. Davis, who held the concession for excavating in the Valley of the Kings at this time.

Horemheb makes an offering to the god Osiris

Not only the royal tomb architecture but also its decorative program and style of painting developed new features in the tomb of Horemheb. The scenes of gods are still to be found in the shaft space and anteroom, as they were before the Amarna period, but the range of deities is extended, and sky blue is used as the background color on the walls. Here Horemheb stands before Osiris, the god of the dead, "Lord of Eternity" to whom he is offering two spherical wine jars.

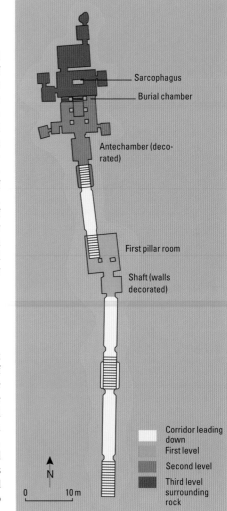

Sarcophagus

Burial chamber

Antechamber (decorated)

First pillar room

Shaft (walls decorated)

Corridor leading down
First level
Second level
Third level surrounding rock

N

0   10 m

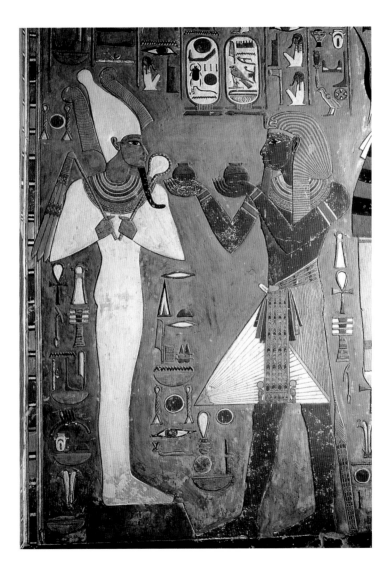

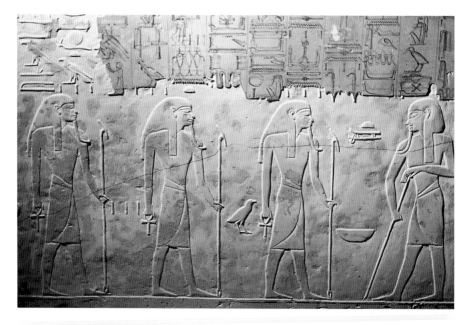

The "Book of Gates" (detail)

Horemheb's burial chamber was the first of its kind to be ornamented with scenes from one of the "Guidebooks to the Netherworld" other than the *Amduat*, which had hitherto been used. This was the "Book of Gates," a religious tract which also concentrates on the nocturnal journey of the sun god; the gates dividing the separate hours of the night and guarded by spirits in the form of serpents are systematically depicted. The incomplete state of these scenes (the figure on the extreme right represents the creator god Atum as an old man leaning on

a stick, the setting sun), provides an insight into the working methods. After the walls had been smoothed, inscriptions and images were drawn on them, corrections being made as the work went along, before the sculptors began carving the reliefs working from bottom to top. The final stage would have been the painting. But all work on the decoration of the tomb was immediately halted when the king died, and preparation for his burial became the sole focus of interest. Even the attempt to execute the missing depictions in painting did not get beyond one scene. So, another unfinished royal tomb challenged eternity.

Tomb of Ramesses I (KV 16)
Nineteenth Dynasty, ca. 1290 B.C.

The souls of Pe and Nekhen

When Ramesses I, founder of the Nine-teenth Dynasty, came to the throne at an advanced age on the death of Horemheb, he had only a few years to reign. As a result no proper royal tomb could be prepared for him. The burial chamber in his complex immediately adjoins two flights of steps leading steeply downward. An unfinished sarcophagus decorated only with painting almost fills the small chamber. The wall paintings, on a blue background, follow those in the tomb of Horemheb in style, and because of the lack of space available show only sections from the "Book of Gates" and a few scenes of divinities. Ramesses himself, in a very unusual depiction, is shown on the back wall, kneeling in a posture of rejoicing between the animal-headed "Souls of Pe and Nekhen," powerful spirits representing the primeval mythological tradition of the united kingdom.

The barque of the sun god

The image of the sun god's journey in his barque goes back to a very ancient system of ideas, and can already be found in the pyramid texts of the Old Kingdom. At an early date daily observation of the rising of the sun, its course across the sky, and its setting in the west suggested the concept of a boat as a suitable means of transport for this process. There are some differences between the form taken by the solar barque in the *Amduat* and the version from the "Book of Gates." It is now being drawn by four men walking ahead of it; their clothing clearly identifies them as the dead souls of the blessed. At every hour of the night, the ram-headed figure of Re in his shrine-like cabin is surrounded and protected by the coiling body of the *mehen* serpent. The sun god's escort on board has also been modified, and now consists of only two divine figures flanking him. Sia, the personification of creative knowledge, stands in the bows, and Heka, symbolizing the power of magic, at the stern. Another of the serpent-guarded gates after which Egyptologists have called this text "Book of the Gates" can be made out on the right.

Tomb of Sety I (KV 17)
Nineteenth Dynasty, ca. 1285 B.C.

The Italian adventurer Giovanni Belzoni was undoubtedly one of the most ambivalent characters ever to set foot in the Valley of the Kings. He carried out many "excavations" all over the country on behalf of the British consul-general Henry Salt. Belzoni's greatest success came in October 1817, when within a few days he discovered the rock-cut tombs of Ramesses I and Sety I, the first two kings of the Nineteenth Dynasty, lying side by side. Even today, "Belzoni's tomb" is still a term in common use for the tomb complex of Sety I. The two axes, with their many corridors and chambers, covering a length of some 328 ft (100 m), run down to the monumental burial chamber. But the discovery of this most beautiful of the royal tombs of the New Kingdom ushered in a series of problems which has brought it to the brink of destruction in less than 200 years. Wanton destruction and the taking of poor copies in the 19th century have done as much harm as modern mass tourism to the reliefs and their original splendid color. The scene showing Sety I seated at the offering table of the funerary repast will serve as an example of the loss of substance that has occurred: the picture above shows its state in Belzoni's publication of 1820, while the same section of the picture below is from a black and white photograph taken in the 1920s by the American Harry Burton.

View of the Burial chamber

Passing through a pillared room, the visitor reaches the slightly sunken burial chamber or crypt. The tomb of Sety I contains the first example of a burial chamber with a vaulted ceiling, decorated with scenes from the *Amduat*. Here, Belzoni found the inner sarcophagus made of calcite still in place, ornamented with a complete version of the "Book of Gates." Today it is in the Soane Museum in London; the price asked by the excavator seemed excessive to the British Museum. A long, undecorated corridor leads directly from the floor where the coffin was found down into the rock, and is blocked up: perhaps the last secret in the Valley of the Kings. As it is in great danger of collapse, it has not yet been explored, but this system of corridors probably has mythological meaning, like the "tomb robbers' shaft" which is to be regarded as a symbolic tomb of the god of the underworld Sokar. The idea was probably to reach groundwater level, thus establishing the connection with the primeval ocean Nun, from which the king was reborn like the sun every morning.

The Astronomical ceiling

The flat ceilings of the royal tombs of the Eighteenth Dynasty were ornamented with a simple decorative motif of five-pointed stars (for instance in the tomb of Amenophis II), intended to represent the firmament. The vaulted ceiling in the burial chamber of Sety I was the first to bear a large-scale depiction of astronomical phenomena, which was to be superseded in the Twentieth Dynasty period (from Ramesses IV onward) by a picture of Nut, the sky goddess. The ceiling of Sety's tomb bears long lists of decanate stars (the southern group, including Orion and Sirius), and depictions of stars and constellations of the northern sky including the Big Dipper (shown as a bull) appear on a midnight-blue background. Other constellations, for instance the hippopotamus standing upright with a crocodile on its back, have so far eluded definite identification. This magnificent view of the heavens was solely for the benefit of the dead king lying here in his set of coffins, so that he could rise to the imperishable stars in the form of a *ba* soul.

Tomb of Merenptah (KV 8)

Nineteenth Dynasty, ca. 1205 B.C.

King Merenptah before Re-Horakhty

From the early Nineteenth Dynasty onward, the "Litany of Re" provided the usual decorative material for the first two corridor areas of a royal tomb. The original title of this netherworld text runs: "Book of the Adoration of Re in the West." A longer text of the Great Litany invokes the sun god by his 75 different names and shapes. Here King Merenptah is shown first, in an elaborately worked garment, standing before the falcon-headed figure of Re-Horakhty, who has the solar disk with the *uraeus* serpent around it on his head. This scene is followed by the title picture and beginning of the text of the "Litany of Re." The god appears in two forms in the central image of the ball of the sun, as a scarab and as a human figure with the head of a ram.

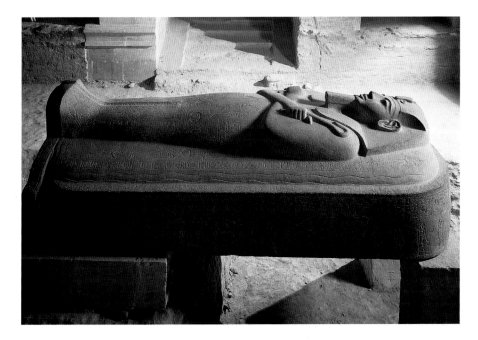

Lid of the Sarcophagus of Merenptah

Monumentalization of the royal sarcophagi developed parallel to the increase in
the size of tombs, and during the
Ramesside period they assumed gigantic
proportions. But even these enormously
heavy resting places for the royal
mummies could not save them from tomb
robbers. The sarcophagus ensemble of
Merenptah consisted of four separate
coffins nesting one inside the other. The
three outer stone sarcophagi were made of
red granite, the anthropoid inner sarcoph-

agus of calcite alabaster. It probably contained further coffins of gilded wood and
pure precious metals, such as those found
in the tomb of Tutankhamun. The burial
chamber of the tomb still contains the lid
of the second sarcophagus (L. 135 in;
345 cm, W. 59 in; 150 cm). Its basic form is
that of a royal cartouche. It depicts the
semi-three-dimensional figure of the king
as Osiris, holding the royal insignia of
crook and flail in his crossed hands. The
inscriptions on the lid are extracts from the
two most prominent funerary texts of the
Amduat and "Book of Gates."

Tomb of Ramesses VI (KV 9)
Twentieth Dynasty, ca. 1135 B.C.

The walls of the burial chamber in the tomb of Ramesses VI were ornamented with scenes from the "Book of the Earth," used in only a few tombs of the Ramesside period, and given here in full. The division of the night into twelve hours, as in the *Amduat* and "Book of Gates," is abandoned in this underworld book. Instead the earth gods Geb, Tatenen, and Aker are the focus of attention. The upper register on the right-hand wall shows the earth god Aker in the form of a double sphinx, carrying the solar barque on his back. The journey of the sun through the interior of the earth is also the subject of the central picture in the bottom register, with the arms of Nun, god of the primeval ocean, raising the solar disk from the depths between the two lion figures of Aker. This important motif is repeated in different ways in the two series of pictures in the other registers.

The Valley of the Queens

A special place was set aside in the south of Western Thebes for the interment of the many queens, princes, and princesses of the New Kingdom, and is known as the Valley of the Queens (Egypt.: Ta set neferu, "Place of Beauty.") Most of the larger tombs are of the Nineteenth and Twentieth Dynasties. The rock-cut tombs laid out at this time consist mainly of a corridor with several small side chambers. In point of size and depth they do not bear comparison with the contemporary tombs of the kings. The difference is also obvious in the program of decoration, which here concentrates on ritual scenes showing the owner of the tomb standing before the gods, and the texts are generally taken from the *Book of the Dead*. Many of the tombs have lost much of their relief pictures, and without exception they were robbed in antiquity. They include the world-famous tomb of Queen Nefertari, which was discovered only at a relatively late date (1904) by an Italian

team directed by Ernesto Schiaparelli of the Museo Egizio in Turin. However, even today the Valley of the Queens may be not completely "exhausted."

Tomb of Nefertari (QV 66)
Nineteenth Dynasty, ca. 1250 B.C.

With the official conclusion in the spring of 1992 of the painstaking restoration work on the endangered murals of the tomb of Nefertari, this jewel of ancient Egyptian art was preserved from final decline. Financed by the Getty Conservation Institute, Malibu, the rescue operation to save the paintings swallowed up around six million Deutschmarks and saw specialists from seven nations involved in the preparations, before a team of conservationists from Italy could begin on the work of restoration.

Despite all their efforts, the loss of some 20% of the wall and ceiling surfaces in the tomb, covering over 5381 ft² (500 m²) had to be accepted. In accordance with her status as "Great Royal Wife" of Ramesses II, Nefertari had a tomb complex of considerable extent laid out for her during her lifetime, and she was interred there in the 24th year of her husband's reign. Only a very few objects (e.g. fragments of the lid from the sarcophagus) survived the robbing of her tomb. An access corridor with 18 steps leads to the upper room, from which another stairway passage leads to the burial chamber on a displaced axis, which has three small side rooms.

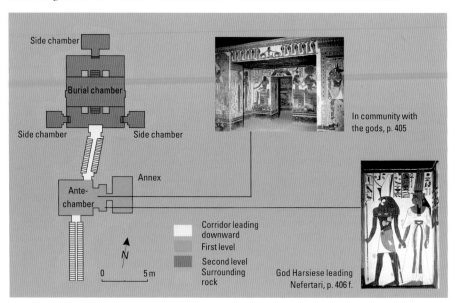

Side chamber

Burial chamber

Side chamber

Side chamber

Annex

Ante-chamber

In community with the gods, p. 405

Corridor leading downward
First level
Second level
Surrounding rock

N

0   5 m

God Harsiese leading Nefertari, p. 406 f.

In community with the gods

The upper level of the tomb has a broad annex to the east of the antechamber. The entrance is flanked by two depictions of the sun god. On the left, the enthroned figure of Khepri appears, symbolizing the rising morning sun in the form of a scarab. He is holding a symbol of life and the *was* scepter carried by male deities. In a short inscription, Khepri promises Nefertari participation in the cycle of eternity and a place in the "Sacred Land." Opposite him, both of them on richly decorated block thrones, sit the falcon-headed god Re-Horakhty, here representing the noonday and evening sun, and the goddess Hathor in her capacity as "lady of the West" of the underworld (with the corresponding symbol over her head). Directly over the doorway, a representation of the vulture goddess Nekhbet catches the eye. Her wings are outspread, and she holds two *shen* rings in her claws.

On each of the narrow walls of the annex to the upper room, the queen is being led by a single deity before the enthroned representations of the solar gods. The eastern wall shows this scene taking place with the falcon-headed god Harsiese ("Horus, son of Isis"), who is holding Nefertari by the hand. The comparable scene of the western wall features the goddess Isis with the queen. Harsiese

Nefertari making offerings

Access to the burial chamber is down a broad corridor, with niche-like recesses on both sides where the corridor begins. The walls of these niches bear scenes of offerings. On the south wall, the queen is giving the goddesses Isis and Nephthys a drink offering, while on the north wall she appears before Hathor and Selket, again with the spherical wine jars in her hands. She is wearing a smooth wig with a vulture's plumage, a magnificent collar in several rows, and what are known as "papyrus flower earrings," symbolically alluding to rebirth.

wears the double crown of Upper and Lower Egypt over his wig, a doublet with shoulder straps, and the short kilt of the gods, with the tail of a bull. The queen wears a diaphanous linen robe with a long red sash around her waist, and is described in the inscription as "justified, may she live under Osiris, the Great god." The area of the wall behind Nefertari bears a full-size depiction of a *djed* pillar, the cult fetish of Osiris. It wears the *atef* crown, and in this instance has arms, which are holding the god's insignia. In addition, the sacred symbol is depicted with the same long sash as shown in the depictions of the queen, who is thus portrayed on her way to "Osiris."

Painting on a Pillar in the Burial chamber

The level of the floor was slightly sunken at the center of the burial chamber, marking the spot where the queen's great stone sarcophagus of red granite once stood. Only fragments of its lid (L. 104 in; 265 cm) have been found, while the sarcophagus itself and the gilded inner coffins containing the mummy of Nefertari have not survived desecration by tomb robbers. Four pillars surround the place where the sarcophagus once stood, bearing up the star-covered ceiling. The two sides of the front pair of pillars turned toward the entrance each show a specific manifestation of the god Horus; he appears in the figure of a *sem* priest, wearing a panther skin, and handing over the dead to the care of Osiris, ruler of the world beyond the tomb. The inner sides of all the pillars, turned toward the sarcophagus, were ornamented with the cult symbol of Osiris, the *djed* pillar.

Tomb of Amenherkhepeshef (QV 55)

Twentieth Dynasty, ca. 1160 B.C.

Ramesses III with the Gods of the Netherworld

Among the tombs discovered by Schiaparelli during his excavations in the Valley of the Queens between 1903 and 1905 is the burial place of Amenherkhepeshef, one of five princes born to Ramesses III who were laid to rest here. The ground plan shows an almost square entrance area with a side chamber adjoining a corridor. It leads to a burial chamber, only roughly hewn out of the rock, where the unfinished stone sarcophagus of the prince still stands. The paintings are not of the very highest quality, but are striking for their well preserved colors and wealth of iconographic detail. All the depictions of the first room show ritual scenes, with the still living king in a dominant position in each of them, appearing before the various deities. The smaller figure of Amenherkhepeshef, serving already as a cavalry commander and being the true owner of the tomb, stands behind him. He is wearing the characteristic princely lock, a lock of hair at the side of his head, and holds a large flail with an ostrich feather. The upper part of the wall is decorated with a broad *kheker* frieze.

Domestic Life in Ancient Egypt

Mighty pyramids, magnificent shrines dedicated to the kings and gods, and the immense wealth of the pharaohs dominate our ideas of ancient Egyptian culture today. The emphasis is on official monuments and royal decrees. But what was daily life like for the subjects of the divine rulers of the land by the Nile? In what kinds of domestic conditions did people live?

Unlike the stone-built temples, the ordinary buildings of Egypt were principally made of mud brick, which the climate favored, and timber: these materials did not survive the millennia so well, for they were always being built over, and had to contend with a rising groundwater level. It is only occasionally that special circumstances provide archeologists

Wall-painting: House of a high-ranking official with garden (lower register), Eighteenth Dynasty, ca. 1420 B.C., Western Thebes, tomb of Djehuty-nefer (TT 80)

with an opportunity to study a large settlement area thoroughly: for instance the pyramid town of Sesostris II (Twelfth Dynasty) at el-Lahun; the capital of Akhenaten at Tell el-Amarna; and Deir el-Medineh, the village built for the craftsmen who worked on the Theban necropolis. In the New Kingdom, depictions of dwelling houses in tombs have supplemented and confirmed the archeological finds. At this period a more or less standard form of dwelling had developed, with its size and furnishings reflecting the social position of the master of the house. There were large villas for high-ranking administrative officials, with an area of up to 4305 ft^2 (400 m^2), and small houses of only 269 to 332 ft^2 (25 to 30 m^2). The outside walls were usually plastered and then painted in a shade of white or yellow. The roof was generally used as a living area, and a high wall around the property was also common, to shelter the family from the wind and the prying eyes of outsiders. However, cellars like those at Deir el-Medineh were the exception and not the rule. A house of good size in el-Amarna, for instance, typically built on a slightly raised masonry base, was entered through a small anteroom, leading into a broad hall supported on four wooden columns and with rooms on both sides of it. From here one would gain access to the main and central room of the

Sarcophagus of Ashait (detail): granary, Eleventh Dynasty, ca. 2040 B.C., Western Thebes, Deir el-Bahri, mortuary temple of Mentuhotep II, limestone, H. 97 cm, Egyptian Museum, Cairo

property, used principally for formal purposes. Its roof was higher than that of the other rooms around it, and spaces left open in the top part of the wall admitted light and air. At the back of the house lay such private living rooms as the sitting room, a bedroom with a niche to take the bed, and a bathroom with a wash basin and lavatory seat. The dwelling house itself could be surrounded by courtyards and gardens, or by such domestic buildings as barns, sheds and stables for animals, ovens, and workshops, so that the whole extensive layout had the character of a manor house and farm.

Although hardly any items of the indoor furnishing of houses have been found during archeological excavations, we are well informed about them. According to Egyptian

beliefs, the dead would require their everyday utensils in the next world as well, and such things are an important component of tomb furnishings. Not all household items, of course, were represented, and many single objects were specially made for use as grave goods. Taken as a whole, however, all these finds from tombs provide a clear picture of the material wealth of Egyptian culture, and it is supplemented by the many detailed depictions on wall reliefs and paintings.

Among the most common items of furniture in prosperous houses were various forms of seating, their manufacture depending on the financial means of the master of the house. Besides simple stools, there were folding chairs and armchairs with high backs. The seat usually had leather stretched over it or was made of woven plant fibers. The low bedsteads, with legs in the shape of the hooves of cattle, were covered with similar materials. The Egyptians had also a great facility for making light furniture for use when travelling or on military campaigns. Most famous is the travelling bedroom set of Queen Hetepheres, mother of Khofu (4th Dynasty, ca. 2560 B.C.). With the tomb equipment of Tutankhamun a

Jewelry casket of Tuya, Eighteenth Dynasty, ca. 1370 B.C., Valley of the Kings, tomb of Yuya and Tuya (KV 46), wood, ivory, faience, H. 43 cm, Egyptian Museum, Cairo

Chair of Kha, Eighteenth Dynasty, ca. 1400 B.C., Western Thebes, Deir el-Medineh, tomb of Kha (TT 8), painted wood, H. 91 cm, Museo Egizio, Turin

Small cosmetic Vessel, Eighteenth Dynasty, ca. 1300 B.C., polychrome glass, H. 10 cm. Musée du Louvre, Paris

Cosmetic container in the shape of the god Bes, Eighteenth Dynasty, 1350 B.C., polychrome faience, H. 8.4 cm. Musée du Louvre, Paris

folding bed was discovered which could not be surpassed by a modern example. Small tables and shelves, usually made of wood, served to hold objects of many different kinds. However, dining tables as we know them were unknown. Chests of various sizes and designs held personal possessions, including jewelry, clothes, wigs, and cosmetics. Just as meticulous cleanliness was observed in the house to keep vermin away, the upper classes paid close attention to their daily personal hygiene. Vessels containing eye make-up, ointments, perfumed essences, combs, hairpins, and mirrors, many of them artistic masterpieces in miniature, were kept in separate little caskets. Cosmetic jars of opaque glass, which was not made in Egypt until the early Eighteenth Dynasty, were regarded as special luxury items in the New Kingdom. The classic forms of cosmetic containers made of stone and faience were now joined by purely figurative types, like the example shown, made in the form of the gnome-like god Bes, who was much venerated as the protective spirit of the home.

The family was at the center of the Egyptian social structure. Normally it was organized around a monogamous marriage, and consisted of the parents and their underage children. This nuclear family formed a household that could be extended by the addition of a varying number of servants. The acknowledged aim of a marriage was to engender children, as stated in Ptahhotep's famous maxim: "If you are prosperous, if you have founded a household, and if you love your wife as you should, then fill her belly and clothe her back. Make her heart rejoice as long as you live, for she is a fruitful field for her lord." The most important task incumbent on children was to perform the mortuary ritual for their dead parents, in order keep their memory alive in the next world and ensure their survival beyond the tomb. From the Old Kingdom onward, countless depictions on tomb walls and stelae show offerings being made to provide for the married couple in the next world. The occupant of the tomb and his wife sit at the funerary repast or with other goods of theirs, or are portrayed in marital or family statuary groups.

In many ways the wife was legally equal to her husband, although that did not in principle affect his superior position as head of the household and breadwinner. Women could appear before a court of law, enter into contracts independently, and even leave their own property as they liked. They were responsible for the raising of children up to a certain age; after that the sons were educated by their father, or if they showed aptitude might attend a temple school, which opened up the chance of a career in the administration. Despite the ideal of lifelong marriage, divorce was not unknown, and a father tells his daughter: "You are my good daughter. Should your husband turn you out of the house you two have prepared, then you can live in the hall of my storehouse."

Right: the mayor Sennefer and his wife Senai, Eighteenth Dynasty, ca. 1410 B.C., Karnak, temple of Amun-Re, granodiorite, H. 120 cm, Egyptian Museum, Cairo

Family group of the dwarf Seneb, Fourth/Fifth Dynasties, ca. 2475 B.C., Giza, mastaba of Seneb, painted limestone, H. 34 cm, Egyptian Museum, Cairo

The Private Tombs of Western Thebes

The western mountain range of Thebes was originally thought to be the border between this world and the next, and served not only the rulers of the New Kingdom and their families as a final resting place, but also many private persons since the time of the Old Kingdom: administrative officials, military officers, and priests. From north to south the private tombs, over 500 of which have been discovered so far, form the necropolis areas of el-Tarif, Dra Abu el-Naga, Asasif, Khokha, Sheikh Abdel-Qurna (picture below), Qurnet Murai, and Deir el-Medineh. As a rule each tomb had an accessible part for the funerary cult, and an inaccessible underground part for the mummy and its grave goods. The cult area consisted of a courtyard and at least one chamber driven into the rock itself—the reverse T-shape with a long hall and a shorter transept is usual—a niche for the dead man's statue, and a small pyramid over the entrance. If the quality of the limestone outcrop was good enough, the ornamentation was carved in relief, but it was generally executed as painting over a layer of plaster thinned with straw. The size of the tomb complex usually allows us to draw conclusions about the social status of its occupant.

Tomb of Rekhmire (TT 100)

Eighteenth Dynasty, ca. 1450 B.C.

Nubian tribute

Rekhmire, vizier under Thutmosis III and Amenophis II, had his tomb laid out on an elevated site in the cemetery of Sheikh Abdel-Qurna. Its size and the wealth of its decorative motifs make it one of the most important tombs in Thebes, and in addition it contains a unique text known as the "Instructions to the Vizier," describing the tasks incumbent on the holder of that office. In the transept of the hall, to the right of the entrance, the decoration includes scenes showing the produce of different parts of the country, the preparation of royal statues for the New Year festival, and the owner of the tomb fowling and fishing in the marshes. On the other side of the entrance hall, Rekhmire is depicted supervising the taxation revenues from Upper Egypt and deliveries of tribute from abroad (Punt, Nubia, Syria, the Aegean). Various exotic animals from Nubia such as cheetahs and giraffes are portrayed, as well as ivory, skins, and ostrich eggs. The long hall, which has a ceiling rising perceptibly in the direction of the false door and the niche for the statue, contains scenes showing a number of craft activities, a royal boat procession, and the ritual of burial in a very detailed version with 50 separate scenes. From the original tomb equipment not a single item had survived, except the monumental granite false door (Louvre, C 74; H. 1.46 m).

Making bricks

The left-hand wall of the long hall in the tomb of Rekhmire contains the famous scenes of craftsmen at work which provide us with much information about the procedures of the time. They include depictions of the making of mud bricks, the most commonly used building material in Egypt. The mass of material, which consisted of diluted Nile mud, sometimes mixed with sand, chaff, or ash, was poured into a wooden frame and smoothed flat. The frame was then removed and used for the next brick. Long rows of such bricks were set out to dry side by side, and in special cases were stamped with the royal seal.

Sandal makers

Although most people in Egypt went barefoot, sandal making was a highly regarded trade. On the one hand fine sandals were regarded as a status symbol, particularly when they were a gift from the king, on the other they were a necessary protection for the feet if one was working in a mountainous region. Leather sandals were as desirable as they were expensive; a pair would cost an ordinary workman almost a quarter of his monthly wages. The depictions here (workers in the upper register) are of the stretching of the leather, the boring of holes in the soles and leather uppers, and the sandal maker's tools.

Rekhmire at the offering table

At the end of the long hall, immediately in front of the back wall with the false door, the occupant of the tomb is shown at the offering table with his wife Merit. This scene is repeated on both right and left, in several registers arranged one above another. Rekhmire is wearing the vizier's kilt and holds a scepter in his right hand; his left hand is stretched out to the offering table. One of his sons was once shown standing in front of the laden sacred table, but his figure has been completely chipped away. The reason for effacing him may lie in the political changes at the beginning of the reign of Amenophis II. The new king seems to have disliked the great influence wielded by Rekhmire and the members of his family, who held many important posts, and he soon retired the vizier. He himself favored another family, that of Sennefer, the friend of his youth. Rekhmire's eldest son, who might perhaps have been expected to succeed to the post of vizier, fell into disfavor, which would explain why his picture was erased, but not the representation of his father.

Tomb of Ramose (TT 55)

Eighteenth Dynasty, ca. 1360 B.C.

Funeral procession (detail)

Ramose, vizier under Amenophis III and during the early years of the reign of Amenophis IV (Akhenaten), also laid out his tomb in Sheikh Abdel-Qurna. Although the tomb was not completed because of his early death, it clearly reflects the upheavals following the change of government. Only the entrance hall with its four sets of eight columns was partially decorated. Larger-scale scenes in fine relief feature on the entrance walls, but the medium changed to painting on the left-hand side wall. The entire length of this wall is devoted to a funeral procession. It shows the coffin and canopic shrine being carried to the tomb, the bearers of offerings and grave goods, the accompanying priests and female mourners, the ritual outside the tomb, and the dead man's meeting with Osiris. Striking features are the diversity of motifs and the manner of composition, with many overlapping and graduated figures. On the back wall of the hall Ramose appears twice before Amenophis IV, who is depicted in the traditional manner on the left, while the right-hand scene (showing the royal family in the Window of Appearance) is executed in the new style of the time, known as the Amarna style.

The Banquet

The couples depicted here are among the guests at a banquet held in honor of the dead vizier. Those present are his relations and high dignitaries from the ranks of the administration, including the famous sage Amenophis, son of Hapu. The importance of the vizier was highlighted by a statement (elsewhere) that: "there was nothing of which he was ignorant in heaven, in earth, or in any quarter of the Netherworld." This banquet is on the left wall of the entrance to the tomb of Ramose. The pictures bear expressive witness to the high quality of relief techniques in the time of Amenophis III. The delicate modeling of the features, the varied details of the wigs, robes and jewelry, executed in the finest carving, are evidence of an artistic desire to achieve the highest esthetic perfection. The painting was not completed; only the black color on the eyes and eyebrows has been applied. Although the figures look almost the same at first sight because of their identical seated attitudes and their arrangement in pairs, even brief examination soon shows that no one figure is exactly like another.

The Ritual of purification

The purification of the tomb owner is depicted on the right-hand wall of the entrance to the tomb. Two priests, one on each side, are pouring water over him. Ramose wears the vizier's robe drawn high up over his chest and held in place by a narrow band around the neck. He is holding a staff and a scepter resembling a key, which should be regarded as a sign of office. He is adorned with the traditional collar and bracelets, and also wears a heavy necklace, the so-called "Gold of Honor" consisting of two rows of disk-shaped golden beads and a long chain with a heart-shaped amulet. The inscription in front of his face gives his name and his vizier's title, and further describes him as "honored by the sun god." In real life we must assume that this act of purification, associated with the "opening of the mouth" ritual, was performed on the mummy as well as the statue of the deceased; he had to be pure on entering the tomb and passing into the next world, as funerary texts emphasize over and over again. This very elaborate ritual involved other actions beside purification, such as censing, anointing and incantations.

Tomb of Sennefer (TT 96)

Eighteenth Dynasty, ca. 1410 B.C.

The tomb owner with his wife

Sennefer, mayor of Thebes, was a boyhood companion and close friend of king Amenophis II. His family also enjoyed high esteem; one of Sennefer's brothers held the office of vizier. Not only the cult area but also the burial chamber of Sennefer's tomb bore fine decoration; the latter lay twelve meters down and was reached along a steep, low-roofed stairway. The elegant style of the murals and a part of the ceiling showing a grape vine have made this complex famous. On the left of the entrance Sennefer is seated with his wife Merit, who held the title of temple singer of Amun. He is holding a scepter signifying high rank, and she has a lotus flower in her hand. After his death, Sennefer was granted the extremely unusual privilege of interment not in his magnificent tomb in Sheikh Abdel-Qurna but in the Valley of the Kings, by order of Amenophis II. Although his burial chamber there was undecorated, its proximity to all the dead divine rulers compensated for that disadvantage.

The voyage to Abydos

The most important series of pictures on the western wall is devoted to the pilgrimage to Abydos, center of the cult of Osiris, the supreme judge of the dead. The official and his wife sit under a canopy in a papyrus skiff which is being pulled along the river by a rowing boat. A priest is in attendance, with offerings. The aim was to win the favor of Osiris so that he would be well disposed to the pilgrims when the dead later came to judgement. Only thus could they be transfigured beyond the tomb and lead eternal life. However, as not everyone could really make this pilgrimage, pictorial magic allowed a depiction of the voyage to Abydos in the tomb to serve as a substitute.

In the Netherworld

Three large scenes occupy the northern wall of the burial chamber: the purification ritual for the owner of the tomb; his mummification; and his meeting with the gods Osiris and Anubis. As part of the ritual of the "opening of the mouth" a *sem* (class of priests, wearing the skin of a leopard) is pouring a stream of water over Sennefer and his wife. Both have already got over the judgement of the dead, and are now moving on "in peace" to meet Osiris. The mayor is wearing a double heart amulet on a chain, and a great deal of jewelry. Merit is holding a *menat* (a collar with a counterweight) in front of her breast, and a hooped sistrum in her left hand, indicating her title of temple singer.

Tomb of Menena (TT 69)

Eighteenth Dynasty, ca. 1395 B.C.

Field inspectors at work

Under King Thutmosis IV the scribe Menena was responsible in Thebes for surveying the agricultural land and assessing the yield of the crops. His tomb, which he had built for him in Sheikh Abdel-Qurna, consists as usual of an entrance passage, a long hall, a transept, and a niche in the rock for a statuary group of Menena and his wife. The scenes showing the occupant of the tomb in the course of his professional work (on the left wall of the entrance to the transept) are particularly detailed. Menena, described here as "Scribe of the Lord of the Two Lands," is standing in a light pavilion supervising work in the fields. Four assistant scribes kneeling on the ground behind him are noting down the yield of the harvest on papyrus rolls. A second group of scribes is standing by the harvested grain itself, noting down every bushel (a measure of capacity, 1 oipe probably = 9 pints; 19.21 l) as the labourers fill the measures before them. Another scribe is sitting in the middle of the pile of grain and seems to be counting along with them on his fingers. Above him there is a chest with a closed lid, probably used to contain the records and the writing utensils needed by the scribes.

The grain harvest

Although the ancient Egyptian calendar indicates that there was only one harvest season, the fertility of the soil in the valley of the Nile made it possible to grow more than one crop a year in many places. The tomb of Menena not only depicts the recording of the yield in detail but also shows work in the fields. After the grain had been cut with sickles, it was put into large baskets and carried by men or donkeys to the threshing floor. Here the

ears were raked into a heap and oxen were driven over them to separate the grain from the husks; the grain was then winnowed to remove the chaff. Most of the harvest yield was then taken to central granaries and distributed by the granary administrators. These processes are shown in a very attractive way, and in great detail, in the tomb murals. The men on the threshing floor, for instance, have tied cloths around their hair to protect it from the chaff and dust, but not the men who are transporting and raking up the ears.

Small genre scenes also feature, like the two girls tussling with each other in the field, and a tree with two workmen sitting under it. One of them has nodded off, while his companion is passing the time by playing a pipe. These subsidiary scenes from life (and shown on a small scale because they are not the main subject) seem to have been regarded as particularly attractive centuries later, since several of them were copied in the tombs of Theban officials of the Late Period (Twenty-fifth/Twenty-sixth Dynasties).

Tomb of Nakht (TT 52)

Eighteenth Dynasty, ca. 1390 B.C.

Ladies at a Banquet

Nakht, scribe and "hour-priest of Amun," lived at the time of Thutmosis IV and Amenophis III. Although his tomb is very small, the scenes in the transept are among the most famous in ancient Egyptian painting because of their high esthetic value and formerly good state of preservation. The back left-hand wall shows scenes of a banquet held in honor of the deceased. The female guests are squatting on papyrus mats in two groups behind a harpist with a very impressive posture of his fingers at play. All ladies are richly robed and wear perfume cones on their wigs. A nearly naked maidservant is helping to adjust their gold earrings.

Three musicians

In the lower register, the guests at the banquet are being entertained by three musicians playing the harp, lute, and double flute. The young women wear wreaths of flowers and ointment cones on their elaborate wigs, rich jewelry, and elegant clothes. While the women on the left and right are clad in white linen robes, the lutenist in the middle wears only the narrow belt of a dancing girl. As she walks forward, she is turning her head to look at the flute player behind her, thus giving coherence to the composition of the group. It is because of the elegance of the girls' movements and the charm of the faces, with their large, slanting almond eyes, that the scene exerts such a powerful fascination on viewers today. However, also here style rules supreme, not individuality.

Hunting in the marshes

A hunt in a papyrus thicket is one of the most traditional themes in the pictorial program of private tombs, found from the Old Kingdom onward. The scene not only conveys the pleasure of a family hunting expedition but must also be seen as a cult action. It is connected on the one hand with the taming and exploitation of nature, and on the other with the mythical nature of the papyrus thicket, which promises protection and regeneration. This scene is located on the right-hand back wall of the transept in the tomb of Nakht. The owner of the tomb is shown twice, in opposite attitudes. In both depictions he is standing on a papyrus skiff, in a striding position with legs wide apart, and accompanied by his wife and daughters. The male figure on the extreme right may be a son. On the right-hand side of the picture Nakht is harpooning two fish, which are being pulled out of the river along with the water around them (the "water mound"). Although the gesture is that of a man harpooning, the weapon in his hand is not rendered. On the other side, he has swung back the throwing stick (originals made from wood; the assumed boomerang effect is uncertain) used to hunt birds, and is already holding a goose by its feet. A flock of startled waterfowl is flying over the stylized plantation of the papyrus thicket.

Tomb of Userhat (TT 56)

Eighteenth Dynasty, ca. 1400 B.C.

Userhat hunting in the desert

The tomb of Userhat, who held many administrative offices under Amenophis II, lies in Sheikh Abdel-Qurna, not far to the south of the great tomb complex of Ramose (TT 55). Userhat's functions included those of a "true royal scribe," and a "scribe of provision in Upper and Lower Egypt," whose duty it was to supply the officials with grain for bread. The architecture of his tomb follows the standard pattern of a Theban private tomb, with a long hall and a transept. Several hunting scenes are united on the left-hand wall of the back room; the desert hunt deserves particular attention. Userhat is pressing forward in his chariot at a gallop, as in scenes showing royal hunts, and has looped the reins of both horses around his body. He is concentrating hard as he bends his bow and lets the arrow fly at the animals, who are shown in wild confusion, their coats colored in different shades of ocher. Various species of gazelles and antelopes, along with hyenas, ostriches, and hares can be made out in this fine composition, showing the animals either struck down or in flight. The whole composition of this marvelous scene demonstrates the outstanding ability of the artists working in Thebes.

In the commissariat

The right-hand back wall of the transept is covered with a pictorial area divided into two. On the inside, Userhat comes before his master King Amenophis II, who is enthroned in a kiosk, and gives him a large arrangement of offerings consisting of flowers and fruits. The accompanying text explains that it shows: "The bringing of all manner of beautiful flowers to his Majesty by the excellent one, the close friend of his lord, he who is commended by the good god (…)." The rest of the wall up to the doorway is occupied by a single large scene illustrating the distribution of provisions to the army. Although Userhat does not appear himself, he was obviously responsible for this function too. On the right is the commissariat building, with two doors leading into it. 14 officers in all are sitting in its courtyard, their differences of rank shown by the way they are arranged on four small registers and the various kinds of supplies with which they are concerned. The soldiers are drawn up in pairs in several ranks outside the gates of the commissariat to receive their bread ration, which is being brought out by the staff of the office (below right). A unique genre scene (below left) concludes the series of pictures, showing soldiers visiting the barber. While most of the men are squatting on the ground or on small folding stools, dozing, two of their comrades are already having their hair cut.

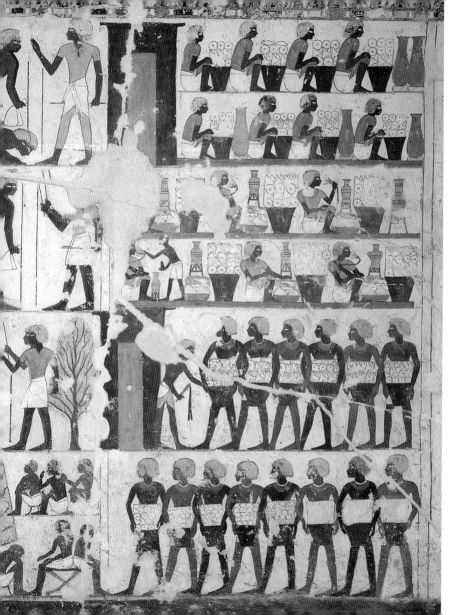

Shabti Figures—Servants for the Netherworld

Among the most typical objects found as grave goods in tombs from the Middle Kingdom onward are the mummiform figurines known as *shabti*s. The oldest examples were shaped like naked human bodies, made of wax or Nile mud, and were regarded as a substitute image in case the mummy in the tomb was destroyed. The change to representing the *shabti*s as mummiform figures took place in the Twelfth Dynasty, and was to remain the rule into the Ptolemaic period. At first the figurines were inscribed with the owner's name alone, and an offering formula was unusual. Not until the time of the transition from the Twelfth to the Thirteenth Dynasties does a longer text first appear, described as the *shabti* formula and quoting Spell 6 of the *Book of the Dead*. It explains the task of the *shabti*, who is to do menial labor instead of the dead person in the next world: "O *shabti*, if I be summoned to do any work which has to be done in the realm of the dead—to make arable the fields, to irrigate the land, or to convey sand from east to west; 'Here am I,' you shall say, 'I shall do it.'" The important point is that the *shabti*s were to obey the orders of the god, deputizing for the occupant of the tomb. The requisite implements—a pick, an adze, bags, baskets, and vessels—

Shabti figure of Sati, Eighteenth Dynasty, ca. 1320 B.C., probably Saqqara, polychrome faience, H. 25 cm, Brooklyn Museum, New York

might be placed in the tomb in the form of small models made of such materials as faience, but were usually painted or incised on the figurines themselves.

While *shabti*s were initially used only for private persons, they began to be placed in the tombs of rulers from the beginning of the New Kingdom. As well as the standard kinds, made of wood or faience, examples in stone now became increasingly frequent. Large shabits made of red granite, for instance, were found in the tomb of Amenophis III. Altogether, the royal tombs revealed a great variety in their size, material and quality. With Tutankhamun a staggering 413 figures were buried, and the final resting place of Sety I once held an even higher number. The number of *shabti*s seems to have been arbitrary until the number of 365 statuettes became established in the Nineteenth Dynasty, a servant for every day of the year. In addition, there could be *shabti* overseers, ideally one for every ten figures. Occasionally they also had a chief overseer. Because of the great demand, mass production of *shabti*s began in the late New Kingdom, and these specimens were seldom of very high quality. The *shabti* figures were put into painted boxes and placed in the burial chamber near the coffin.

Shabti figure of Sety I, Nineteenth Dynasty, ca. 1280 B.C., Western Thebes, Valley of the Kings, blue faience, H. 22.4 cm, British Museum, London

Shabti figure of Upuat-mes, early Nineteenth Dynasty, ca. 1280 B.C., Saqqara, ebony, H. 25 cm, Rijksmuseum van Oudheden, Leiden

Deir el-Medineh

At the beginning of the Eighteenth Dynasty, by order of King Thutmosis I, a well-guarded settlement was founded in a small depression of the mountains at Western Thebes, at a place now known as Deir el-Medineh. The craftsmen who worked on the royal necropolises, the Valley of the Kings, lived here with their families. They were called "servants in the place of truth," were regarded as the guardians of secrets because they knew so much about the situation and contents of the royal tombs, and were directly answerable to the vizier. The houses, in Deir el-Medineh laid out along a broad main street and several side streets, were enclosed by a town wall. Each house had four to five rooms, a cellar, and an upper floor with a terrace. We are very well informed about the community of artists and workmen who lived here, because a considerable number of the outdated daily notes and documents they made have been found in the large pit dug to take the garbage of the village. The people of Deir el-Medineh used the mountain slope rising behind the settlement to the east for making their tombs, which were of only modest extent, but are among the finest examples of ancient Egyptian art because of the brilliance and individuality of their paintings.

Tomb of Sennedjem (TT 1)

Nineteenth Dynasty, ca. 1250 B.C.

In February 1886 the family tomb of Sennedjem, a worker in the necropolis at the time of Ramesses II, was uncovered at Deir el-Medineh and found to have escaped the attention of tomb robbers. Although the superstructure of the tomb, consisting of an entrance pylon, an open courtyard, and three brick pyramids, had been largely destroyed, the underground part was extremely well preserved. One of three shafts led to a painted and sealed wooden door (H. 135 cm, Egyptian Museum, Cairo). The outside of the door bears representations of Sennedjem and his family before the gods Osiris and Ptah-Sokar-Osiris; the inside shows Sennedjem and his wife playing a board game. They are both wearing long pleated garments, and are sitting on chairs with feet shaped like lion's claws, in front of the *senet* game board and a richly laden offering table. A long inscription contains Spell 72 of the *Book of the Dead*, supposed to guarantee the care of the dead and their free movement in the Netherworld. The excavators found 20 mummies behind this door, some of them in anthropoid coffins, and the entire funerary furnishings of the tomb. The burial chamber itself is completely painted, and depicts motifs such as: the voyage of the sun god through the underworld; Osiris, the god of the dead; the Field of Reeds; and the mummification of the dead man by Anubis.

The Blessed in the "Field of Reeds" (with detail)

The Field of Reeds is depicted on the eastern wall of Sennedjem's burial chamber; at the top, the falcon-headed sun god is traveling in his barque, and is greeted by the raised arms of two solar monkeys (hamadryas baboons). This representation of the "Iaru" fields is a vignette associated with Spell 110 from the *Book of the Dead*, which was thought to ensure the existence of the deceased in the next world. The heading states this idea very explicitly: "Spells of the fields of offerings (…) to till the soil and gather harvest there, to eat and drink there, to have sexual intercourse there and do everything that is done on earth." The picture associated with these words shows a region surrounded by the underground Nile, with various motifs. In the upper register, Sennedjem and his wife are praying before a group of gods squatting on the ground, headed by the great national triad of the Ramesside period: "A prayer to Re-Horakhty, we kiss the ground before Osiris, first among those of the west, may he praise the *ka* of Sennedjem, servant in the places of truth, the justified one, to Ptah, lord of *maat*." Next comes Sennedjem's son Rahotep in a papyrus skiff, while his other son Khonsu is performing the ceremony of the opening of the mouth for his father's mummy. In the two registers below, husband and wife are shown working the soil, sowing grain, and then harvesting wheat and flax. On the extreme right the occupant of the tomb kneels at an offering table, smelling an outsize lotus flower. Two narrow registers at the bottom show a rich flora, with sycamore fig trees, doum palms and date palms, poppies and cornflowers, and beautiful mandragora blooms.

The solar barque

Vignettes illustrating the most important spells from the *Book of the Dead* are depicted on the vaulted ceiling of the funeral chamber. They include Spell 100, which assures the deceased that he can travel in the sun god's barque "to any place where he would wish to be." The pictorial motif shows the solar barque, with its bows and stern formed like papyrus umbels. The *benu* bird, described by the Greeks as a phoenix and resembling a heron, stands at the front of the barque, wearing the *atef* crown, as a symbol of regeneration. Its cult in the "Phoenix House" of Heliopolis was mentioned as early as the pyramid texts of the Old Kingdom. It is followed by the falcon-headed sun god Re-Horakhty-Atum, and by a group of five gods standing in the boat to represent the great Ennead as we learn by the given inscription.

The "Sycamore of heaven"

Care for the dead is the central concern of the 59th spell in the *Book of the Dead*: "that they may breathe air and having power over water in the realm of the dead." Sennedjem and his wife Iineferti, clothed in fine linen robes and wearing festival wigs with tall ointment cones, are kneeling on top of their tomb, holding up their hands up in a beseeching gesture. Nut, the sky goddess, rises from the trunk of a sycamore or mulberry fig to receive them as souls found righteous in the judgment of the dead, and to give them food and drink. This idea is conveyed in pictorial terms by the way in which Nut pours water over the couple's outstretched hands and gives them food standing on a mat. The brief inscription merely states the names and titles of the participants.

Tomb of Onuris-kha (TT 359)

Twentieth Dynasty, ca. 1140 B.C.

Ceiling painting with heads of bulls

The last resting place of Onuris-kha (or Inherkan) who was in office as foreman of a workgang at Deir el-Medineh for over thirty years (time of Ramesses III – Ramesses VI) lies close to the tomb of Sennedjem. The shaft running down from the forecourt of the tomb leads to two richly decorated underground chambers. The scenes in the upper anteroom are mainly from the "Book of Gates" and the *Book of the Dead*, and there is also a brief list

of kings, with the patrons of Deir el-Medineh, king Amenophis I, and his mother Ahmes-Nefertari. The ceiling was decorated with separate ornamental fields and lines of inscription. The field with the repeated motif of bulls' heads facing forward, each with a solar disk on its head, is outstanding. The "bukranion," or bull's head, first features in the iconography of Egypt during the New Kingdom and probably came from Crete and the Minoan region in the first place. A floral collar of red and green rows of petals can be seen below each head. Bands of yellow spirals separate the rows of bulls' heads from each other laterally.

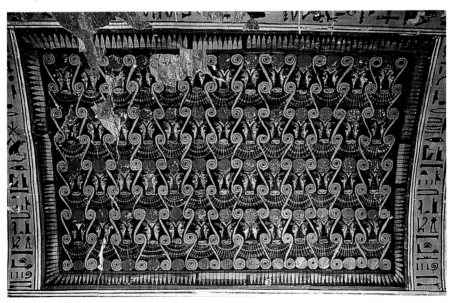

The family of Onuris-kha

The walls of the burial chamber of Onuris-kha are entirely covered with pictures arranged in three registers on a yellow ground. The bottom register rises from a broad base decorated with the highly stylized representation of a palace façade. The right wall shows the occupant of the tomb seated, with his entire family. His wife has placed one arm around his shoulders; the other is raised in greeting. They are both looking towards funerary objects given to them by one of their sons: a small painted figure of the Osiris and a wooden box (probably for shabti figures). The couple's four grandchildren are playing in the foreground. As children they are depicted naked, but already wear collars, bracelets and earrings. The girls' hairstyle—single locks, with the head shaven in between them—is unusual, and so is the gesture of Onuris-kha, who appears to be running his fingers lovingly through one of these locks of hair of his favorite granddaughter.

The Harper and his Song

This scene depicts an older musician, a harper squatting on a mat and playing to the owner of the tomb and his wife. While Onuris-Kha holds a scepter as a sign of his dignity, his wife has one hand raised in greeting. The harper has both hands on the strings of the instrument before him, and his mouth is open to sing. His eyes are shown closed, which may be taken to indicate either that he is blind or that he is concentrating on his singing. The text of his song is contained in the inscription behind him. This text, the "harper's song," already known in the Middle Kingdom, speaks of the transience of life, the beauty of this world, and the uncertainty of the next. It therefore urges listeners to enjoy life to the full and not to complain, for "none who departs comes back again, and none is allowed to take his goods with him."

Temple of Hathor at Deir el-Medineh

Ptolemaic period, 3rd–1st century B.C.

This small Ptolemaic temple lies slightly to the north of the settlement inside a high brick wall, and was dedicated to Hathor as the goddess who protected the dead, and to Maat as the goddess presiding over their judgment. The interior of the temple (founded in the time of Amenophis III, 18th Dynasty) consists of three sanctuary rooms, with depictions showing Ptolemy IV with his sister Arsinoë, Ptolemy VI, and Ptolemy VII before the gods. The close connection of the temple with the mortuary cult is particularly clear in the left-hand chapel, where there is an extensive representation of the judgment of the dead. The slightly raised offering table area in front of the chapels, from which steps lead up to the roof, again shows the Ptolemaic rulers making offerings before two rows of gods (right). Two columns with composite capitals and columnar barriers mark the transition to the undecorated entrance area. Many graffiti inscribed on the stone show that this temple was converted into a Coptic monastery in the Christian era, as the modern place-name Deir el-Medineh—"Monastery of the town"—indicates.

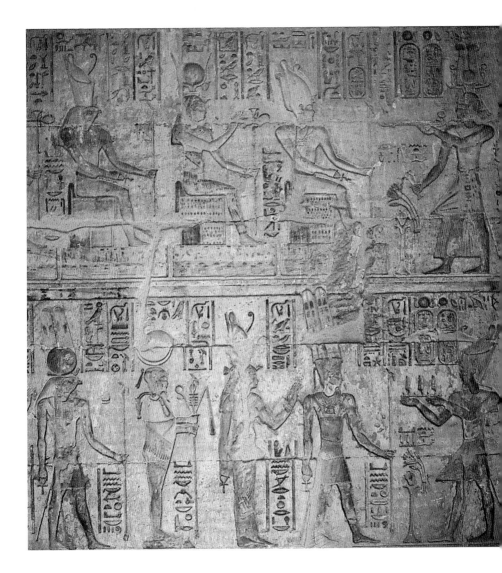

In the Words of the Tomb Robbers

The late Twentieth Dynasty period was marked by internal unrest and a noticeable rise in the crime rate. The dead themselves were not safe from thieves, and even the royal graves in the necropolis of Western Thebes were robbed. A series of papyri from the time of Ramesses IX (1125–1107 B.C.) and Ramesses XI (1103–1070/1069 B.C.), containing records of trials, lists of suspects, descriptions of impounded loot and accounts of tomb inspections give a picture of the situation. The discovery of the first robberies came about as the result of a political conflict between the mayor of the eastern bank of Thebes, Paser, and the mayor of the western bank, Pawer-aa. Intending to harm his rival, Paser went to the vizier claiming that the tombs in the Valley of the Kings and Queens, for which Pawer-aa was responsible, had been plundered. The accusation in fact turned out to be false, but nonetheless, it was found that several private tombs had indeed been robbed, and so had the tomb of King Sobekemsaf II and his wife of the Seventeenth Dynasty (ca. 1600 B.C.), which was a particularly serious matter. The

Papyrus Abbot: record of the trial of tomb robbers, Twentieth Dynasty, ca. 1100 B.C., papyrus, L. 218 cm, The British Museum, London

trial records from the 16th year of the reign of Ramesses IX (1110 B.C.) contain the full confession of the criminals. It runs, literally: "We opened their sarcophagi (…) and found the venerable mummy of this king (…). It was all covered with gold, and its coffins were adorned with gold and silver both inside and out, and inlaid with many precious stones. We collected the gold (…) together with his amulets and jewels (…). We found the queen in exactly the same state (i.e. adorned). We gathered up what we found and set fire to their coffins. We divided the gold (…) into eight parts, 20 *deben* (4 lb; 1.82 kg of gold) for each of us."

View into the burial chamber with its robbed sarcophagus at the time of its discovery in 1908, Valley of the Kings, tomb of Horemheb (KV 57), Eighteenth Dynasty, ca. 1300 B.C.

The flourishing trade in tomb robbery in the Theban necropolis toward the end of the New Kingdom, and during the following Twenty-first Dynasty, was certainly encouraged by the country's poor economic state, but its extent can hardly be regarded as the sole work of bands of tomb robbers in the classic sense. Instead, the threatened bankruptcy of the state (among other problems, no more gold was coming in from Nubia) forced its rulers to resort to its only available resources of any value, the gold in the royal tombs. Under orders from the authorities in Upper Egypt and the high priesthood of Amun, and in an operation carried out by their officials with the requisite secrecy, the objects in the tombs were stripped of even the thinnest covering of gold leaf, and items made of solid precious metals were melted down. Piety did still extend to reburial of the mummies of the divine kings themselves (see p. 116 ff) in a hidden communal tomb, the famous Royal cache of Deir el-Bahri at Western Thebes. With the rediscovery of Egypt in the 19th century, modern forms of tomb robbery and illegal trade immediately developed, and are practised to the present day.

From Esna to Kom Ombo

Esna

Previous pages: The great courtyard in the Horus Temple of Edfu, from: David Roberts, "Egypt and Nubia," London 1846–1850

Temple of Khnum
Ptolemaic and Roman Period,
2nd century B.C. – 3rd century A.D.

Around 37 miles (60 km) south of Luxor on the west bank of the Nile lies the city of Esna. Here, only the spectacular pronaos remains of the town's temple to Khnum, the ram-headed god of creation. As Esna's ground level has been raised by some 30 ft. (9 m) since antiquity the visitor now has to descend a ladder to view the site. The Greco-Roman building replaced an older temple complex which had stood in Esna since the Eighteenth Dynasty of the New Kingdom. Begun under Ptolemy VI (221–204 B.C.), the decoration of the new building was largely carried out in the 1st and 2nd centuries A.D. during Roman rule (by the emperors Claudius, Vespasian and Trajan among others), though the most recent relief dates from the reign of Emperor Decius (249–251 A.D.). The façade of the pronaos features characteristically high partition walls (intercolumnar slabs) which separate the rear temple building from the courtyard. Inside, the roof is supported by a total of 24 columns whose capitals, with their elaborately carved plant motifs, are among the finest of their kind. One of the most interesting features in the Esna temple are the detailed texts on the

column shafts whose contents are largely taken from mythology (such as the story of creation).

On the walls, Roman emperors in the regalia of the pharaohs can be seen making offerings to a number of gods. Of historical interest is the depiction of the emperor Septimius Severus with his wife, Julia Domna, and their sons, Caracalla and Geta, who visited Egypt in 199 A.D., (south wall). After his murder in 212 A.D., both the figure and name of Geta were chiseled out —as indeed they were elsewhere in the Roman Empire. Two cryptographic hymns in the interior above the external partition wall are also worthy of interest. They consist almost exclusively of ram and crocodile hieroglyphs and have so far escaped a satisfactory interpretation.

Emperor Commodus hunting birds
Roman Period, end of the 2nd century A.D.

This depiction stands out from the surrounding offering scenes on the basis of its size alone. It shows the pharaoh—here, the Emperor Commodus—in mid stride holding the rope from a vast net filled with birds and fish. The monarch is flanked by the gods Khnum and Horus who assist him in drawing the net tight. The image does not refer to an actual hunt but is instead borrowed from the symbolic vocabulary used for Egypt's enemies. Hunting birds was synonymous with destroying the enemies of the king; this kind of magic spell in artistic form could therefore help to render these foes harmless and defeated.

Elkab

The City

The city of Elkab lies on the banks of the Nile around 50 miles (80 km) south of Luxor and today it is easily reached by the Aswan road. Together with its sister city Hierakonpolis on the west bank, Elkab—known as Nekheb in ancient times—is one of the most respected sites in Egypt and has a tradition of settlement stretching back to the Early dynastic era. Elkab was considered the main cult site of the vulture goddess Nekhbet, the goddess of the crown and land of Upper Egypt. This deity was equated by the Greeks with their goddess Eileithyia, for which reason Elkab is also known as Eileithiaspolis. The city is surrounded by a massive enclosure wall (621 × 588 yds, 570 × 540 m) of unfired mud brick pierced by three entry gates. The enclosure wall as well as the residential areas within the precinct were grievously damaged in the 19th century when local farmers dug up the ruins in order to use the bricks as fertilizer for their fields. The condition of the various temples is scarcely any better: situated in the southwest corner of the city they have been virtually razed to their foundations.

From the New Kingdom on, a number of kings modified the main temple of

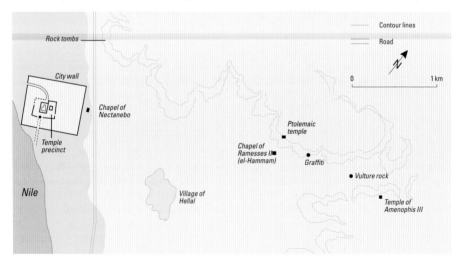

Nekhbet; the most recent phase is associated with the names of Nectanebo I and II (Thirtieth Dynasty). Another temple, dedicated to the god Thoth, is directly adjacent on the western side. This structure dates back to Amenophis II, (Eighteenth Dynasty) was extended under Ramesses II, and its newest additions were completed during the Roman imperial period. In the east of the Nekhbet-temple the remains of the sacred lake and other ancillary buildings can be seen. To the east outside the city walls is a chapel from the Thirtieth Dynasty and, somewhat farther away in the northwest, a small building was erected by Thutmosis III.

The Rock Tombs

Just 500 m away from the city the rock tombs of the provincial governors and other high officials were hewn into a range of hills. Their entrances are situated directly next to each other and can now be reached by a modern stairway. The tombs generally consist of a single, small cult chamber with vaulted ceiling and a statue niche at the rear wall. The complexes from the early Eighteenth Dynasty are particularly interesting; their vivid depictions and inscriptions are a valuable source of information on the art and history of this epoch.

Tomb of Paheri (No. 3)

Eighteenth Dynasty, ca. 1450 B.C.

Inspection of the gold delivery

The tomb´s owner, Paheri, was the mayor of Elkab and therefore at the top of the provincial administration of the third Upper Egyptian nome. At the same time he was head of the prophets in the cult of Nekhbet, the goddess represented dominion over Upper Egypt wearing therefore the "white crown" of this part of the country. His long career ended during the reign of Thutmosis III and it is probably from this period that his tomb dates. Along with depictions of the burial, detailed relief cycles on the left wall show the various activities carried out by Paheri during his time in office. Among his most important tasks, as this picture shows, was supervising gold deliveries from mines in the eastern desert. Seated on a cube-shaped chair with a low backrest, the official holds a scepter and long staff in his hands as signs of his authority. Before him, gold ingots in the form of rings are being delivered by a group of workers before being weighed on large scales. The result is then recorded by a scribe. In the second smaller register at the bottom still more gold rings and sacks of gold dust are pictured along with other objects.

Grain and flax harvest

Paheri and Prince Wadjmose

Although scenes of agricultural activities are among the most common themes in private tombs they are only rarely characterized as matters of official business—as they are here in the tomb of Paheri. Part of his duties on behalf of the vizier was to ensure the orderly conduct of the grain harvest and its delivery to the administrators of the local silos. This entailed recording the yield of the harvest, a task performed with measuring vessels. Almost as important was the flax harvest: linseed oil was made from the seeds of the plant while its fibers were used to produce linen for textiles.

In addition to his important position as mayor of Elkab, Paheri was entrusted with an honorary function normally reserved for the very highest of officials: he became the tutor of Prince Wadjmose, son of Thutmosis I. The child died at an early age however and never ascended to the throne, a destiny of many of the royal heirs. This close relationship to the Thutmoside kings was depicted by Paheri in a small side scene. Seated on an elegant chair, the official holds the prince—pictured as a small, naked boy—on his knee. Wadjmose wears a close-fitting cap with the long sidelocks appropriate to a boy of his years.

Tomb of Ahmose, Son of Ibana (No. 5)

Eighteenth Dynasty, ca. 1450 B.C.

Autobiography of Ahmose

The significance of Ahmose's modest rock tomb lies in the long, so-called autobiographical inscription of the tomb´s owner rather than in its extensive pictorial programme. As captain of the Egyptian fleet his long career encompassed the reigns of the first three rulers of the Eighteenth Dynasty—kings Ahmose I, Amenophis I and Thutmosis I. His father before him had already taken part in the Thebans' wars of liberation under Seqenenre Taa II against the foreign rule of the Hyksos. There are detailed descriptions of the Hyksos capital, Avaris, being conquered by the founder of the New Kingdom, Ahmose I, and of the resulting three year siege of Sharuhen (southern Palestine) where the Hyksos had fled with their followers. Ahmose accompanied Amenophis I on a successful campaign to Nubia and returned to that country once again under the next pharaoh, Thutmosis I, with whom he also ventured to Syria where the first undefinable contacts between the Egyptians and Mitanni were made near the Euphrates river. In the final part of the inscription the by then retired captain tells of his rewards in the form of land and slaves.

Desert Temple of Amenophis III

Eighteenth Dynasty, ca. 1380 B.C.

To the east of the rock tombs and at the entrance to a broad desert valley lie two cult structures in close proximity. One of these is a severely damaged hemispeos from the Ptolemaic era, the other a small chapel built by Setau, viceroy of Nubia under Ramesses II, to honor the god Thoth. Today it is known by the local people as el-Hammam ("the bath"). The desert temple of Amenophis III, built still deeper into the desert, is reached after passing a geological formation known as Vulture Rock. This somewhat obscure location is neither unique nor arbitrary; instead it is based on a mythological idea which saw the temple as a place to welcome the gods returning from abroad. In the sanctuary the roof is supported by four columns with Hathor capitals. Reliefs on the walls show Amenophis III and his father Thutmosis IV sacrificing to various gods. Amenophis (illustration bottom) stands before the enthroned falcon god, Horus of Hierakonpolis, and offers two vessels of wine to the city's goddess, Nekhbet. The upper section of the walls is decorated by a frieze of alternating Hathor-head emblems and royal cartouches. At the right of the entrance (external wall) is a short inscription from Prince Khaemwaset proclaiming the fifth *Sed* festival of his father, Ramesses II.

The Egyptian Book of the Dead

Many ancient Egyptian texts are concerned with the hereafter and were intended to guarantee a continued existence in the afterlife. This group of texts includes the Pyramid and Coffin Texts as well as the Guidebooks to the Netherworld and Books of Heaven. The so-called Book of the Dead forms a category of its own; it was written in order to introduce the deceased to the secrets of the realm of the dead in order to provide him or her with protection. Ordinarily, extracts from the book with relevant illustrations were copied onto a papyrus scroll and placed in the tomb, though various parts of the text were also inscribed on coffins, tomb and temple walls as well as statues and amulets. The roots of the collection of verses which make up the Book of the Dead date back to the age of the pyramids. Despite this, the book is essentially a creation of the New Kingdom which was to endure until the Graeco-Roman period. The spells themselves all had different purposes and were meant to provide for the protection, freedom of movement and material needs of the deceased in the land of the dead and in heaven. There are, therefore, spells which enable the deceased to escape from dangerous places and reach the 'field of offerings' (the Egyptian equivalent of

Papyrus of Ani—Judgment of the dead and weighing of the heart (detail), Nineteenth Dynasty, ca. 1250 b.c., Papyrus, H. 38 cm, The British Museum, London

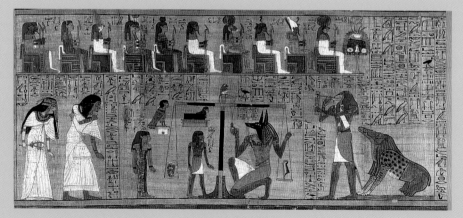

Papyrus of Anhai: Worship of the sungod in the form of a falcon (detail), Twentieth Dynasty, ca. 1150 B.C., papyrus, H. 37.5 cm, The British Museum, London

the Elysian Fields). There, they would meet the sun god in his barque and ascend to heaven in order to join the Lord of Death, Osiris, and the other gods.

Another category was concerned with the appropriate embalming of the corpse and its burial, the judgment of the deceased in the afterlife, protection from punishment and eventual regeneration. Several spells had a special significance and were therefore more widely used. This group includes spells concerning the judgment of the dead in which the heart of the deceased—the seat of understanding and conscience—was weighed against the feather of the goddess Maat who represented order and justice. If the deceased had led an upstanding life the scales were evenly balanced and he or she was then considered one of the righteous and able to ascend to heaven; the decision was affirmed by 42 judges of the dead and the supreme head of the court, Osiris. Whoever did not pass this test was thrown to the great devourer of the dead, a mythical creature composed of several different wild beasts. In the same context another important spell was directed at the heart of the deceased so that it would not give evidence against him. In order to reinforce the magical effect of this spell it would be written on the bottom of a large stone scarab which was then buried together with the mummy.

Edfu

Temple of Horus
Ptolemaic period, 3rd–1st centuries B.C.

Naos in the sanctuary, p. 465

Several miles south of Elkab on the west bank of the Nile lies Edfu, the Greek city of Apollinopolis and former capital of the second Upper Egyptian nome known as the "Throne of Horus." In the center of the modern city stands the great towering temple of the falcon god, Horus. He was the head of the local divine family whose other members were Hathor from Dendera and their son Harsomtus. The temple is a purely Ptolemaic structure begun in 237 B.C. under Ptolemy III Euergetes I with the final work completed 180 years later at the time of Ptolemy XII Neos Dionysos. On completion in 57 B.C., it was the greatest religious building of its age. Even today it still impresses with its almost perfectly preserved architecture and nowhere else can the effects of space and the play of light in an ancient Egyptian temple be so power-fully experienced as in Edfu. As with other temples from the Greco-Roman era the site has a long architectural history dating back to the third millennium B.C., although the earliest definite archeological evidence is from the Ramesside period. Investigations several years ago in the great courtyard uncovered a number of decorated stone blocks from the Twenty-fifth and Twenty-sixth Dynasties which had been used as paving stones by the Ptolemaic builders.

The first Hypostyle Hall
(pronaos), p. 464

Temple of Horus
(Pylon), p. 460 ff.

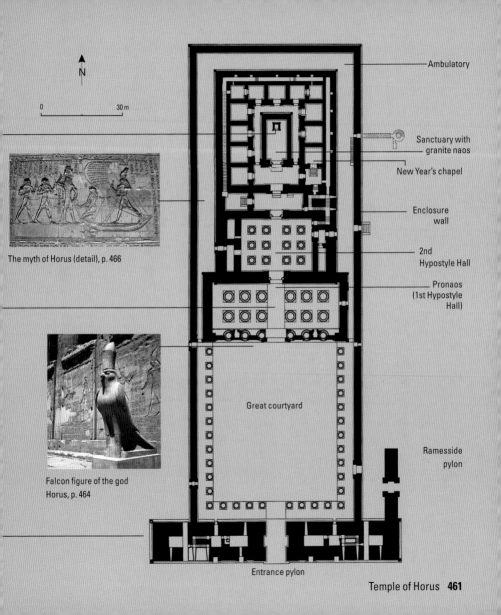

N

0   30 m

Ambulatory

Sanctuary with
granite naos

New Year's chapel

Enclosure
wall

2nd
Hypostyle Hall

Pronaos
(1st Hypostyle
Hall)

Great courtyard

Ramesside
pylon

The myth of Horus (detail), p. 466

Falcon figure of the god
Horus, p. 464

Entrance pylon

At present a team of German Egyptologists are studying the temple's vast collection of texts. The scale of the gigantic entrance pylon (118 × 243 ft, 36 × 74 m) is only overshadowed by a similar structure at the temple of Karnak. On both sides of the gateway can be seen four vertical niches in the towers which mark the place where the great flag posts once stood. The decoration on the façade is dominated by canonic images of the "Smiting of the Enemies," an action dedicated to the two main gods of Edfu, Horus and Hathor.

The Façade of the Pronaos (detail)

In the highly conventionalized spatial arrangement of a Graeco-Roman temple the sphere of the gods began with the pronaos, the great hypostyle hall situated behind the pylon and courtyard and at right angles to them. The columns on the courtyard side (illustration right) are connected by high partition walls (intercolumnar slabs), each of which is crowned by a frieze of *uraeus* snakes. Several of the reliefs on these walls were even ornamented with gold foil overlays—indicated by the still prominent holes for dowel plugs.

Falcon figure of the god Horus

The entrance to the pronaos is flanked on both sides by large falcon figures of the god Horus in dark gray granite; only the statue on the left has been preserved intact. This deity, who bore the epithet "Brightly Feathered One," wears a separately sculpted double crown of Upper and Lower Egypt. Although this work has a timeless elegance, the modern visitor should bear in mind that it was once painted and would therefore have inspired a completely different effect. The two falcon figures (H. 10.5 ft, 3.20 m) possibly decorated an earlier building and might therefore not be contemporaneous with the present Ptolemaic architecture.

The first Hypostyle hall

A total of 18 monumental papyrus columns with various capitals dominate the great hypostyle hall. Astronomical depictions decorate the ceiling while the walls—divided into strict series of registers—depict Ptolemaic rulers making sacrifices and performing rituals before the gods. The schematic nature of the relief cycles also has a purely formal structure so that while the gods, for example, are shown standing in the lowest register, they are then pictured seated on thrones in the upper-most register. Two small rooms at each of the central columns partitions served as a temple library (right) and storeroom for recipes for oils and essences respectively.

The naos in the sanctuary

Today the view from the great hall of pillars is directed along the building's central axis to the inner sanctum unhindered by the doors of the intervening rooms. The further one advances into the interior of the temple the darker it becomes. Tiny windows and skylights allow only enough light to create a diffuse twilight glow. The path becomes slightly steeper as one moves towards the sanctuary while the ceilings become progressively lower. The pronaos is followed by another hall of columns and two antechambers before the inner sanctum—the real dwelling place of the god Horus—is reached. Here, shrouded in the mystic gloom, there still stands a pedestal for the sacred barque and a mono- lithic granite shrine dating, according to an inscription, from the reign of Nectanebo II (Thirtieth Dynasty, H. 13.8 ft, 4.20 m). Originally it housed a small wooden naos with the golden cult image of Horus. Wall reliefs show scenes from the daily cult image ritual and depic- tions of Ptolemy IV bringing offerings to the sacred barques of Hathor and Horus. The first builder of the temple, Ptolemy III, and his wife, Berenice II, are included in these events. A free-standing building, the sanctuary is surrounded by a ring of chapels whose rooms all served various cult functions. Directly to the right of the inner sanctum— as in the temple at Dendera—is the "Wabet," the structure used for the New Year festival. It consists of a small courtyard which leads to a chapel via a short stairway where lustration ceremonies were performed.

The myth of Horus

On both sides of the pronaos, a narrow passageway leads to the great temple ambulatory whose high outer walls surround the temple thus separating the sacral sphere from other areas of the temple precincts. The extensive relief cycles on the western inner wall are entirely devoted to events of the Horus myth, a story of the elementary conflict between Good and Evil. Both texts and images depict in detail the victorious battle of Horus with his uncle, Seth, who embodied all hostile and sinister forces and who was responsible for the murder of his father, Osiris. Seth is pictured as a small hippopotamus (seen partly on his back), the size of the animal already indicating its status as a vanquished opponent. Together with his mother Isis, who kneels at the bow, Horus stands in the center of his sail-driven barque and harpoons his foe. Horus's successful act of revenge assured him of sole dominion over the ordered world—the principle that the Egyptians called *maat*. Each Egyptian pharaoh ascended to the throne as the direct descendants of Horus, and therefore ruled with devine powers over Egypt. It is in this context that the Ptolemaic monarch is seen contributing to the gods' battle by using his lance from the river bank. This rather late version of the Horus myth is an impressive proof for the longevity of the ancient legend.

Coronation of Ptolemy VIII

The walls of the temple are covered with a vast mass of depictions and inscriptions. Taken as a whole they provide details on Edfu's cult traditions, reveal the theological concepts underpinning the temple and therefore offer insights into the knowledge of the priesthood. Thanks to their detailed inscriptions, Graeco-Roman religious structures can also be important tools for interpreting the meanings of even older, more familiar images. This individual scene of the symbolic coronation of Ptolemy VIII Energetes II by the two tutelary goddesses of Egypt, Nekhbet (right) and Uto/Wadjyt (left), is part of the classical repertoire of temple scenes. Over headdresses of vulture skins the goddesses (the "two ladies") wear the crowns of Upper or Lower Egypt while the king is adorned with the double crown (Egyptian: pshent) and wears the classical short kilt of his pharaonic forebears.

The Egyptian Scribe

In ancient times, Egypt was a rigidly centralized state with an extremely effective administrative apparatus. The basis for the smooth functioning of the state was a broad class of literate officials who were employed in either the temple, central or local administration. Pupils at the schools for scribes were first given instruction in writing but they were also taught the fundamentals of literature. Specialized knowledge could then be gained by undertaking further training in the

Figure of a high official as a scribe, Fourth Dynasty, ca. 2550 B.C., Saqqara, painted limestone, H. 53 cm, Musée du Louvre, Paris

various administrative departments or with the temples' own scribal teams. Generally the profession was handed down from father to son but there were times when increased demand meant it became necessary to recruit people from other classes. The high status accorded to scribes and their profession is expressed in several passages in the various *Instructions*. These texts also emphasized the advantages of the scribes' lot compared with other professions, as in the instruction of Dua-kheti: "Behold, there is not a single profession without a supervisor except for that of the scribe for he alone is the supervisor." Essentially it was knowledge of hieroglyphics which enabled a scribe to rise through the ranks of the official hierarchy and scribes were correspondingly well-respected. This is the reason why even the highest state officials thought it appropriate to refer to their position as scribes in their biographies and to have themselves depicted seated on the ground with crossed legs in the typical manner of a scribe. Indeed, such figures of dignitaries—shown writing or reading—were known throughout Ancient Egyptian history, starting as early as the Old Kingdom.

The tools of the scribe included material on which to write (e.g. papyrus, leather, wooden slates, pottery or limestone shards for notes), a small bag for the soot and red ochre from which ink was made, a palette on which to mix the ink and reed pens.

Scribes of the army at work, Eighteenth Dynasty, ca. 1320 B.C., Saqqara, Tomb of Horemheb, limestone, H. 36 cm, Museo Archeologico, Florence

The depiction of this ensemble of palette, reed pen and sack was used as a character to denote both the concept of writing as well as the word "scribe." It could also be carved on the shoulder of statues to indicate the profession of the person represented. The status of scribes should not merely be seen then as reflecting their privileged position in the administration. Rather, it indicated the high educational level of a person fully integrated into the system of the Egyptian state which, ultimately, was pleasing in the eyes of god. Wisdom and order were thought to be the same thing in Egypt and for this reason the god Thot, embodiment of wisdom, was himself the patron deity of all scribes.

Kom Ombo

Twin Temple of Sobek and Haroëris
Ptolemaic and Roman period,
2nd century B.C.–3rd century A.D.

Around 25 miles (40 km) north of Aswan on a small hillock on the eastern bank of the Nile stands the twin temple of Kom Ombo. Its proximity to the river has unfor-

tunately meant that parts of the ancillary buildings, such as the mammisi and the great entry gate of Ptolemy XII, have fallen victim to the annual floods. Most of the temple lay buried under sand before it was excavated by the department of antiquities in 1893. In Kom Ombo, too, architectural history is much older than the structures which presently occupy the site. The first buildings on the site were erected as long

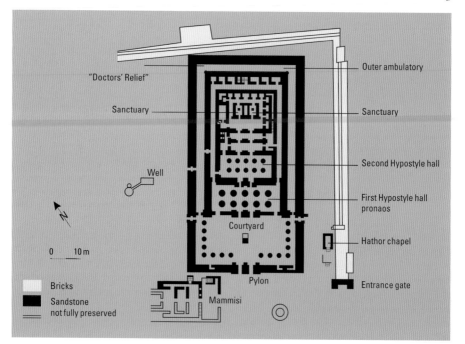

"Doctors' Relief"

Sanctuary

Well

Courtyard

Pylon

Mammisi

0   10 m

Bricks

Sandstone

not fully preserved

Outer ambulatory

Sanctuary

Second Hypostyle hall

First Hypostyle hall
pronaos

Hathor chapel

Entrance gate

ago as the Middle Kingdom.

The temple in its present form was begun under Ptolemy VI Philometor (2nd century B.C.) but most of its reliefs were not made until the Roman period. While the names of Tiberius and Augustus appear on the much destroyed pylon and stumps of columns in the courtyard, the eastern wing of the outer ambulatory has preserved a more recent image in a scene depicting the Emperor Macrinus (217/18 A.D.) with his son, Diadumenianus. The temple was dedicated to two main gods: the right half belonged

to Sobek, while the left was the domain of the falcon-headed god, Haroëris. Both were heads of a family of gods: Sobek (as the dominant god) was associated with Hathor and the moon god Khonsu, while Haroëris's bride was Tasenetneferet ("The beautiful sister") and his son, Panebtawi ("The lord of the two lands").

First Hypostyle hall (pronaos)

From the river Nile the great hall of pillars, the best preserved part of the temple at Kom Ombo, can be seen from a great distance. True to its nature as a dual temple the façade features two independent portals which give onto two parallel axes. This spatial structure begins at the pylon and continues on to the small sanctuaries each of which has a barque pedestal of black granite. The pronaos features altogether fifteen columns with composite, papyrus and palm brunch capitals; of particular interest are the scenes of lustration and coronation rituals on the partitions between the columns (intercolumnar slabs). Their expansive style is typical for the reliefs of the late Ptolemaic era. On the ceiling of the pronaos, the astronomical scenes decorating the architraves may still be discerned (the gods of the stars in their barques, some only as sketches in red ink).

Scene from the Temple Foundation Ritual

Among those depictions whose traditions date back to the time of the Old Kingdom are scenes from the so-called temple foundation ritual. Complete series of images from the temples at Edfu and Dendera provide information on the individual actions performed by the king together with the main local deities. These include: preparation of the building site, marking out the foundations, transporting the stone blocks, making mud bricks, purifying the building and, finally, handing it over to its divine occupant. In Kom Ombo a relatively well-preserved scene from the reign of Ptolemy VI shows the ceremony of "stretching the cord" which traditionally features the goddess Seshat and the monarch. The appearance of a goddess of literacy and numeracy is especially appropriate as the process was concerned with surveying the area for the temple complex. Seshat is clad in a panther skin and wears a finely braided wig with a band around her forehead from which rises her divine symbol—a single star shaped rosette with inverted cow's horns. In her right hand the goddess holds a long peg which she drives into the ground with a large club-like hammer. Her royal counterpart (since destroyed) formed a mirror image. A measuring tape wound around both markers and a short inscription explains the ceremony: "Stretching the cord in the temple together with His Majesty himself." Behind Seshat stands the falcon god Heroëris, lord of this half of the temple, who appears as though indifferent to proceedings. He wears the double crown of the two lands on top of his headdress and holds the traditional sign of life *(ankh)* and long *was* scepter in his hands.

The god Sobek

The crocodile was widespread in Pharaonic Egypt and the dangers it presented to both man and beast led to it being regarded as a god at an early stage of the country's history. Throughout the country temple complexes were built to honor the god Sobek and pacify him in cult ceremonies. In Upper Egypt Kom Ombo was one of his chief places of worship. Some distance away from the temple existed an animal cemetery in which there were found a number of well-preserved crocodile mummies. Today they are stored in the small Hathor chapel from the reign of Hadrian (2nd century A.D.) situated to the immediate right of the main building.

The "Doctors' Relief"

At the rear of the temple ambulatory on the eastern side of the wall a famous depiction has been preserved which is without parallel in Egypt: this is the so-called "doctors' relief" of Kom Ombo. It shows the Roman emperor Trajan (98–117 A.D.) bringing offerings and kneeling before the divine trinity of the northern half of the temple. Standing on a pedestal between the figures is a small cupboard with open doors in which can be seen four registers displaying various surgical instruments (including pincers, hooks and a saw) and healing amulets (*Wdjat* eyes). At the right, and shown in pseudo-perspective, is a high pedestal with a bowl for consecrated water.

The Sacred Animals

Even though the Greeks thought of the Egyptians as a particularly pious people whose religion had inspired their own, they were always mystified by the Egyptian veneration of sacred animals. Even the Romans were unable to understand these animal cults—with the result that several authors even lampooned the practice. Both attitudes however were based on a fundamental misunderstanding because the Egyptians never actually worshipped animals. The basis for their veneration of these sacred creatures was the notion that all parts of creation were interconnected and this meant that a god could manifest itself in anything that existed, even an animal.

There was a close association between the king and the sacred animals. Every king existed in some sense in a supreme god and, conversely, every supreme god existed in the king. But because every god was able to establish such a connection with a favored sacred animal, this relationship was also transferred to the king. The relationship of the king himself to other human beings was similar to that between a sacred animal and its lesser kind.

The sacred herds constituted a special case; these

Ram figure of the god Amun, Eighteenth Dynasty, ca. 1380 B.C., Soleb (Nubia), granite, L. 207 cm, Ägyptisches Museum, Staatliche Museen Preußischer Kulturbesitz, Berlin

were animals which seemed particularly well suited to the god because of certain characteristics. In the late period there was an increase in the number of cult communities which provided for the sacred animals and who were thereby able to supplement their incomes. They were very closely associated with the royal cult though their herds did not exclusively contain animals thought to embody the king such as falcons, bulls or crocodiles. Other creatures—such as the cats of the goddess Bastet—which were associated with protective or maternal characteristics also came to be included. Because these sacred animals were creatures which metamorphose into divine or royal forms of being they were mummified after death and given a proper burial. The great animal cemeteries such as the Serapeum for the sacred bulls of Apis (see p. 204) or the subterranean complexes for the sacred ibises and baboons of the god Thot in Tuna el-Gebel (see p. 281) are evidence of these practices. However, just as it was possible for an animal to be invested with the divine nature of a god, in other circumstances it might also be thought of as negative and dangerous and in such cases the creature was killed and even cremated. Generally, it was believed that the divine principle was able to manifest itself in all forms of existence irrespective of whether these were humans, animals, plants or inanimate objects.

Cat figure of the goddess Bastet, Late Period, 7th/6th centuries B.C., bronze and precious metals, H. 38 cm, The British Museum, London

Aswan and its Surroundings

Aswan and its Surroundings

The area surrounding the modern city of Aswan, known to the Greeks as Syene, is home to an overwhelming number of archaeological monuments which bear lasting witness to the region's importance. During the early years of the Old Kingdom, Egypt's southern frontier was established here, not far from the rapids of the First Cataract, marking the limits of the southernmost Upper Egyptian province of "Taseti." Up to the beginning of the Ptolemaic period, Elephantine (Egyptian: Abu, "elephant fortress"), an island in the river Nile, served as the region's seat of administration and main settlement, housing its various shrines as well. Its favorable strategic position resulted in the city becoming the point of departure for military operations in the Nubian region, and led to an important part of Egypt's trade with the south being conducted in Elephantine. In addition to the valuable imports being brought in, Aswan itself possessed highly prized natural products in the form of the red granite and other hard stone extracted from its extensive quarry areas. Opposite Elephantine, on the hill of the Qubbet el-Hawa, lie the rock tombs of regional governors of the Old and Middle Kingdoms. Other highlights are the temples at Kalabsha and on the island of Philae.

Previous pages: view of the temple island of Philae (after its relocation)

Tomb of Sarenput II (No. 31), p. 490 f.

Temple of Satet, New Kingdom, p. 483

The quarries with unfnished obelisk, p

Trajan's Great Kiosk, p. 499

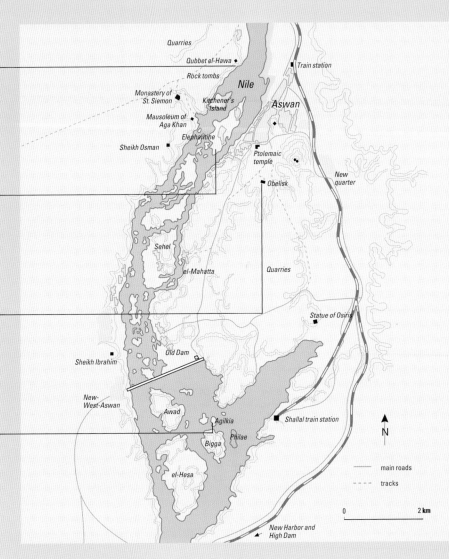

Quarries

Qubbet el-Hawa ◆

Train station ■

Rock tombs

Nile

Monastery of St. Siemon ◆

Kitchener's Island

Aswan

Mausoleum of Aga Khan ◆

Elephantine

Sheikh Osman ■

Ptolemaic temple ■

New quarter

Obelisk ■

Sehel

Quarries

el-Mahatta

Statue of Osiris ■

Sheikh Ibrahim ■

Old Dam

New-West-Aswan

Awad

Agilkia

Philae

Shallal train station ■

Bigga

N

el-Hesa

main roads

tracks

0   2 km

New Harbor and High Dam ▲

Aswan and its Surroundings **479**

Elephantine

Elephantine Island, whose settlement history embraces nearly all the different periods of the country's history, is without doubt one of the most fascinating archaeological sites in the "Land of the Nile." A mere 1.5 km (1 mile) long and no more than 500 m wide, the island's monuments are concentrated in a small area towards its southern tip. Due to its rocky subsoil, archaeological excavations can proceed without any danger of being disrupted by ground water, which now represents one of the major threats to the survival of ancient monuments. Since 1969, a team of German and Swiss archaeologists has been excavating and carrying out research on Elephantine with considerable success. The main deity worshiped throughout the Cataract region was the ram-headed god, Khnum, whose spouse was the gazelle goddess Satet. Their shrines are the most important on Elephantine, although Khnum's temple complex has been badly damaged and only the final building phase, dating from the Thirtieth Dynasty, is represented. The monumental granite Alexander IV gateway (c. 310 B.C.) alone gives an idea of

its former size. Immediately next to the temple of Khnum lies the smaller shrine of Satet, which dates from the Eighteenth Dynasty, now reconstructed. In close proximity to these is the sanctuary of Heqaib, a deified governor of the Sixth Dynasty, a site which developed during the Middle Kingdom from a collection of smaller shrines. Bordering on the shrines to the north are the actual settlement areas (consisting of Nile mud-brick buildings) which date back to the Old Kingdom. The impressive riverbank fortifications were constructed much later, during the Graeco-Roman period.

Barque shrine of Amenophis III
M. Adolphe Linant, c. 1820, watercolor, Griffith Institute, Oxford, Bankes MS. No. IV C 6

Near to the temple of Satet, facing north, is the site where a barque shrine of Amenophis III once stood, with a pillared ambulatory and papyrus bundle columns along each of its smaller sides. Sadly, this jewel of ancient Egyptian architecture was completely demolished in 1822 in order to provide building stone for local use. The only surviving evidence of its existence are a few pictures dating from the early 19th century.

Grotto of the Temple of Satet
Sixth Dynasty, ca. 2270 B.C.

One of the most important results of the German excavations on Elephantine was the clarification of the different building phases of the temple of Satet, which had hitherto been a mystery. This established a building history that ran from the Early dynastic Period right up to the Ptolemaic era. At the outset there was just a small rock grotto whose floor area yielded a wealth of faience figurines, in all likelihood votive offerings, similar to those found in Abydos and Hierakonpolis. The place was remarkably extended in the Sixth Dynasty, under Pepy I, through the addition of a small granite Naos (original: Louvre, Paris). In order to open up access to these ancient beginnings of the cult tradition on Elephantine, a reinforced concrete platform was built over the site, which today supports the large Eighteenth Dynasty structure above.

New Kingdom Temple of Satet

Eighteenth Dynasty, ca. 1470 B.C.

Following the completion of a new building of fine limestone by Senusret I at the beginning of the Twelfth Dynasty, the next phase of construction occurred during the early New Kingdom. The older building was demolished in order to make way for an even bigger shrine, this time of sandstone, the construction of which began under Queen Hatshepsut (1479–1459/58 B.C.).

Around half the relief blocks used for this building were recovered from the foundations of the structure which in turn replaced it during the Ptolemaic period. Further material has been provided by casts of blocks which have been in the collections of various museums (e.g. Musée du Louvre, Paris). The successful reconstruction of this building has produced a 20 × 14 m shrine with an external ambulatory comprising a total of 32 pillars and a non-axial entrance. A vestibule with two Hathor pillars leads to the adjoining cult rooms of Satet and Amun.

Thutmosis III with the Goddess Satet

The reliefs on the pillars of the ambulatory depict the royal builder in the company of various gods. The cartouche in this scene replaces an earlier one naming his unloved stepmother Hatshepsut, and gives Thutmosis III's throne name of Men-Kheper-Re. The figure of the ruler, wearing a high, feathered crown, a short kilt with pearl sash and holding a mace, is being embraced warmly by Satet, an indication of his close relationship with the goddess. She is wearing a long woman's tunic and her characteristic headgear, which consists of an Upper-Egyptian crown with gazelle horns on either side. Some other unique reliefs showing scenes related to a ritual about Elephantine as a place for the mythical spring of the Nile. The decoration of the New Kingdom blocks was by and large preserved during their recycling in the Ptolemaic period.

Nilometer

Thirtieth Dynasty, ca. 370 B.C.

Because of Elephantine's long history, not just one but several nilometers, used for measuring the water level of the Nile, were constructed over the course of time, employing a variety of different methods. With the arrival of the annual inundation at Egypt's southern frontier, this system of measuring the water level provided reliable data on the extent of this natural phenomenon. Agricultural work was organized and taxes calculated on the basis of these measurements. In the event of a flood of catastrophic proportions, they allowed for the implementation of such security measures as could still be taken. A simple inlet in the eastern river wall caused the water to flow into a 16 m-high stairwell which today still displays a measuring scale dating from the Roman period. In the 19th century this nilometer was brought back into operation as displayed by the later scale markings on marble plaques. The nilom-

eter immediately to the south of the Khnum temple terrace is of a completely different design. The measuring well (approx. 11 × 8 m) built of large square blocks of stone was described by the Greek geographer Strabo (1st century B.C.) and displays two scales, one of which indicates the flood level over and above the average height of the fields of Upper Egypt.

The Rediscovery of Egypt during the 19th Century

Already the Greeks and the Romans were fascinated by ancient Egyptian culture. They visited the pyramids and stood in uncomprehending amazement in the kings' tombs of Western Thebes. Even Roman emperors such as Hadrian (130 A.D.) visited Egypt. The cult of the gods Isis and Osiris reached as far as Rome, and many obelisks were transported back there. Interest in ancient Egypt disappeared with the arrival of Christianity in many parts of the Mediterranean region, and the country sank into insignificance. Only 1,000 years later, during the 17th and 18th centuries, did occasional European travelers start to visit Egypt again, enduring considerable hardship along the way, and publish accounts of their experiences. Among these were the Italian Pietro della Valle (1586–1632), who described the pyramids of Giza and Dahshur, and the English clergyman Richard Pococke (1704–1765). The Danish captain Frederik L. Norden (1708–1742), who explored Egypt in 1738 in the service of King Christian VI, produced an exhaustively illustrated account of his travels which proved especially popular. But it was a military expedition that really lit the touch-paper for the modern rediscovery of the culture of the pharaohs: that of Napoleon Bonaparte. When he set sail for Alexandria in 1798, not only did the Corsican have 34,000 troops with him, but also 65 members of the so-called Commission for Science and the Arts which formed part of his Army of the Orient. Right up to the French surrender in 1801, this elite unit dedicated itself to the study and recording in graphic form of the ancient Egyptian monuments. The resulting wealth of plans and sketches later formed the

The search for mummies in Saqqara: Pietro della Valle, "Description of Travels through various Parts of the World (…)," engraving, Geneva 1674

Transporting a colossal bust of Ramesses II (now in the British Museum, London) from the Ramesseum, lithograph. G. Belzoni, Six New Plates, London 1822

basis of the monumental multi-volume work "Description de l'Égypte," which was the first of all comprehensive descriptions of Egypt's monuments. This work also came to the attention of Jean-François Champollion (1790–1832), who a little later, in 1822, became the first person to decipher hieroglyphics. With the help of the famous "Rosetta Stone" (today in the British Museum, London), he unearthed the principles behind the Egyptian writing system and thus founded modern Egyptology.

Along with serious researchers, who painstakingly uncovered the secrets of various inscriptions piece by piece, this enthusiasm for Egypt also lured numerous adventurers and unscrupulous treasure hunters. The Italian Giovanni Battista Belzoni (1778–1823) features prominently among these. Belzoni, who was in the service of the British Consul General Henry Salt, was one of the most prolific plunderers of art of his time. At Salt's instigation he transported a colossal bust of Ramesses II, weighing several tons, from Thebes, managed to gain entrance to the rock temple of Abu Simbel and was the first to enter the pyramid of Chephren in Giza. He pulled off his greatest coup, however, in October 1817, when he discovered the magnificent tomb of Sety I in the Valley of the Kings, thus earning himself fame which has endured right up to the present day.

The Burial Hill of Aswan

Opposite the northern part of Aswan, on the western bank of the Nile, lies the distinctive burial hill known today as Qubbet el-Hawa ("the dome of the winds"). At its summit is the tomb of Sheikh Osman, its domed roof forming a landmark visible from far and wide. Numerous decorated rock tombs dating from the Old and Middle Kingdoms and belonging to Elephantine's governors and dignitaries are built into the hillside along various terraces. The larger complexes possess a small forecourt and a steep causeway leading down to the river. Inside, the tombs are decorated with wall paintings or reliefs on a layer of stucco, whose style would generally only have satisfied provincial tastes. Of great interest, on the other hand, are the many inscriptions telling of officials who led trading expeditions into Nubia. The intensive trade connections of these nomarchs from the very south of Egypt are well attested by the discovery of a pretty Minoan vase at the Qubbet el-Hawa.

Tomb of Mekhu and Sabni (No. 25/26)

Sixth Dynasty, ca. 2300 B.C.

Fishing and bird hunting

At the southern end of the middle terrace, the governors Mekhu and Sabni built a massive double tomb whose cult chambers are furnished with several rows of columns and pillars. While the entrance to Mekhu's cult chamber is marked by two impressive obelisks without inscription, the visitor's attention is drawn in particular to the inscription on the facade of Sabni's. Here the governor tells of leaving for Nubia upon hearing news of his father's natural death there and gives an account of transporting the body back to Aswan and burying him with full honors. The rear wall of Sabni's burial chamber contains the most attractive individual picture of the complex, a typical Old Kingdom scene of fishing and bird hunting ("fishing and fowling"). The owner of the tomb is shown standing in a simple barque on either side of a papyrus thicket: to the left he is seen spearing two fishes and on the right he is using a throwing stick to kill waders.

conducted four successful trips following different routes and returned from the south bearing highly-prized goods such as ivory, ebony, incense and leopard skins. But none of these items aroused as much interest on the part of Pepy II as a dwarf Harkhuf brought back with him from his final expedition. The king expressly warned his officials: "When he (the dwarf) gets on the ship with you, please charge some reliable men with the responsibility of making sure he does not fall into the water."

Tomb of Sarenput II (No. 31)
Twelfth Dynasty, ca. 1900 B.C.

Sarenput II before the repast table

The tradition of constructing tombs on the burial hill at Aswan reached its peak with the impressive burial complex of Sarenput II, mayor of Elephantine under Senusret II. As in Egypt's other provinces, the extensive autonomy enjoyed by the governors of this region was finally brought to an end by the strong rulers of the Twelfth Dynasty, who once again administered the country centrally. A broad staircase leads up from a large pillared hall into a corridor with a lightly vaulted roof which in turn leads to a small room containing four pillars. The cult niche is positioned against its rear wall. The central scene depicts the deceased seated on a chair with his hand stretching out towards a richly laden funerary table.

Tomb of Harkhuf (No. 34)
Sixth Dynasty, ca. 2200 B.C.

Autobiographical Inscription

Among the best known tombs on Qubbet el-Hawa is the rock tomb of Harkhuf, who undertook a number of expeditions to Nubia and the Sudan during the Sixth Dynasty under kings Merenra I (Nemtyemsaf I) and Pepy II. The owner of the tomb tells of these spectacular trading expeditions in a long autobiographical inscription on the façade of his tomb to either side of the entrance. Harkhuf

Mausoleum of the Aga Khan

The view from the terrace of the venerable Old Cataract Hotel leads across Elephantine's southern tip to the west bank of the Nile, on a rocky outcrop of which is the tomb built by Aga Sultan Sir Mohammed Shah (1877–1957). The Aga Khan III was leader of the Ismaili Hodja sect (a branch of Shiite Muslims), who also worshiped him as their hereditary imam. In honor of his elevated status, his followers used at one time to present him annually with his own weight in gold, a practice his adherents have decided is no longer in keeping with the times. A broad outdoor staircase leads up from the banks of the Nile to the domed mausoleum, which is based on the Guyushi Mosque near Cairo and decorated inside with polished granite. The tomb remained unfinished at the time of the Aga Khan's death, and his remains could not be interred in the splendid tomb decorated with Koranic inscriptions until 1959. Below the mausoleum, built in neo-Fatimid style, is the white villa named Nur el-Salam ("Light of Peace") of the Begum, who died just some years ago and was laid to rest alongside her husband.

The Monastery of St. Simeon

Coptic, 7/8th centuries A.D.

The Monastery of St. Simeon was built during the 7/8th centuries in the middle of the desert on the west bank of the Nile, but had to be abandoned in the 13th century as a result of water shortages and repeated Bedouin attacks. With its well-preserved architecture, this is one of Egypt's most important monastery sites. Constructed on a two-level cliff terrace, the monastery buildings are surrounded by a wall which is a good six meters high. Its lower parts are built of undressed stone, while unbaked Nile mud bricks were used for the upper portion. Directly opposite the entrance to the monastery on the lower level stands the church, a triple-aisled basilica dating from the 9th century. Fragments of wall frescos can be seen in the main apse, including Christ seated on his throne in the central vault. The upper level to the right houses the monks' cells along with the refectory where they would have eaten their meals together. The remaining rooms were used for sundry household and sanitary purposes.

The Temple Island of Philae

The island of Philae, with justification, has earned itself the nickname "Pearl of Egypt" for its unique ensemble of sacred buildings and harmonious natural surroundings. Squeezed together on the small island (approx. 460 × 150 m) lay an entire city of temples that had been built in honor of the goddess Isis. During the course of moving the shrines to the neighboring island of Agilkia in the 1970s, hundreds of recycled stone blocks were recovered from the foundations, which allowed the cult and building tradition on Philae to be dated back to as early as the Twenty-fifth or Twenty-sixth Dynasties. The earliest reliably known building patron on the island was Nectanebo I (Thirtieth Dynasty), while the main buildings date from the Greco-Roman period. Some of the relief decoration even extends up to the time of emperors Marcus Aurelius and Commodus (late 2nd century A.D.). As the great mother goddess, Isis was so popular that her cult on Philae lasted longer than that of any of the other Egyptian gods. The latest graffito, inscribed into stone in Demotic script by a pilgrim, dates from 452 A.D. Not until the reign of Justinian in the 6th century was her shrine finally closed and part of it converted into a church—that of St. Stephen. Coptic Christianity went on to have a similarly long history on Philae, lasting until the 12th or 13th centuries.

The Temple of Isis, p. 496 f.

Great Kiosk of Trajan, p. 499

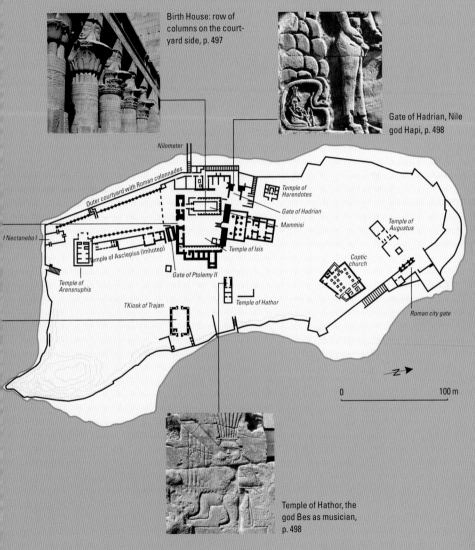

Birth House: row of columns on the court-yard side, p. 497

Gate of Hadrian, Nile god Hapi, p. 498

Nilometer

Outer courtyard with Roman colonnades

Temple of Harendotes

Gate of Hadrian

Mammisi

Temple of Augustus

f Nectanebo I

Temple of Asclepius (Imhotep)

Temple of Isis

Coptic church

Temple of Arensnuphis

Gate of Ptolemy II

TKiosk of Trajan

Temple of Hathor

Roman city gate

0   100 m

Temple of Hathor, the god Bes as musician, p. 498

Temple of Isis

Ptolemaic period, 3rd–1st centuries B.C.

The main temple on Philae was dedicated to Isis and her son Harpocrates ("Horus the child"). Its ground plan does not correspond to the traditional schema of a Ptolemaic shrine either in terms of the configuration of its rooms or its orientation. Particularly striking is the deviation from the axis which commences with the second pylon; this is no doubt explained by the rocky geological conditions below ground. Today the large outer courtyard, lined with long colonnades whose decoration dates from the early Roman empire, is entered through a kiosk built by Nectanebo I (Thirtieth Dynasty). Two granite lion statues and a pair of obelisks once stood in front of the mighty entrance pylon (45.5 × 18 m), but these were removed at the beginning of the 19th century by the Italian adventurer Giovanni Battista Belzoni. The reliefs on the first pylon show Ptolemy XII Neos Dionysos "smiting the enemies." Above these triumphant scenes, the ruler is shown in several smaller reliefs making sacrifices to the gods. On the eastern tower he can be seen handing the crowns of the kingdom to Horus and Nephthys and burning incense before Osiris, Isis and Harpocrates. Set at a diagonal immediately in front of the eastern tower of the pylon is the large gate of

Ptolemy II Philadelphos, while the central entrance portal is a Thirtieth Dynasty structure built by Nectanebo I which was later integrated into the Ptolemaic temple. The inner courtyard of the temple of Isis is bordered by the birth house to the left and a sequence of priests' rooms to the right. A flight of steps leads up to the second pylon (32 × 12 m), which was also decorated during the reign of Neos Dionysos. Incorporated in the stonework of the tower on the right is a granite outcrop that has been smoothed down and inscribed with a dedicatory text from the 24th year of Ptolemy VI Philometor's reign. Behind the pylon lies a small courtyard which can be covered with an awning as necessary. Behind this is a vestibule containing eight pillars which once housed a Christian church (6th century A.D.). This is revealed by the crosses carved into the walls and a small apse set into the wall. Various further rooms lead eventually to the inner sanctum at the end of the temple axis, where the large pedestal for the cult barque of Isis still stands. The high-quality bas-reliefs (depicting ritual scenes) were completed during the time of the temple's first patron, Ptolemy II Philadelphos.

Birth House: Row of columns on the courtyard side
Ptolemaic period, 2nd /1st centuries B.C.

Traditionally, the birth houses or *mammisi* of the later shrines are situated outside the main temple as independent structures. Philae is the only known example where the *mammisi* is incorporated as a peripteral structure into the western side of the first courtyard. The birth house is entered through a small door in the western tower of the main pylon. The central tableau of its inner sanctum, reached via a vestibule and two further rooms, depicts the youthful god Horus as a falcon in the marshes of the Delta where, according to legend, he was brought up under the protection of his mother.

Gate of Hadrian (Detail)
Roman period, 2nd century A.D.

Nile god Hapi

To the northwest of the temple of Isis, against the perimeter wall of the complex, is a gatehouse dating from the time of Emperor Hadrian (117–138 A.D.). Below the main reliefs of the largely destroyed antechamber, which relate to the cult of Osiris, one scene in particular, located on the left end of the north wall, deserves closer attention. It depicts the mythical sources of the Nile and is probably the most famous individual scene on all the shrines on Philae. The Nile god Hapi, encircled by a snake, kneels in his grotto at the foot of a towering rock formation (signifying the cataract area) and pours out the water of the river from two vessels, or rather simply lets it gush out of the pots in which it originates.

Temple of Hathor (Detail)
Ptolemaic period, 2nd/1st centuries B.C.

The god Bes as musician

Somewhat to the east of the Isis temple, a small shrine was raised to the goddess Hathor. Originally constructed during the middle Ptolemaic period (Ptolemies VI and VII), its forecourt and inner sanctuary were only added under Emperor Augustus (30 B.C.–14 A.D.). The columns and masonry partitions of the courtyard display some extremely attractive scenes, which have a cult background despite their apparently profane character, for music and dance played an important part in the temple festivals and processions. Flute and harp players, apes playing lutes and the figure of the gnome-like Bes, banging a hand drum and moving in time to the sound of the harp, are all visible here.

Great Kiosk of Trajan
Roman period, 2nd century A.D.

This great kiosk (H. 50 ft), which dates from the Roman period, stands on the eastern bank of the island. Although its relief decoration remains incomplete, the capitals of the plant-motif columns impress with the richness of their detail. Kiosk structures of widely varying sizes are a characteristic Graeco-Roman architectural form in Egypt. Today, their open construction (wooden roof gone) allowed the sunlight to enter unimpeded. To the front of the structure is a quay area where barques carrying the cult image of Isis would once have landed and cast off from when she was being taken to visit the Abaton, the tomb of Osiris on the neighboring island of Biga.

Philae—An Island is Relocated

The trials and tribulations of the temple sites on Philae began with the construction of the first Aswan dam between 1898–1902. The initial consequence of the new dam was that the shrines on Philae were largely submerged between January to July, the months of the Nile inundation, meaning that the great Temple of Isis could only be visited by rowing boat, and the island could only be visited without visitors getting their feet wet during August and September. This regular bathing of the temple buildings had positive and negative aspects. On the one hand the water dissolved the salts which had collected in the sandstone, but on the other it also washed away the colored reliefs in all their splendor. These had been praised at the beginning of the 19th century by the scientists who accompanied Napoleon on his Egyptian expedition. Philae's architecture, meanwhile, remained undamaged. This situation changed dramatically, however, when the immense High Dam, the Sadd el-Ali, finally came into service in 1971.

The western colonnade of the Temple of Isis under flood, Philae, 1962

The Temple of Isis during the move, Philae, ca. 1975

Situated about seven kilometers (4¹/₂ miles) upstream from the old Aswan Dam, the High Dam blocks off the Nile completely and extends across a width of 3,600 m (11,800 feet). The supply of water to the river is regulated exclusively by the six turbine tunnels of its large power station. The shrines on Philae, which suddenly lay between the two dams, were now severely endangered by the daily fluctuating water level and considerable swell.

Within the framework of an international initiative to save the ancient monuments of Nubia under the patronage of UNESCO, various suggestions were also examined for the preservation of the ancient temple city of Philae. The solution that was finally opted for was the complete dismantling of the buildings and their reconstruction on the island of Agilkia, just 300 m away, which offered the necessary safety from the water due to its higher elevation. Before the dismantling of the buildings could begin, however, Philae first had to be drained. This involved laying an enormous steel sheet-pile wall around the most important structures prior to pumping out the water. The shrines were then carried away stone by stone, a total of 40,000 blocks. Work started simultaneously on Agilkia, where extensive blasting was needed in order to prepare the ground for the concrete foundations which all the buildings were to have. The transfer to the new location was complete by spring 1980. The incomparable magic of this architectural ensemble in its antique site could not, however, be transplanted.

The Quarries

Egypt has been called a "state built on stone," and with good reason. The geological formations on either side of the Nile, in both the Eastern and Western Deserts, yielded a wide variety of stone types. With the founding of a unified state during the early years of the third millennium B.C., an intensive bout of prospecting and quarrying took place, leading too to the working of quarries great distances away. Numerous expedition reports tell of the logistical expense involved in the quarrying of building materials for pyramids, temples and statues. The extensive quarries south of Aswan played a very special role in this, as it is here that along with other stones (such as quartzite), the highly-prized varieties of red granite were found. An excellent illustration of ancient working methods is provided by an unfinished obelisk which was not ultimately freed from the rock bed because of a material defect. At 42 m long and weighing an estimated 1,168 tons, this would have been the largest obelisk ever. It can be dated with certainty to the Eighteenth Dynasty and was possibly destined for the national shrine at Karnak.

The Temple of Kalabsha

Ptolemaic and Roman periods, 1st century B.C.

The great temple of Kalabsha (72 × 35.5 m), was re-erected on the west bank close to the Aswan High Dam to prevent it sinking beneath the waters of Lake Nasser, 50 km (31 miles) to the south. The relocation work, the official contribution of the Federal Republic of Germany to the UNESCO-sponsored rescue of the ancient Nubian monuments, began in 1961 and was finished two years later. A total of 13,110 blocks of stone (up to 20 tons) had to be moved. The shrine replaced an older structure dating from the reign of Amenophis II in the Eighteenth Dynasty. It owes much of its decoration to the time of the Roman emperor Augustus, although its reliefwork was never completed. The complex was dedicated to the local Nubian god Mandulis, whose cult has only been traced back as far as the Ptolemaic era. Close connections existed with the goddess Isis on Philae, who visited her fellow cult in Kalabsha annually in a procession of ships. As with so many other sacred buildings, the temple of Mandulis was transformed into a church during the 6th century.

The Pronaos

The great courtyard of the shrine, which has colonnading along three of its sides, is entered via a largely undecorated pylon (H. 14.5 m). Behind it is the hall of columns (pronaos) whose roof has collapsed, giving it more the appearance of a light kiosk. The columns of the façade are linked by high intercolumnar slabs on the left of which a scene representing the royal purification can be seen. This act was traditionally performed by the gods of the two parts of the country, Upper and Lower Egypt, and is being carried out here by Horus and Thoth in the presence of Harsiese of Talmis (the district to which Kalabsha once belonged). Preserved on the masonry slab to the right is an inscription from 248/49 A.D. in which the military governor Aurelius Besarion orders shepherds to keep their animals away from the temple precincts. Further to the right is a depiction of the victory of petty Nubian king Silko (5th century A.D.) over the nomadic Blemyer tribe at Taffa and Talmis.

Relief showing the god Mandulis

As the actual temple building, which was the dwelling place of a god, could only be entered by the ruler or by the priests responsible for cult ceremonial, subsidiary cult buildings were often erected alongside major shrines. These were usually positioned at the rear or in the ambulatory of the main temple and could thus be entered by pilgrims and other visitors to the temple wishing to supplicate the gods and pray. While the ritual acts of the priests were being performed in front of or on a figure of the relevant god, the divine being was deemed to inhabit the representation of him in these secondary places of prayer. The temple of Kalabsha also possessed a place of prayer of this kind, on the rear wall of its inner ambulatory. It shows the local Nubian god Mandulis (left) and the pharaoh (Double Crown in front view!) flanking a offering table. Several postholes are visible around the scene, which would have supported the wooden framework surrounding the shrine.

Temple of Beit el-Wali

Nineteenth Dynasty, ca. 1270 B.C.

The small rock-hewn temple of Beit el-Wali, situated close behind the temple of Kalabsha, is another shrine rescued from the floodwaters of the reservoir. This modest construction was built during the early years of Ramesses II's reign. Behind the entrance portal stretches a long vestibule which was originally covered by a barrel-vaulted ceiling made of Nile mud bricks. The northern wall contains individual scenes from the king's military campaigns against the Syrians and Libyans, and the main images on the southern wall depict battles against the Nubians and the payment of tribute. Three doorways lead through to a transverse hall containing two simple columns with polygonal shafts. In addition to the colorful reliefs, two small statue niches are also distinctive. These contain figures of Ramesses II between Isis and Horus of Kuban on the left and Ramesses II between the ram-headed god Khnum and his wife Anuket on the right. It is probable that the adjoining sanctuary room would also have contained a further triad of figures.

The Nubian Tribute (detail)

Egypt regained control over Nubia, which was governed by a high official known as the "Viceroy of Kush," shortly after the founding of the New Kingdom. The reason for Egypt's interest in this area was the opportunity to plunder its rich deposits of gold and carry off other valuable natural products. Representations in temples of a triumphant king and the ensuing tribute payments from the southern regions are not to be seen so much as depictions of concrete historical situations but rather as symbols of the eternal claim over this area exercised by succeeding pharaohs. In Beit el-Wali such scenes feature in a rich geographical setting on the southern wall of the vestibule, executed in sunken relief. The delivery of the tribute is conducted by the Viceroy Amenemope as well as the Vizier and the crown prince of those days, Amenhirwenemef. Among the duty being paid to the king there are also exotic creatures such as apes, wild cats, a giraffe and, as a particular curiosity, an ostrich. Since women and children also appear in this long procession of tribute items, it seems likely that campaigns to Nubia of this type were more like small punitive expeditions. Groups of prisoners from the captured village are shown alongside, whose ethnic origins, as elsewhere, are clearly shown in their hairstyles and facial features.

The Island of Sehel

Approximately three kilometers (2 miles) south of Elephantine lies the small island of Sehel, on which the principal gods of the cataract region were worshiped. Sehel is well known for the inscriptions, of which there are over 200, on its heaps of granite boulders. These were produced mainly by high state officials who stopped off at this last domestic cult district and left these "visiting cards" before continuing their journey to Nubia. Among them are such well-known personalities as the vizier Ramose, who held office under Amenophis III, and Setau, viceroy of Kush during the reign of Ramesses II, pictured in many places making a supplicatory gesture with raised arms. These inscriptions and pictures were not executed using the traditional relief technique; instead, the contours were produced by exploiting the difference in color between the weathered surface of the stone and the natural color underneath.

The "Famine Stele"

Ptolemaic period, 3rd century B.C.

Sehel's most interesting inscription is set into an enormous boulder, the so-called "Famine stele" on the eastern peak of the island's granite hill. The long text (decree) is accompanied by a small picture in a square frame showing King Djoser (Third Dynasty) sacrificing to the triad of cataract gods, Khnum, Satet and Anuket. The beginning of the text (top right) names this king of the Old Kingdom and dates the event precisely to the 19th year of his reign. But all is not what it seems. In reality the inscription was created during the reign of Ptolemy IV (221–205 B.C.) with the intention of ascribing an ancient and therefore untouchable tradition to the claims of the priests of this region to tax local produce. The inscription tells of a severe drought and famine under Djoser which was only overcome when the king made renewed sacrificial offerings to the cataract god Khnum. The horizontal split in the boulder seems to have occurred after the inscription was made.

The Nubian Museum

The Nubian Museum, one of Egypt's most modern, opened on November 16, 1997. Not far from Aswan's city center (on the road to the airport), the museum is surrounded by an extensive park in which numerous monuments and exhibits are on display. In addition to the many individual artifacts there is a whole collection of Islamic tombs and a model of a Nubian house. The main museum building, of lightly curved design and dominated by the lavish use of red granite in its interior decoration, extends over three levels and provides comprehensive service facilities in addition to the exhibition rooms themselves. The artifacts on display have been chosen to reflect the settlement history of the Nubian region; all periods, from prehistoric times to the Christian and Islamic era, are represented with interesting ex-

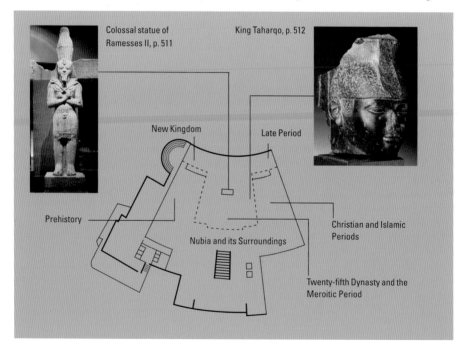

Colossal statue of Ramesses II, p. 511

King Taharqo, p. 512

New Kingdom

Late Period

Prehistory

Nubia and its Surroundings

Christian and Islamic Periods

Twenty-fifth Dynasty and the Meroitic Period

hibits. Further interesting information is provided by models and documentary material (UNESCO projects).

Colossal statue figure of Ramesses II
Nineteenth Dynasty, ca. 1235 B.C., Gerf Hussein, painted sandstone, H. ca. 5.20 m

Upon entering the central exhibition room in the basement, the visitor is greeted by the colossal standing figure of Ramesses II taken from his Nubian temple at Gerf Hussein (approx. 100 km—62 miles—south of Aswan), which was dedicated to the Memphite gods (Ptah, Ptah-Tatenen and Hathor) and the deified ruler himself ("Ramesses, the Great God"). Only a few elements from the building, such as this pillar statue, were dismantled from the rock temple and thus saved; the rest of the architecture was left to the mercy of Lake Nasser. The pharaoh is wearing the *nemes* headcloth with the double crown, the *uraeus* on his brow and a broad ceremonial beard. His arms are crossed in front of his chest and he is holding the crook and flail as insignia. His regalia is completed by a knee-length kilt decorated with a panther's head and *uraeus* trim. Several standing figures of this type, depicting the pharaoh with feet together and assembled from a number of separate pieces, once flanked the shrine's great forecourt. Although impressive in scale, they are only of moderate artistic interest by showing a rather heavy, brutal style.

King Taharqo

3rd Intermediate Period, Twenty-fifth Dynasty, ca.
670 B.C., probably Karnak, temple of Amun-Re,
dark-gray granite, H. 36.5 cm

This famous head, which was moved to the
Nubian Museum from Cairo, is part of a
larger than life-size statue, probably a standing figure of King Taharqo. Taharqo's reign
represented the culmination of Kushite
rule. He left his mark as a patron of building, in the Theban region in particular.
Here the pharaoh wears the characteristic
Kushite cap with a double *uraeus* (now, like
the top part of the crown, broken off) and
rounded earflaps to the sides. The surface
of the headdress has been left unpolished
in order to facilitate the adhesion of the
gilding with which it was once decorated.
The face combines features typical of King
Taharqo's African origins with the ideal-
izing tendency of the Egyptian tradition.

Standing figure of Horemakhet

3rd Intermediate Period, Twenty-fifth Dynasty,
ca. 690 B.C., Karnak, temple of Amun-Re,
red quartzite, H. 66 cm

This standing figure of Horemakhet is
another of the artworks brought to Aswan
from the Egyptian Museum in Cairo. Under
his father, King Shabaqo, Horemakhet held
office as the high priest of Amun in the
national temple at Karnak. The statue was
hidden there in the famous "cachette" close
to the seventh pylon. Horemakhet is
wearing the short, three-part kilt and a
collar consisting of several different bands.
He also has a chain around his neck from
which hangs an amulet in the form of the
sign of life (Egypt. "ankh"). As a reference
to his priestly status, the king's son is
depicted with shaven head.

Nubia and its Temples

Nubia

Today Nubia is divided between the two modern states of Egypt and Sudan. During pharaonic times, Lower Nubia, which stretched from Aswan as far as Wadi Halfa, was known as Wawat, and Upper Nubia, the region which extended south from there, was called Kush. Intensive settlement of the area had already begun during the Neolithic age (5th/4th millennia B.C.), but with the First Dynasty there began a long period of economic and cultural interaction of these neighboring southerly regions with Egypt, whose main interest was to secure the trade in valuable goods. Exotic goods were imported from or via Nubia, including high-grade timber, ivory, incense, oils and rare types of stone. First and foremost, though, Nubia was the supplier of gold of varying qualities. While the rulers of the Twelfth Dynasty had managed to consolidate their influence (by building massive fortresses, such as Buhen and Semna) as far south as the Second Cataract, it remained for the pharaohs of the New Kingdom (Thutmosis I and III) to bring the region completely under Egypt's control and to unite it administratively with the mother country. In the 1st millennium B.C., however, it was the Kushite kings who in turn overran Egypt and ruled as the Twenty-fifth Dynasty.

Previous pages: the Great Temple of Ramesses II at Abu Simbel

Temple of el-Dakka, p. 533

Statue of Ramesses II as a standard-bearer, p. 532

Great Temple of Ramesses II, p. 518 ff.

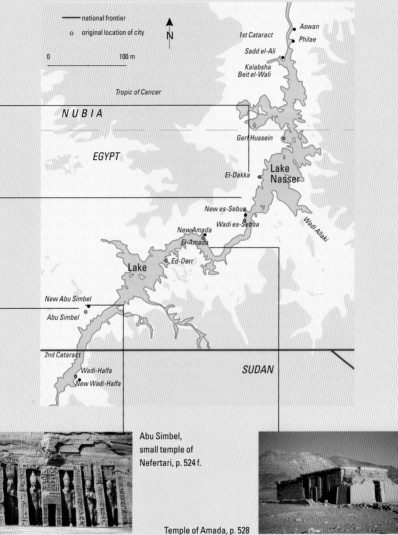

national frontier
o   original location of city

0   100 m

N

1st Cataract
Aswan
Philae
Sadd el-Ali
Kalabsha
Beit el-Wali

Tropic of Cancer

N U B I A

EGYPT

Gerf Hussein

El-Dakka

Lake Nasser

New es-Sebua
Wadi es-Sebua
New Amada
El-Amada
Lake
Ed-Derr

Wadi Allaki

New Abu Simbel

Abu Simbel

2nd Cataract

SUDAN

Wadi-Halfa
New Wadi-Halfa

Abu Simbel,
small temple of
Nefertari, p. 524 f.

Temple of Amada, p. 528

Abu Simbel

Great Temple of Ramesses II
Nineteenth Dynasty, ca. 1260 B.C.

The two rock temples of Abu Simbel are located around 40 km north of the Sudanese border on the west bank of the modern reservoir (Lake Nasser). Originally hewn into the cliffs of the Nile riverbank, these two temples, were rediscovered buried in sand by the Swiss traveler Johann L. Burckhardt in 1813. Following their successful rescue, they now stand like skittles in the Nubian desert. Ramesses II dedicated the larger temple to the national gods Re-Horakhty, Amun-Re, Ptah and his own divine self. Constructed in pylon form, the façade is taken up by four colossal seated figures (H. some 20 m, 68 ft.) of the pharaoh, which flank the entrance in pairs. The ruler wears the Nemes headcloth with the Double Crown and a short loincloth. By his legs are statues of the princes and princesses, and also of the pharaoh's mother and his main wife, Nefertari. The upper body of the figure to the left of the entrance collapsed in an earthquake that occurred already in ancient times.

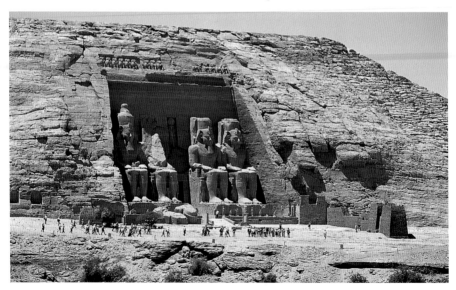

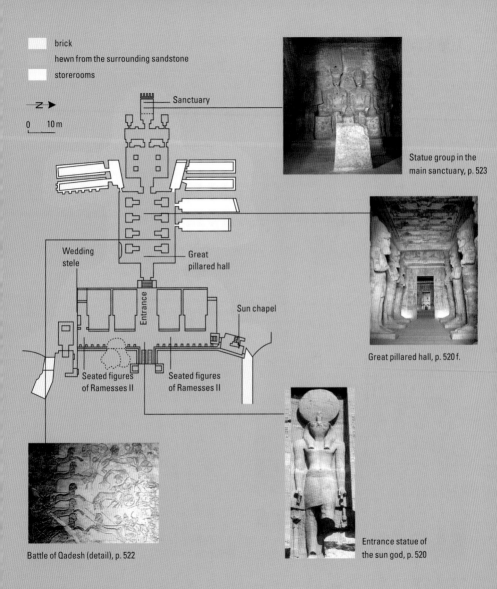

brick

hewn from the surrounding sandstone

storerooms

N →

0   10 m

Sanctuary

Statue group in the
main sanctuary, p. 523

Great pillared hall, p. 520 f.

Wedding
stele

Great
pillared hall

Entrance

Sun chapel

Seated figures
of Ramesses II

Seated figures
of Ramesses II

Battle of Qadesh (detail), p. 522

Entrance statue of
the sun god, p. 520

Entrance statue of the sun god

In a high niche immediately above the temple entrance is a statue of falcon-headed sun god Re-Harakhty. Looking east, the divinity wears the symbolic sun disk on its head and a short loincloth. His arms hang down by the side of his body and are "supported" by two hypostatized hieroglyphs next to its legs: the dog-headed staff (left) with the sound value "user" and the figure of the goddess Maat, wearing a crown of feathers. In the form of a rebus, these two symbols make up the throne name of Ramesses II, User-Maat-Re, when combined with the name of the god, being present in his statue.

The great pillared hall

The entrance of the temple leads into the great pillared hall, whose function corresponds to the courtyard of a traditional temple building. Four immense statues of the pharaoh (H. 10 m, 33 ft.) stand against the front of the pillars on either side of the axis. As with the façade statues, an individual name, expressing a specific divine quality of the ruler, was chiseled onto the shoulder of each of the statues. The long northern wall is completely given over to scenes depicting the battle of Qadesh against the Hittites, while on the opposite wall just the lower register is decorated, by three large sized battle scenes of Syrian, libyan and Nubian war campaigns.

Battle of Qadesh (detail)

No other event in the sphere of foreign affairs affected Ramesses II's reign to the extent that the battle of Qadesh against the Hittites did. In spite of a not exactly glorious outcome, the pharaoh had all the major temples in the country decorated with detailed representations of the campaign, thus celebrating a heroic victory for the ruler, very much in the style of dynastic propaganda. With their scenic construc-tion, the pictures of the battle of Qadesh are convincing due to a hitherto unknown narrative tautness, which nevertheless makes use of traditional set pieces. One of these is the scene showing the chariot divi-sion on the left attacking in orderly fashion and causing chaos in the enemy ranks facing it. This contrast clearly conveys an Egyptian victory, which is a rather liberal interpretation of the historical facts. The dynamics of the battle are emphasized by the free composition without register lines.

Statue group in the main sanctuary

The temple's inner sanctum is situated at the far end of the structure, which measures 63 m (207 ft.) in length, in the depths of the hillside. The entire width of its rear wall is occupied by a group of statues. The four seated figures have been hewn directly from the cliff face and are raised forward on a shared throne bench. On the outside left is the figure of the god of creation, Ptah of Memphis, next to him the national deity Amun-Re of Thebes, then the divine Ramesses wearing a blue crown, and on the other end, to the right, the sun god Re-Horakhty of Heliopolis. Even after the relocation of the temple, the so-called sun miracle of Abu Simbel still takes place twice a year around the time of the equinox (now 21 February and 21 October). When the doors are open, the light of the rising sun penetrates through to the sanctuary and the group of gods is illuminated. While the statue of Ptah, on the outside of the row, remains mostly in semi-darkness, the central fall of the light reduces the group of gods to a triad, with the pharaoh enthroned in the middle between the two most important gods Amun-Re (representing the south, Thebes) and Re-Horakhty (representing the north, Heliopolis). The inscription above the Sun-god gives the ancient name of the shrine as the "House of Ramesses, beloved of Amun."

Small Temple of Nefertari
Nineteenth Dynasty, ca. 1260 B.C.

The so-called Small Temple of Abu Simbel, dedicated by Ramesses II to his wife Nefertari and the goddess Hathor, was constructed slightly further north from the main temple. Against its sloping façade (12 × 28 m) with a cavetto molding now largely broken off, stand six colossal figures of the ruler and his wife. These are over 10 m high and flank the entrance in groups of three. The figures on either side of the portal embody Ramesses II's divine nature and through the choice of crowns have also been given separate attributes in terms of the different regions of the kingdom: the figure on the left is wearing the white crown and the figure on the right the double crown. The statues at either end depict the pharaoh as the reigning monarch on the throne of Horus. Between these two royal manifestations in each set stands Queen Nefertari, who has been made to resemble the goddess Hathor with her headdress featuring cow horns, double feathers and a sun disk.

The pillared hall

In keeping with the temple's function as a shrine to Hathor, the great hall has been furnished with six pillars whose inward-facing sides are decorated with a sistrum (musical instrument that is rattled) with the head of the goddess. Each of the hall's long walls is decorated with four ritual scenes, among which the second picture on the northern (right-hand) wall stands out in particular. Here we see Ramesses II bringing the ram-god Heryshef of Herakleopolis, a city situated at the entrance to the oasis of

Faiyum, a gift of water. The presence of Heryshef in a Nubian temple may at first seem peculiar, but it begins to make sense when we define the rock temple as a place representing above all fertility and regeneration. A subliminal relationship with a "green" area such as Faiyum does, therefore, exist. This important aspect is also represented by the goddess Hathor when she emerges in the small sanctuary (rock-cut figure), as if from the cliffside, in the form of a cow holding the pharaoh protectively under her chin and thus guaranteeing the cyclical renewal of the kingdom.

The World Saves Abu Simbel

A dramatic race against time to rescue the cultural treasures of the Nubian region from the vast waters of the new Lake Nasser was unleashed by the decision of the Egyptian government to construct the new high dam at Aswan. On January 9, 1960, the day blasting for

Relocation work (face of one of the colossi) in progress; Great Temple in Abu Simbel, 1965

the dam commenced, the clock started to tick relentlessly and the rescue problem grew more acute with each passing month. It also became clear that the countries affected, Egypt and Sudan, would not be able to carry out the necessary work without international assistance, both financial and scientific. In March that year, therefore, UNESCO appealed to all its member states for support, and this appeal met with a generous response. While countless teams of archaeologists and technicians went on to carry out excavations and relocation work with great success over the following years, the central problem of how to save Ramesses II's two rock temples in Abu Simbel from the artificial lake remained unsolved at this stage. More and more rescue plans were discussed and rejected. At the same time, work on the high dam was proceeding swiftly and as 1962 gave way to 1963, the threat to these unique sacred buildings started to become more and more real. At almost the last minute, Egypt and UNESCO agreed on a solution which was acceptable in terms of both cost and the desperate time situation. This solution consisted of dismembering the temples into the largest possible individual blocks and then reassembling the complexes 65 m higher and 180 m further back from the river. Responsibility for this work was entrusted to an international consortium under the overall control of Hochtief of Essen, Federal Republic of

Germany. The first phase of work consisted of constructing a sheet pile bulkhead in front of the temples to hold back the rising water. Next the façades were embedded for protection, meaning that the shrines could only be entered through specially installed steel culverts. After the stone of the surrounding cliff area had been removed, the actual wall surfaces and façade area were sawn into individual blocks no heavier that 20 to 30 tons using handsaws with a mere 6 mm cutting width. 807 blocks were lifted by special crane from the Great Temple and 235 from the Nefertari temple and transported to a holding depot. The last block was loaded on April 16, 1966, marking the successful completion of the dismantling process three months ahead of schedule. The reconstruction had already got underway during the final phase of the dismantling process, and this was finished in mid-1968. As

Façade of the Great Temple in Abu Simbel before dismantling, 1964

the reinforced concrete used in the walls and façade structures of both temples could not be expected to support the weight of the stone newly positioned on top, they were covered by a spherical roof. In the case of the Great Temple the resulting dome can be viewed by visitors and is a cause of no less astonishment than the buildings of Ramesses II themselves. However, both temples of Abu Simbel have to cope with their new positions in the desert in the long run. Only time will tell the results.

The Temple of Amada

Eighteenth Dynasty, ca. 1450–1400 B.C.

The Temple of Amada is another of the Nubian buildings that were rescued. It was built or extended by three great pharaohs of the Eighteenth Dynasty, Thutmosis III, Amenophis II and Thutmosis IV and dedicated to the gods Re-Horakhty and Amun-Re. While its exterior walls remained undecorated, the fine reliefs adorning its internal walls are remarkable for the well-preserved state of their paintwork. Following building work carried out by Thutmosis IV, the temple comprised a pylon followed by a pillared hall, a transverse hall, two side rooms and the main sanctuary. The rear wall of the sanctuary displays an interesting inscription from the third year of Amenophis II's reign, which describes among other things a military campaign led by the king to Syria. To facilitate the shrine's relocation, a concrete platform was inserted underneath the temple building, which was then, with the help of hydraulic winches, moved as a unit on rollers to its new site around 2.5 km (1.5 miles) away.

The Temple of ed-Derr

Nineteenth Dynasty, ca. 1250 B.C.

New Amada is also where the rock temple of ed-Derr, built by Ramesses II, was reconstructed. Today, this temple consists merely of two large pillared halls and a sanctuary with side chambers. The unspectacular architecture of the temple has nevertheless managed to preserve numerous vividly-colored reliefs, as the walls were covered with a protective layer of stucco when the temple was converted into a Coptic church. In the second hall, which has six pillars, the last picture field on the northern wall (left) shows the gods handing the pharaoh his years. For this, Ramesses stands in full regalia under the sacred *ished* tree (or persea tree) of Heliopolis, on whose leaves the pharaohs' titulary was traditionally inscribed. The Memphite god Ptah and the lion-headed goddess Sekhmet represent Lower Egypt here, while behind the pharaoh the god of wisdom, Thoth, in walking position, records the unending jubilees (*sed* festival) on a palm branch (Egyp. *renpet* for year).

The Temple of Wadi es-Sebua

Nineteenth Dynasty, ca. 1240 B.C.

In New Sebua there are also a number of shrines that were moved to a place of safety from the floodwaters of Lake Nasser. At the center of the present-day ensemble of temples stands the Wadi es-Sebua complex of Ramesses II, built for the ruler by the viceroy of Nubia, Setau, in the fourth decade of the pharaoh's reign. The modern Arabic name for this place, meaning "valley of lions" was given to the temple, whose original position was approximately 5 km (3 miles) to the west, because of its avenue of sphinxes, which passes also through two forecourts. From the second courtyard, steps lead up to the entrance pylon (H. 20.5 m), situated on a slightly higher level, which is followed by the great courtyard. The construction of the pillared hall is rather unusual. Cut out of the cliff side, it is almost completely filled by the twelve structural supports it contains. Next comes a transverse room vestibule which leads directly to the sanctuary and its two side chambers.

Sphinx of Ramesses II

Before the Aswan High Dam was built, Sebua offered its visitors a magnificent sight nearly every year at flood time. As the water level rose, the lower forecourts gradually sank beneath the floodwater until the sphinxes of Ramesses II lay on the surface like sculpted stone islands. The axis of the first forecourt is flanked on either side by three sphinxes of the ruler made of local sandstone, which rise up above plinths inscribed with the pharaoh's titulary. Today,

these in turn rest on high stone pedestals. The artistic execution of the figures is of local quality only, showing a very "putty" style. The pharaoh wears the nemes head-cloth with double crown, along with the uraeus on his brow and a wide ceremonial beard. In the second forecourt a far less common variant takes over from this clas-sical design of sphinx. Here the creatures line the central aisle in pairs. Instead of the head of the pharaoh, the lions' bodies bear falcon's heads as evidence of a cult associa-tion with the sun god.

Statue of Ramesses II as a standard-bearer

From the New Kingdom onwards, the colossal architectural sculptures positioned in front of the pylon towers generally took one of two forms: they could either be standing or enthroned figures of the pharaoh. The few known exceptions almost all date back to the 19th / 20th Dynasties, with the temple of Wadi es-Sebua providing the most striking example. In front of each of the pylon's towers there originally stood two enormous statues of Ramesses II holding a staff (H. 9.50 m, 31 ft.). Only one of these is still standing, another lies beside it on the ground. This particular type of royal statue was introduced under Amenophis III and enjoyed great popularity during the Ramesside period. It shows the ruler holding a long divine staff (sometimes two) surmounted by the head of a god. The staffs of the four statues of Sebua comprised a pair with falcon heads, representing Re-Horakhty, and a pair with ram's heads, representing Amun-Re, as the shrine's two main gods.

The Temple of el-Dakka

Meroitic, Ptolemaic and Roman period,
3rd / 1st centuries B.C.

The temple of el-Dakka was originally positioned 40 km (25 miles) north of its present site. Its building history begins with the Meroitic king Arkamani II (Greek Ergamenes, ca. 218–195 B.C.) and his younger contemporary, Ptolemy IV Philopator (221–204 B.C.) and extends up to the early imperial Roman period to Augustus (30 B.C.–14 A.D.) and Tiberius (14–37 A.D.). The shrine was dedicated to the local god Thoth of Pnubs and his spouse, the goddess Tefnut. The magnificent entrance pylon (W.

24.5 m; largely undecorated) and actual temple building lie isolated from each other, as the connecting courtyard area and perimeter wall have been completely destroyed. The ritual images in the pronaos and adjoining transverse hall are examples of Ptolemaic work (Ptolemy VIII) which are surpassed in quality by those in the Ergamenes chapel which follows after. The crude execution of the images in the final room, the Roman sanctuary, however, leave no doubt about their later genesis. In the time of moving some reused blocks of a much earlier temple at Dakka (New Kingdom) were found.

Sinai

Sinai

Previous pages: Mountain range in Sinai with Mount Moses in the foreground

Familiar as a theater of war over the past few decades Sinai also has a rich cultural heritage concentrated predominantly into the southern tip of the peninsula, which is dominated by an impressive mountain landscape. Sinai was yielding up valuable mineral resources, the most important of which were copper and turquoise, as long ago as the 3rd millennium B.C. Evidence of this is provided by the numerous rock inscriptions (dating from the Old Kingdom onwards) found in the quarrying area of Wadi Maghara. Several well-preserved reliefs were even sawn off and taken for safekeeping by Flinders Petrie to the museum in Cairo, among them the famous depiction of King Snefru smiting an Asiatic enemy (picture on the left; red sandstone, H. 112 cm). Alongside his titulary, the accompanying text describes him as the "Conqueror of the Foreign Lands." This main heraldic motif is extended through the addition on the right of Snefru's Horus name in large format, with the figure

of the falcon representing the ruler pictorially above the palace façade (Egyp.: serekh). The ancient inscriptions dating from the Middle and New Kingdoms on and in the temple of Hathor at Serabit el-Khadim, with its unique architecture, indicate the continuity of this mining activity. The Sinai is a holy place for Jews and Christians alike. Moses received the commandment tablets from God on Mount Horeb, and ever since the building of St. Catherine's Monastery in the 6th century, this has also been the location of Egypt's most important Christian site.

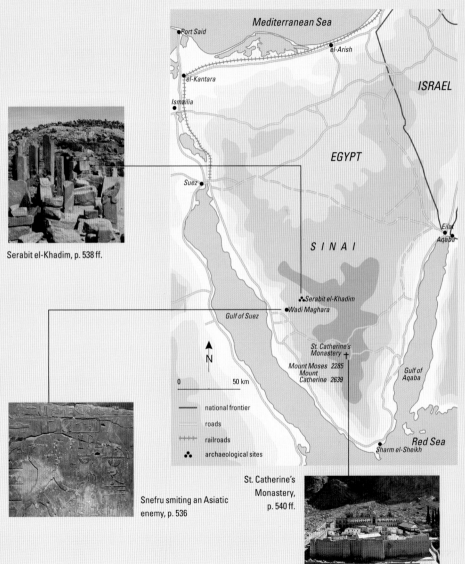

Serabit el-Khadim, p. 538 ff.

Snefru smiting an Asiatic
enemy, p. 536

St. Catherine's
Monastery,
p. 540 ff.

Mediterranean Sea

Port Said

el-Arish

el-Kantara

Ismailia

ISRAEL

EGYPT

Suez

Eilat
Aqaba

S I N A I

Serabit el-Khadim
Wadi Maghara

Gulf of Suez

St. Catherine's
Monastery

Mount Moses 2285
Mount
Catherine 2639

Gulf of
Aqaba

N

0   50 km

Red Sea

Sharm el-Sheikh

national frontier

roads

railroads

archaeological sites

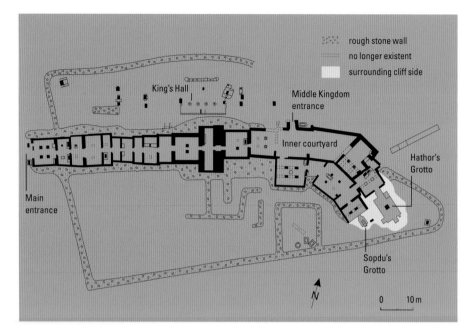

rough stone wall
no longer existent
surrounding cliff side

King's Hall

Middle Kingdom
entrance

Inner courtyard

Hathor's
Grotto

Main
entrance

Sopdu's
Grotto

N

0   10 m

Serabit el-Khadim

Middle and New Kingdoms, 2nd millennium B.C.

Sinai's largest pharaonic shrine, the elongated temple of Serabit el-Khadim (excavated by Petrie in 1905), is situated on an
850 m (2,800 ft) high rocky plateau in the
middle of the former turquoise-mining
area. The patron deity worshiped here
was Hathor, who also bore the epithet
"Mistress of the Turquoise," although
Sopdu, god of the Eastern Desert, the
moon god Thoth and the deified early

Fourth-Dynasty king, Snefru, also had
cults here. With its succession of open
courtyards, this temple complex, which
also possesses a sanctuary built into the
cliff side, falls outside the framework of
traditional sacred architecture of its time,
and the number of monumental stelae,
erected on behalf of the king by the officials leading the turquoise expeditions is
quite bewildering. These start with the
Twelfth Dynasty, take in all the great
rulers of the Eighteenth Dynasty, and end
with a memorial stone slabs from the time
of Ramesses VI (Twentieth Dynasty).

St. Catherine's Monastery

Byzantine period, 6th century A.D.

The immense, 1,570 m (5,150 ft) high complex of St. Catherine's Monastery lies in a hollow at the foot of Mount Sinai (2,285 m/ 10,795 ft) like a siege castle. Founded by the Byzantine emperor Justinian I (527– 565), the monastery was built over the site of the legendary burning bush, where it replaced an earlier fortified church. Its unfavorable site prompted the emperor furthermore to station 200 Roman and Egyptian soldiers there, by deed of gift, for the protection of the monks. At the time of its foundation, the monastery was dedicated to the Virgin Mary and only later rededicated to St. Catherine. Legend has it that the mortal remains of the martyr were found at the summit of nearby Mount Catherine following a dream experienced by one of the monks. Since the 16th century the monastery has been an independent archbishopric of the Greek Orthodox Church. After falling for several

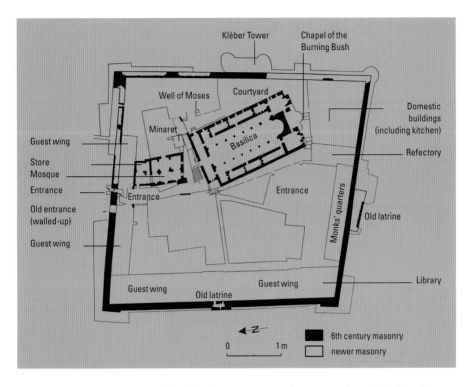

Kléber Tower

Chapel of the Burning Bush

Courtyard

Well of Moses

Domestic buildings (including kitchen)

Minaret

Basilica

Guest wing

Refectory

Store

Mosque

Entrance

Entrance

Entrance

Monks' quarters

Old entrance (walled-up)

Old latrine

Guest wing

Library

Guest wing

Guest wing

Old latrine

N

0   1 m

■ 6th century masonry

□ newer masonry

decades, the number of monks who live here today is on the increase again. The monastery complex, covering an area of 85 × 76 m, is surrounded by a 12 to 15 m-high protective wall made of granite blocks. This wall is of irregular construction to accommodate the unevenness of the site, and only on the southwestern side has its Justinian stonework been substantially preserved, all other parts of it having undergone frequent restoration work. For reasons of security, the original main gate had to be walled up early in the monastery's history and was finally replaced by a small gateway on the left-hand side at the beginning of the 19th century, when the old basket lift for both goods and people ceased to be used. Once inside the walls, visitors are confronted by a labyrinth of alleyways, staircases, entrances and buildings housing the sacred and secular facilities of the monastery.

The Basilica

The dominant feature of the monastery is its large basilica dating from the time of Justinian, which is entered through a Fatimid-era (11th century) door. The triple-aisled main body of the church, with its two rows of six granite columns, extends from the other side of the narthex, which is positioned at right angles to the main aisle. The two side aisles contain chapels dedicated to the saints of the Orthodox Church. The colored stone floor, made of marble and porphyry, was installed relatively recently, in 1714, and the flat ceiling was also put up during the 18th century. Three of the beams of the original roof truss, covered by a lead roof since the 14th century, bear inscriptions which refer to the imperial couple Justinian ("God protect our pious emperor Justinian") and Theodora and also the church's building master, Stephanos Ailisios. A richly painted and gilded iconostasis from 1612 separates the main body of the church from the choir, where the marble sarcophagus of St. Catherine (18th century), under a baldachin on the right, and the world-famous apse mosaic can be found. The most recent addition to the church is its bell tower built in 1871, whose nine bronze bells were donated by the imperial family of Russia.

The Great Apse Mosaic

The mosaics in the apse, commissioned by Emperor Justinian II (527–565) from a Byzantine court artist and his assistants, are of exceptional quality. Even a brief glance captures something of their clarity of composition, which is impressive for the monumentality of its figures. The central double window on the end wall is flanked by two scenes: on the left, Moses in the burning bush, and on the right, Moses receiving the commandment tablets. Underneath are two hovering angels and two medallions containing portrait heads presumed to be those of Emperor Justinian himself and his wife Theodora, orientated towards the lamb of God, which forms the central motif beneath the window arch. The figure of Christ, in the mandorla, dominates the vault of the apse. The prophets Elias and Moses stand on his left and right respectively, while the three disciples John, James and Peter can be seen at his feet. A chain of medallions featuring busts of 16 prophets and the 12 disciples runs around the edges of the vault, relieved on the central axis by medallions containing a crucifix (top) and a picture of David (bottom).

Chapel of the Burning Bush

Icon displaying a view of the monastery

The holiest place in the monastery, the Chapel of the Burning Bush, is located behind the choir. The walls of this room, which was created after the main church, are covered with faience tiles and decorated with numerous icons. In the small apse stands a small altar under which an eternally-lit lamp indicates the site of the Burning Bush. This spot is now covered by a silver plate bearing an inscription from the year 1696.

Its collection of icons is probably the monastery's greatest art-historical treasure. Over 2,000 individual items, displaying the widest possible styles and originating over the widest possible period (6th c. to the modern era) form a collection unrivaled throughout the world. The early Byzantine icons in particular are priceless. The monastery and its surrounding area have also been the subject of artists, as this icon (17th c.), which was executed in Sinai, reveals.

The Copts—Christianity on the Nile

ΕΝΗΡΗΝΗΤΗΑΝΑ
ΠΑΥCΑΜΕΝΗΘΕΟΔΟΡΑ

Theodora's grave stele, 6th century, Faiyum, limestone, H. 75 cm,
Early Christian and Byzantine Collection, Staatliche Museen
Preußischer Kulturbesitz, Berlin

Most of the Christians living in Egypt today belong to the Coptic Orthodox Church. In contrast to the Muslims, who see themselves at least in part as the descendants of the Arab conquerors, the Copts regard themselves as the direct descendants of the ancient Egyptians. Christianity played an important role in Egypt from a very early stage. It is supposed to have been brought to Egypt by Mark the evangelist during the 1st century A.D. The saint is believed to have established the first bishopric in Alexandria, where he was also martyred. The development of the early Christian church was beset by two serious problems: the argument over the true doctrine, which ultimately led to the schism between the churches, and the large-scale persecution of Christians during the 3rd and 4th centuries A.D. The terror of this era of martyrdom could never be forgotten, and the Coptic calendar also refers to it, as it commenced with the

Diocletian's reign in 284 A.D., under which the worst persecution took place. Once Christianity was finally tolerated, many Egyptians embraced the new religion, which gave them a renewed sense of self-esteem despite their poverty and despite being subjected to foreign rule. Some of the faithful withdrew to the desert and sought their own path to God as hermits. Others banded together to form communities, and strictly hierarchical monasteries developed, led by such great men as abbots Pachomius (died 346 A.D.) and Shenoute of Atripe (348–466 A.D.). The monasteries were also cultural centers in which, in addition to the bible being translated into Egyptian, a new literature also developed. The written form of language used for this was no longer complicated hieroglyphics, but Greek letters supplemented by certain additional Egyptian characters. Although the Coptic script and language were later superseded by Arabic, they retained an essential role in the country's Orthodox church liturgy. Art and architecture also experienced a golden age, and the Coptic textiles with floral and figurative motifs produced during this period, which have survived well in the dry Egyptian climate, were to become especially famous. In their heydays (4th–7th Centuries) the different products of the looms were highly esteemed all over Egypt. Monasteries and places of pilgrimage still play an important part in religious life today and are widely visited on religious holidays. For many young Copts in particular, a short stay in a monastery is seen not only as satisfying an inner need, but also as an expression of their Christian cultural identity in a world dominated by Islam.

Robe trim with a bird motif and "ankh" symbol, 5th century, wool and linen, 22 × 22 cm, The British Museum, London

Robe trim featuring a sea scene, 5th/6th centuries, wool, 31 × 29.5 cm, Musée du Louvre, Paris

Appendix

Chronology (Selection)

Previous double page: Papyrus with the Book of the Dead of Amenemope (detail), Eighteenth Dynasty, ca. 1400 B.C., Thebes, H. 35 cm, Museo Gregoriano Egizio, Vatican

Prehistory, 5th–4th millenia B.C.

Dynasty 0	**before 3000**
Narmer	before 3000

Early Dynastic Period

1st/2nd Dynasty	**3007–2682**
Aha (Menes)	3000–2975

Old Kingdom

3rd Dynasty	**2682–2614**
Nebka	2682–2665
Djoser	2665–2645
Huni	–2614
4th Dynasty	**2614–2479**
Snefru	2614–2579
Cheops	2579–2556
Djedefre	2556–2547
Chephren	2547–2521
Mycerinos	2514–2486
Shepseskaf	2486–2479
5th Dynasty	**2479–2322**
Userkaf	2479–2471
Sahure	2471–2458
Neferirkare	2458–2438
Neferefre	2431–2420
Niuserre	2420–2389
Menkauhor	2389–2380
Djedkare Asosi	2380–2342
Unas	2342–2322
6th Dynasty	**2322–2191**
Teti	2322–2312
Pepy I	2310–2260
Pepy II	2254–2194
Nitokris	2193–2191

(7th)/8th Dynasty	**2191–2145**

First Intermediate Period

9th/10th Dynasty	**2145–2025**

Middle Kingdom

11th Dynasty	**2119–1976**
Intef I, II, III	2119–2046
Mentuhotep II	2046–1995
Mentuhotep III	1995–1983
12th Dynasty	**1976–1794**
Amenemhet I	1976–1947
Senusret I	1956–1911
Amenemhet II	1914–1879
Senusret II	1882–1872
Senusret III	1872–1853
Amenemhet III	1853–1806
Amenemhet IV	1806–1798
13th Dynasty	**1794–1648**

Second Intermediate Period

14th Dynasty (in the delta)	**? –1648**
15th/16th Dynasty (Hyksos)	**1648–1539**
17th Dynasty	**1645–1550**
Seqenenre Taa II	–1556
Kamose	1556–1550

New Kingdom

18th Dynasty	**1550–1292**
Ahmose	1550–1525
Amenophis I	1525–1504
Thutmosis I	1504–1492
Thutmosis II	1492–1279

Hatshepsut	1479–1458		Takelot I	890–877
Thutmosis III	1479–1425		Shoshenq II	877–875
Amenophis II	1428–1397		Osorkon II	875–837
Thutmosis IV	1397–1388		Shoshenq III	837–785
Amenophis III	1388–1351		Shoshenq V	774–736
Amenophis IV (Akhenaten)	1351–1334		**23rd/24th Dynasty**	**756/740–712**
Semenkhkare	1337–1333		Pedubastis	756–730
Tutankhamun	1333–1323		Tefnakhte	740–718
Ay	1323–1319		**25th Dynasty (Kushite)**	**before 746–655**
Horemheb	1319–1292		Piy	746–715
19th Dynasty	**1292–1186**		Shabaqo	713–698
Ramesses I	1292–1290		Shebitqo	698–690
Sety I	1290–1279		Taharqo	690–664
Ramesses II	1279–1213		Tanutamani	664–655
Merenptah	1213–1203			
Amenmesse	1203–1199		**Late Period**	
Sety II	1199–1194			
Siptah/Tausret	1194–1186		**26th Dynasty (Saite)**	**664–525**
20th Dynasty	**1186–1070**		Psametik I	664–610
Sethnakht	1186–1183		Nekau II	610–595
Ramesses III	1183–1152		Psametik II	595–589
Ramesses IV	1152–1145		Apries	589–570
Ramesses V	1145–1142		Amasis	570–526
Ramesses VI	1142–1134		Psametik III	526–525
Ramesses VII	1134–1126		**27th Dynasty (1st Persian Period)**	**525–401**
Ramesses VIII	1126–1125		Cambyses (in Egypt)	525–522
Ramesses IX	1125–1107		Dareios I	522–486
Ramesses X	1107–1103		Xerxes I	486–465
Ramesses XI	1103–1070		Artaxerxes I	465–424
			Xerxes II/Dareios II	424–405
Third Intermediate Period			**28th/29th Dynasty**	**405–380**
			Amyrtaios	405–399
			Nepherites I	399–393
21st Dynasty (in Tanis)	**1070–946**		Psamuthis/Achoris	393–380
Smendes	1070–1044		**30th Dynasty**	**380–342**
Psusennes I	1044–994		Netanebo I	380–362
Amenemope	994–985		Teos	364–360
Siamum	979–960		Netanebo II	360–342
Psusennes II	960–946		**31st Dynasty (2nd Persian Period)**	**342–332**
22nd Dynasty (in Bubastis)	**946–736**		Artaxerxes III (in Egypt)	342–337
Shoshenq I	946–925		Dareios III	337–332
Osorkon I	925–890			

Graeco-Roman Period

The Macedonians (Argaeid Dynasty)	**332–310**
Alexander the Great	332–305
Philippos Arrhidaios	323–317
Alexander IV	317–306
The Ptolemies	**305–30**
Ptolemy I Soter .	305–282
Ptolemy II Philadelphos	285–246
Ptolemy III Euergetes I	246–221
Ptolemy IV. Philopator	221–204
Ptolemy V Epiphanes	204–180
Harwennefer/Ankhwennefer	205–186
Ptolemy VI Philometor and	
Ptolemy VII Neos Philopator	180–145
Ptolemy VIII Euergetes II	145–116
Ptolemy IX Soter II	116–107
Ptolemy X Alexander I	88
Ptolemy XI Alexander II	88–80
Ptolemy XII Neos Dionysos (Auletes)	80–51
Cleopatra VII	51–30
Roman (Imperial) Period	**30 B.C.–324 A.D.**
Augustus	27 B.C.–14 A.D.
Tiberius	14–37
Caligula	37–41
Claudius	41–54
Nero	54–68
Galba/Otho/Vitellius	68–69
Vespasian	69–79
Titus	79–81
Domitian	81–96
Nerva	96–98
Trajan	98–117
Hadrian	117–138
Antoninus Pius	138–161
Marcus Aurelius/Lucius Verus	161–180
Commodus	180–192
Septimius Severus	193–211
Caracalla/Geta	211–217
Macrinus/Diadumenianus	217–218
Elagabalus	218–222

Philippus Arabus	244–249
Decius	249–251
Valerian/Gallienus	253–268
Diocletian	284–305
Maximinus Daia	305–313
Byzantine (East Roman) Period	**324–641**
Constantine I, the Great	324–337
Constantinos II and Julian	337–363
Jovian	363–364
Valens	364–378
Theodosius I	379–395
Arcadios	395–408
Theodosius II	408–450
Markian	450–457
Leon I/Leon II	457–474
Zenon/Basiliskos	474–491
Anastasios	491–518
Justinian I	527–565
Justinian II	565–578
Tiberios I Constantinos	578–582
Maurikios	582–602
Phokas	602–610
Herakleios	610–641

Islamic Period

Caliphs	**632–661**
Omar	634–644
Otman	644–656
Ali	656–661
Omyyads (in Damascus)	**661–750**
Muaviya I	661–680
Yazid I	680–683
Muaviya II/Mervan I	683–685
Abdul Malik	685–705
Walid I	705–715
Suleyman	715–717
Omar II	717–720
Yazid II	720–724
Hisham	724–743
Walid II/Yazid III	743–744
Merwan II.	744–750

Abbasids (Baghdad)	**750–868**	**Bahri-Mamluks (25 rulers)**	**1250–1382**
Abu l'Abbas	750–754	El-Muizz Aybak	1250–1257
Al-Mansur	754–775	El-Zahir Bey Bars I	1260–1277
Al-Mahdi and Al-Hadi	775–786	El-Mansur Qalaun	1279–1290
Haroun Al-Rashid	786–809	El-Nasir Mohammed I	1294–1340
Mohammed Al-Emin	809–813	El-Nasir Hassan	1347–1361
Abdallah Al-Mamun	813–833	**Burgi-Mamluks (24 rulers)**	**1382–1517**
Al-Mutasim Billahi	833–842	Ez-Zahir Barkuk	1382–1399
Al-Watik Billahi	842–847	En-Nasir Farag	1399–1412
Djafar Al-Mutawakkil	847–861	El-Ashraf Bars Bey	1422–1437
Al-Muntasir	861–862	El-Ashraf Qait Bey	1468–1496
Al-Mustain Billahi	862–866	Qansuh II El Ghauri	1501–1517
Al-Mutaz	866–869	**Ottoman (18 rulers)**	**1512–1773**
Tulunids (Cairo)	**868–905**	Selim I Yavuz	1512–1520
Achmed Ibn Tulun	868–883	Suleyman II, the Magnificent	1520–1566
Chumaraweh/Yaysh	883–896	Murat III	1577–1595
Haroun/Shayban	896–905	Murat IV	1623–1640
Abbasids (Baghdad)	**905–935**	Ahmed III	1703–1730
Governors in Cairo		Mustafa III	1757–1773
Ikhshidids	**935–969**	**Mamluks (again)**	**1768–1798**
Mohammed, Al-Ichshid	935–946	Ali Bey	1768–1773
Unujur	946–961	*(French Occupation)*	*1798–1805*
Ali, Kafur und Ahmed	961–969	**Khedeval Period**	**1805–1953**
Fatimids	**909–1171**	Muhammad Ali	1805–1848
Al-Muizz	953–975	Abbas Helmi I	1848–1854
Al-Aziz	975–996	Muhammad Said	1854–1863
Al-Hakim	996–1021	Ismail	1863–1879
Ez-Zahir	1021–1036	Tawfiq	1879–1892
Al-Mustansir	1036–1094	*(British Protectorate)*	*1882–1922*
Al-Mustali	1094–1101	Abbas Helmi II	1892–1914
Al-Amir	1101–1131	Hussein Kamil	1914–1917
Al-Hafiz	1131–1149	**Monarchy**	**1917–1953**
Ez-Zafir	1149–1154	Ahmed Fuad I	1917–1936
Al-Faiz	1154–1160	Farouk	1937–1952
Al-Adid	1160–1171	**Republic**	**since 1953**
Ayyubids	**1171–1250**	Mohammed Nagib	1953–1954
Salah Ed-Din (Saladin)	1171–1193	Gamal Abdel Nasser	1954–1970
Al-Aziz and El-Mansur	1193–1200	Anwar El-Sadat	1970–1981
Al-Adil I	1200–1218	Moh. Hosni Mubarak	since 1981
Al-Kamil and al-Adil II	1218–1240		
Es-Salih Ayub	1240–1249		

Seated figure of Mentuhotep II, 11th Dynasty, ca. 2030 B.C.

Mentuhotep II reunifies the kingdom (11th Dynasty, ca. 2050 B.C.). Thebes is the seat of government. The following 12th Dynasty (Kings named Senusret and Amenemhet) is regarded as the classical epoch of the language and fine arts; intensive trade with other countries and policy of conquest in Nubia.

Senusret III praying, 12th Dynasty, ca. 1850 B.C.

Head of an Osiride figure of Queen Hatshepsut, 18th Dynasty, ca. 1470 B.C.

Middle Kingdom
ca. 2050 – 1650

Western Thebes, Mortuary Temple of Mentuhotep II, 11th Dynasty, ca. 2030 B.C.

Karnak, Barque Sanctuary, "The White Chapel" of Senusret I, 12th Dynasty, ca. 1930 B.C.

Faiyum, Temple of Qasr es-Sagha, 12th Dynasty, ca. 1800 B.C.

Karnak, Alabaster Shrine of Amenophis I, 18th Dynasty, ca. 1500 B.C.

Karnak, Osiride Pillar of Senusret I, 12th Dynasty, ca. 1930 B.C.

Seated Figure of Queen Nefertite, 12th Dynasty, ca. 1880 B.C.

Double statue: The "fish-offerers" of Amenemhet III, 12th Dynasty, ca. 1820 B.C.

Kneeling Figure of Thutmosis III, 18th Dynasty, ca. 1450 B.C.

Relief on the Sarcophagus of Kawit, 11th Dynasty, ca. 2050 B.C.

Senusret I with the God Ptah, 12th Dynasty, ca. 1940 B.C.

Aswan, The Nomarch Sarenput II at the offering Table, 12th Dynasty, ca. 1880 B.C.

The King and Queen of Punt, 18th Dynasty, ca. 1470 B.C.

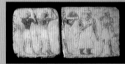

Statuette of a Woman bearing Offerings, 11th / 12th Dynasty, ca. 1990 B.C.

Pectoral bearing the Name of Amenemhet III, 12th Dynasty, ca. 1840 B.C.

Figure of a Hippopotamus Standing, from a Tomb, 17th Dynasty, ca. 1600 B.C.

Papyrus with the Book of the Dead of Maiherperi, ca. 1450 B.C.

History

The unification of Egypt in the making: the great palette of King Narmer, Dynasty 0, ca. 3100 B.C.

Seated figure of King Djoser, 3rd Dynasty, ca. 2650 B.C.

First peak of ancient Egyptian culture, symbolized in the great pyramids of King Snefru, King Cheops and King Chephren (4th Dynasty); the sacral kingdom develops, with the pharaoh at its head and Memphis as the capital. At the end of the 6th Dynasty (ca. 2180 B.C.) the Old Kingdom collapses for internal reasons.

Seated figure of King Chephren, Giza, 4th Dynasty, ca. 2530 B.C.

B.C.

Dynasty 0/Early Dynastic Period ca. 3100–2700

Old Kingdom ca. 2700–2150

Architecture

Abydos, Tomb of King Qa'a, 1st Dynasty, ca. 2900 B.C.

Step Pyramid of King Djoser in Saqqara, 3rd Dynasty, ca. 2650 B.C.

King Chephren's Pyramid in Giza, 4th Dynasty, ca. 2530 B.C.

King Unas' Pyramid in Saqqara, 5th Dynasty, ca. 2330 B.C.

Sculpture

Figure of the god "Great White" as a Baboon, Dynasty 0, ca. 3100 B.C.

Seated Figures of Prince Rahotep and his wife Nofret, 4th Dynasty, ca. 2600 B.C.

Standing Figure of the Official Ti from Saqqara, 5th Dynasty, ca. 2450 B.C.

Figure of an Anonymous Scribe, 5th Dynasty, ca. 2450 B.C.

Reliefs/ Painting

Ceremonial palette, Dynasty 0, ca. 3100 B.C.

Wooden Panel of Hesire from Saqqara, 3rd Dynasty, ca. 2650 B.C.

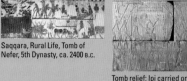

Saqqara, Rural Life, Tomb of Nefer, 5th Dynasty, ca. 2400 B.C.

Tomb relief: Ipi carried on a Litter, 6th Dynasty, ca. 2300 B.C.

Funerary and Minor Arts

Stone Vessels, 1st/2nd Dynasties, ca. 2900/ 2800 B.C.

Large Jubilee Vase, 3rd Dynasty, ca. 2650 B.C.

Throne of Queen Hetepheres, 4th Dynasty, ca. 2550 B.C.

Servant Girl brewing Beer, 5th Dynasty, ca. 2350 B.C.

Head of King Taharqo, 25th Dynasty, ca. 680 B.C.

In 728 B.C., the 20th year of his reign, King Pije conquers Egypt and establishes the Kushite rule for the 25th Dynasty. Only a short time later he launches attacks on Assyria. His successor Tanutamani has to withdraw to his Nubian homeland and a city prince of Sais founds the 26th Dynasty in 664 B.C., ruling as Psammetich I.

After the death of Alexander the Great Ptolemy I assumes power in Egypt in 304/05 B.C. and establishes the Ptolemaic Dynasty. Alexandria was established as capital with its landmark, the lighthouse of Pharos. The defeat of Cleopatra VII in the battle of Actium (30 B.C.) against Rome marked the end of Ptolemaic reign.

Marble bust of Cleopatra VII, ca. 30 B.C.

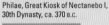

Late Period
ca. 664–332

Ptolemaic Period
332–30

History

B.C.

Karnak, Column of Taharqo in the First Court, 25th Dynasty, ca. 680 B.C.

Philae, Great Kiosk of Nectanebo I, 30th Dynasty, ca. 370 B.C.

Edfu, Pylon and Court of the Horus Temple, 2nd/1st century B.C.

Dendera, Pronaos of the Hathor Temple, 1st century B.C.

Architecture

Standing Figure of the Governor Monthemhat, 25th Dynasty, ca. 680 B.C.

Head of King Amasis, 26th Dynasty, ca. 550 B.C.

Horus Falcon in the Temple at Edfu, 2nd century B.C.

Standing Figure of Horsitutu, 3rd century B.C.

Sculpture

El Kurru, Tomb Painting: King Tanutamani, 25th Dynasty, ca. 650 B.C.

Tomb Relief: Women making Perfume, 30th Dynasty, ca. 350 B.C.

Edfu, Coronation Scene in the Horus Temple, 2nd century B.C.

Dendera, Astronomical Ceiling in the Pronaos, 1st century B.C.

Reliefs/ Painting

Great Wdjat-Eye, faience, 25th Dynasty, ca. 700 B.C.

Bronze Figure of the Cat Goddess Bastet, 26th Dynasty, ca. 600 B.C.

Sculptor's Model with Two Vultures, 3rd/2nd century B.C.

Small Chest, faience, 3rd century B.C.

Funerary and Minor Arts

Standing figure of Thutmosis III, 18th Dynasty, ca. 1450 B.C.

After conquering the Hyksos King Ahmose is the first ruler of the 18th Dynasty to ascend the throne; he founds the New Kingdom. In the official dogma the pharaoh is now regarded as the son of the state god Amun-Re of Thebes. Thutmosis III's many campaigns in Syria-Palestine make Egypt the undisputed hegemonial power in the Middle East. After the religious and political crisis in the time of Amarna (Akhenaton) the royal blood line dies out on the death of Tutankhamun. Ramesses II is the outstanding monarch in the following period of rule by the Ramessides (19th/20th Dynasties, 1292–1069 B.C.), reigning for 67 years, pursuing a successful foreign policy (peace treaty with the Hittites) and winning lasting glory with a great building program at home.

Colossal figure Akhenaton from Karnak, 18th Dynasty, ca. 1350 B.C.

Bust of a seated figure of Ramesses II, 19th Dynasty, ca. 1250 B.C.

New Kingdom
ca. 1550 – 1070

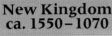

Obelisk of Hatshepsut, 18th Dynasty, ca. 1470 B.C.

Papyrus Column in the Temple of Luxor, 18th Dynasty, ca. 1370 B.C.

Entrance Pylon in the Temple of Luxor, 19th Dynasty, ca. 1270 B.C.

Abu Simbel, Small Temple of Nefertari, 19th Dynasty, ca. 1260 B.C.

Group of Amenophis III with the God Sobek, 18th Dynasty, ca. 1370 B.C.

Bust of Queen Nefertiti, 18th Dynasty, ca. 1340 B.C.

The Wife of General Nakhtmin, 18th Dynasty, ca. 1320 B.C.

Figure of Ramsesnakht as a scribe, 20th Dynasty, ca. 1140 B.C.

Western Thebes, The 4th Hour of the Amduat in the Tomb of Tutmosis III, 18th Dynasty, ca. 1450 B.C.

Western Thebes, The Mayor Sennefer and his Wife, 18th Dynasty, ca. 1420 B.C.

Western Thebes, The King between two Genies in the Tomb of Ramesses I, 19th Dynasty, ca. 1290 B.C.

Western Thebes, The sun god Re-Horakhty in his barque 19th Dynasty, ca. 1250 B.C.

Chest of Tja, 18th Dynasty, ca. 1370 B.C.

Canopic Jar of a Queen, 18th Dynasty, ca. 1340 B.C.

Gold Mask of Tutankhamun, 18th Dynasty, ca. 1330 B.C.

Portable Shrine with a Figure of god Anubis, 18th Dynasty, ca. 1330 B.C.

The Names of the Kings in Hieroglyphs (Selection)

Early Dynastic Period and Old Kingdom, 0–3rd Dynasties

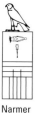

Narmer

Aha

Wadj

Den

Netjerikhet
(Djoser)

4th – 6th Dynasties

Snefru

Cheops

Chephren

Mycerinos

Shepseskaf

Userkaf

Sahure

Neferirkare

Niuserre

Djedkare

Unas

Teti

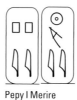

Pepy I Merire

Merenre Nemtiemsaf

Pepy II Neferkare

Middle Kingdom
11th–12th Dynasties

Intef I   Intef II

Mentuhotep II

Mentuhotep III

Mentuhotep IV

Amenemhet I

Senusret I

Amenemhet II

Senusret II

Senusret III

Amenemhet III

New Kingdom
18th Dynasty

Ahmose

Amenophis I

Thutmosis I

Thutmosis II

Hatshepsut

Thutmosis III

Amenophis II

Thutmosis IV

Amenophis III

Amenophis IV

18th Dynasty

Akhenaten

Semenkhkare

Tutankhamun

Ay

Horemheb

19th–20th Dynasties

Ramesses I

Sety I

Ramesses II

Merenptah

Sety II

Ramesses III

Ramesses IV

Ramesses VI

Ramesses XI

Herihor

Third Intermediate Period, 21st–22nd Dynasties and 25th Dynasty

Smendes

Psusennes I

Amenemope

Shoshenq I

Osorkon II

25th Dynasty

 Piy

 Shabaqo

 Shabitqo

 Taharqo

 Tanutamani

Late Period, 26th–30th Dynasties

 Psametik I

 Nekau II

 Psametik II

 Apries

Amasis

 Psametik III

 Cambyses

 Dareios

 Nectanebo I

 Nectanebo II

The Argaeid and the Ptolemaic Dynasties

 Alexander the Great

 Ptolemy I

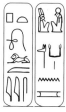 Ptolemy II

 Ptolemy III

 Cleopatra VII

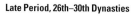

The Calendar

Martina Ullmann

The "official" calendar that was used by the administration and by which historical inscriptions, for example, were dated, was based on the sun year. This was divided into three seasons, "Akhet" (the flood), "Peret" (seed time) annd "Shemu" (the hot season). Each season lasted four months of 30 days each. The individual months in the three seasons were simply numbered through from one to four, for example the third month of Akhet, Day 15.

Five more days, the "Epagomenes" or festival days, were added, so that the Egyptian year had 365 days, deviating from the sun year by only one quarter of a day. The Epagomenes were public holidays and the birthdays of the gods Osiris, Horus, Seth, Isis and Nephthys. The fact that the Egyptian calendar was based on the sun year made it pioneering for later calendars, in contrast to the calendars of other peoples who generally measured their time by natural events that occurred irregularly. Hence the Egyptian calendar also influenced our modern version.

List of kings: Rulers of the Eighteenth Dynasty with their throne names (detail), Abydos, Temple of Ramesses II, limestone, painted, H. of detail ca. 45 cm, Nineteenth Dynasty, ca. 1270 B.C., The British Museum, London

But the deviation of the calendar from the sun year by about one quarter of a day per year meant that the Egyptian calendar shifted from the cosmic year by one day every four years. Hence a few centuries after the calendar was introduced, which was presumably in the early Dynastic period, around 3000 B.C., the seasons no longer conincided with the natural course of events. Only after 1460 years (or, more accurately 1456 years) did the dates of the cosmic year again coincide with those of the Egyptian civil year or "wandering year"— the Sothis Period, from the ascent of Sothis, the fixed star Sirius, that marked the start of the year. But the calendar was never reformed in ancient Egyptian times, presumably because the official way of counting time had a tradition going back for centuries, if not thousands of years, and was regarded as sacred and so untouchable. Moreover, the calendar, like other cultural achievements, was linked to the gods in Egyptian belief, it was held to be their work, and part of the divinely sanctioned world order ("Maat" in Egyptian). Sirius, the fixed star, whose annual re-ascent in the sky marked the start of the year, was often shown personified as a goddess. The Greek name "Sothis (or Seirius, sirius)" derives from the Egyptian "Sepdet." As Sirius reappears in northern Egypt in mid-July after being invisible for a time, and the Nile swelled each year at about the same time, Sothis was regarded as the bringer of the Nile floods. The ascent of Sothis and the Nile flood together marked the start of the year, and so the goddess Sothis was believed to be the incarnation of the year. Although two important records of Sothic risings (12th and 18th Dynasties) are known to us the assigned absolute dates by them may be not so certain as they look. The main reason: without real evidence we can only speculate about the location (Memphis, Elephantine?) where the astronomical observation took place.

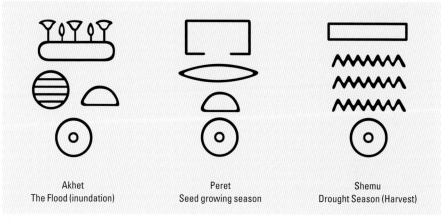

Akhet	Peret	Shemu
The Flood (inundation)	Seed growing season	Drought Season (Harvest)

The Three Seasons of the year in the Egyptian Calendar

All the data that has survived on Egyptian documents or monuments of any kind—stelae, temple walls, tomb walls, statues etc.—refer to this "official" calendar. In early Dynastic times the individual years were named after important events that took place in them, like religious festivals, the building of temples or the creation of statues of the gods, and that were listed by years. In the Old Kingdom the cattle count made every two years, or every year in some cases, to establish property as a basis for collecting taxes was the event used for dating, e.g. "the year of the third time (or the year after the third time) of counting under King Cheops." Extracts of these lists of the names of years from very Early times and following the Old Kingdom have survived in later copies, and they are a very important source for the reconstruction of Egyptian history or its chronology.

About the start of the Middle Kingdom (ca. 2000 B.C.) the method was changed to counting by the years of a king's reign. First the year of the reign of a certain king was given; this was followed by the month, the season and finally the day. For example, "25th Year of the Reign of His Majesty King User-Maat-Re (Ramesses II), 2nd month of the Peret season, Day 10." This method of dating was retained until the end of ancient Egyptian history, that is, until the time of Roman rule in the first centuries A.D. The practice of dating the reigns of the individual kings in chronological order, as in the lists of kings, as they are called, of which extracts have also survived (best known is the Turin Royal Canon), not only provided the basis for the recording of Ancient Egyptian history but is also of great importance for the modern reconstruction of Egyptian chronology.

In addition to the "official" calendar the natural year had existed since earliest times, and it was oriented to the phases of the moon, that could easily be observed with great precision. They lasted 29 or 30 days, so that with 12 moon months the year had only 354 days. But as the cosmic year has 365 and a quarter days, and the start of the year was linked with a annual event that occurred every year at the same time—the rise of the Nile and the ascent of Sothis that followed immediately after—a thirteenth month occasionally had to be inserted in the moon calendar.

The Ancient Egyptian Nomes

Already at the beginning of its Unification, Egypt was divided into Upper and Lower Egypt: the southern area along the course of the Nile, and the northern Delta region. The two parts of the country were further subdivided into 22 southern and 20 northern provinces, known to us as nomes. The nome system was introduced, at the latest, in the time of King Djoser (Third Dynasty), and remained in force until the Greco-Roman period, although with changes to the borders and the capital cities. In writing, the older nome hieroglyphs are combined with the sign of a standard, and frequently still indicate the original powers supposed to protect a region, such as the crocodile, snake, or bitch. However,

these powers are usually not the same as those of the chief divinity of the later nome. The names of the nomes formed at a later date dispensed with the sign of the standard and are written on their own. Initially, royal administrators presided over the nomes; they were succeeded by nomarchs, who could officiate with considerable autonomy. At its height, this extensive independence from the royal central power lasted from the end of the Old Kingdom until the middle of the Twelfth Dynasty. Thereafter the nomarch families were superseded by military officials, and in the New Kingdom "mayors" were responsible for the various nome regions.

The Upper Egyptian Nomes

1st Upper Egyptian nome Ta-seti, "Nubian land" Capital: Elephantine Chief gods: Khnum, Satet Other center: Kom Ombo	4th Upper Egyptian nome Waset, "scepter nome" Capital: Armant Chief gods: Montu, Amun Other center: Thebes
2nd Upper Egyptian nome Wetjset-Hor, "Horus throne" Capital: Edfu Chief god: Horus of Edfu	5th Upper Egyptian nome Netjerui, "the two divine ones" Capital: Koptos Chief god: Min Other center: Ombos
3rd Upper Egyptian nome Nekhen, "landing place" Capital: Hierakonpolis Chief gods: Horus, Nekhbet Other center: Esna	6th Upper Egyptian nome Iqer, "crocodile nome" Capital: Dendera Chief goddess: Hathor

7th Upper Egyptian nome "Bat nome" Capital: Hut-sekhem Chief goddess: Bat Other center: Diospolis Parva	13th Upper Egyptian nome Nedjfit khentit, "near pomegra- nate nome" Capital: Asyut Chief god: Upuaut
8th Upper Egyptian nome Ta-wer, "oldest land" Capital: Thinis Chief gods: Onuris, Osiris Main cult center: Abydos	14th Upper Egyptian nome Nedjfit pekhtit, "far pomegranate nome" Capital: Qusae Chief goddess: Hathor
9th Upper Egyptian nome "Min nome" Capital: Akhmim Chief god: Min of Ipu Other center: Sohag	15th Upper Egyptian nome Wenet, "hare nome" Capital: Hermopolis Magna Chief god: Thoth Other centers: Neferusi, el-Amarna
10th Upper Egyptian nome Wadjt, "serpent nome" Capital: Qaw el Kebir Chief god: Antiui (Horus and Seth)	16th Upper Egyptian nome Ma-hedj, "gazelle nome" Capital: Hebenu Chief god: Horus Other center: Menat-Khufu
11th Upper Egyptian nome "Seth nome" Capital: Skhashotep Chief gods: Horus/Seth Important center: Deir Rifeh	17th Upper Egyptian nome Input, "female whelp nome" Capitals: Henu, Sako Chief god: Anubis Other center: Hardai
12th Upper Egyptian nome Atfet, "mountain viper nome" Capital: Iakmet Chief goddess: Matit Other center: Deir el-Gabrawi	18th Upper Egyptian nome Nemti, "falcon nome" Capital: Hut-nesut Chief god: Horus-Dunanui Other center: Hut-benu

19th Upper Egyptian nome
Wabui, "double scepter nome"
Capital: Seper-meru
Chief gods: Den, Seth
Other center: Oxyrhynchos

21st Upper Egyptian nome
Naret pekhtit, "far oleander nome,"
sometimes including the Faiyum
Capital: Kafr Ammar
Chief god: Khnum

20th Upper Egyptian nome
Naret khentit, "near oleander nome"
Capital: Herakleopolis Magna
Chief god: Harsaphes

22nd Upper Egyptian nome
Medenit, "knife nome"
Capital: Atfih
Chief gods: Hathor, Neith

The Lower Egyptian nomes

1st Lower Egyptian nome
Inebu-hedj, "white wall nome"
Capital: Memphis
Chief god: Ptah
Other center: Itj-taui

5th Lower Egyptian nome
Neith mekhit, "northern Neith nome"
Capital: Sais
Chief goddess: Neith

2nd Lower Egyptian nome
Khepesh, "ox-leg nome"
Capital: Letopolis
Chief god: Horus

6th Lower Egyptian nome
Khasuw, "mountain bull nome"
Capital: Xois
Chief gods: Khasu, Re, Amun-Re, Horus

3rd Lower Egyptian nome
Imentet, "western nome"
Capital: Kom el-Hisn
Chief goddess: Hathor
Other center: Hut-ihit

7th Lower Egyptian nome
Wa-em-Huu-ges-imentet, "harpoon nome, western half"
Capital: Besta

4th Lower Egyptian nome
Neith resit, "southern Neith nome"
Capital: Sais
Chief goddess: Neith

8th Lower Egyptian nome
Wa-em-Huu-ges-iabtet, "harpoon nome, eastern half"
Capital: Pithom
Chief gods: Atum, Osiris

9th Lower Egyptian nome
Anedjti, "god of grazing region nome"
Capital: Busiris
Chief god: Osiris

15th Lower Egyptian nome
"Ibis nome"
Capital: Hermopolis Parva
Chief god: Thoth

10th Lower Egyptian nome
Kem-wer, "great black (bull) nome"
Capital: Athribis
Chief god: Khentekhtai

16th Lower Egyptian nome
Hat-mehit, "tip of the fish nome"
Capital: Mendes
Chief god: Hat mehit
Twin city: Thmuis

11th Lower Egyptian nome
Hesbu, "nome of the slaughtered"
Capital: Leontopolis
Chief gods: Miysis, Bastet
Other center: Tell el-Yahudiya

17th Lower Egyptian nome
"Behedet nome"
Capital: Sema-Behedet
Chief gods: Amun-Re, Ptah, Horus

12th Lower Egyptian nome
Tjeb netjeret, "calf and divine cow nome"
Capital: Sebennytos
Chief god: Onuris

18th Lower Egyptian nome
Imet khenti, "near king's child nome"
Capital: Bubastis
Chief goddess: Bastet

13th Lower Egyptian nome
Heka-andju, "the ruler is safe nome"
Capital: Heliopolis
Chief god: Re-Horakhty
Other center: Su

19th Lower Egyptian nome
Imet pekhti, "far king's child nome"
Capital: Buto
Chief goddess: Uto
Other center: Tanis

14th Lower Egyptian nome
Japti, "eastern nome," later Khenti-japti, "near eastern nome"
Capital: Sile
Chief god: Horus of Mesen

20th Lower Egyptian nome
"Sopdu nome"
Capital: Per-Sopdu (Saft el-Henneh)
Chief god: Sopdu

The Names of Old Kingdom Pyramids

The royal pyramids of the Old and Middle Kingdoms had their own names which generally contained a state-ment about the king. Less frequently they referred to the building itself, as in the pyramid of Cheops.

Saqqara, Step Pyramid of Djoser:
"Horus is the star in the zenith of heaven"

Dahshur, Red Pyramid of Snefru:
"Snefru appears"

Dahshur, Bent Pyramid of Snefru:
"Snefru appears in the south"

Giza, Pyramid of Cheops:
"Horizon of Cheops"

Giza, Pyramid of Chephren:
"Great is Chephren"

Giza, Pyramid of Mycerinos:
"Divine is Mycerinus"

Abusir, Pyramid of Sahure:
"The *ba* of Sahure appears"

Saqqara, Pyramid of Unas:
"Perfect are the places of Unas"

Saqqara, Pyramid of Teti:
"Eternal are the places of Teti"

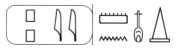

Saqqara, Pyramid of Pepy I:
"The perfection of Pepi endures"

Numbers, Weights and Measures in Ancient Egypt

Numbers

	wa	1	udjat	1/1	
∩	medj	10		1/2	
℮	shet	100	○	1/4	
	kha	1000	~	1/8	
	djeba	10 000		1/16	
	hefen	100 000		1/32	
	heh	1 000 000		1/64	

Weights

	deben	weight, 3.2 oz (91 g)
	qedet	weight, 0.32 oz (9.1 g)

Capacities

	hekat	measure of grain, 1.27 gallons (4.81 = 10 hinu)
	hinu	measure, 1.02 pints (0.48 l)
	des	jug (measure of beer)
	ra	mouthful, 0.5 fl. oz. (0.015 l) (320 ra = 1 heqat)

Lengths and Areas

	meh	cubit (7 hands), 20.7 inches (52.5 cm)
	shesep	handbreadth (= 4 fingers), 2.95 inches (7.5 cm)
	djeba	finger, 0.73 inches (1.85 cm)
	khet	100 cubits, 57.4 yds (52.5 m)
	setjat	arure, $2/3$ acre (2 756.5 m^2 or 100 cubits square

Scepters and Symbols of Kings and Gods

Royal power was expressed by the images and insignia —scepters, weapons and other objects—which the king wore or carried when he appeared in public. The position of the king as a supernatural individual whose life, reign and good fortune were vouchsafed by the gods was both confirmed and demonstrated by those symbols which the gods can also own.

Crook
"Authority"
Egyptian: hekat

Scepter
"Power"
Egyptian: sekhem

Flail
"Royal dignity"
Egyptian: nekhakha

Mekes symbol;
also a scroll case
Egyptian: mekes

Mace
Egyptian:
hedsh

Sandal straps
"Life"
Egyptian: ankh

Scimitar
Egyptian:
khepesh

Scepter
"Good fortune, dominion"
Egyptian: was

Dagger
Egyptian:
bagesu

Pillar
"Permanence, stability"
Egyptian: djed

Crowns

As well as the crowns from Upper and Lower Egypt forming together the Double Crown, the king's regalia included a variety of headdresses made from or representing feathers, the stems of plants, ram's horns, cobras and sun discs. Unfortunately not even one example of all royal crowns has survived the course of time.

Lower Egyptian
or Red Crown
Egyptian: mehus, deshret

Royal helmet
or Blue Crown
Egyptian: khepresh

Upper Egyptian
or White Crown
Egyptian: shemas, hedjet

Royal headcloth
Egyptian: nemes

Double crown
or pshent
Egyptian: sekhemti

Bag wig
Egyptian: khat

Double plumed crown
with ram's horns
Egyptian: shuti

Crown with ostrich
plumes and ram's horns
Egyptian: atef

Ostrich plume crown
with ram's horns
Egyptian: henu

Triple *atef* crown
Egyptian: hemhemet

The Gods of Ancient Egypt

Amun

Amun, as "king of the gods," was central to the Egyptian pantheon from the 2nd millennium B.C. onward. With Ptah and Re, he was one of the national gods, and chose the earthly king. As Amun-Re he had the capacity for constant regeneration, and under the title of Amun-Re-Kamutef he was the primeval god. He, Mut, and Khonsu formed the sacred triad of Thebes, worshipped at Karnak, and with the goddess Amaunet he was one of the creator deities of Hermopolis. He was depicted in anthropoid form, with a tall plumed crown, or in the shape of a man with a ram's head surmounted by the solar disk. He could also appear in animal form as a ram or a goose.

Anubis

Anubis, "Lord of the Sacred Land" (= necropolis), the "Embalmer," and "Guardian of Secrets," was depicted in the form of a jackal or as a man with a jackal's head. His main tasks were to preserve the corpse through its embalming, to guarantee the ritual of the "opening of the mouth" so that the mummy could regain the use of its senses, and to care for the dead. He was regarded as judge of the dead, and was their guardian through the hours of the night. His qualities as protector and preserver also accounted for his appearance at the birth of the children of kings or gods.

Atum

The theological system of Heliopolis described Atum as the creator god who had brought space and time, men and gods into being out of himself, but who could also destroy them again. His symbol was the monolithic *benben* stone marking the site of the first primeval mound when it emerged from the waters of the floods. He was associated with the constantly regenerating sun god Re in maintaining the creation, and personified the aspect of Re in age (= the setting sun). In this capacity he was shown in human form with the double crown, but when his aspect as the primeval deity was to be emphasized he appeared in the form of a snake.

Bastet

The goddess of Bubastis, portrayed as a cat or a cat-headed woman, was originally a patron deity of the king. As early as the Old Kingdom, she was equated with the lion goddess Sekhmet, and like her was originally represented in the form of a lioness. She was also associated with Hathor, Mut, and Tefnut, and was regarded as a daughter of the Atum. As time went on, more and more emphasis was laid on her peaceful and protective characteristics. Bastet became increasingly popular, as witness countless bronze figures of cats (from the Late Period onward), and many cemeteries all over the country containing the mummies of cats, as well as the Bastet festival mentioned by Herodotus.

Khnum

Khnum, shown as a ram or the hybrid figure of a man with a ram's head, was one of the oldest gods of Egypt. One of his most important cult centers was at Elephantine, near the first cataract of the Nile, where he formed a triad family with the goddesses Satet and Anuket, and was worshipped as god of the sources of the Nile and of fertility. In Esna he was regarded as the primeval god and was associated with the lion-headed Mehit and Neith, goddess of the primeval waters. As creator, he was shown forming the bodies of mankind on the potter's wheel, and was often accompanied by the frog-headed midwife goddess Heket, who breathed life into human bodies.

Khonsu

The moon god Khonsu, who appears in the netherworld texts of the Old and Middle Kingdoms as a punitive deity, did not rise to mythical and cultic prominence until the New Kingdom. As the son of Amun and Mut in the Theban triad, he was the protector of life and healing, and was also god of oracles. He was further associated with the moon god Thoth, the god of the air Shu, and several child deities. Depictions show him with the crescent moon and the black lunar disk on his head, either mummiform with a human head and a sidelock of youth, or as a man with a falcon's head striding out; he also appears, but far less frequently, in the figure of a crocodile.

Hathor

The goddess Hathor, usually represented as a woman or a cow, always wears a headdress of cow's horns and the solar disk. At her main cult center of Dendera she was one of a triad with the Horus of Edfu and the god of music Ihy. She was regarded as the daughter of the sun god Re, a royal goddess like Bastet, a mother goddess like Isis, and a goddess of the dead like Imentet. However, many other goddesses were also called by the name of Hathor, as if it were a title. She united elements of heaven and earth, this world and the next, the indigenous and the foreign, but the main ideas connected with Hathor, shared by all her manifestations, were of love, protection, and joy.

Horus

The term Horus, "the distant one," designated several gods depicted as a falcon or as a man with a falcon's head. Among the most important were Horus the god of the sky and kingship (whose name was used in the earliest royal titles), the Horus of Edfu (with the symbol of the winged solar disk,) and Horus son of Isis (Harsiese, also Harpocrates). The last-named was regarded as successor to his father Osiris, and guaranteed legitimate rule in the next world. He represented the ordered and cultivated world, and was constantly at odds with Seth, the powerful god of wild, untamed nature.

Isis

The great mother goddess Isis was one of the most important deities of Egypt from the late Old Kingdom onward, together with her husband Osiris. In the myth she succeeds in reviving Osiris by her magic powers when Seth has killed him, and bears him his son and successor Horus. Her magic makes her a protecting goddess, and she therefore accompanies the sun god on his journey through the hours of the night. In the second half of the 1st century B.C. Isis finally acquired the status of the "One" goddess, standing for all the others, and later she was even worshiped throughout the Roman Empire.

Maat

The concept of *maat* stood for the ancient Egyptian system of order and values; it denoted equilibrium, justice, and truth. The ethical opposite was Isfet, standing for disorder, injustice and falsehood. Every ruler had to maintain *maat* and guarantee it to the gods. However, even ordinary people must follow the dictates of *maat*, or they would not survive when they died and came to judgment. As a goddess, Maat was personified as a woman with an ostrich plume on her head. Regarded as the daughter of Re, she was worshiped in a cult of her own from the New Kingdom at the latest, as her temple at Karnak indicates.

Mut

From the New Kingdom onward, the goddess Mut was one of the Theban triad with her husband the national god Amun, and her son the moon god Khonsu. The identification of Amun with the sun god, in his capacity as Amun-Re, meant that she was simultaneously the god's mother, wife, and daughter. However, her chief aspect was maternal, and Mut was regarded as the divine personification of the great and wise woman. She is represented as a woman wearing the royal double crown, or—like other mother goddesses—as a vulture.

Osiris

Osiris, supreme god of the underworld and judge of the dead, was originally a vegetation god and the adversary of the desert god Seth. In the myth, he was an ideal ruler murdered by his brother Seth. Brought back to life by his wife Isis, he became the guarantee of life after death for those who had lived according to ethical standards. Although he was worshiped in many places throughout the country, and in all necropolises, his main cult centers were Busiris in the Delta and Abydos in Upper Egypt. He is represented as a mummiform figure, with the symbols of royal rule in his hands.

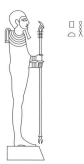

Ptah

Ptah, god of the city of Memphis, was regarded as a creator deity who had made the world through his thoughts and words. He was the divine personification of human creativity, and was thus patron of the visual arts. With the lion goddess Sekhmet and the lotus blossom god Nefertem, he formed a triad uniting not only the various forms of life—human, animal, and plant—but also such ideas as creation, protection, and regeneration. He was depicted as a mummiform figure, with a close-fitting cap and a long composite scepter in his hands, consisting of the symbols for "life," "long duration," and "well-being."

Re

The sun god Re, depicted as a falcon or a man with the head of a falcon surmounted by the solar disc, stood for the regenerative forces of nature, and was thought of as the father of the king. During the cyclical course of the sun through twelve diurnal and twelve nocturnal hours, he appeared in various forms: in the day as the falcon-headed Re-Horakhty, in the evening in anthropomorphic form as Atum, and in the morning as Khepri in the shape of a scarab. Later, the ram-headed figure of Amun-Re reviving the blessed souls in the underworld was added to these manifestations. The main center of the cult of Re was Heliopolis, where the primeval mound had risen from the waves of the ocean at the time of the creation.

Sekhmet

Sekhmet, depicted as a lion-headed woman (with the solar disk on her head after the New Kingdom period), was a powerful protective goddess who formed the triad of Memphis with Ptah and Nefertem. She was thought of as the goddess of healing, and her priesthood may be regarded as the first community of doctors. Sekhmet also had wild and dangerous aspects which come to the fore in the myth of the destruction of mankind, where it is her function to strike down those human beings who rebel against the sun god. Her warlike nature is also evident in her support of the king in every battle against his enemies.

Seth

The mighty desert god Seth was seen as the personification of wild, untamed nature. He was the adversary of the god of vegetation and cultivation, Osiris, the rightful ruler of the well-ordered world. In the legend, Seth murders his brother Osiris. A power struggle then breaks out between him and Horus, the son of Osiris. Horus and Seth thus represent the two aspects of creation; chaos and structure. In the other world, however, Seth appears as the companion of the sun god, whose function is to preserve creation from the attacks of Apophis, the serpent-shaped destroyer of the world.

Sobek

Originally, the crocodile god Sobek was probably a fertility god, and was honored in various places, including the oasis of the Faiyum. Later he was also regarded as the son of Neith, goddess of the primeval waters, and thus as a primeval god himself, with the task of protecting the world. Sobek was worshiped in many different parts of Egypt (for instance in Kom Ombo), and associated with a wide range of deities, even including the sun god Re. The great attraction of this deity will have been based on the danger of the animal associated with him, and the idea that its great power could be used to protect mankind.

Thoth

The god Thoth was the moon god, represented in the form of an ibis or baboon, or as a man with the head of an ibis (surmounted from the time of the New Kingdom by a crescent moon and lunar disk). He was also regarded as the creator god and the god of wisdom, and was credited with the invention of writing and the legal code. His origin is uncertain, but after the Middle Kingdom his main cult center may be considered to be Hermopolis. Here he was at the head of a group of eight deities who were regarded as the source of creation. Countless numbers of the animals sacred to him were buried in underground tomb complexes in nearby Tuna el-Gebel.

A Short Guide to Architectural Forms

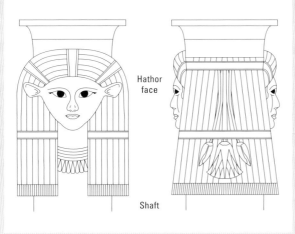

Hathor face

Shaft

Hathor Capital

The crown of a type of column familiar from the Middle Kingdom onwards which took the form of a sistrum (sistrum column). The capital reveals the face of Hathor on either two or four of its sides, often with the three-dimensional depiction of a naos (chapel) between two volutes above. In addition to the classical column form, of widely diverging sizes and materials (stone, wood etc.), the sistrum emblem also occurs in raised relief against a pillar, as in the Nefertari temple in Abu Simbel. This form of structural support was used in shrines dedicated to female divinities, e.g. Bastet, Isis, Hathor.

Hypostyle Hall (Hall of Columns)

Term used in Egyptian architecture to denote a hall of columns with elevated nave, typical for the time of the New Kingdom. The most monumental example is the great 19th Dynasty hypostyle hall of Karnak, as shown here. The hall is lit by means of enormous ridge windows in the walls of the nave. While the campaniform papyrus columns of the wide nave have open-flower capitals, those in the side-aisles have been given closed capitals, representing papyrus bud Columns.

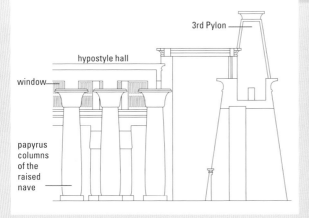

3rd Pylon

hypostyle hall

window

papyrus columns of the raised nave

Pylon

Monumental temple facade comprising two towers either side of an entrance. The towers are characterized by sloping walls and their edges are reinforced with torus molding (originally wound reeds used to protect the edges of prehistoric brick buildings) and are crowned with a cavetto molding. Against the outside of the pylons, fixed into niches in the wall, were enormous flagpoles from which colorful pennants were flown. These conifer flagpoles would have soared high above the building and were therefore additionally secured by wooden brackets positioned halfway up. The first pylons made of brick started being built as early as the Eleventh Dynasty, and stone was introduced as a construction material during the New Kingdom. The largest pylon of all time was constructed during the Thirtieth Dynasty in Karnak and was 112 meters wide. In the conception of the temple as a reflection of the cosmos, the pylon repre-

sented the mountains of the horizon and therefore also denoted the place where the sun rose. The common theme used in the decoration of the external walls, the heraldic image of the king "smiting the enemies," symbolized the repulsion of all hostile powers (chaos) potentially harmful to the carefully ordered world of the temple. Furthermore, these main scenes, representing the most important theme, were incised more deeply into the stone of the pylon towers than the subsidiary images so that by making use of the fall of the light they could be seen from a great distance. The decoration of a pylon was probably not carried out as the building ramps were removed but once the construction work was completely finished, by means of scaffolding. With the immense pylons of the Ramesside period, narrow staircases were built inside the structures which led up to platforms on top of the entrance and towers. Some pylons of the Graeco-Roman period even incorporated internal stairwells leading up to rooms of different levels.

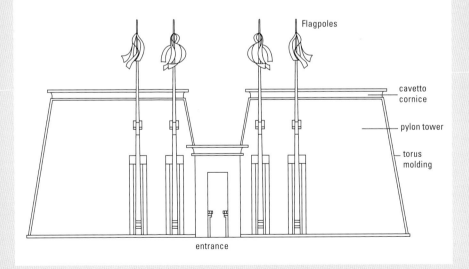

Flagpoles

cavetto cornice

pylon tower

torus molding

entrance

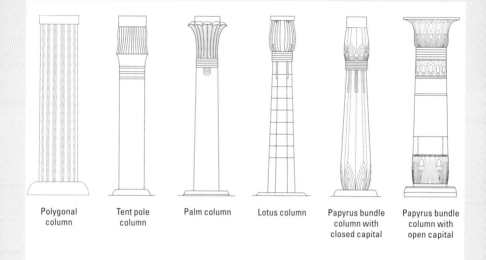

| Polygonal column | Tent pole column | Palm column | Lotus column | Papyrus bundle column with closed capital | Papyrus bundle column with open capital |

Columns

Sacred architecture in Egypt had a rich repertoire of column types at its disposal, most of which were based on vegetal motifs. They have a base, a square slab (abacus) covering the capital, and were generally painted. While hard stone was used to make single-piece, monolithic columns, limestone and sandstone columns were usually composed of cylindrical and half-cylindrical sections pegged together. In this case the individual units would only be smoothed and shaped once the columns were erected.

1. Polygonal columns—with up to 32 sides, derived from the octagonal structural support. Examples of effectively fluted polygonal columns therefore resemble the shafts of Greek Doric columns, although they differ significantly from these.

2. Tent pole columns—a stone column of this type has only been found in Thutmosis III's Festival Hall at Karnak. Its capital consists of a bell-shaped pommel separated from the smooth shaft by a circular ridge.

3. Palm columns—a style in use from the Old Kingdom right up to the Greco-Roman period. The capital at the top of the cylindrical shaft imitates vertical, lightly curved palm fronds.

4. Lotus columns—the shaft imitates a sheaf of between four and eight plant stalks and has a capital in the shape a closed flower separated from the lower column by a band effect. In contrast to the papyrus bundle column, the shaft rises straight up from the base.

5. Papyrus bundle columns—a number of different variants with open or closed flower capitals. The shafts, which taper into the bases and are decorated with a flower design around the foot, were initially ribbed to imitate papyrus stalks, but from the 19th Dynasty onwards were usually smooth. The shafts also commonly bore inscriptions displaying the pharaoh's titulary as well as relief decoration.

False Door

As the main cult focus of a mastaba tomb during the Old Kingdom, the false door is the magical place where the deceased was believed to appear in order to receive his funerary gifts. In its standard form it consists of a single or double niche with a door roll (in imitation of a rolled-up curtain) above the actual doorway. Above this is a lintel and adjoining picture area (tablet) depicting the deceased before an offering table. The outer frame consists of two traditional architectural elements: a torus molding, which runs around three sides of the doorway and a projecting cornice in the form of a concave molding, whose origins go back to the palm fronds once inserted into the top of brick walls. In addition to this standard type of false door, which was highly variable in terms of its individual components, and could be made of a variety of materials (e.g. wood), the cult chambers of larger tombs were often also equipped with another type, the so-called palatial false door. Unlike the normal type, the decoration of the palatial false door is not dominated by exhaustive inscriptions (offering formulae, titles and names of the deceased) and the indispensable funerary repast scene, but exhibits instead an intricate niche construction modelled on the perimeter walls of the early palaces.

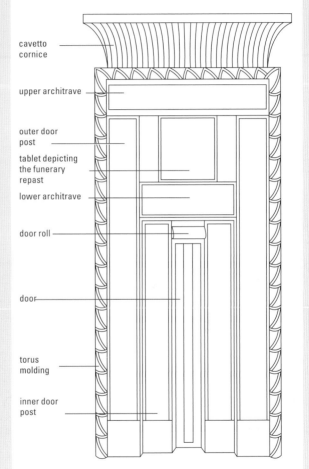

cavetto cornice

upper architrave

outer door post

tablet depicting the funerary repast

lower architrave

door roll

door

torus molding

inner door post

Glossary

Akh (Egyptian: "Blessed One"). Refers to the spirit of the dead invested with magical powers. In Ancient Egypt everyone had the ambition—from king to commoner—to enjoy eternal life in heaven in the divine form of the Akh (see also **Ba** and **Ka**).

Ankh (Egyptian: "Life, vital force"). The *ankh* symbol was often depicted being held in front of the king by the gods, who thereby bestowed the "vital force" upon him. Because of its magical and religious meaning, it often appears on tomb furnishings and objects associated with the mortuary cult. As an emblem representing eternal life it continued to be used until late into the Coptic period (e.g. on funerary stelae).

Ba. Complex Egyptian concept which has various levels of meaning. As *Ka* and *Akh*, *Ba* denoted a form of being common to both gods and men. Gods and kings possessed a multitude of *Ba* which manifested their power and influence to the outside world. The *Ba* was the personification of all the vital forces of the deceased and, in contrast to the mummy, it formed the active and unfettered element of the dead person. It was therefore often represented as a bird with a human head, especially in the private tombs of the New Kingdom. The *Ba* of the dead resided in heaven but regularly returned to "their" tomb on earth in order to accept offerings.

Barque sanctuary (or shrine). Important room in most of the larger Egyptian temples in which the portable cult barque of a god (or of a king) was stored and ritualistically provided for. These barques were lavishly constructed from precious materials. During large festival processions, a small scale statue of a god or king was placed in a shrine in the middle of the barque and then carried out of the temple to visit other cult sites. The barque and other ritual ceremonies were often depicted on the walls of the sanctuary which is usually situated on the main axis of the temple. The barque itself is placed on a stone pedestal in the middle of the room.

Birth legend. Traditional textual and figurative myth of the divine origin of the Egyptian king. According to the myth the god Amun-Re comes to earth in the form of the king in order to betake himself to the queen, to whom he reveals his divine nature. Together they conceive the heir to the throne. After his birth he is cared for by divine wet nurses and recognized by his father Amun-Re as his son. This dual nature of the Egyptian king—both divine and human—is represented in several temples of the New Kingdom (e.g. the Temple at Luxor and the Mortuary temple of Hatshepsut in Deir al-Bahri).

Book of the Dead Modern term for a large collection of texts and illustrations concerning Egyptian beliefs on death and intended to secure a continued life in

Papyrus of the Book of the Dead belonging to Maiherperi showing the Ba as a bird in front of the tomb entrance. Eighteenth Dynasty, ca. 1450 B.C., Western Thebes, Valley of the Kings (KV 36), Egyptian Museum, Cairo

the hereafter. Different types of Books of the Dead were interred with the deceased from the New Kingdom onwards. In contrast to the **Books of the Netherworld** they were available to non-royal persons from the very beginnings of Egyptian culture. They are often written on long papyrus scrolls, while individual sayings or depictions are found on grave walls, coffins, statues etc.

Books of the Netherworld. A series of illustrated didactic "books" (including the **Amduat**, the **Book of Gates** and the **Book of Caverns**) which describes and depicts the Egyptian vision of the hereafter. The systematic description of what awaited the deceased in the afterlife was intended to enable him to join the eternal cycle of life and thereby achieve immortality. Initially, the Books of the Netherworld were almost always the exclusive preserve of the king. They form the most important part of the wall decorations of the royal graves of the New Kingdom. Later, they were increasingly used by private citizens on coffins and papyri.

Canon of proportions. A set of rules governing the relationship of the sizes of various parts of a sculpture or painting to each other. The basis of the Ancient Egyptian "canon" was formed by the proportions of the human body. Modern reconstructions of these theories of proportions are supported by the partially preserved guidelines which were sketched by artists on walls and statues. The actual size of the units of measurement and the way in which the rules were applied by Old Egyptian artists are still a matter for conjecture however.

Canopic jars. Vessels in which the embalmed entrails of the corpse were placed. Often of calcite-alabaster or limestone, they take the shape of a tall vase with a convex lid and were generally grouped in fours in the grave. Their contents were wrapped in bandages and guarded by the **Sons of Horus**. From the Middle Kingdom onwards the lids of the jars were shaped like human heads, but later also took the form of baboon, jackal and falcon heads.

Relief showing Sety I. bestowing the gold of honor, Nineteenth Dynasty, ca. 1280 B.C., Saqqara, limestone, H. 123 cm, Musée du Louvre, Paris

Cartouche (French). The oval frame around the nomen and prenomen of the King. Originally it was a rope whose tied ends extended slightly beyond the knot; later, these came to be represented by a stroke made at right angles to the end of the oval. The circular or oval form symbolized eternity and placed the person named under the magical protection of the gods.

Cataracts. Greek term for the rapids in the southern, Nubian part of the Nile valley. At six places between Aswan and Khartoum the hard rock stratum of the Eastern desert juts through the sandstone of the Nile floor and forms rocky barriers several kilometers long in the course of the river. The first cataract at Aswan had always formed a natural border between Egypt and Nubia.

Cavetto cornice Typical element of Egyptian religious architecture, which generally appears together with torus moldings as a decorative feature on the top of buildings. Vertical strips with rounded upper ends were often painted above concave moldings, and this indicates that their origins can probably be traced back to rows of palm fronds which were once set atop walls of mud brick. Cavetto cornices are therefore an abstract form in stone of an older architectural ornament. They first appeared in the temple architecture of the early Old Kingdom.

Cuboid statue or Block statue Genuinely Egyptian type of statue in which the figure has its legs drawn up, its arms crossed on its knees and is shown squatting either on the ground or on a cushion. The body is often covered by a cloth, thus giving the statue a cube-like appearance. Produced in great numbers from the beginning of the Middle Kingdom up until Roman times and used exclusively by private persons.

Cycle of offerings. The redistribution of an offering (food, clothing, ointments, flowers etc.), which was first made to a god, to other recipients. Often these recipients were first the statues of kings and then later those of individuals in temples or private tombs. This cycle of sacrificial offerings was governed by individual sets of rules; ultimately, they were used to pay the priest of the very last sacrificial recipient.

Deben. Egyptian unit of weight in the form of stones used for weighing out. In the Old Kingdom a deben weighed around 0.5 oz (13.6 g) but changed over time to become 3.2 oz (91 g) in the New Kingdom.

Djed pillar. A pole around which were coiled bundles of plants in several tiers and which was worshipped as a fetish from earliest times. It became a symbol for permanence and constancy and, as such, was very popular as an amulet.

Electrum. Alloy of gold and silver which occurs

Amulet figures of the four Sons of Horus, Twentieth Dynasty, ca. 1100 B.C., polychrome faience, H. 14.6 cm, The British Museum, London

naturally in the desert areas bordering Egypt but which can also be made artificially. Used in jewelry since the early Old Kingdom and later in large quantities as an inlay or an embellishment for temple walls and doors.

Ennead. The gods grouped around the main divinity of a particular area. The number nine represented a squaring of the number three, which the Egyptians believed was an indefinite quantity; it therefore stood for a vast number. The groups of gods described in this manner do not necessarily have to number nine and the composition of the groups may also change. The best known are the enneads of Heliopolis, Memphis, Abydos and Thebes, the latter having generally 15 members.

Eye of Horus Eye of the falcon god Horus which, according to myth, was stolen and injured but always brought back and healed. A complex cycle of myths developed around the Eyes of Horus which were equated with the sun and moon. The eternally recurring injury to and healing of the eye reflected the setting of the constellations or the changing phases of the moon. Because the Eye of Horus, like the sun and moon, always returned whole it became one of the most popular symbols of regeneration and, as such, was often depicted or worn as an amulet (Wdjat-Eye). The earliest Wdjat-Eyes of Cornelian were made in the 6th Dynasty.

False door. Stone, sometimes wooden, imitation of a door with a closed-off entrance (see p. 583). False doors mark the division between this world and the hereafter. In the private tombs of the Old Kingdom, they represent the central cult site in front of which offerings to the deceased were placed; they were also an important decorative element in royal buildings, temples and later tombs. The required elements of doorframe, lintel and recessed center section could be designed in different ways so that a variety of types of false doors developed.

Festival of the Valley. Besides the Opet Festival, the most important annual processional festival held in Thebes. Presumably since the early Middle Kingdom the barque of Amun, accompanied by gods and statues of the kings (both living and dead), was taken out of his temple in Karnak and over the Nile to the West Bank on great river boats to visit the royal funerary temples. This festival was of great importance for the royal cult and a large proportion of the population actively participated in it; it was a time for visiting deceased family members at their tombs in Western Thebes and for feasting.

Flag poles. Flag poles, sometimes over 34 yards (36 m) high, flanked the entrances to temples. They consisted of a smooth tree trunk and were lowered into niches in the façades of pylons. The very top of the mast was partly plated with electrum and decorated with bright pennants.

Funerary repast. Refers to portrayals of the deceased which show him or her seated at a table of offerings. Frequently occurring motif, showing the material provision of the dead, and seen from the beginnings of Egyptian culture. In the graves of the Old Kingdom the funerary repast was often related to the false door. In the broader sense the expression is also used for depictions of gods or kings seated before a meal (offering table).

Divine Adoratrice. Generally used as the title of the high priestess of the Temple of Amun in Thebes; during the New Kingdom it was held by the wives and daughters of the kings. The office holder was considered the bride of the god Amun and her person guaranteed the eternally recurring creation of the world through the primeval life-giving powers of the god. In the 3rd Intermediate Period the title holder was the religious head of the Theban theocracy of Amun and the office was exercised by unmarried daughters of the royal house who thereby secured political influence for themselves in Upper Egypt. Heirs to the office were adopted.

Gold of honor. The Egyptian custom of rewarding deserving officials with gold is recorded in Egypt from the Old Kingdom onward. In the New Kingdom the public award of such distinctions is often pictured in private tombs. The king stands at the "Window of Appearances" giving the gold of honor to the official standing below. Usually the gold takes the form of various kinds of jewelry, such as gold bracelets and collars of lenticular gold beads. These decorative items were often shown in depictions of the person thus distinguished, for instance on his statues.

Heka(t) scepter (Egyptian: "ruler" or "scepter of Kingship"). As part of the king's ceremonial costume this scepter was an important component of the royal insignia. It was a crook which the king (or a god e.g. Osiris) usually held in his right hand as a sign of the power of his office.

High Priest. Head of the priesthood of a temple; corresponds to the title "First servant of God." The high priests represented the king concerning the rituals and managed the personnel, administration and finances of their temples. These sometimes possessed large estates and great wealth.

House of Millions of Years. Traces its origin to an Egyptian term for temple complexes, especially those of the New Kingdom, in which the veneration of royal statues closely associated with the cult of the gods was particularly important. The cult sought

Osiride pillars of Ramesses II, Nineteenth Dynasty, ca. 1250 B.C., Western Thebes, Ramesseum, 2nd courtyard, sandstone, H. 10.5 m (34 ft.)

to preserve the reign of the king and confer eternal life on him, thus making him king of Upper and Lower Egypt for millions of years. The funerary temples of the New Kingdom in Western Thebes were a special type of "House of Millions of Years."

Instructions. Egyptian literary genre which enjoyed great popularity, as can be seen from the countless copies made at scribes' schools. At least 16 individual works have been preserved completely or in part. They attempt to teach the new generation of officials the basic rules of Egyptian society and to educate them in the fundamental ethics of the state. They are, therefore, important documentary sources for the Egyptian conception of mankind and the world. Their influence extended beyond Egypt, evidence for which can be found, for example, in the Bible.

Incense cones. Small cones of ointment worn on the head on festive occasions. The cones were made of animal fat mixed with aromatic substances. Depictions of banqueting scenes in the tombs of the New Kingdom often show them on the heads of the participants. During the banquet the cone would melt, anointing the hair and upper body of the person wearing it.

Journey to Abydos.
Representation of a boat trip of the mummy or a statue of the deceased since the Middle Kingdom. In the course of a funeral this ritual journey to Abydos was performed so that the dead person could participate in the Festivals of Osiris held there. The death and resurrection in the afterlife of the god Osiris was observed annually in Abydos.

Ka. Complex Egyptian concept pertaining to an aspect of the personality of gods and men. (see also **Akh** and **Ba**.) Ka was considered the bearer of generative, life-giving forces and a symbol of uninterrupted vital force which passed from generation to generation. It came into existence at the birth of a person and continued to exist after his death. Like the **Ba** it also accepted offerings and guaranteed eternal life after death.

King List. Written inventory of kings' names in chronological order with a note on the length of their reign. An example is the famous Turin Royal Canon. Used for purposes of dating in administration and historiography, the King Lists are today one of the most important documentary sources for reconstructing Egyptian chronology.

Kiosk. In Egyptian architecture the term for a light, open-sided pavilion often made of stone. Kiosks were built with partition walls (intercolumnar slabs) of medium height between the outer columns or pillars and had a wooden or canvas roof. They were often found nearby the entrances to great temple complexes or along processional routes.

Mammisi. Expression borrowed from the Egyptian-Coptic meaning "birth-house;" refers to small temples proved to be in existence by archaeologists from the Late period onwards. They stand within the outer ramparts of a larger main temple. Generally situated at right angles to these on processional routes, they often featured an ambulatory. On particular ceremonial days, the processions of the gods entered the mammisi in order to celebrate the birth of the god-child of the local divine trinity (father, mother and child deities) with whom the young king was identified.

Mastaba. (Arabic: "bank") Royal and private tombs whose superstructure consisted of a solid, square area of bricks or stone with sloping sides. The burial usually took place in a subterranean chamber surrounded by storerooms. Common in the early dynastic era and in the Old Kingdom.

Mortuary Cult. Rites carried out for the dead in order to secure their continued existence after death date from the prehistorical period. The mortuary cult of the king, however, was different from that of private individuals because of his dual human-divine nature. The notions of preserving the body (through mummification and biographical texts in the grave) and providing for it (furnishings and offerings placed in the tomb) were central to the mortuary cult. Having one's own tomb built was necessary for the private individual to establish a mortuary cult. When the rites had been completed after embalming and interring, the cult was set in motion by daily offerings performed by the eldest son or a priest employed for this purpose.

Mortuary temple. Refers to two diverse types of funerary temple: 1. Temples attached to the pyramids of kings in the Old and Middle Kingdoms at which rituals relating to the perpetual renewal of power and the mortuary cult were performed for the benefit of the monarch; these are also known as pyramid temples. 2. Religious sites of the New Kingdom in Western Thebes (which differ from 1. in their architecture and religion) where a royal statue cult was practiced, closely related to that of Amun in Karnak (see **House of Millions of Years**).

Mummy. Derived from an Arabic word meaning "asphalt." Today the term means a corpse protected from decay either by artificial means or by natural desiccation. Certain forms of embalming took place in Egypt during the Early Dynastic period. Later, the embalming process lasted 70 days after which the mummified corpse was buried. According to Egyptian beliefs on death, the preservation of the corpse was absolutely necessary for ensuring life after death.

Naos. (Greek: "temple, house of the gods") Lockable shrine for storing religious images; generally made of wood or hard stone and placed in temples or tombs. The term is also occasionally used for the sanctum of the inner temple where the cult statue of the god was housed in a shrine.

Ostracon depicting a princess dining, Eighteenth Dynasty, ca. 1340 B.C., el-Amarna, limestone, H. 23.5 cm, Egyptian Museum, Cairo

Pyramidion with coronation scene from a toppled obelisk of Hatshepsut, Eighteenth Dynasty, ca. 1470 B.C., Karnak, Temple of Amun-Re, red granite, H. ca. 3.50 m

Natron. Naturally occurring mineral compound of sodium carbonate and sodium bicarbonate; mined in Lower Egypt in Wadi Natrun. Used for drying the corpse during mummification and for purification and incensing in cult ceremonies.

Nilometer. A narrow canal or well shaft connected to the Nile whose walls had a scale marked on them, by means of which the height of the Nile could be read. The systematic observation of the level of the Nile was carried out from the early Dynastic period. It was important for monitoring the Nile inundation, for distributing irrigation water correctly and therefore for determining the annual taxes.

Nubians. Term generally used for the inhabitants of the Nile valley south of the first cataract who were ethnically and linguistically distinct from the Egyptians. From the ancient Egyptian point of view Nubians were foreigners and, as a potential threat to Egypt, they had to be politically and militarily subdued. Contacts with Nubians existed from the earliest times and these were partly military, partly peaceful (trade); there was also a considerable Nubian population in Egypt.

Offering table A stone slab on which the offerings for the dead were laid; associated with the false door as the main cult area of the tomb as well as with the mortuary cult. It usually had hollows to hold food and beverage. Typical offerings such as different kinds of bread were often shown in decoration on the upper surface of the table.

Opening of the mouth ritual This ceremony, for which there is evidence from the Old Kingdom onward, was seen as giving life to cult objects that were lifeless in themselves. Recorded in texts and depictions on papyri and on the walls of temples and tombs until the Roman period, the ritual involved many very complex actions and was most frequently performed on statues into which it was supposed to "breathe life." They would then take part in ritual acts and be capable of accepting the offerings made to them. In this way the mummies of the dead and of sacred animals were "awakened" to life in the next world. A key episode in the rite, often shown in depictions, was the opening of the mouth with a tool shaped rather like the blade of an adze.

Opet festival. The Opet festival, one of the most important in the ancient Egyptian calendar, was held annually in Thebes and lasted for up to 27 days. Its high point was the procession, attended by great pomp, of the cult barque of Amun of Karnak to the temple of Luxor 1.5 miles (2.5 km) away. There, the statue of the god remained for several days before the procession returned. The rituals carried out during the visit to Luxor were thought to renew the royal claim to rule which were vouchsafed by Amun.

Osiride pillar (Pillar figure). A statue of the king resting with its back to a wall or pillar. The somewhat misleading term has found its way into the language because of the form of the pillars which are often in the shape of a mummy and therefore similar to depictions of the god Osiris. Osirid pillars and their precursors date from the reign of Senusret I. and are mainly found in the façades and courtyards of the great royal temples of the New Kingdom.

Ostracon. (Greek: "potsherd") Sherd of pottery or smooth flake of limestone which bore an inscription. Thousands of ostraca have been found from the New Kingdom in particular when they were used for a variety of texts in daily life (letters, bills, notes, school exercises) as they were much cheaper than papyrus. They were also used by artists as surfaces for sketching.

Sea Peoples. Modern term for a number of different peoples, most of whom probably lived on the west coast of Asia Minor and in the Aegean. In the 12th and 13th centuries B.C. they migrated in several waves (first attack in the fifth year of Merenptah) through Asia Minor and as far as Egypt. They caused enormous political and ethnic upheavals, especially in Syria-Palestine. Several Egyptian kings led campaigns against them in order to prevent them settling on the Egyptian coast. Battles against the Sea Peoples can be seen depicted in the decorations of Theban temple (e.g. Medinet Habu time of Ramesses III).

Pharaoh. From the Egyptian per-aa, meaning "Great House." From the beginnings of Egyptian culture it meant the royal palace and its occupants i.e. the court. Used from the 18th Dynasty on for the person of the king and later as the title of the ruler.

Primeval Mound. The Primeval Mound was of paramount importance in ancient Egyptian cosmogony. From the Primeval Waters, which represented chaotic forces, arose the first land, the Primeval Mound, upon which the first god created the world. In architecture, literature and art the Primeval Mound is an important motif and a symbol for the eternally recurring process of creation.

Pronaos. (Greek) A hall of columns situated in front of a temple. Its front is either open, or—more frequently—closed by slabs of medium height between the columns in the foremost row. The architectural form of the pronaos was developed during the 18th and early 19th dynasties. It later became a magnificently designed element of Egyptian temples in Ptolemaic and Roman times.

Pylon. (Greek: "large portal, gatehouse") In Egyptology, a monumental gateway to a temple flanked by two towers. The passage through the middle was blocked by two large double-winged wooden doors, often with inlays and surfaces of precious metals, as can be read in many construction texts. The interiors of these towers frequently had either steps leading up to a roof or rooms which were reached by a staircase.

Pyramid Text(s). Modern name for the religious texts found in the pyramids of some kings and queens of the Old Kingdom. The oldest known example is from the burial chambers of the pyramid of Unas in Saqqara. The pyramid texts were not a homoge-

Married couple at a funerary repast, Eighteenth Dynasty, ca. 1450 B.C., Western Thebes, tomb of Benja (TT 343)

neous text corpus but rather a collection of some 800 spells consisting of hymns, litanies, incantations etc. which had as their theme the eternal life of the king in the hereafter.

Pyramid town. Settlement planned and financed by the state and situated next to the royal pyramids. The first of these settlements was next to Sneferu's pyramids in Meidum and Dahshur. Inhabitants of these cities belonged to the royal Endowment to the Dead and were therefore priests, tradesmen and officials who administered the endowment, together with its agricultural production, and who carried out sacred rites in the pyramid complex.

Pyramidion. Term derived from the Greek for the apex of pyramids and obelisks; in the case of pyramids it was made separately, usually from stone, and decorated with pictures and texts related to the course of the sun. On obelisks it formed the pyramid-like peak on top of the monolithic shaft and was often coated with electrum.

Royal ideology. Totality of concepts and beliefs associated with the Egyptian kings. According to the Egyptians the king represented the gods on earth and in his person he embodied the Egyptian state. He was the representative of the people of Egypt in the world of the gods and was responsible for maintaining the divine world order (Egyptian: "maat") which was guaranteed by his historical deeds, ritually exaggerated innumerable times in the depictions on temple walls. By virtue of his office, granted him by the gods, the king was also invested with divine qualities. For this reason he was not only the highest priest of the land, but was himself the object of worship during his lifetime.

Sanctuary (Lat.: "holy place") The term can be used for an entire cult building devoted to a deity, but is generally applied only to the room in the god's temple where his or her statue was worshipped daily. As a rule this room lies at the very back of the chamber and its walls are ornamented with scenes from the daily ritual.

Amulet in the form of an Wdjat eye, Twenty-fifth Dynasty, ca. 700 B.C., polychrome faience, L. 6.7 cm, The British Museum, London

Sed festival (Egyptian *heb-sed*: "royal jubilee") Royal festival documented from the beginnings of Egyptian culture up to the Graeco-Roman period. During the festival, complex rituals lasting several days renewed the physical and magical powers of the king in order to effect a continuation of his reign. The influence of Sed festival celebrations was thought to carry over to the hereafter so that the rule of the king could be perpetuated for all eternity.

Senet game. An ancient board game for two people first documented in the Early dynastic era and extremely popular throughout Egyptian history. The game could be interpreted religiously: moving the pieces over the board was considered the equivalent of the journey of the dead through the afterlife and winning guaranteed the victor's re-birth.

Sistrum A musical instrument resembling a rattle, especially important in the worship of goddesses. It consisted of a handle with a metal hoop containing holes through which metal rods were passed; the ends of the rods were then bent. Shaking the instrument produced a rattling sound used to mark the rhythm of liturgical ceremonies in temples.

Solar barque. The course which the sun seemed to take every day around the earth was interpreted in

Egyptian myth and religion as the journey of the sun-god in his barque. With his escort, he crossed the underworld at night unseen in the Night Barque before emerging in the Morning Barque to cross the sky in the opposite direction.

Sons of Horus. The four tutelary gods Hapi, Amset, Duamutef and Qebehsenuef were considered the children of Horus. They participated in the ritual resurrection of Osiris and therefore of every deceased individual transmuted into Osiris. In particular, they protected the inner organs of the dead as lords of the **Canopic jars** in which the embalmed innards of the dead were stored.

Sphinx. (Greek) A hybrid of lion's body and human head. Sphinxes were frequently depicted in a variety of forms—sculpted, painted and in relief—from the early Old Kingdom on. The best known example is the Great Sphinx of Giza. In the New Kingdom sphinxes were erected in large numbers on both sides of processional routes ("avenues of the sphinx"). In Thebes, sphinxes of the god Amun can be seen with a ram's head on a lion's body.

Stele. (Greek) Upright slab of stone (and later often of wood), generally in the shape of a tall rectangle and often rounded at the top. Stelae frequently bore texts and pictures referring to a wide range of subjects; for instance, they could be erected in memory of the dead in or near a tomb, or as the public record of various events or political treaties. Such stelae are often of great size, and most of them stood at the gates or in the courtyards of temple complexes.

Wdjat eye See **Eye of Horus**

Unification of the Two Lands. Refers to the presum-ably long historical process during which the various areas of Egypt came to form a political whole. A unified state arose from the different regions and ethnic groups of Upper and Lower Egypt in the fourth millennium B.C. Later historical records condensed this to the deeds of one man—Menes, the first king of Egypt. An echo of these historical events can be found in the ritual of "the unification of the two lands" which was performed at the coro-nation of every king.

Uraeus. (Greek) Term for the image of a rearing cobra worn on the brow of kings or gods. An impor-tant part of royal regalia from the Old Kingdom on, its implied threat of a poisonous bite was said to ward off danger and served as a symbol of royal power.

Votive offering In the narrower sense, an offering dedicated to a deity in its sanctuary as the result of a vow. In Egyptology, however, the term is often used for any kind of object donated to a temple. Usually these offerings were rather small figures of gods, symbols connected with the deity, or stelae.

Viceroy of Kush. The office of the so-called "King´s son of Kush" was established in the early 18th Dynasty, about 1530 B.C. Appointed by the king, this high official governed the whole of Nubia. His most important duty was the control of the gold mines and the collection of the highly valued "Nubian Tribute."

Was scepter. Staff with a forked lower end and a stylized animal's head at the upper end. Seen from the Early dynastic period and carried as a symbol of power by the gods who bestowed it on the king.

Way stations. Refers to small cult structures along a processional route in which the statue of a god or king carried in his barque could be temporarily placed. Many such structures have been preserved in the Theban area.

Window of Appearance. Balcony in the royal palace with a low balustrade, overhung by a baldachin, where the king appeared to the public to bestow, for example, the **Gold of honor** on deserving officials. A variant of the Window of Appearance with a relig-ious function is found in the temples of the New Kingdom in Western Thebes.

Basic Concepts of Islamic Architecture

Cairo, south minaret (with tower-like surround) of the great courtyard mosque of Caliph el-Hakim, Fatimid period, 1012

Arabic military commander Amr ibn al-As in el-Fustat (later Cairo) at first consisted of a simple building with six doors and no inner courtyard. Numerous later extensions, conversions and additions transformed its original appearance beyond recognition, however. It was given its present form, of a courtyard mosque with arcading which forms multi-aisled halls (called riwaqs) around a central courtyard (sahn) by the Abbasids in 827. The arcading is generally deeper on the sanctuary (qibla) side than on the other three sides.

Some of Egypt's most famous mosques, the Mosque of Ahmed ibn Tulun (9th century) and the al-Azhar Mosque (10th century), for example, follow this courtyard plan at the same time as displaying distinctive architectonic features based on their respective models—the art of the Abbasid court based in Samarra in the case of the first and North African elements in the case of the second. The courtyard mosque remained in use throughout the Middle Ages, especially for the Friday mosques (or congregational mosques) in which the faithful gather for communal prayers on the Muslim holy day. The main mosque of a city or city district is always a Friday mosque.

Courtyard mosque The very first mosques consisted of a simple, open courtyard, separated from its surroundings by a wall. The large courtyard of the Prophet Muhammad's house in Medina, where the community used to gather for prayers, thus served as a mosque (from the Arabic masjid meaning "place of prostration"). Egypt's oldest mosque, which was built by the

Dikka High platform (podium or gallery) resting on pillars near the minbar. The prayer leader takes up position here during communal prayers.

Four-Iwan mosque Developed from the basic Iwan mosque type during the early Mamluk period. Four barrel-vaulted halls, or iwans, of varying sizes, positioned opposite each other, open onto a communal inner courtyard, resulting in a cruciform ground plan. The iwan orientated towards Mecca stands out in terms of both its size and its decoration. The space between the iwans is given over to the living accommodation and support functions of by the madrasa. The best known example of this is the Sultan Hasan Mosque from the middle of the Mamluk period (mid-14th century). During the Mamluk period it was also customary for the Sultan who founded the madrasa to integrate his—usually dome-vaulted—mausoleum into the complex.

Iwan mosque Design of mosque used predominantly in madrasa (Islamic theological university, lit. "a place of study") architecture. An iwan is a hall completely open on one side with a barrel-vaulted or flat roof. Early examples of madrasas in Egypt, from the Ayyubid period in the early 13th century, consist of two iwans positioned opposite each other across an open courtyard. Alongside these were the living quarters of the students and teachers as well as the secondary facilities such as kitchens and washrooms.

Hanafia The original domed structure over a fountain in the middle of a mosque courtyard, eventually replaced during the Ottoman period by a well for the performance of ritual ablutions before prayer.

Mabkhara, lit. "incense pot," referring to the chape of early Ayyubid and Mamluk minaret finials.

Madrasa Form of religious university introduced into Egypt by Sultan Saladin (Salah al-Din) in 1180 in an attempt to assert the Sunni branch of Islam over the Shiite orientation of the preceding Fatimid rule. The sheikh of the al-Azhar Mosque in Cairo is still the supreme authority in all matters relating to Sunni Islam.

Mihrab Prayer niche indicating the direction of Mecca. The mihrab usually takes the form of an arch flanked by columns with a half-dome ceiling, and is often richly decorated with stones.

Minaret Characteristic tower (Arabic manara, "place of light") of a mosque, from where the muezzin summons the Muslim faithful to prayer. In emulation of the spiral minaret of the ibn Tulun Mosque, these towers were given a square ground plan (11th century) and crowned with a domed kiosk (finial). Further developments led to a tripartite design, the octagonal shafts of the Mamluks and the slender "foundation minarets" (e.g. the Muhammad Ali Mosque) of the Ottoman rulers.

Minbar The pulpit is positioned next to the prayer niche and is an essential element of the Friday mosque. Its sides take the form of two triangles made of wood or stone (marble), whose surfaces are often lavishly decorated with calligraphy and arabesques. The steps in between, for which there is no fixed number, lead up to a small platform (from where the sermon is given) covered by a baldachin.

Mosque type of the late Mamluk period, (15th century, early 16th century) Modification of the four-iwan mosque-madrasa which involved the scaling-down of the halls, flattening of their roofs and the reduction in size and roofing-over of the central courtyard. The building decoration, on the other hand, grew increasingly lavish, as can be seen in the magnificent burial mosque of Sultan Qait Bey (15th century).

Ottoman-period domed mosque Based in Egypt on the courtyard mosque design. This classical Ottoman mosque type involves the rows of arcades on the sanctuary side being closed off to the courtyard and a large domed roof being superposed. The courtyard's side arcading consists of a single row resembling a portico. The most famous Egyptian example of this is the alabaster mosque of Muhammad Ali in the Citadel of Cairo, which dates from the 19th century.

Qibla, designates the direction of prayer towards Mecca, as prescribed by the Prophet Muhammad in 624. All Cairo's mosques (and their prayer niches) are thus orientated towards the south east.

Sahn, large central courtyard of a mosque containing a fountain at its center. The oldest courtyard in Cairo is that of the Amr Mosque, dating from its first phase of enlargement in 667.

Bibliography

Ägypten. Schätze aus dem Wüstensand, Kunst und Kultur der Christen am Nil, Wiesbaden 1996

Dieter Arnold, Die Tempel Ägyptens. Götterwohnungen, Kultstätten, Baudenkmäler, Zürich 1992

idem, Lexikon der ägyptischen Baukunst, Zürich 1994

Jan Assmann, Ägypten. Theologie und Frömmigkeit einer frühen Hochkultur, Stuttgart 1984

idem, Stein und Zeit: Mensch und Gesellschaft im alten Ägypten, München 1991

idem, Ägypten. Eine Sinngeschichte, Darmstadt 1996

Kathryn A. Bard (Hg.), Encyclopedia of the Archaeology of Ancient Egypt, London/New York 1999

Jürgen von Beckerath, Chronologie des pharaonischen Ägypten. Die Zeitbestimmung der ägyptischen Geschichte von der Vorzeit bis 332 v. Chr., Mainz 1997

Doris Behrens-Abouseif, Islamic Architecture in Cairo. An Introduction, Leiden 1989

Hellmut Brunner, Grundzüge einer Geschichte der altägyptischen Literatur, Darmstadt 1986

idem, Die Weisheitsbücher der Ägypter. Lehren für das Leben, Zürich/München 1991

Helmut Buschhausen (Hg.), Der Lebenskreis der Kopten. Dokumente, Textilien, Funde, Ausgrabungen, Wien 1995

Peter A. Clayton, Das wiederentdeckte alte Ägypten. In Reiseberichten und Gemälden des 19. Jahrhunderts, Bindlach 1987

Mark Collier - Bill Manley, How to read Egyptian Hieroglyphs, London 1999

Vivian Davies u. Renée Friedman, Unbekanntes Ägypten. Mit neuen Methoden alten Geheimnissen auf der Spur, Stuttgart 1999

Sergio Donadoni, Theben. Heilige Stadt der Pharaonen, München 2000

Aidan Dodson - Dyan Hilton, Royal Families of Ancient Egypt, London 2004

Arne Eggebrecht (Hg.), Das Alte Ägypten. 3000 Jahre Geschichte und Kultur des Pharaonenreiches, München 1984

John Galey, Das Katharinenkloster auf dem Sinai, Stuttgart/Zürich 1990

Albert Gerhards u. Heinzgerd Brakmann (Hg.), Die koptische Kirche. Einführung in das ägyptische Christentum, Stuttgart/Berlin/Köln 1994

Renate Germer, Mumien. Zeugen des Pharaonenreiches, Zürich/München 1991

Jean-Claude Golvin u. Jean-Claude Goyon, Karnak – Ägypten. Anatomie eines Tempels, Tübingen 1990

Günter Grimm, Alexandria. Die erste Königsstadt der hellenistischen Welt, Mainz 1998

Rolf Gundlach, Der Pharao und sein Staat. Die Grundlegung der ägyptischen Königsideologie im 4. und 3. Jahrtausend, Darmstadt 1998

Manfred Gutgesell, Arbeiter und Pharaonen. Wirtschafts- und Sozialgeschichte im Alten Ägypten, Hildesheim 1989

Zahi Hawass (ed.), The Treasures of the Pyramids, New York 2003

Wolfgang Helck u. Eberhard Otto, Kleines Lexikon der Ägyptologie, Wiesbaden 1999

Friedhelm Hoffmann, Ägypten: Kultur und Lebenswelt in griechisch-römischer Zeit. Eine Darstellung nach den demotischen Quellen, Berlin 2000

Günther Hölbl, Geschichte des Ptolemäerreiches. Politik, Ideologie und religiöse Kultur von Alexander dem Großen bis zur römischen Eroberung, Darmstadt 1994

Erik Hornung, Tal der Könige – Die Ruhestätte der Pharaonen, Zürich/München 1982

idem, Grundzüge der ägyptischen Geschichte, Darmstadt 1988

idem, Der Eine und die Vielen. Ägyptische Gottesvorstellungen, Darmstadt 1990

idem, Das Totenbuch der Ägypter, Zürich/München 1990

idem, Altägyptische Jenseitsbücher. Ein einführender Überblick, Darmstadt 1997

idem, Das esoterische Ägypten. Das geheime Wissen der Ägypter und sein Einfluß auf das Abendland, München 1999

Fouad N. Ibrahim, Ägypten. Eine geographische Landeskunde, Darmstadt 1996

Rosemarie Klemm u. Dietrich D. Klemm, Steine und Steinbrüche im Alten Ägypten, Berlin 1992

Klaus Koch, Geschichte der ägyptischen Religion. Von den Pyramiden bis zu den Mysterien der Isis, Stuttgart 1993

Dieter Kurth, Treffpunkt der Götter. Inschriften aus dem Tempel des Horus von Edfu, Zürich/München 1994

Jean Leclant (Hg.), Ägypten, 3 Bde., München 1979–1981

Mark Lehner, Das Geheimnis der Pyramiden in Ägypten, München 1999

Emmanuel Le Roy Ladurie u. Dietrich Wildung (Hg.), Pharaonendämmerung. Wiedergeburt des Alten Ägypten, Straßburg 1990

Jaromir Malek (Hg.), Ägypten: Geschichte – Kunst – Das Leben heute, München 1993

Hans Wolfgang Müller u. Eberhard Thiem, Die Schätze der Pharaonen, Augsburg 1998

Klaus Parlasca u. Hellmut Seemann, Augenblicke. Mumienporträts und ägyptische Grabkunst aus römischer Zeit, München 1999

Nicholas Reeves, The Complete Tutankhamun. The King – The Tomb – The Royal Treasure, London 1990

Mohamed Saleh u. Hourig Sourouzian, Das Ägyptische Museum Kairo, Mainz 1986

Wolfgang Schenkel, Einführung in die altägyptische Sprachwissenschaft, Darmstadt 1990

Heike C. Schmidt u. Joachim Willeitner, Nefertari: Gemahlin Ramses' II., Mainz 1994

Thomas Schneider, Lexikon der Pharaonen. Die altägyptischen Könige von der Frühzeit bis zur Römerherrschaft, Zürich 1994

Regine Schulz u. Matthias Seidel (Hg.), Ägypten. Die Welt der Pharaonen, Köln 1997

Wilfried Seipel (Hg.), Gott – Mensch – Pharao. Viertausend Jahre Menschenbild in der Skulptur des Alten Ägypten, Wien 1992

Ian Shaw (ed.), The Oxford History of Ancient Egypt, Oxford 2000

Abdel Ghaffar Shedid, Das Grab des Sennedjem. Ein Künstlergrab der 19. Dynastie in Deir el-Medineh, Mainz 1994

idem, Die Felsgräber von Beni Hassan in Mittelägypten, Mainz 1994

Abdel Ghaffar Shedid u. Matthias Seidel, Das Grab des Nacht. Kunst und Geschichte eines Beamtengrabes der 18. Dynastie in Theben-West, Mainz 1991

David P. Silverman (Hg.), Das Alte Ägypten, München 1997

Rainer Stadelmann, Die ägyptischen Pyramiden. Vom Ziegelbau zum Weltwunder, Mainz 1985

idem, Die großen Pyramiden von Giza, Graz 1990

Nigel u. Helen Strudwick, Thebes in Egypt. A Guide to the Tombs and Temples of Ancient Luxor, London 1999

Miroslav Verner, Verlorene Pyramiden, vergessene Pharaonen. Abusir, Prag 1994

Oleg V. Volkoff, 1000 Jahre Kairo. Die Geschichte einer verzaubernden Stadt, Mainz 1984

Kent Weeks, Ramses II. Das Totenhaus der Söhne. Die sensationelle Ausgrabung im Tal der Könige, München 1999

idem (ed.), Valley of the Kings, New York 2001

Dietrich Wildung, Die Kunst des alten Ägypten, Freiburg i. Br. 1988

Dietrich Wildung u. Sylvia Schoske, Kleopatra. Ägypten um die Zeitenwende, Mainz 1989

Richard H. Wilkinson, Temples of Ancient Egypt, London 2000

Joachim Willeitner, Nubien. Antike Monumente zwischen Assuan und Khartum, München 1997

Karl-Theodor Zauzich, Hieroglyphen ohne Geheimnis. Eine Einführung in die Altägyptische Schrift für Museumsbesucher und Ägyptentouristen, Mainz 1980

Index of Names and General Index

Djet 211
Djoser **10**, 93, 94, 95, 172, 194, 196, 197, 201, 238, 347, 509
Dourgnon, Marcel 88
Duamutef 391
al-Akhraf Bars Bay 84
al-Shafii, Imam 84
al-Zahir Barkuk 84
al-Nasir Muhammad I 81
Gabriel, St. 153, 155
Geb 402
George, St. 154, 155
Hadrian 486, 498
Hapy 391
Hapy, Nile god **57**, 498
Harkhuf 490
Harmachis 169
Haroëris 470, 471, 472
Harpocrates 39, 496
Harsiese 406, 504
Harsomtus 460
Hasan, Sultan 76
Hathor 298, 301, 302, 304
Hatshepsut 18, 19, **113**, 297, 315, 338, 340, 341, 345, 363
Heka 396
Heqaib 481
Herihor 23, 24, 346
Herodotus 10, 56, 57
Hesyra 94
Hetepdief 95
Hetepheres II 178
Hittites 19, 21, 322, 323, **371**, 520, **522**
Hor 109
Horemakhet 513
Horemheb 21, 319, 329, 334, 337, 392, 469
Horus 47, 244, 256, 292, 294
Horus Aha 9
Hunefer, Priest 307
Hyksos **16**, 17, 456
Idu 177
Ihy 298, 304
Imhotep 196, 347

Intef I 14
Intef II 14
Intef III 14
Isis, goddess 46, 54, 55, 290, 292, 294, 302, 391
James 543
John, St. 152, 543
John the Baptist 154, 155
Julius Caesar 52, 53
Junker, Hermann 156
Justinian I 494, 540, 542, 543
Ka'aper 101
Kamose 17
Kamutef 349
Kawab 178
Khaemwaset 203, 206
Kheti 251, 252, 253
Khnum 480, 481, 485, 506, 509
Khnumhotep, Nomarch 12th Dyn. 228, 250, **254**, **256**, 257
Khnumhotep, Official 5th Dyn. 228
Khonsu 313, 319, 346, 358, 471
Khonsu, Son of Sennedjem 439
Kircher, Athanasius 130
Libyans 23, 376, 506
Loret, Victor 380
Louis Philippe 82
Maat 191, 444, 459, 466
Macrinus 471
Maketaten 268
Mandulis 503, 505
Marcus Aurelius 494
Mariette, Auguste 58, 88, 94, **202**, **203**, 212, 238, 301, 331
Mark Anthony 53
Mark, St. 43, 546
Maspero, Gaston 116 – 118
Mehu 230
Mekhu 489
Memnon 367
Menena 426
Menes, see Horus Aha
Mentuemhat 143
Mentuhotep II **14**, 298, 310

Index of places

Picture credits

The publisher would like to thank all contributing museums, archives and photographers for granting the right to reproduce images, and Cleo Huggins, Dover (New Hampshire) for providing the hieroglyphic fonts.

The publisher has made every effort to secure copyright for all the images reproduced in this book. Any individuals or institutions claiming copyright who may not have been contacted are asked to direct their concerns to the publisher.

© Ägyptologisches Seminar, Universität Basel (384, 398); © AKG, Berlin (42, 202, 406)—Photograph: Henning Bock (338/339)/W. Forman (16, 238); © Antiquities Service Cairo (174); after: Dieter Arnold, Die Tempel Ägyptens, Zürich 1991, p. 213/Rolli Arts, Essen (59 tl)/p. 224 (538)/(287 l); after: Dieter Arnold, Lexikon der ägyptischen Baukunst, Zürich 1994, p. 195/Rolli Arts, Essen (160 b)/p. 203 (172)/p. 294 (173); from: Arte sublime nell' antico Eggito, Artificio Skira, Florence/Milan , Special exhibition 1999, No. 4, p. 85 (210); © Ashmolean Museum, Oxford (265); from: G. B. Belzoni, Narrative of the operations and recent discoveries in Egypt and Nubia, London 1820 (397 t); © Bildarchiv Preußischer Kulturbesitz, Berlin (486, 546)—Photograph: Margarete Büsing (122 b, 262 b, 271, 272 l)/Ingrid Geske (27, 557/558: 1. reg. 5)/Jürgen Liepe (25, 190, 272 r, 273, 557/558: 3. reg. 6, 8)/Museum für Islamische Kunst, SMB/Georg Niedermeiser (86); © The Bridgeman Art Library, London (6 bl, 284/285, 448/449, 554/559)/Charles Edwin Wilbour Fund (443); The British Library, London (487), © The British Museum, London (14, 131, 246, 259, 307, 435 o, 446, 458/459, 475, 547 t, 557/558: 5. reg. 5, 564, 586, 592); © Maximilien Bruggmann, Yverdon (217, 298 m, 305, 310 t, 336, 472, 473 l, 480, 489, 525); from: Century Illustrated Magazine, 1887 (116); from: Jean-François Champollion, Grammaire égyptienne, 1836 (132); © CNRS—CFETK, Paris—Photograph: A. Bellod (6 r, 308/309, 356/357); from: Coptic Art II, Cairo, undated, 49 b(151), 93 t (71 b, 152 t); © Giovanni Dagli Orti, Paris (79); from: N. de G. Davies, El-Amarna V. London 1908, Pl. 39 (269); © Peter Der Manuelian, Boston (156 m, 162); after: Sketch by Peter Der Manuelian/Rolli Arts, Essen (263 r); from: Chr. Desroches-Noblecourt, Die Welt rettet Abu Simbel, Berlin, Vienna (Koschka): 1968, ill. 3, 82 (527); © Documentation Center, Zamalek, Cairo (180); © G. Dreyer, Cairo (555/556: 2. reg. 1); from: Rainer Droste/Rolli Arts, Essen (11, 20); Rome: M. S. Drower, Ägypten in Farben, Munich 1964, Tf. 7 (201)/Tf. 9 (222)/Tf. 11 (205 b); © Editions Errance, Paris (330); © Forschungszentrum Griechisch-Römisches Ägypten der Universität Trier (36 tl, 38); © Das Photographarchiv, Essen/Andreas Riedmüller (537 br, 540); from: G. Gabra, Cairo—The Coptic Museum, Cairo 1993. No. 21 (152 b); © Geodia, Verona/Andrea Siliotti (165, 243, 362 tl, 366 b); © Georg Gerster, Zürich (359 bl, 368, 526); © Grabung Qantir-Piramesse, Hildesheim (66); © Andrea Grahmann, Munich (54/55, 58 t, 59 br, 60, 61 l, 232–235); © The Griffith Institute, Ashmolean Museum, Oxford (387); transcription: © Rainer Hannig, Marburg (133); from: J. E. Harris and K. Weeks, X-Raying the Pharaohs, London 1973, p. 43 (118); © Zahi Hawass, Cairo (182, 183); © Hirmer Verlag, Munich (231, 287 r, 291); Rome: Erich Hornung, Das Grab Sethos' I., 1991, Nr. 96 (397 b); © Andrea Jemolo, Rome (164, 168, 228, 555/556: 2. reg. 3); from: Hermann Junker, Giza I, Vienna 1929 (163); © Könemann Verlagsgesellschaft mbH, Köln/Photograph: Andrea Jemolo (12, 195 tl, 207, 208, 218/219, 221, 223, 224, 333 t/br, 342–344, 454, 455 l, 555/556: 2. reg. 4)/Rolli Arts, Essen (28)/Matthias Seidel, Munich: Götterzeichnungen (574–579)/Studio für Landkartentechnik, Norderstedt (endpaper, 34, 70); © Kunsthistorisches Museum, Vienna (17); from: Richard Lepsius, Denkmäler aus Aegypten and Aethiopien, 12 vols., Berlin 1849–1858, (6 tl, 248/249); © laif, Cologne/Martin Kirchner (534/535)/Axel Krause (57); from: G. Legrain, Statues et Statuettes, Cairo 1909, Pl. 28 (191); © Jürgen Liepe, Berlin (2, 10, 89 tl/bl, 90 tr, 92/93, 97, 103, 104, 108 b, 117, 121, 125 t, 166 br, 555/556: 1. reg. 1, 2, 4); © Lotos Film, Kaufbeuren (13, 58 m, 65, 67, 171, 189, 230, 318, 322, 373 br, 374, 388, 409, 423, 492)/E. Thiem (358 b, 363, 371, 373 bl, 375, 377, 382, 417, 426/427); © Giacomo Lovera, Turin (412 u, 444); from: L. Macadam, in: JEA 32, 1932, Tf. 7 (481); © The Metropolitan Museum of Art, New York (18, 270, 282, 297)/Museum Excavations, 1919–20, Rogers Fund, supplemented by contribution of Edward S. Harkness (20.3.203) (260/261); from: The Monastery of St. Catherine, 1976, p. 23 (543)/p. 9 (545); © Museo Gregoriano Egizio, Vatikan (7 bl, 548/549);